PERSONALITY AND
DEMOCRATIC POLITICS

PERSONALITY
AND DEMOCRATIC
POLITICS

Paul M. Sniderman

UNIVERSITY OF CALIFORNIA PRESS

Berkeley   Los Angeles   London

University of California Press
Berkeley and Los Angeles, California

University of California Press, Ltd.
London, England

ISBN:9780520303843
Library of Congress Catalog Card Number: 72-87201

To

HERBERT McCLOSKY

sine qua non

CONTENTS

PREFACE

It can scarcely be questioned that personality may affect political attitudes or actions; indeed, it has become an article of faith. Yet, it must largely be accepted on the grounds of faith, not of science. The study of personality and politics abounds in individual case studies, conceptual discussions, methodological debates, psychological analyses of entire nations; unfortunately, it lacks studies based on systematic evidence and quantitative analysis. This study is an attempt to redress the balance.

Two problems stand out, in my view, in the literature on personality and politics. First, it has become increasingly plain that the same personality characteristic sometimes leads to one consequence and sometimes to another. My assumption was that this puzzling phenomenon was not merely random but worth working out, certainly if we wish to understand why the world is as complex in fact as it often is in appearance. And my suspicion was that much of the previous research had been misdirected: it had attempted to learn whether personality affects belief, not how it does so. That is why I have concentrated on analyzing the process by which a personality characteristic becomes translated into a political belief. The results of this study, I trust, will help make plain why the same personality characteristic may, and frequently will, lead to very different political views, depending on time, place, and circumstance.

Second, the political man and the common man are not the same. Previous studies of personality and politics have gathered systematic evidence on the latter but not the former. Does personality shape the political convictions of activists as it does the opinions of ordinary citizens? Do

personality differences help determine who becomes a political leader and who a follower? Happily, we are for the first
time in a position to address such questions as these, to
initiate a quantitative analysis of personality and political
leadership.

If a distinction can be maintained between blame and
responsibility, this is the place to draw it. The responsibility
for this book, in my view, is Herbert McClosky's: he introduced me to survey research and political psychology; the
years working for and with him at the Survey Research
Center were the core of my education in graduate school;
the data he made available to me made this study possible;
his continuing work on personality and politics provided the
stimulus — and many of the major ideas — for this study;
and his comments on drafts of the manuscript and his
encouragement were invaluable.

If the responsibility is his, the blame must be mine. Though
I would be delighted to be as generous with the one as the
other, unfortunately I cannot find anyone else to accept
liability for errors of fact, interpretation, and analysis. Happily, there is less for me to bear because of the inestimable
assistance of numerous colleagues and friends — Nelson W.
Polsby, Stanley Coopersmith, Jack Citrin, J. Merrill Shanks,
Carol Wallin, Alexander L. George, Fred I. Greenstein, Robert Jervis, and particularly, Robert Axelrod, a reader every
writer should have.

I should also like to thank those who gave me so much
assistance in processing the data and preparing the manuscript — Cynthia Tablak, Julie Serences, Charles Goldman,
Margaret McKean, Kim Takata and Scott Brickner. Their
cheerfulness, industry, and patience in the face of my continuous demands were exceptional.

In addition, I should like to thank those whose financial
assistance and encouragement speeded completion of this
book—the Chairman of the Department of Political Science
at Stanford, Heinz Eulau; the Dean of Graduate Studies,
Lincoln Moses; the Center for Research in International
Studies at Stanford; the Canada Council; and the Survey
Research Center, University of California, Berkeley.

Finally, in conformity with custom, I should like to thank my wife. I owe her a special debt. I would not have completed this book were it not for her unreasonable insistence that I begin my dissertation — and that I finish it. Also, for my awareness of the imperfections in this work, I have her to thank.

Chapter 1 · INTRODUCTION

The democratic idea is always at risk. For free citizens cannot be forced to be free. They may reject the democratic idea outright; they may be so indifferent to it that apathy rather than participation is the result; or they may so misunderstand it that acceptance is tantamount to rejection. This study is an attempt to explore how the personality of citizens influences the extent to which they embrace democratic politics.

Two questions stand out: First, why do some citizens accept and others reject democratic values? Second, why do some chose to participate in democratic politics and a few even seek to become political leaders?

These two questions at once raise a host of others. How strong an influence do personality factors exert over political belief and behavior? Do basic personality factors exert as much influence on the political ideas of the politically influential as on those of the ordinary citizen? Do men seek the power and prestige of high office in politics in order to overcome feelings of personal inadequacy? How do basic psychological predispositions become translated into political beliefs? And most broadly, what do the answers to all these questions have to say about our understanding of democratic theory and politics? I shall address all of these questions as I explore the relevance of personality for the study of democratic commitment and political leadership.

My first objective, then, is to analyze the connection between personality and commitment to democratic values. This task may not be novel, but my approach to it is. Previous investigators have concentrated on identifying the various personality characteristics that may predispose an individual to support democratic norms, hoping thereby to draw a psychological profile of the democratic personality.[1] My aim is different. It is not a profile I shall attempt to trace but a process. Specifically, I shall explore how personality characteristics become translated into political belief.

The scholarly literature to date has been largely confined to identifying psychological traits that deter commitment to democratic values — for example, authoritarianism, intolerance of ambiguity, low self-esteem, and hostility. In this study, however, I take these findings as given and ask not whether personality and democratic commitment are related but how they are related. So far, the psychological processes by which personality gives rise to democratic commitment remain a mystery. Consequently, I shall proceed to construct and test a formal causal model, identifying and evaluating the importance of the various paths leading from basic personality characteristics to support for democratic values.

A number of attempts at unraveling the ties between personality and belief have been made. But these attempts have tended to explain adherence to a particular belief in terms of the psychological benefits it brings to individuals with particular personality characteristics. Thus, authoritarian personalities, it has been suggested, gravitate to anti-Semitism because of the interplay of developmental vicissitudes (for example, failure to achieve an adequate solution to the Oedipal complex); deep-seated fears and feelings born of this failure (such as fears of personal weakness); subsequent efforts to defend the sense of well-being and personal worth (for example, by projection); and last, the psychological functions served by anti-Semitism (such as reduction

---

[1] This question will be discussed in detail in Chapter 5. For examples of this analytic approach see Harold D. Lasswell, *Political Writings of Harold D. Lasswell* (Glencoe, Ill.: Free Press, 1951), pp. 465-525; Alex Inkeles and Daniel Levinson, "National Character: The Study of Modal Personality and Socio-Cultural System," Gardner Lindzey and Elliot Aronson, eds., *Handbook of Social Psychology* 2d ed. (Reading, Mass.: Addison-Wesley, 1969), vol. 4, pp. 418-506; Robert Lane, *Political Ideology* (New York: Free Press of Glencoe, 1962), pp. 400-413.

of anxiety and ventilation of hostility).[2] Plainly, this type of explanation of a link between authoritarianism and anti-Semitism is centered on the psychodynamics of deep-seated motives, inner needs pressing for relief. For convenience of reference, I shall call this type of explanation of the link between personality and belief "motivational."[3]

In this study I shall put forward a rather different explanation of how personality dispositions become translated into belief. My basic hypothesis is that the connection between personality and political belief is not entirely — and sometimes not even predominantly — a matter of psychological benefits gained or functions served by holding some attitude or point of view. Rather, I shall argue that the relationship between personality and commitment to democratic values

[2] For a fuller exposition, see Nevitt Sanford, "The Approach of the Authoritarian Personality," in J. L. McCary, ed., *Psychology of Personality* (New York: Logos Press, 1956), pp. 253-320. The major volume on authoritarianism, of course, was W. Adorno, Else Frenkel-Brunswick, Daniel J. Levinson, and R. Nevitt Sanford, *The Authoritarian Personality* (New York: Harper, 1950). This book was the outgrowth of a variety of earlier influences, among them Erich Fromm, *Escape from Freedom* (New York: Holt, 1941), and Abraham H. Maslow, "Authoritarian Character Structure," *Journal of Social Psychology* 18 (1943): 401-411. See also Nathan W. Ackerman and Marie Jahoda, *Anti-Semitism and Emotional Disorder* (New York: Harper, 1950). The best indication of the later, critical reaction is in Richard Christie and Marie Jahoda, eds., *Studies in the Scope and Method of "The Authoritarian Personality"* (Glencoe, Ill.: Free Press, 1954). A recent review of research on authoritarianism is also available: John P. Kirscht and Ronald C. Dillehay, *Dimensions of Authoritarianism* (Lexington: University of Kentucky Press, 1967). For research on authoritarianism of the left see Gabriel Almond, *The Appeals of Communism* (Princeton, N. J.: Princeton University Press, 1954). Also see Milton Rokeach, "Generalized Mental Rigidity as a Factor in Ethnocentrism," *JASP* 43 (1948): 259-278; *The Open and Closed Mind* (New York: Basic Books, 1960); and C. Hanley, "Eysenck's Tender Mindedness Demension: A Critique," *Psychological Bulletin* 53 (1956): 159-176.

[3] I am using the term "Motivational" for convenience, not precision. As I shall later show, at least three distinct explanatory approaches can be distinguished, but since it is a key point of similarity among them which is of chief importance I have placed them all in the same broad category, labeled here "motivational."

has as much to do with the impact of personality factors on an individual's capacity for social learning as with their impact on the satisfaction of particular personality needs and motives.[4] For convenience of reference I shall call·this the "social learning" hypothesis.

The distinction between these two hypotheses will later be set out in detail, but a specific example that highlights the difference between them may be of value here. Let us assume that we wish to explore the connection between a particular personality characteristic, say, hostility, and a particular attitude commonly associated with it, say, opposition to fluoridation. Following the motivational approach would entail analyzing psychological themes characteristic of the anti-fluoridation movement. Proceeding in this fashion, one might well stress the characteristic stridency of opponents of fluoridation and their quasi-paranoid insistence on the existence of conspiratorial forces bent on adding mysterious substances to municipal water supplies. More generally, one would note that opposition to fluoridation is also associated with an animus against many of the established institutions and norms in the society. It would seem to follow, according to this line of analysis, that the relationship between opposition to fluoridation and the personality characteristic of hostility arises because such opposition stimulates and provides for the release of aggressive feelings, and so ought to have strong appeal for the hostile personality. This reasoning may well prove valid. What I shall propose, however, is a different approach. Let us suppose that a personality characteristic such as hostility tends to reduce or eliminate altogether exposure to information favorable

[4] For recent works which emphasize, as I do, questions of social learning see Giuseppe DiPalma and Herbert McClosky, "Personality and Conformity: The Learning of Political Attitudes," *APSR* 64 (1970): 1054-1073; William J. McGuire, "The Nature of Attitudes and Attitude Change," *The Handbook of Social Psychology*, 2d ed. (Reading, Mass.: Addison-Wesley, 1969), vol. 3, pp. 136-314; William J. McGuire, "Personality and Susceptibility to Social Influence," in E. F. Borgotta and W. W. Lambert, *Handbook of Personality Theory and Research* (Chicago: Rand McNally, 1968), pp. 1130-1188.

to fluoridation. In that case, another explanation for a link between hostility and opposition to fluoridation might stress the impact of personality on opportunities for learning the pro-fluoridation rationale rather than emphasizing the opportunity that the anti-fluoridation posture offers for the expression of hostility.

The example of fluoridation, then, illustrates two different ways of understanding how personality becomes translated into belief. According to the first approach, a common one in the study of personality and politics, personality exerts its influence by arousal of particular needs and feelings which find expression in particular political attitudes or actions. But according to the second approach, which I shall later treat in detail, the link between personality and belief may largely depend on the ways in which basic personality characteristics facilitate or inhibit the learning of political values. Of course, these two approaches are not mutually exclusive. Indeed, one objective of this study is to develop causal models incorporating both approaches and mapping the interconnections between them.

Yet much depends on which of the two is the more important. Consider, for example, the relationship between authoritarianism and opposition to democratic values. If authoritarianism inclines individuals to reject democratic values chiefly because of psychodynamic processes such as are identified in studies of the authoritarian personality, then it may well take radical intervention more or less modeled after psychotherapeutic treatment to sway the authoritarian individual to a more democratic point of view. On the other hand, if the chief effect of an authoritarian personality is that it prevents its possessor from effectively learning the values of democratic politics, then a rather different procedure to influence his or her opinions may be called for — a procedure more like remedial education than like psychoanalysis.[5] What is more, to the extent that the connection

[5] A similar line of argument, based on somewhat different theoretical grounds, was developed in the studies of attitude change directed by Daniel Katz and Irving Sarnoff. For an exposition of this earlier work

between personality and democratic commitment depends on learning rather than on motivation, the more likely the "democratic personality" will subscribe to nondemocratic values in a nondemocratic culture.[6] The good man (defined psychologically) may turn out to be the good citizen — even in the bad society. Equally important, to the extent that learning proclivities as well as motivational factors play a vital role, the very personality characteristics that lead many individuals to oppose democratic values also tend to disarm them as adversaries of democratic institutions, as I shall later show.

Our second concern is the connection between personality and political leadership. Hitherto quantitative studies of personality and politics have dealt only with the ordinary citizen. There has been virtually no systematic objective research on political leaders.[7] In this study I shall undertake exploratory analysis of the impact of personality on the politically active and influential.

The connection between political leadership and personality has often been asserted, but it has yet to be convincingly established. To date, the chief evidence available is an occa-

---

see Daniel Katz, Irving Sarnoff, and Charles McClintock, "Ego Defense and Attitude Change," *Human Relations* 9 (1956): 27-46; Daniel Katz, "The Functional Approach to the Study of Attitudes," *Public Opinion Quarterly* 24 (1960): 163-204.

[6] The rationale behind this argument is set out in detail in chapters 4 and 8. See in particular the arguments on the relationship between self-esteem and conformity to social values.

[7] Unfortunately, the major exceptions are studies also employing McClosky's data, see: Giuseppe DiPalma and Herbert McClosky, "Personality and Conformity: The Learning of Political Attitudes," and Herbert McClosky, "Personality and Attitude Correlates of Foreign Policy Orientation," in James Rosenau, *Domestic Sources of Foreign Policy* (New York: Free Press, 1967), pp. 51-110; Paul M. Sniderman and Jack Citrin, "Psychological Sources of Political Belief: Self Esteem and Isolationist Attitudes," *APSR* 65 (1971): 401-417. However, see chapter 5 for a critique of a number of smaller studies which have collected some psychological data on American political elites.

sional case study of a historical figure.[8] Whether personality factors regularly play an important role in impelling men to seek political influence remains to be shown.

My interest in the connection between personality and political leadership, I must emphasize, is narrow. It centers chiefly on one particular hypothesis, first put forward explicitly by Harold Lasswell in his classic study, *Power and Personality*, and long suspected by other students of political leadership. As Lasswell put it, "Our key hypothesis about the power seeker is that he pursues power as a means of compensation against deprivation. *Power is expected to overcome low estimates of the self.*"[9] This, of course, is the classic compensation hypothesis. Political man, according to this hypothesis, is impelled into political life to compensate for low self-esteem, because politics offers an opportunity to win power and prestige and so overcome feelings of personal inadequacy.

The idea of compensatory striving is the most popular psychologically oriented explanation of the drive for political leadership. It is an idea ingrained in the popular culture as well as in the scholarly literature. But popularity and validity are two different things. A rough count suggests that studies that seemingly confirm the notion of compensation and those that apparently disconfirm it are approximately equal in number.[10] Moreover, most of the previous studies which bear

[8] Among the more outstanding are: Alexander George and Juliette George, *Woodrow Wilson and Colonel House* (New York: Dover Publications, Inc., 1964); Erik Erikson, *Young Man Luther* (New York: Norton, 1958); *Gandhi's Truth* (New York: Norton, 1969). Also see E. Victor Wolfenstein, *Revolutionary Personality: Lenin, Trotsky and Gandhi* (Princeton, N. J.: Princeton University Press, 1967); Arnold Rogow, *James Forrestal: A Study of Personality, Politics, and Policy* (New York: MacMillan, 1963); Lewis J. Edinger, *Kurt Schumacher: A Study of Personality and Political Behavior* (Stanford, Calif.: Stanford University Press, 1965).

[9] Harold D. Lasswell, *Power and Personality* (New York: Viking Press, 1948), p. 39.

[10] See Chapter 6 for a detailed evaluation of empirical studies with a bearing on the "compensation" hypothesis.

on the compensation hypothesis prove on close examination to be at best inconclusive and turn out as a rule to be ill conceived or poorly executed or both. And last, close analysis shows that there are in fact a number of compensation hypotheses, a family so to speak, closely related but distinct nonetheless.

Happily, we are in a position to conduct a fair test of the compensation hypothesis or, more exactly, of the versions of it most frequently advanced by students of personality and politics. Indeed, it is my hope to settle, once and for all, the question of its validity. To this end, I have developed an alternative theory of the psychological motives that impel individuals to participate in politics and to contend for political influence. For convenience I have labeled it the competence hypothesis and hope to show it to be sounder than any of the versions of the compensation hypothesis.

Once established, a connection between personality and political leadership raises many questions. Not the least important of these is the extent to which personality factors shape the political opinions and convictions of the politically active and influential. That personality can shape the political beliefs of the common man can no longer be seriously questioned. But the common man and the political man are scarcely the same. To show, for example, that classical conservatism and hostility are related in the general public is by no means to prove that the two are similarly related among the more reflective and politically influential. Compared to the average citizen, the political leader is far better informed about politics; more articulate; more likely to understand and to make use of abstract political ideas; better able to relate general values to specific opinions; more likely to select reference groups appropriate to his overall ideological orientation; more highly involved in political activities and so more frequently exposed to social pressures that constrain idiosyncratic opinions, not the least of these constraints being the political roles political leaders hold.[11] By

[11] See, for example, Herbert McClosky, "Consensus and Ideology in American Politics," *APSR* 58 (1964): 361-382; Herbert McClosky, Paul J. Hoffman, and Rosemary O'Hara, "Issue Conflict and Consensus Among Party Leaders and Followers," *APSR* 54 (1960): 406-427; Angus Campbell,

contrast, the political ideas of the mass public tend to be rudimentary, easily changeable, inconsistent, frequently sketchy and shallow — in a word, unconstrained.

Not surprisingly, then, it has been argued that personality has far less impact on the politically well informed and influential than on the politically unsophisticated citizen.[12] Such arguments are not without merit, but they underestimate the pervasive influence of personality. Political elites may be better informed, more consistent in their views, and possibly in some sense more rational in their reactions to political issues, but as I shall demonstrate, the personality characteristics of political leaders permeate their ideas about society, history and politics, their attitudes toward other people, and even their most basic convictions about the values of democratic politics. And I shall also show the connection between personality and political belief in general is strong both among those with power and those without it — a finding that has some bearing on an adequate understanding of democratic theory and politics.

These, then, are the principal topics I shall address. But before dealing directly with them, I will describe the approach to the notion of personality that guides this study.

Personality and Self-Esteem

Discussions of personality and politics often begin with a discussion of the meaning of the term *personality*. These

---

Philip Converse, Warren Miller, Donald Stokes, *The American Voter* (New York: John Wiley and Sons Inc., 1960), especially pp. 168-265; Philip Converse, "The Nature of Belief Systems in Mass Publics," in David Apter, *Ideology and Discontent* (New York: Free Press, 1964), pp. 206-261; V. O. Key, *Public Opinion in American Democracy* (New York: Knopf, 1961), especially pp. 182-206; Samuel Stouffer, *Communism, Conformity and Civil Liberties* (New York: Doubleday, 1955); Heinz Eulau, *The Behavioral Persuasion* (New York: Random House, 1967), especially pp. 100-109.

[12] For two arguments which lead in this direction, though neither explicitly draws this conclusion, see Sidney Verba, "Assumptions of Rationality and Non Rationality in models of the International System," *World Politics* 14 (1961): p. 100 or Fred I. Greenstein, *Personality and Politics* (Chicago: Markham, 1969), p. 51.

discussions usually take one of two turns: either the reader is treated to an extended tour of the extraordinary variety of definitions which have been assigned to this term, or a single definition is laid down more or less by fiat. Both alternatives have their drawbacks: the first, faithful to the complexity of the issues involved, can bewilder the intelligent reader by the very number and fineness of the distinctions it draws; the second, admirable in its forthrightness, can provoke a certain uneasiness and even outright opposition by the abruptness with which it disposes of issues others deal with at such length.

Consider some definitions of personality put forward by prominent personality theorists:[13]

> Personality is the dynamic organization within the individual of those psycho-physical systems that determine his unique adjustments to his environment. [Gordon Allport]

> The organized aggregate of psychological processes and status pertaining to the individual. [Ralph Linton]

> Characteristic modes of tension reduction are learned by the individual as a function of his past experiences of success or failure with them and of the opportunity for employment of them within the confines of his particular culture. *Personality* may be described as the pattern of the relative importance of these various modes of adjustment to tension which uniquely characterizes the individual. [Krech and Crutchfield]

> Personality is the more or less stable and enduring organization of a person's character, temperament, intellect, and physique which determines his unique adjustment to his environment. [Eysenck]

> [Personality is the] relatively enduring pattern of recurrent interpersonal situations which characterizes a human life. [Harry Stack Sullivan]

[13] The problem of defining personality is a well-recognized one; these definitions were selected from among those listed by Nevitt Sanford in a perceptive and wide-ranging treatment of the issues the problems of

> [Personality is] the most adequate conceptualization of
> a person's behavior in all of its detail that a scientist
> can give at a moment in time. [David McClelland]

There is, apparently, some measure of agreement among these psychologists on what personality means, for all the differences in their definitions. Most appear to abide with a definition of personality that includes the following elements: certain more or less enduring needs or motives a person strives to satisfy; certain more or less stable preferences for or inclinations against goal objects depending on whether they are satisfying or frustrating; certain characteristic response patterns to tension, that is, modes of adjustment and mechanisms of defense; and certain typical ways of striving for goals, perceiving objects, and expressing feelings.

Yet it would be foolish to deny the persistent disagreement over the meaning of personality, particularly about its scope. Some theorists treat personality as co-terminous with the totality of a person's response probabilities; thus McClelland identifies personality as the most comprehensive conceptualization of a person's behavior. Other definitions are narrower in scope, though how much narrower is rather difficult to determine. Some subsume both role behavior and attitudes under personality; others exclude one or the other or both. Plainly, the boundaries of the term personality are not well fixed.

Plainly, too, for us to focus on the whole of an individual's personality is not practical. If we are to analyze in some depth the questions we want to answer, we must select some aspect of personality for attention. The choice may be made on purely theoretical grounds or on basically pragmatic ones. Thus, one way to decide which aspect of personality to study is to rely on some theory that specifies which elements are the most central in the personality system. Unfortunately,

definition raises. "Personality: Its Place in Psychology," in S. Koch, ed., *Psychology: A Study of a Science* (New York: McGraw-Hill, 1963), vol. 5, pp. 488-592. See especially pp. 494-497. |

there are many different theories of personality,[14] and the conceptualization of "structure" and "dynamics" of personality differs greatly from theory to theory.

At this point in time no one can predict which theory or combination of theories will emerge as most valid. It seems prudent, therefore, to focus on an aspect of personality that many theories agree is of strategic importance—the dimension of self-esteem. Self-esteem appears to lie at or near the center, rather than the periphery, of the personality system. It appears to be bound up with our most central needs and values, our conception of ourselves and of others, our aspirations and our actions. Our sense of worth seems to become identified with the groups to which we belong, our beliefs and practices, and the symbolic objects on which we place a high value. To demean them is, somehow, to demean ourselves. William McDougall's classic description of self-esteem captures the idea that it lies at the very center of personality by referring to it as the "master sentiment."[15]

In addition, self-esteem meets two further requirements for usefulness as a personality variable in this study: it has been extensively researched and it has been shown empirically to be a significant determinant of socially relevant behavior. Thus, evidence of the far-reaching influence of self-esteem has appeared in studies of attitude change,[16]

[14] For an introductory account of the major approaches to personality, see Calvin S. Hall and Gardner Lindzey, *Theories of Personality* (New York: John Wiley, 1957).

[15] See William L. McDougall, *An Introduction to Social Psychology* (New York: Barnes and Noble, University Paperbacks, 1960), especially Chapters 7 and 8.

[16] See especially William J. McGuire, "Personality and Susceptibility to Social Influence," R. E. Nisbett and A. Gordon, "Self-Esteem and Susceptibility to Social Influence," *Journal of Personality and Social Psychology* 5 (1967): 268-276; Irwin Silverman, Leroy H. Ford, Jr., and John B. Morganti, "Inter-related effects of Social Desirability, Sex, Self-Esteem and Complexity of Argument on Persuasibility," *Journal of Personality* 34 (1966): 555-568; Irwin Silverman, "Differential Effects of Ego Threat Upon Persuasibility for High and Low Self-Esteem Sub-

interpersonal attraction,[17] conformity and deviation,[18] psychological adjustment,[19] school achievement,[20] perception

---

jects," *JASP* 69 (1964): 567-572; James M. Dabbs, Jr., "Self-Esteem, Communicator Characteristics and Attitude Change," *JASP* 69 (1964): 173-181; Arthur R. Cohen, *Attitude Change and Social Influence* (New York: Basic Books, 1964), pp. 44-46; Arthur R. Cohen, "Some Implications of Self-Esteem for Social Influence," in C. I. Hovland and I. Janis, eds., *Personality and Persuasibility* (New Haven: Yale University Press, 1959), pp. 102-120; H. F. Gollob and J. E. Dittes, "Effects of Manipulated Self-Esteem on Persuasibility Depending on Threat and Complexity of Communication," *Journal of Personality and Social Psychology* 2 (1965): 195-201.

[17] See, for example, Morris Rosenberg, *Society and the Adolescent Self-Image* (Princeton: Princeton University Press, 1965); Stanley Coopersmith, *Antecedents of Self-Esteem* (San Francisco: W. H. Freeman, 1967), especially Chapter 3, "Some Expressions of Self-Esteem," pp. 45-71; W. B. Griffitt, "Interpersonal Attraction as a Function of Self Concept and Personality Similarity-Dissimilarity," *Journal of Personality and Social Psychology* 4 1966): 581-584.

[18] K. J. Gergen and R. A. Bauer, "Interactive Effects of Self-Esteem and Task Difficulty on Social Conformity," *Journal of Personality and Social Psychology* 6 (1967): 16-22; B. J. League and D. N. Jackson, "Conformity, Veridicality and Self-Esteem," *JASP* 68, (1964) pp. 113-115; Richard Crutchfield, "Conformity and Character," *American Psychologist* 10 (1955): 191-198; Frank Barron, "Some Personality Correlates of Independence of Judgment," *Journal of Personality* 21 (1953): 287-297. For general reviews of self-esteem, conformity, and persuasibility see Arthur Cohen, *Attitude Change and Social Influence*, especially pp. 44-46; William McGuire, "Personality and Susceptibility to Social Influence."

[19] Jack Block and Thomas Hobart, "Is Satisfaction with Self a Measure of Adjustment?" *JASP* 51 (1955): 254-259; R. H. Turner and R. H. Vanderlippe, "Self-Ideal Congruence as an Index of Adjustment," *JASP* 57 (1958): 202-206; B. M. Smith, "Six Measures of Self-Concept Discrepancy and Instability: Their Interrelations, Reliability, and Relations to Other Personality Variables," *Journal of Consulting Psychology* 22 (1958): 101-112.

[20] R. H. Coombs and V. Davies, "Self-Conception and the Relationship Between High School and College Scholastic Achievement," *Sociology and Social Research* 50 (July 1966): 460-471; Virginia C. Crandall, "Personality Characteristics and Social and Achievement Behaviors Associated with Children's Social Desirability Response Tendencies," *Journal of Personality and Social Psychology* 4 (1966): 477-486.

and learning,[21] creativity,[22] and success and failure in therapy.[23] Researchers have also observed a connection between self-esteem and such phenomena as day-dreaming,[24] depression,[25] social interaction,[26] political participation,[27] suicide

[21] S. Shrauger and John Attrocchi, "The Personality of the Perceiver as a Factor in Person Perception," *Psychological Bulletin* 62 (Nov. 1964): 289-308; S. Coopersmith, "Studies in Self-Esteem," *Scientific American* 218 (Feb. 1968): 96-106; "Relationship Between Self-Esteem and Sensory (Perceptual) Constancy," *JASP* 68 (1964): 217-221; D. M. Gelfand, "The Influence of Self-Esteem on Rate of Verbal Conditioning and Social Matching Behavior," *JASP* 65 (1965): 259-265.

[22] S. Coopersmith, "Studies in Self-Esteem," *Scientific American* 218 (1968): 96-106.

[23] The dominant tendency in this area of research is to treat psychotherapy as the independent variable and self-esteem as the dependent variable, sometimes in effect, as an index of therapeutic success. For a critical review of this area of research, see Ruth Wylie, *The Self-Concept* (Lincoln: University of Nebraska Press, 1961), pp. 161-183.

[24] M. Rosenberg, *Society and the Adolescent Self-Image*, pp. 218-219.

[25] J. Richard Wittenborn, "Depression," in Benjamin B. Wolman, ed., *Handbook of Clinical Psychology* (New York: McGraw-Hill, 1965), pp. 1030-1057; A. P. Noyes and L. C. Kolb, *Modern Clinical Psychiatry* (Philadelphia: W. B. Saunders's Co., 1964).

[26] Robert H. Coombs, "Social Participation, Self-Concept and Interpersonal Evaluation," *Sociometry* 32 (Sept. 1969): 460-471. For a review of the research literature on groups, see Richard D. Mann, "View of the Relationships Between Personality and Performance in Small Groups," *Psychological Bulletin* 4 (July 1959): 241-270.

[27] See, for example, P. H. Mussen and A. B. Wyszynski, "Personality and Political Participation," *Human Relations* 5 (1952): 65-82; H. Lasswell, *Power and Personality* (New York: Viking Press, 1962); Alexander L. George, "Power as a Compensatory Value for Political Leaders," *Journal of Social Issues* 24 (1968): 29-49; James D. Barber, *The Lawmakers* (New Haven: Yale University, 1965). For a full review of previous research and theoretical issues in the compensation hypothesis, see Chapter 6 of this study.

attempts,[28] and racial discrimination.[29] And psychologists, sociologists, and historians have frequently suggested that the need for esteem is deeply implicated in the psychology of social movements.[30] The number and variety of these studies testify to the significance that the psychologist attaches to the concept of self-esteem. What is more important in the present context, many of the phenomena to which self-esteem has been linked are of immediate interest to the sociologist and political scientist.

Succeeding chapters will confirm the close connection between the value a person places on himself and his perception of the political world. What is worth noting at this point is the special dividends we can gain from the voluminous research on self-esteem already conducted. All too often studies of personality and politics find themselves without a solid foundation in psychological research. Brief references are made to a certain area of inquiry, for example, achievement motivation, no doubt to suggest that there is a secure foundation developed by psychologists upon which further research may be built. But rarely does the political scientist present a detailed evaluation of past and on-going research by psychologists — that is, a consideration of the major findings and newly promising lines of inquiry, of inconsistent

[28] S. Farnham Diggory, "Self-Evaluation and Subjective Life Expectancy Among Suicidal and Non-Suicidal Psychotic Males," *JASP* 69 (1966): 628-634.

[29] A. Kardiner and L. Ovesey, *The Mark of Oppression* (Cleveland: The World Publishing Co., 1962). More recently this relationship has come under challenge. See particularly William L. Yancey, Leo Rigsby, and John McCarthy, "Social Position and Self Evaluation: The Relative Importance of Race," *AJS* 78 (1972): 338-359; John McCarthy and William Yancey, "Uncle Tom and Mr. Charley: Metaphysical Pathos in the Study of Racism and Personality Disorganization," *AJS* 76 (1971): 648-672. For a dissenting view of the revisionist interpretation see Jerold Heiss and Susan Owens, "Self Evaluations of Blacks and Whites," *AJS* 78 (1972): 360-370.

[30] Hadley Cantril, *The Psychology of Social Movements* (New York: Wiley, Science Editions, 1963).

and mixed results, of failings in method and weaknesses in theory, or of the likelihood that original findings will prove valid for other persons in different settings. Consequently, the field of personality and politics has acquired a jerry-built appearance. Observation suggests that political scientists inspect the array of psychological hypotheses, personality theories, and experimental findings like single-minded customers at a bargain counter, each bent on obtaining whatever suits his or her immediate purpose. The upshot is a melange of ideas, borrowed from disparate sources, sometimes tested but more often intuitive and anecdotal in character. Political scientists who have entered the field of psychological research have also actively exercised the right to put forward their own constructs and measures, and political science has suffered the inevitable confusion and disarray. The decisive experiments to perform, even the main questions at issue, are obscure.

For several reasons, then, the extensive research on self-esteem is invaluable. Psychologists have located some of the larger theoretical and methodological pitfalls, making it possible for this study to avoid them. My study has also profited by the enormous effort that has been spent in conceptualizing and measuring self-esteem. And I have been able to check my findings against the results of a large body of previous research. The greater the convergence, the more confidence I can place in the validity of the measures of self-esteem I have constructed. The very bulk and diversity of previous research has allowed me to evaluate certain hypotheses such as the linkage between self-esteem and social learning, even though my own data are persuasive but not always absolutely conclusive. Occasionally, these studies have permitted me to choose the better of two or more equally plausible interpretations of my results. Perhaps most importantly, previous research provided a broad and relatively secure base for the major hypotheses of this study. For the most part, my hypotheses have been derived from, or suggested by, prior work on self-esteem; in a sense, then, it is the insights of many researchers, who have worked on a great number of different problems and have confirmed and refined their ideas by empirical test, which provided the underpinnings of this study.

An Introduction to the Data

The data I shall use are drawn from two studies conducted by Herbert McClosky.[31] The *Marginal Believer* (MB) study, carried out in 1955, includes a representative cross-sectional sample (N = 1,082), selected by the Minnesota Poll, of the adult population of Minnesota. The *Political Affiliation, Activity and Belief* (PAB) study, conducted in 1958, consists of two samples. One is a cross-sectional, national sample of adults (N = 1,484) labeled the General Population or Follower sample, drawn by the American Institute of Public Opinion. The social characteristics of respondents in the sample have been compared with those of other national samples conducted at approximately the same time, including one drawn by the Michigan Survey Research Center (1956 presidential election) and one by the Gallup Poll organization. In addition, comparable census data were compiled on available

[31] For a description of these studies, see Herbert McClosky, "Political Participation and Apathy," in David Sills, *International Encyclopedia of the Social Sciences*, (Macmillan, 1968) pp. 253-265; "Survey Research in Political Science," in C. Y. Glock, ed., *Survey Research in the Social Sciences* (New York: Russell Sage Foundation, 1967), pp. 63-143; "Personality and Attitude Correlates of Foreign Policy Orientation," in James Rosenau, ed., *Domestic Sources of Foreign Policy* (New York: The Free Press, 1967), pp. 51-110; "Consensus and Ideology in American Politics," *APSR* 58 (June 1964): 361-382; "Conservatism and Personality," *APSR* 52 (1958): 27-45; H. McClosky and John H. Schaar, "Psychological Dimensions of Anomy," *American Sociological Review* 30 (1965): 14-40; H. McClosky, Paul J. Hoffman, and Rosemary O'Hara, "Issue Conflict and Consensus Among Party Leaders and Followers," *APSR* 54 (June 1960): 406-427; H. McClosky and Paul E. Meehl, "Personality, Attitudes, and Liberal-Conservative Belief Systems," Preliminary Draft, August 1967; H. McClosky and Paul E. Meehl, "Inflexibility," unpublished manuscript; H. McClosky and Eugene Bardach, "Psychological Correlates of Democratic Commitment," forthcoming.

socio-demographic characteristics. Thus, systematic comparisons were made with respect to a whole variety of personal characteristics, including sex, age, race, place of residence, religion, income, and party preference, all in an effort to show that the PAB population was indeed a representative sample of American adults. All the relevant statistics, originally compiled and presented by McClosky, are reproduced in Appendix 1. As these statistics make plain, the PAB general population matches (allowing for sampling error) the other three samples and the census data in every respect but one: the PAB General Population sample slightly overrepresents the very well educated and slightly underrepresents the poorly educated.

The second PAB sample, for convenience called the Leader sample, consists of delegates and alternates to the 1956 national conventions of the two major political parties (N = 3,020, comprising 1,788 Democrats and 1,232 Republicans). Included, then, are major public officials at all levels of government, national committeemen and party officers, leaders of state and local party organizations, prominent financial contributors, even party regulars honored for years of service by a convention invitation. Needless to say, not all in our leader sample have equal power, nor are all who have political power included in our sample. Nevertheless, we believe the differences between the Leader and Follower samples to be a fair reflection of the difference between the relatively narrow stratum of the politically active and influential and the general population as a whole.

An omnibus questionnaire was administered to all three samples. It was designed to elicit information on, among other things, political attitudes and values; opinions on specific issues; political knowledge, interest, and awareness; commitment to democratic norms and to ideological orientations; and attitudes toward political figures, political involvement, and key political institutions such as the party system. In addition, information was collected about group memberships and reference group identifications, general social attitudes, socio-psychological states, aspects of personal adjustment, clinical personality traits, and of course, standard socio-demographic characteristics such as income, education, religion, place of residence, and the like. In short, these studies obtained data on a wide range of personal characteristics–attitudinal, social, psychological, and political.

The original questionnaire was constructed by McClosky, in collaboration with Paul E. Meehl and Kenneth E. Clark. All subsequent versions of the questionnaire include an assortment of question formats. Some questions are accompanied by a list of alternative answers, and respondents are invited to select the alternative closest to their own opinions. For instance, respondents are asked whether America should increase its reliance on the United Nations, should lessen it, or should let it remain unchanged. Other questionnaire items, indeed the largest number of them, consist of short, declarative assertions (for example, "When I disagree with people it generally turns out later that I was in the right.") with which respondents are asked to agree or to disagree.

The questionnaires used in our study, it should be emphasized, were the product of five years of painstaking development, experimentation, statistical evaluation, and cross-validation. The original form of the questionnaire was in the first instance the object of a massive validation and scale-building study, based on a cross-sectional sample of the Minneapolis-St. Paul area (N = 1,200). The second form of the questionnaire, revised and refined, was put to the test of a full-scale field study, employing both a specially selected sample of different types of leaders (such as labor, business, and P.T.A.) and a fresh cross-sectional sample of the Twin Cities area (N = 1,211). Thus, the questionnaire was tested and then retested in two separate studies using two entirely independent samples before being tested and retested again in the two studies with three independent samples that I have relied on. Questionnaire items and measures surviving nearly a decade of rigorous screening, refinement, and evaluation provide, I believe, a uniquely reliable measuring instrument on which to base my study of personality and politics.

For the record I should point out that the MB and the PAB questionnaires are not the same in every detail. Although most of the items are identical in wording and format, some questions were asked of one sample but not the others to capitalize on the differences among samples. For instance, leaders were asked in detail about their political careers (they were asked, for example, to indicate their official position in the party), while the general population samples in both MB and PAB were not. Also, the MB includes items (and scales) that the PAB does not, partly because the PAB's research objective was somewhat different, partly because the three years intervening between the two studies required certain questions such as those touching on current issues to be changed. But in nearly all respects important for our analysis, the PAB and MB questionnaires are identical. In effect, one questionnaire, developed and refined in a series of large-scale studies spanning half a decade, has been administered to three wholly independent samples over a period of a further three years, thereby presenting us with an uncommon opportunity to cross-validate our measures and findings.

An Overview of the Book

This study addresses three major questions. First, what do we mean by self-esteem and how should we measure it? Second, is there a connection between self-esteem and democratic commitment and, if so, how does the connection arise? And last, what influence does an individual's self-esteem have over whether he will participate in politics, and more importantly, whether he will become a political leader?

PART I: SELF-ESTEEM

Chapter 2: The Meaning and Measurement of Self-esteem

Self-esteem, like a number of constructs in social science, is rather difficult to conceptualize and measure in any exact fashion. This chapter opens with an introduction to some of the problems that complicate the task of definition and a number of the definitions which have been offered by men such as Sigmund Freud, William James, Leon Festinger, and Abraham Maslow. This survey helps unearth a basic proposition to which most researchers would subscribe and which serves as a starting pont for a definition of self-esteem. The thicket of specific definitions is then trimmed somewhat by identifying the three main conceptual approaches to self-esteem — need, structure, and attitudes — and by arguing for the superiority of the third approach for this study. Finally, a working definition of self-esteem is set forth, the measurement procedure is discussed, and certain major conceptual and operational issues in the measurement of self-esteem are considered.

Chapter 3: The Syndrome of Self-Esteem

This chapter presents a theoretical conception of self-esteem so that we may anticipate and interpret the ways in which people with high and low self-esteem differ. To give added credence to this conception, but more importantly, to convey some sense of what variations in self-esteem mean psychologically, I examine some of the strands which tie a lack of self-esteem into a larger web encompassing, among other things, feelings of inadequacy, of helplessness and hopelessness, and of disaffection, defensive withdrawal, and social entrangement.

PART II: POLITICAL BELIEF

Chapter 4: The Acquisition of Political Knowledge

How does personality affect political belief? This chapter addresses that question. It opens by reviewing the kinds of answers students of personality and politics have offered in the past. My aim is to show that theorists have taken too narrow a view of the role of personality, and in particular, have neglected the connection between personality and social learning. The chapter then proceeds with the formulation of a general model to account for the connection between personality and political belief, and concludes with an elaboration of this model, outlining how self-esteem affects the acquisition of political knowledge.

Chapter 5: Democratic Commitment and the Democratic Personality
This chapter takes up a classical problem in political theory and psychology, the idea of the democratic personality. Certain conceptual problems in the notion of a democratic personality are examined, and empirical evidence documenting the impact of self-esteem on democratic commitment is presented. The main object of the chapter is to examine the idea of the democratic personality in the context of the general model of self-esteem and political belief advanced in Chapter 4. This model casts a rather different light on how personality traits tie in with democratic commitment, emphasizing as it does cognitive as well as motivational interpretations. The model is translated from verbal to mathematical terms and tested, and the test results confirm that the connection between democratic commitment and self-esteem depends as heavily on social learning as on motivation.

PART III: POLITICAL PARTICIPATION

Chapter 6: The Idea of Compensation
This chapter is devoted to a critical examination of the compensation hypothesis, that is, the idea that people enter politics to overcome a sense of personal inadequacy. The task of this chapter is two-fold: first, to subject that hypothesis to analysis in order to separate a number of tightly connected, but essentially independent ideas; and second, to assess critically the scholarly literature on the hypothesized connection between compensatory striving and political leadership in order to determine if the empirical evidence, on balance, supports it, disconfirms it, or as I shall argue, is too inconsistent, fragmentary, and poor in quality to permit us to accept or reject the hypothesis in any of its versions.

Chapter 7: Participation and Political Leadership
The first section of this chapter presents my interpretation of the dynamics of self-esteem and social activity, thereby laying the basis for the two rival hypotheses this chapter explores — compensation and competence. The classic compensation hypothesis is tested and rejected. The chapter then

proceeds to test a number of variations on the two major hypotheses which center on the interaction of self-esteem and socio-psychological factors. In short, this chapter explores the variety of ways in which self-esteem affects participation and political leadership.

CONCLUSION

Chapter 8: Personality and Democratic Politics

In this last chapter I shall attempt to suggest some of the broader implications of this study's findings, considering, among other questions, personality and political extremism, elites and masses, participatory theories of democracy, and the connection between the good man and the good citizen.

THE MEANING
Chapter 2 · AND MEASUREMENT
OF SELF-ESTEEM

Self-esteem is like a shadow: easy to point to but impossible to grasp. The task of this chapter is to secure at least an outline of self-esteem — what it means and how to measure it. To do so, we shall have to consider two sets of issues — the first, conceptual, and the second, operational —which in the end are intertwined. For to measure self-esteem we must know what it means, and to know what it means we must know how to measure it.

Conceptual Issues

Disagreement is inevitable, if only because the concept of self-esteem is tied to the problematical idea of the self. Particularly since the English attempt to marry psychological empiricism and analytic philosophy, the notion of the self has provoked disputes that continue to divide both philosophers and psychologists. The problems of personal identity and individuation, of the nature of self-knowledge, and of the relationship between mind and body are among the more persistent problems begotten by the concept of the self.[1]

[1] For an excellent historical overview of many of these problems from the vantage point of a psychologist, see James C. Diggory, *Self-Evaluation* (New York: Wiley, 1966), especially Chapters 1 and 3. For a view from the perspective of linguistic philosophy, see J. Wisdom, *Other Minds* (Oxford: Blackwell, 1952), and G. Ryle, *The Concept of Mind* (London: Hutchinson's University Library, 1949). See also, Donald F. Gustafson,

The meaning of the term *self* is itself a matter of controversy. Beyond the well-established distinction between the self which knows and the self which is known, there are as many distinctions as one has the patience and ingenuity to draw. Lowe, for example, has suggested six different meanings of self — the knowing self of structural psychology, the self-as-motivator, "the humanistic semi-religious conception of the self as that which experiences itself," the self-as-organizer (providing an internal frame of reference or meaning), the self-as-pacifier (serving as a mechanism of adjustment), and the self "as the subjective voice of the culture" (that is, the internal and personal representation of social values).[2] One may look at many such lists, say, that of Hall and Lindzey[3] or that of Gordon Allport,[4] and see correspondence or divergence, depending on one's temperament and professional inclinations. In general, the more abstract the meanings assigned to the idea of the self, the more agreement there appears to be, and the more specific the operational definitions, the more disagreement there appears to be. It is better, I believe, to acknowledge and tolerate the existence of these disagreements, rather than surrender to the temptation to pronounce on the "true" meaning of the self.

Tolerance usually has a price — in this instance, uncertainty about the scope of self-esteem: What does it include? What does it exclude? The answers to these questions are surprisingly elusive, for our self-esteem, as William McDougall long ago observed, appears to be bound up with every part of our selves. Our regard for our selves can change as

---

ed., *Essays in Philosophical Psychology* (Garden City, N.Y.: Doubleday, Anchor Books, 1964), and Kenneth J. Gergen, *The Concept of Self* (New York: Holt, Rinehart and Winston, Inc., 1971).

[2] C. Marshall Lowe, "The Self-Concept: Fact or Artifact?" *Psychological Bulletin* 58, no. 4 (1961): 325-336.

[3] C. S. Hall and G. Lindzey, *Theories of Personality* (New York: John Wiley and Sons, Inc., 1957), pp. 469-475.

[4] Gordon Allport, *Personality and Social Encounter* (Boston: Beacon Press, 1964), pp. 71-94.

our wishes and desires change, rising when they command our approval, falling when they provoke our disapproval. Self-regard can be excited by our achievements and wounded by our failings. More than that, as we identify with others, their fortunes become entwined with ours and our self-regard entwined with theirs. Discussing the meaning for an individual of membership in a family, McDougall writes,

> the family of which he is a part has a capacity for collective suffering and collective prosperity. . . and is the collective object of the judgments, emotions, and sentiments of other men; he recognizes that he, being a member of the whole, is in part the object of all these regards. . . Therefore he desires that his family shall prosper and shall stand well in the eyes of men; and that this desire may become a motive hardly less strong than the care for his own welfare and position. The mere community of name of all the members of the family goes a long way to bring about this identification of the self with the family and the consequent extension of the self-regarding sentiment, results which are described by the popular phrase, "Blood is thicker than water."[5]

Plainly, the objects and persons to which our self-esteem can become attached may vary with the individual, time, and circumstance. And the more indefinite the boundaries of self-esteem, the more difficult it is to determine what to take account of.

The absence of fixed and definite boundaries gives rise to a series of questions, among them whether the concept of self-esteem refers to many things or to one. On this issue opinion is divided. Some personality theorists speak of self-esteem as if it involves one attribute of the personality system, complex to be sure, but essentially unitary in character. Certainly, this has been the dominant view when researchers have proceeded to measure self-esteem. Whatever the differences in their theoretical orientation or their specific measurement technique, with few exceptions their aim

[5] William McDougall, *Introduction to Social Psychology* (New York: Barnes and Noble, 1961), p. 178.

has been the same: to arrive in the end at a single summary score which indicates a person's level of self-esteem. Gough's Adjective Check List, Rogers and Dymond's Q Sort, and Bill's Index of Adjustment and Values, though vastly different in design and application, are alike in one respect: each measure yields a single overall self-esteem score. This practice of deriving a single summary score is obviously congruent with the view that self-esteem is unitary in character.

By contrast, a competing view contends that self-esteem is multi-dimensional.[6] According to this second view, self-esteem involves a number of distinct judgments a person makes in a variety of areas about his or her abilities and achievements. The standards for self-evaluation may vary from one area to another, as may the specific judgments. In one area (say, achievement at school) a person may think highly of himself, and in another (say, skill at sports), he may think poorly of himself. This second approach seeks to differentiate and study separately these different areas or dimensions of evaluation. It makes no assumption at the outset about the number of dimensions involved, or about the nature of their interrelationships. These are empirical questions to be answered in the course of study, not matters to be settled in advance by definition or assumption.

This study follows the second approach. To a reader of the research literature, it is clear that self-esteem has often meant different things to different people. The fact that researchers have not agreed on an understanding of the term is a strong indication that self-esteem is a complex, multifaceted concept. More than this, the use of one global, undifferentiated concept helps obscure points of similarity and dissimilarity among definitions, both theoretical and operational, which different investigators have adopted. As a consequence, it is more difficult than need be to assess the research literature: conflicting results among studies or findings apparently disconfirming a widely-held hypothesis may frequently be traced to divergent definitions of self-esteem.

[6] J. C. Diggory, *Self-Evaluation*, pp. 107-109.

The concept of self-esteem is too vague, too subject to idiosyncratic interpretation. At a minimum, the multidimensional approach encourages the investigator to specify the elements which go to make up the concept of self-esteem. By focusing on the constituent parts rather than the global concept, we gain specificity, and thereby, clarity. Last, the multi-dimensional approach leaves us free to choose alternative conceptions of self-esteem, for in practice the different dimensions may be analyzed separately or summed up together. The basic question, then, is not whether the concept of self-esteem is in fact multi- or uni-dimensional; rather it is whether, or more precisely, when, it is more useful to think of it in one way or the other. And being in a position to make this choice at any point in a study, rather than having it made at the very outset of research, is no small advantage. Indeed, my own findings will show first, that it can be quite useful for purposes of analysis to combine different aspects of self-esteem, and second, that it can be invaluable to separate them.

Yet the multi-dimensional approach brings up other conceptual issues, among them, the question of generality.[7] To what extent, one may ask, is there a tendency toward consistency in the way individuals evaluate their abilities and achievements in different areas of life? Are certain aspects or dimensions of self-esteem in some sense more fundamental than others? To what extent are people's evaluations of some aspect of themselves at one point in time or in one situation similar to their evaluations at some other point or in some other situation? By what standards do people evaluate themselves, which standards are the most common, for whom, and under what circumstances?

Such questions have no simple answers, for they raise matters of theory as well as of fact. For instance, should self-esteem be viewed as a social or a personal attribute? This distinction is by no means scholastic. Festinger's Theory

[7] On this point, see Douglas P. Crowne and Mark W. Stephens, "Self-Acceptance and Self-Evaluative Behavior: A Critique of Methodology," *Psychological Bulletin* 58, no. 2 (1961): 104-121, especially pp. 117-118.

of Social Comparison, to cite only one example, accents the social nature of self-evaluation, and in so doing derives a conception of the dynamics of self-esteem radically different than that of, say, psychoanalytic theory.[8] According to Social Comparison Theory, all individuals have a fundamental "drive" to evaluate themselves; to do this, they compare their abilities and achievements with those of others around them, judging themselves accordingly. Thus, both the standards and the process of comparison underlying self-evaluation are social. This suggests that self-esteem is variable rather than constant, for whether people think well or ill of themselves depends largely on whom they compare themselves with, which in turn varies with time, circumstance, and place. In short, to accept the idea that self-esteem is social in character is to reject the view that it is an aspect of personality, if by personality we mean basic features of an individual's psychological makeup that tend to be relatively enduring.[9]

It is my belief that self-esteem can be put to profitable use at either conceptual level — personal or social. There is evidence to suggest that self-ratings are in part situationally determined, as there is reason to believe that at a deeper level self-esteem is an integral part of the personality system. But two points of warning ought to be kept in mind: first, these two levels of analysis should be kept distinct, and second, the warrant for either is the same, namely, how fruitful each proves in the research enterprise.

Beyond this lies the further issue of whether to draw distinctions of kind as well as of degree. According to the customary view, self-esteem may be thought of as a continuum along which individuals may be ranked according to their level of self-regard. This view suggests that differences

[8] Leon Festinger, "A Theory of Social Comparison Processes," *Human Relations* 7 (1954): 117-140.

[9] To say "relatively enduring" is not to say "permanent." Obviously, the same personality trait can give rise to different behaviors, or vary in strength, from one developmental stage to another; to declare otherwise is to rule out personality as an explanatory construct in developmental psychology.

in self-esteem are essentially a matter of more or less, differences of degree rather than of kind. But there is reason to doubt whether such a view is altogether valid.

It appears that there are varieties as well as degrees of self-esteem. McDougall, for example, drew a distinction between "self-respect," a sentiment which encompasses "negative self-feelings as well as . . . positive self-feelings," and "pride," an exaggerated form of self-regard which admits of no personal failing or limitation.[10] The emblems of pride are boundless ambition and a desire to rise, a refusal to accept realistic limits, an unresponsiveness to criticism and guidance from others, and a vulnerability to self-destruction, whose full-blown expression Murray captures in his concept of the Icarus Complex. One feature of this complex is "a craving for unsolicited attention and admiration, a desire to attract and enchant all eyes like a star in the firmament." In contrast to this "gratuitous pride" stands another species of pride or self-respect, described by Murray as the Solar Complex. More mature and realistic, it is marked by "a relatively strong ego structure supported by tested abilities, which serves to constrain the reckless aspirations of youth within the bounds of realizable achievements."[11]

The ease with which distinctions among the varieties of self-feelings can be overlooked points to one final problem: self-esteem lacks a clear and widely agreed-on meaning. In broad terms, of course, it refers to the measure of respect, praise, admiration, or approval we believe we merit. But where is the line that divides high self-esteem from pride,

[10] W. McDougall, *Introduction to Social Psychology,* pp. 165-166.

[11] Henry A. Murray, "An American Icarus," in G. Lindzey and C. S. Hall, *Theories of Personality: Primary Sources and Research* (New York: Wiley, 1965), pp. 162-175; see also Murray's brilliant analysis of malevolent pride — especially the intertwining of "Egoistic Self-Inflation and Unleashed Wrath in Captain Ahab," in G. Lindzey and C. S. Hall, *Theories of Personality: Primary Sources and Research,* pp. 153-161; for a valuable discussion of the difference between gratuitous and realistic pride, see J. Diggory, *Self-Evaluation,* pp. 110-114.

vanity, or vainglory, or low self-esteem from shame, despair, or mortification?[12] Are we able to distinguish self-esteem from self-satisfaction, self-respect, self-acceptance, self-love, or self-confidence?[13] Who has high self-esteem — those who are pleased with themselves without qualification or those who, acknowledging their limitations, accept themselves as they are, awarding themselves the praise they deserve? Who has low self-esteem — those who have little respect for their achievements and abilities or those who disapprove of themselves? These questions have no simple answers. But to throw some light on the meaning of self-esteem, let us consider some of the definitions others have proposed.

A Preliminary Definition of Self-Esteem

As we have observed, there is very little agreement on the meaning of self-esteem. The range and variety in definitions is striking. Some researchers treat self-esteem as synonymous with such seemingly diverse notions as self-acceptance or self-satisfaction.[14] Others proceed in a different direction, on the assumption that the main distinction is between self-respect and self-love. Yet, scholars taking this path often diverge at this point: some view self-esteem and self-respect as one and the same, while others take the opposite view.[15] Another route is to think of self-esteem as a need, but here, too, we encounter some difference of opinion as to which need (or needs) it involves. Self-esteem has been taken to refer to, among other things, desires for achievement, superi-

[12] These examples are drawn from James' discussion of self-complacency and self-dissatisfaction. See William James, *The Principles of Psychology* (New York: Dover, 1950), vol. 1, pp. 305-307.

[13] For a negative opinion, see Ruth C. Wylie, *The Self Concept* (Lincoln: University of Nebraska Press, 1961), p. 40.

[14] Crowne and Stephens, "Self-Acceptance and Self-Evaluative Behavior: A Critique of Methodology."

[15] See the discussion below of the views of Freud and White.

ority, autonomy, self-confidence, security, prestige, approval, dominance, deference, and abasement.[16]

The reasons for such discord over the definition of self-esteem are varied. Some of the confusion no doubt arises because of the use of very different operational measures. Thus, the Q Sort technique asks the respondent to sort statements into different piles, depending, first, on how well a statement describes himself as he actually is and, then, on how well it describes him as he ideally would like to be.[17] Such a measure natually inclines a researcher to think of self-esteem as related in some fashion to the degree of difference between the ideal self and the actual self. But a different measurement instrument, say, Maslow's Security-Insecurity Test, where respondents are asked to indicate whether they agree or disagree with a particular set of statements, may lead to a very different conception of self-esteem.[18] This instrument inclines one to the view that self-esteem refers to a need for some form of security and satisfaction, which is present in all persons but which varies in strength from one to another. These are two very different meanings to ascribe to the concept of self-esteem.

Another reason for the discord over the meaning of self-esteem is theoretical rather than operational. The source of the difficulty is the connection between definition and hypothesis. In practice, the connection between the two is so close that agreeing to the former means accepting the latter. The problem, we should emphasize, is not that the two cannot be distinguished, at least in the sense of being separately stated. Rather it is that definitions of self-esteem

[16] White, for example, mentions the last four needs as indicators of a sense of interpersonal competence. See Robert W. White, "Sense of Interpersonal Competence: Two Case Studies and Some Reflections on Origins," in Robert W. White, ed., The Study of Lives (New York: Atherton, 1966), pp. 172-193, especially pp. 79-80.

[17] See W. Stephenson, The Study of Behavior (Chicago: University of Chicago Press, 1953).

[18] A. H. Maslow, The S-I Test: A Measure of Psychological Security-Insecurity (Stanford: Stanford University Press, 1952).

frequently do more than they should. The proper task of a definition is "to point to" a phenomenon, not to give an account of it.[19] But all too often, agreement with a definition of self-esteem entails a commitment to a particular theory of personality, or to a specific set of hypotheses concerning the sources or consequences of self-esteem, or to a particular strategy or method of measuring it. To illustrate this problem, let us compare three major views of the meaning of self-esteem.

In his analysis of self-esteem, Freud insisted on the ties between self-regard and narcissism. Self-esteem is subject to the economy of libido theory: there is a fixed amount of libido to apportion to all objects, including the self. An early discussion of narcissism presented this interpretation.

> Self-regard has a very intimate connection with the narcissistic libido. . . It is easy to observe that libidinal object-cathexsis does not raise self-regard. The effect of dependence upon the loved object is to lower that feeling: a person in love is humble. A person who loves has, so to speak, forfeited a part of his narcissism, and it can only be replaced by his being loved. In all these respects self-regard seems to remain related to the narcissistic element in love.[20]

For Freud, then, self-esteem is in essence self-love.

This self-love changes in character in the course of development. Initially, it involves the libido children naturally and freely bestow on themselves, a phenomenon Freud labeled primary narcissism.[21] As a child develops, the denial of complete gratification and the inevitable criticism and

[19] Donald T. Campbell, "Social Attitudes and Other Acquired Behavioral Dispositions," in Sigmund Koch, ed., *Psychology: A Study of a Science*, vol. 6, (1963), pp. 91-177, especially p. 96.

[20] Quoted by Robert W. White, "Ego and Reality in Psychoanalytic Theory," *Psychological Issues*, monograph 11, vol. 3, (1960), p. 127.

[21] An excellent short summary of Freud's views on this subject is James F. Bing, Francis McLaughlin and Rudolf Marburg, "The Metapsychology of Narcissim," *The Psychoanalytic Study of the Child* (New York: International Universities Press, 1959), 14, pp. 9-29.

punishments of parents attack his or her original sense of omnipotence. The child acquires a "narcissistic scar" in the form of a sense of inferiority and unworthiness[22] and an image of a self that he or she ought to be. This image or 'ego-ideal' becomes the object of the original narcissism, and according to standard psychoanlytic formulations, a measure of self-esteem of adults is the discrepancy between their ego-ideal and their ego in actuality.[23]

Robert White, however, charges Freud with a failure to distinguish between respect and love.[24] Self-respect usually accompanies self-love, but need not. As White points out, a classic example of a person simultaneously high in self-love but not in self-respect is a schizophrenic who believes himself to be Napoleon. In his delusion he regards himself as infintely clever and powerful, but in everyday life he lacks the confidence to attempt his ambitions: the Emperor of France sweeps the hospital corridors.[25] According to White, a man of strong self-esteem is confident of his abilities and achievements. The hallmark of self-esteem, then, is not self-love; it is self-respect.

What must a person do to earn self-respect? White speaks rather broadly of winning mastery over the environment and inner impulses. William James, however, takes a narrower view of the kind of success necessary to sustain a person's self-esteem. What matters is not a *general* sense of confidence or self-respect, but the achievement of *specific* aspirations. For James, every man must choose among the selves (or roles) open to him at the outset ". . . and pick out the one on which to stake his salvation."[26] He wrote of himself:

[22] Diggory, *Self-Evaluation*, pp. 99-100.

[23] For a succinct summary of psychoanalytic theories of self-esteem, see Robert W. White, "Ego and Reality in Psychoanalytic Theory," in *Psychological Issues*, pp. 126-129.

[24] White, "Ego and Reality in Psychoanalytic Theory," p. 129 ff.

[25] *Ibid.*, p. 131.

[26] James, *Principles of Psychology*, p. 310.

I, who for the time have staked my all on being a psychologist, am mortified if others know much more psychology than I. But I am contented to wallow in the grossest ignorance of Greek. My deficiencies give me no sense of personal humiliation at all. Had I 'pretensions' to be a linguist, it would have been just the reverse. So we have the paradox of a man shamed to death because he is only the second pugilist or the second oarsman in the world. That he is able to beat the whole population of the globe minus one is nothing; he has 'pitted' himself to beat that one; and as long as he doesn't do that nothing else counts. He is to his own regard as if he were not, indeed he *is* not.[27]

For James, then, self-esteem hinges on relationship between a person's achievements and his aspirations. And it is from his understanding of the dynamics of self-feeling that James derives his famous definition of self-esteem: "With no attempt there can be no future; with no failure no humiliation. So our self-feeling in this world depends entirely on what we *back* ourselves to be and do. It is determined by the ratio of our actualities to our supposed potentialities; a fraction of which our pretensions are the denominator and the numerator our success: thus,

Self-esteem = Success/Pretensions."[28]

The definitions of Freud, White, and James cannot readily be reconciled, in part because the differences between them are rooted in fundamental disagreements of theory and method. Each definition fits into a different cluster of hypotheses. Each, for example, directs attention to different sources of self-esteem. White's stress on achievement and self-respect leads to a postulate of autonomous ego energies, while Freud's emphasis on narcissism and introjection points in another direction entirely — to the id and the superego. And each cluster of hypotheses fits into a larger intellectual framework: Freud's presupposes libido theory, White's contemporary ego psychology, and James' turn-of-the-century introspective psychology.

[27] *Ibid.,* p. 310.

[28] *Ibid.*

This close connection between definition and theory is particularly risky in research on personality. In view of the number and variety of personality theories which command support, for research results to be comparable and cumulative, definitions should be framed so as to apply to more than one theory. I have, therefore, sought a definition for self-esteem that would fit a wide range of theories. To accomplish this, I have searched for a point of agreement about the meaning of self-esteem, to which most, if not all, researchers and readers subscribe. On reflection, it seemed that self-esteem, as it is commonly understood, refers to a product of a process of self-evaluation. The idea of self-evaluation and of self-esteem are intertwined. Whatever else Freud and James may disagree about, on this they agree, as do current personality theorists and researchers.[29]

I suggest, therefore, as a preliminary definition that self-esteem refers to how favorably (or unfavorably) a person evaluates his or her self. To refine this definition further, we must review the three main conceptual approaches to self-esteem and determine which one is the most appropriate for use in this particular study.

Conceptual Approaches to Self-Esteem: Toward a Working Definition

One conceptual approach speaks in terms of a *need* for esteem. In eighteenth-century psychology, self-esteem was understood as "the desire for, and pleasure in, the esteem, admiration, or applause of others, especially the craving for 'distinction.' "[30] There has continued to be widespread agreement that men share a universal drive to think well of themselves and to encourage others to think well of them too. This drive received its most systematic attention in the psychology of Adler and his followers. In their view, a need

[29] For a review of psychologists' position on this question, see Diggory, *Self-Evaluation,* pp. 115-204.

[30] Diggory, *Self-Evaluation,* p. 95. For elaboration on this point, see A. O. Lovejoy, " 'Pride' in Eighteenth Century Thought," *Essays in the History of Ideas* (New York: Braziller, 1955).

for esteem plays a major role in governing people's social conduct, shaping their styles of life and spurring them to seek recognition, deference, and social approval.[31]

Views differ, to be sure, on the actual role this need plays, on whether, for example, it warrants the hegemony over psychic life that Adlerians award it. Thus, cognitive theorists such as Festinger acknowledge that there may well be a universal drive to evaluate oneself favorably, but insist that men share another drive as well, in effect a need to appraise accurately their own abilities and achievements.[32] This need to know, according to Festinger, Pepitone, and other cognitive theorists, has sufficient strength to overcome (if necessary) the need for esteem. Nevertheless, the idea of a need for esteem is frequently at the center even of psychological theories which are otherwise very dissimilar. Carl Rogers, who has repudiated much of Freudian theory and therapeutic methods, is still in essential agreement with Freud on the central role this need plays in a person's development, a point of view that Rogers makes even more explicit and emphatic in his later work.[33] And in a classic essay, Gordon Allport notes a persistent tendency in ego psychology to recognize esteem needs. In the history of psychology, the ego has been pictured in different ways, but one of the most persistent and popular conceptions has been "the ego as dominance drive," that is, as an organized striving for esteem. "From this point of approach," Allport writes, "the ego is that portion of the personality that demands status and recognition. The negative states of anxiety, insecurity, defensiveness, resistance are just as truly indicators that, whenever the

---

[31] For an introduction to the complex and somewhat changing views of Adler, see Heinz and Rowena Ansbacher, *The Individual Psychology of Alfred Adler: A Systematic Presentation in Selections from His Writing* (New York: Harper Torch Books, 1962).

[32] See for example Leon Festinger, "Theory of Social Comparison Processes," or Albert Pepitone, *Attraction and Hostility* (New York: Atherton Press, 1964), especially pp. 3-72.

[33] See Hall and Lindzey, *Theories of Personality*, pp. 488-489.

ego is debased, there will rise impulses for its defense and a restoration to status."[34]

Among contemporary psychologists, Maslow has argued forcefully for the view that self-esteem is a basic need of the personality. He distinguishes, in all, five basic needs — physiological, safety, belongingness and love, esteem, and self-actualization.[35] For Maslow, all basic needs are instinctive, that is, they are innate and inherent in all people and are not the product of culture and society. But this does not mean that the need for esteem is of equal importance to all people or even to the same person at every stage of his or her development. According to Maslow, the five basic needs form a hierarchy: only after the lower needs are satisfied do higher needs emerge to govern human behavior. Thus, it is first necessary to satisfy the needs of physiological gratification, for safety, and for love and belongingness before the need for esteem will come into play. This need for esteem actually has two components — a need for self-respect and approval and a need for the respect and approval of others.[36] There is not, therefore, one need but two, and each has many forms of expression. There is "the desire for stength, for achievement, for adequacy, for mastery and competence, for confidence in the face of the world, and for independence and freedom. Second, we have what we may call the desire for reputation or prestige (defining it as respect or esteem from other people), status, dominance, recognition, attention, importance, or appreciation."[37]

Obviously, interpretations very different from Maslow's can be given to the idea of self-esteem as a need. For example, analysts such as Robert White and M. Brewster Smith view

[34] Gordon Allport, *Personality and Social Encounter*, p. 74.

[35] A. H. Maslow, *Motivation and Personality* (New York: Harper and Row, 1954), Chapter 5.

[36] A. H. Maslow, *Motivation and Personality*, p. 90.

[37] *Ibid.*

it as a primary drive derived from autonomous energies of the ego, which makes itself apparent in a person's continuous striving for competence and knowledge.[38] Nevertheless, in their conception as in Maslow's there is a common tendency (though not always a consistent one) to regard self-esteem as a need or drive which energizes people's actions and directs them toward the goal of obtaining respect and approval.

The second approach treats self-esteem not as a need but as a ratio between a person's achievements and his aspirations: the greater the difference between what an individual is and what he aspires to be, the lower his self-esteem; the smaller the difference, the higher his self-esteem. A classic expression of this approach of course, is James' formula for self-esteem: Self-esteem = Success/Pretentions.[39]

A similar interpretation is voiced by Freud when he speaks of self-esteem as "the feeling of triumph when ego corresponds to ego-ideal;" conversely, "the sense of guilt (as well as the sense of inferiority) can be also understood as the expression of tension between the ego and ego-ideal."[40] Freud's formulation has won over psychologists of very different theoretical persuasions. His structural approach to self-esteem has lent impetus to the introduction of numerous operational measures of self-regard, which aim to assess the distance between individuals as they are and as they wish they were.[41]

[38] White, "Ego and Reality in Psychoanalytic Theory"; M. Brewster Smith, "Competence and Socialization," in John A. Clausen, ed., *Socialization and Society* (Boston: Little, Brown and Company, 1968), pp. 270-320.

[39] James, *Principles of Psychology,* p. 310.

[40] Sigmund Freud, "On Narcissism: An Introduction," in *Collected Papers* (London: Hogarth, 1925), vol. 4, pp. 60-83.

[41] See, for example, J. M. Butler and G. V. Haigh, "Changes in the Relation Between Self-Concepts and Ideal Concepts Consequent upon Client-Centered Counseling," in C. R. Rogers and Rosalind F. Dymond, eds., *Psychotherapy and Personality Change* (Chicago: University of

This approach to self-esteem represents one family of measurement models. There are some rather important differences within this family in the conception of the two variables basic to this approach. Thus, a person's actual self may refer to his overall evaluation of himself; or it may variously refer to his judgment about the likelihood of success in a specific task, about the desirability of some personal characteristic, or about the chances of meeting a particular set of social expectations. On the other hand, a person's ideal self may refer to the type of person one believes it is desirable to be, or to the type it is praiseworthy to be, or to the type it is morally obligatory to be. Clearly, there are distinct versions of this approach to self-esteem; nevertheless, it differs markedly from both the first and the third approach.

The third approach is to analyze self-esteem in terms of self-attitudes. The term attitude, as used here, refers to "a relatively enduring organization of beliefs around an object or a situation predisposing one to respond in some preferential manner."[42] Self-esteem, in this third approach, becomes identified with evaluative self-attitudes. Self-attitudes are much like other attitudes.[43] Thus, they are conceived to have three components: cognitive, affective and conative; they include, in other words, beliefs about what is true and

Chicago Press, 1954), pp. 55-75; R. E. Bills, E. L. Vance, and O. S. McLean, "An Index of Adjustment and Values," *Journal of Consulting Psychology* 51 (1951): 254-259; for a critical review see Wylie, *The Self Concept*, pp. 41-64; and Lee J. Cronbach, "Proposals Leading to Analytic Treatment of Social Perception Scores," in R. Tagiuri and L. Petrillo, *Person Perception and Interpersonal Behavior* (Stanford: Stanford University Press, 1969).

[42] Milton Rokeach, *Beliefs, Attitudes and Values* (San Francisco: Jossey-Bass, 1969), p. 112.

[43] The discussion which follows draws on Morris Rosenberg, *Society and the Adolescent Self-Image* (Princeton, N. J.: Princeton University Press, 1965), Chapter 1; Stanley Coopersmith, *The Antecedents of Self-Esteem* (San Francisco: W. H. Freeman, 1967), Chapter 2; and Rokeach, *Beliefs, Attitudes and Values,* Chapter 5.

desirable and good; feelings of like and dislike attached to a particular object or situation; and an organized set of response dispositions or action tendencies. But self-attitudes may also differ in several respects from other attitudes.[44] There are differences of degree (for example, a person's self-image is usually of importance to him while his attitudes toward other objects often are not). There are also differences of kind: perhaps the most important is that attitudes are usually organized about a common object — for example, attitudes about the current President all refer to the same man; but every person's self-attitudes are necessarily centered on different objects — every person's own self.[45] Nevertheless, the close resemblance between attitudes toward the self and attitudes toward other objects allows us to conceptualize (and measure) both of them in the same way.[46] According to this third approach, then, we ought to assess a person's self-esteem in the same way as we do his or her beliefs about politics or religion, although the substance of these self-attitudes — what exactly they include and exclude — is by no means obvious or agreed on.

Of the three approaches to self-esteem, I have chosen the third. The first two approaches rely heavily on a number of assumptions about the nature of personality for their persuasiveness, assumptions which it may be neither wise nor necessary to make. The second approach, for example, commits one to a structural conception of personality, whose basic components include ego, ego-ideal, and superego, and inclines one to postulate certain hypotheses about the way these components are interrelated, as for example, the customary view that the formation of the ego-ideal depends on the processes of identification and introjection. But the

[44] For an elaboration of the points of similarity and dissimilarity, see especially Rosenberg, *Society and Adolescent Self-Image*, Chapter 1.

[45] *Ibid.*

[46] For a similar argument, see Coopersmith, *The Antecedents of Self-Esteem,* p. 22.

warrant for these assumptions and hypotheses remains uncertain as long as psychologists remain in fundamental disagreement over the basic components of personality and the nature of their interconnection.

The first approach, viewing self-esteem as a need, requires a belief in the utility of some psychological construct close to the notion of "instinctive ego drives," a notion which Sherif and Cantril, among others, have made the target of cogent criticism.[47] But the third approach, unlike the first two, requires no commitment to a particular conception of personality or to more or less controversial psychological constructs: it suits a wide variety of personality theories because it avoids speculation about the basic elements, dynamisms, and structure of personality. This flexibility, of course, has a price. The attitude approach focuses on the "surface" aspects of personality, and to adopt it is to eschew ambitions to penetrate to deeper layers of personality. But this restriction involves no major concession. Rather, it merely makes explicit a limitation inherent in this type of study. The object of these studies is to unravel the relationship between politics and personality, not to settle fundamental issues in psychological theory and method. In view of the continuing schisms in personality theory and research, it is both proper and prudent to make use of concepts such as attitude, located at an intermediate level of psychological analysis, and to leave more recondite questions for psychologists to answer.

In addition, both the first and second approaches are particularly beset by ambiguity and uncertainty. Take, for example, the relationship between a person's ideal and actual self. Presumably, the smaller the difference between the two, the higher a person's self-esteem. But the closer we look at the relationship between the two, the more perplexed we become. A person's ego-ideal presumably sets the image of who he ought to be and so establishes the standards against

[47] Muzafer Sherif and Hadley Cantril, *The Psychology of Ego-Involvements* (New York: Wiley, Science Editions, 1966), especially Chapter 5.

which he should measure himself. The customary usage, both theoretical and operational, assumes that at best a person can meet these standards. Under certain conditions, however, a person can exceed, not just equal, these standards — for example, if they refer to a particular task that he performs rather than to a personal quality that he wants to possess such as honesty. There are further uncertainties of meaning in the notion of an ideal self. It may refer to the sort of person he wants to be now or to the sort of person he wishes ultimately to become. Then, too, the ideal self may incorporate standards a person feels it is desirable to meet or those a person not only wants to meet but feels he must meet, in order to maintain a sense of decency and personal worth. There is also disagreement over whether these standards are personal or social, as we have observed. Even scholars who agree in the abstract tend to disagree in the specific instance. By social standards Festinger means performance expectations for specific tasks while Snygg and Combs mean a global judgment about personal "worth." By personal standards James has in mind certain self-selected aims, particularly those which involve productive achievements and occupational roles, while George Herbert Mead has in mind a process by which individuals realize the innate qualities which confirm their distinctiveness.[48] Last, this approach suggests that a person's score on a measure of self-esteem is some function of his scores on the two component measures of actual self and ideal self, and in fact this is standard practice in self concept measures.[49] But empirical studies have found that people tend to agree on what a person ideally should be like; where they disagree is on how close they come to this standard. Measures of self-esteem, which compute a score of the difference between scores on measures of actual self and ideal self tend to conceal the fact that there is variation in one component measure but not in the other. Of course,

[48] For a general review of these positions, see Diggory, *Self-Evaluation,* Chapter 3.

[49] See Wylie, *The Self Concept,* Chapter 2.

under these circumstances, the index of self-esteem is a person's actual judgment of himself as he is, not the discrepancy between that judgment and the standards that he sets for himself.[50]

The first approach, viewing self-esteem as a need, suffers comparable drawbacks. We have already observed the diversity of specific needs psychologists have in mind when they speak of a need for esteem. But the problem is even more difficult than we have suggested. Consider what the object of such a need might be. A person may identify himself with an endless number of external objects or symbols; he also may become ego-involved with any of his activities or values. These may all serve as the objects of a need for esteem: examples of the person who seeks to prove his personal worth by achievement in his occupation or by identification with some social group can be multiplied many times over. To define such a motive is extraordinarily difficult, for it may be engaged in many different circumstances and it may propel a person in many different directions. One cannot say with confidence what such a need includes because one cannot say with certainty what it excludes.

I have chosen, therefore, to define self-esteem in terms of self-attitudes. Self-esteem, as it is used here, refers to a particular aspect of the attitudes individuals hold about themselves, embracing what they believe to be their desirable (and undesirable) qualities and whether they like (or dislike) themselves. Taken together, these beliefs and feelings constitute the evaluative dimension[51] of self-attitudes, which may

[50] Cronbach, "Proposals Leading to Analytic Treatment of Social Perception Scores."

[51] I am aware that the "evaluative" dimension includes two components — affects and cognitions — which are not perfectly correlated; that is, one can like what one believes to be bad and dislike what one believes to be good. But in fact the association between the two is so close that Scott, after an extensive review, suggests that (except in rare instances) they may be operationally indistinguishable. See William A. Scott, "Attitude Assessment," in Lindzey and Aronson, eds., *Handbook of Social Psychology* (Reading, Mass.: Addison-Wesley, 1969), vol 2, pp. 204-273. No measure of self-esteem has been able to separate affect and cognition. So in this study we make no use of the distinction between them.

vary from favorable to unfavorable. High self-esteem, then, refers to favorable self-attitudes, low self-esteem to unfavorable self-attitudes.

Measurement Procedure

Self-esteem, then, refers to a set of evaluative attitudes one holds about oneself. But which self-attitudes ought to be included and which excluded? To locate the boundary of this attitude domain, all forty-seven attitudinal and psychological scales in McClosky's PAB study were factor analyzed.[52] These scales are quite varied in content, and include, among other things measures of general social attitudes (such as chauvinism, ethocentrism); of attitudes toward politics (such as political cynicism, party loyalty); of political ideology (such as democratic values, liberalism-conservatism, extreme political belief); of personal adjustment and of a number of clinical personality traits (such as dominance, social responsibility, obsessiveness, paranoia, and hostility). Scales rather than items were the unit of analysis because inter-scale correlations as a rule are both more variable and larger in magnitude than inter-item correlations. Correlations among a pool of items, particularly if they are dichotomous as these are, tend to be so low as to be less likely to generate factors which are internally coherent, clearly distinguishable from one another, or very stable over time.[53] An orthogonal factor analysis, using a varimax rotation, located one and only one factor which appeared to have some bearing on self-esteem.[54] Scales with a loading of greater than

[52] The details of this analysis by Herbert McClosky will be reported separately.

[53] J. Nunally, *Psychometric Theory* (New York: McGraw-Hill, 1967), pp. 255-258.

[54] This factor analysis was done by Jack Citrin and Herbert McClosky for a different purpose. The detailed findings of this analysis of the PAB studies will be available in a forthcoming volume by Herbert McClosky. For the purposes of this study, only one factor is of interest. It is worth noting that the classification of this factor as the self-esteem factor was independently agreed upon by both McClosky and Citrin, *before* the present study got under way.

.4 (an arbitrary cutting point chosen beforehand) on this factor were selected for further analysis. All items in these scales then formed a pool of indicators from which to construct a measure of self-esteem. Thus, the factor analysis established the limits of the pool of eligible items and also provided some assurance of the homogeneity of this pool.

Previous measurement strategies have generally attempted to select a set of items which would provide an indication of a person's overall self-esteem, that is, of whether his evaluation of himself tends, in general, to be favorable or unfavorable. This global approach to self-assessment, however, has critical shortcomings. For one thing, this approach rests on the presumption that all forms of self-evaluation are in essence the same and can therefore be considered together. But lumping them together forecloses any opportunity to confirm this presumption. It is likely that many of the evaluative attitudes which people form about themselves reflect a relatively consistent disposition to evaluate themselves either favorably or unfavorably. But it is also obvious that some people may evaluate themselves favorably in some respects and less favorably—or even unfavorably—in other respects. We have no exact idea of the interrelationships of evaluative self-attitudes. Moreover, these various attitudes may have different consequences, as this study will demonstrate. In brief, we simply cannot tell whether or not these attitudes affect political belief and behavior in the same way unless we investigate them separately rather than lumping them together in some global index.

In addition, the practice of constructing global measures has contributed to confusion in the research on self-esteem and accounts for some of the apparently contradictory findings. Consider, for example, the relationship between self-esteem and psychological adjustment. Following the lead of Carl Rogers, who has contended that low self-esteem (by which he means a large discrepancy between a person's actual self and ideal self) leads to excessive anxiety and psychological stress, a number of investigators have hypothesized that there is a positive linear relationship between self-esteem and psychological adjustment. And indeed several studies have reported a significant association between low self-esteem and psychological maladjustment.[55] But these studies have come under fire from other researchers who have argued that very favorable self-ratings frequently represent efforts by a person to deny his inner conflicts and limitations; they postulate, therefore, that persons with either low or very high self-esteem should show signs of psychological maladjustment and in fact several studies have uncovered evidence of such a curvilinear relationship between self-esteem and personal adjustment.[56] We cannot make much of these contradictory sets of findings, primarily because we have no assurance that the measures of self-esteem that these various studies employed are equivalent. To estimate their equivalence, we must at least know their parameters, that is, specifically what they include and what they exclude as part of the idea of self-esteem.[57] One measure may be very much like another, or it may be quite different. To build a global measure and label it an index of self-esteem provides no clue as to its specific content.

Since self-esteem is a complex concept, too broad and multi-facted to define and measure easily, we must identify component elements which are simpler and more specific

---

[55] R. H. Turner and R. H. Vanderlippe, "Self-Ideal Congruence as an Index of Adjustment," *JASP* 57 (1958): 202-206; G. M. Smith, "Six Measures of Self-Concept Discrepancy and Instability; Their Interrelations, Reliability and Relations to Other Personality Variables," *Journal of Consulting Psychology* 22 (1958): 101-112. For a discussion of the rationale for a positive relationship, and for a negative one, see D. Byrne, *An Introduction to Personality* (Englewood Cliffs, N. J.: Prentice-Hall, 1966), pp. 438-440 and pp. 452-455 respectively.

[56] Jack Block and Thomas Hobart, "Is Satisfaction with Self a Measure of Adjustment?" *JASP* 51 (1955): 254-259; M. Zuckerman and I. Monashkin, "Self-Acceptance and Psychopathology," *Journal of Consulting Psychology* 22 (1957): 165-171.

[57] For a discussion of some of the issues and problems of stimulus-sampling and the self-concept, see Wylie, *The Self Concept*, pp. 44-46.

and define and measure each independently. After reviewing numerous theoretical and empirical studies, I have located three dimensions of self-esteem which (1) other researchers have employed and (2) were incorporated in the data available to me. The first dimension focuses on the feelings of *personal unworthiness*. Persons lacking self-esteem in this sense are acutely aware of their imperfections in character, believing they have violated important moral standards and, in extreme cases, judging themselves to be unforgivably flawed. The second dimension refers to feeling of *interpersonal competence* — an individual's self-confidence about his capacity to deal with other objects in his environment. Feelings of ineffectiveness and vulnerability are among the signs of this form of low self-esteem. The third dimension taps feelings of *status inferiority*, which can find expression, for example, in embarrassment about one's manners, social background, or schooling.

These three "dimensions," it should be noted, were derived on conceptual and not empirical grounds. Strictly empirical procedures such as factor or cluster analysis were rejected for a number of reasons. McClosky's questionnaire had not originally been drafted with an eye to building self-esteem measures, so no systematic effort had been made to ensure that the questionnaire tapped all aspects of self-esteem. Consequently, there would be no justification for any assumption that "factors" extracted from such an item pool would truly represent the main dimensions of self-esteem. Moreover, strictly empirical procedures for data reduction, *which are not directed by preconceived ideas as to the nature and number of the underlying attributes*, have properly come under attack.[58] In this instance, we lack a clear idea as to the scope of evaluative self-attitudes, the character of more basic components which may underlie them, or the interrela-

[58] Nunally, *Psychometric Theory*, pp. 255-258; J. Scott Armstrong, "Derivation of Theory by Means of Factor Analysis or Tom Swift and His Electric Factor Analysis Machine," *The American Statistician* 21 (1967): 7-21; and Robert A. Gordon, "Issues in Multiple Regression," *AJS* 73 (1963): 592-616.

tionship among these components; that is, we are not certain whether they should be thought of as independent or related to one another. In these circumstances, the optimal procedure is to select a number of dimensions that are part of the notion of self-esteem as it is commonly understood and only then determine which items, if any, assess these particular dimensions of self-regard.

This is my strategy. At the very least, it should make plain the meaning of self-esteem in this study. My aim, then, is to construct separate measures for three dimensions of self-esteem — personal unworthiness, interpersonal competence, and status inferiority — not merely to put together a single global measure based on some general notion of self-regard.

The first step was to assemble a panel of judges whose task would be the preliminary classification of the available questionnaire items. In view of the difficulty of the task, the panel had to possess an uncommon degree of skill and professional commitment. Consequently, all judges on the panel had to meet stringent criteria. All nine of the judges selected possessed doctorates in psychology; all held positions in a university department of psychology, though in the case of two, their major commitments were to research in a university-affiliated institute; and all had had previous experience in the administration and interpretation of psychological tests comprised of statements similar in format and design to the items they were asked to evaluate.

Moreover, a deliberate effort was made to recruit judges whose theoretical orientations and research experience differed.[59] Five classified themselves as clinical psychologists, two as social psychologists, and two as research psychologists in personality. The purpose, quite simply, was to assure the representation of various opinions concerning the nature of self-esteem — to avoid, in other words, theoretical censorship at the very outset of this study.

[59] In addition to these judges, two others, both practicing psychiatrists were subsequently polled. In every instance the psychiatrists confirmed the panel's judgments.

All items in the eight scales pinpointed by the factor analysis were presented to the panel. The judges, working independently, were to identify which of these statements, if any, measured the three dimensions of self-esteem I had singled out for study. Every statement had to be placed in one of six categories: self-esteem in the sense of personal unworthiness; self-esteem in the sense of interpersonal competence; self-esteem in the sense of status inferiority; self-esteem in any sense other than the three described above; any attribute other than self-esteem; and any statement that cannot be classified into one of the five preceding categories.

The panel of judges received a written set of instructions,[60] seventy-five scale items arranged in random order, and a scoring sheet to record their decisions. The judges were directed to base their evaluation of the items on their professional interpretation of what agreement (or disagreement) with an item would indicate about a person's self-esteem. This procedure, then, departed to a certain extent from customary practice. As a rule, investigators aim to identify items which, on their face, reflect, or refer to, or exemplify the attribute which they wish to measure; items selected on this basis are said to have "face validity." Here, however, my aim was to evaluate statements not as they would be understood by the average reader or respondent but as they would be interpreted by a person professionally trained in psychology. The judges, therefore, were instructed to identify all items, which in their opinion, assessed an aspect of self-esteem, whether or not they contained an obvious, direct reference to a person's evaluation of himself.

Because all scale items are inherently multi-faceted, they can be interpreted differently by different persons, including of course, the expert panel. It was necessary, therefore, to establish beforehand a minimum level of agreement necessary among the judges for an item to be selected. An arbitrary

[60] Personal discussions with judges after they had executed their assignment indicated they had found both the instructions and the scoring procedures clear and easy to execute.

but stringent standard was imposed: at least six of the nine judges had to concur. Note that the judges had to agree on exactly which one of the three aspects of self-esteem an item measured, not merely that it reflected some form or degree of self-regard. Thirty items from the original pool of seventy-five met this standard, but it is of interest to note that on more than half of these thirty items more than six of the judges were in exact agreement.

Preliminary versions of the three measures of self-esteem were built from the items surviving the screening of the judges. Indices of personal unworthiness, interprersonal competence, and status inferiority were constructed by summing responses to items the panel regarded as measures of each aspect of self-esteem. Multiple regression analyses, regressing the items in each index on the total index score, were performed, enabling me to estimate the direct and indirect effects of items on index scores. This procedure was adopted because a simple correlation between an index and one of its component items can be due to a direct connection between the two, or alternatively, to a connection between one component item and another which is independently related to the index. Thus, I could take into account the interactions among all the items that composed an index, and thereby identify and eliminate any item whose correlation with an index was due primarily to its association with one of the other items and not to its relationship to the overall index. Of the thirty items which had survived the screening of the judges, the regression analysis eliminated fifteen.

Responses to the remaining fifteen items were summed, again separately for the three dimensions of self-esteem, to construct criterion versions for the three indices. At this point I turned to another form of item analysis, computing point bi-serial correlations betweeen the criterion versions of the three indices and all of the items in the original pool (with the exception, of course, of those items which comprise the three criterion indices). This procedure was designed to achieve a number of objectives. One of my aims was to increase the length of the criterion versions of the three indices, without, however, sacrificing their homogeneity and validity. Another was to locate additional items which measured one of these aspects of self-esteem, *even if they contained no direct reference to a person's evaluation of himself.* In the measurement of a psychological trait such as self-esteem, where responses to items may fall under the influence of determinants other than a person's self-evaluation, such as the desire to present a socially acceptable image, it is of particular importance to locate such disguised indicators: the less apparent the intent of the item, the less likely a person will fabricate, deliberately or unconsciously, a misleading description of himself. The item-index correlations provide an economical search procedure to locate items which, regardless of their face content, belong to the same empirical domain as an index.

There was a third objective of the item-index analysis. The three indices are all measures of self-esteem, but they are supposed to tap different dimensions of self-evaluation. The issue, then, is the discriminant validity of the three indices of self-esteem. The item-index correlations provided a method of assuring that the indices measured dimensions of self-esteem which can be discriminated on empirical as well as conceptual grounds. To achieve these three objectives,[61] I added to the criterion versions of the three indices items that met two criteria: (1) demonstration of a significant point bi-serial correlation (= .30) with one but only one of the three indices and (2) agreement by at least five judges that it was this dimension of self-esteem which the item tapped. Cumulation of the responses to items in each of the three indices generated the final versions of the indices of

---

[61] Another consideration that I had in mind is more technical in nature. Item-discriminant analysis, another form of item analysis whose objective is to locate items which best discriminate high and low scorers on a particular index, favors the selection of items with extremes accepting or rejecting. The point bi-serial correlation, on the other hand, favors the selection of mid-range items, which in turn yield index scores with a more normal distribution, a point of some importance in constructing a measure for use in a variety of samples.

personal unworthiness, interpersonal competence, and status inferiority. The final twenty-two items that make up the three indices are:

Personal Unworthiness

I do many things which I regret afterwards.

There is no such thing as being "too strict" where conscience and morals are concerned.

A large number of people are guilty of bad sexual conduct.

I think that in some ways I am really an unworthy person.

People today have forgotten how to feel properly ashamed of themselves.

I never try to do more than I know I can, for fear of failure.

When I look back on it, I guess I really haven't gotten as much out of life as I had once hoped.

I often have the feeling I have done something wrong or evil.

Status Inferiority

I have often had to take orders from someone who did not know as much as I did.

I must admit that rich, successful people are generally more pleasant to be with than poor people.

I would like to wear more expensive clothes than I do.

It bothers me that I do not have more education.

I sometimes run into people who make me feel ashamed of my background..

I prefer to be with people of wealth and good breeding.

I often wish I could have been born into a high position in life.

Interpersonal Competence

I often wish I could act free and easy with the people who count.

I wish I could be as carefree about my actions as others are.

I hate to have to tell other people what to do.

I would rather not have very much responsibility for other people.

When I disagree with people it turns out later that I was in the right.

I dislike to have to talk in front of a group of people.

I doubt whether I would make a good leader.

The Question of Social Desirability[62]

To learn what people think of themselves, we must ask them. But what assurance do we have that their answers will be accurate and candid? Some are likely to attribute to themselves desirable qualities which they do not have or conceal undesirable ones which they do have. Others may admit to personal flaws because they have an uncommon measure of self-awareness and insight, not because they have unfavorable attitudes toward themselves. How serious are these threats to the measurement of self-esteem? How likely are our respondents to give misleading descriptions of how they feel toward themselves?

The key issue, it must be emphasized, is not whether introspective data (or survey questionnaires) are reliable. At the outset, let us concede that this type of data is vulnerable to error. In exchange, though, let us also acknowledge that other types of data used in the measurement of psychological attributes (for example, reports of trained observers) are similarly vulnerable to error. Estimates of error which are based only on the type of data and which do not take into account the details of the test situation and procedure have

[62] I have chosen to discuss here the question of social desirability and not the more familiar problem of acquiescence for two reasons. First, I happen to have in this study a measure of acquiescence and not one of social desirability, so I am in a position to determine how serious a risk to my findings acquiescence poses. As I shall show the risk is slight. Second, the accumulating literature on acquiescence has persuaded me that its seriousness as a source of measurement error has been greatly exaggerated. Earlier studies initially persuaded me of this view. See Jack Block, *The Challenge of Response Sets*; Dean Peabody, "Attitude Content and Agreement Set in Scales of Authoritarianism, Dogmatism, Anti-Semitism and Economic Conservatism," *JASP* 63 (1961): 1-11; Douglas N. Jackson and Samuel Messick, "Response Styles on the MMPI: Comparison of Clinical and Normal Samples," *JASP* 65 (1962): 285-299; Leonard G. Rorer, "The Great Response Style Myth," *Psychological Bulletin* 65 (1965): 129-156; Donald T. Campbell, Carole R. Siegman and Matilda B. Rees, "Direction-of-Wording Effects in the Relationship Between Scales," *Psychological Bulletin* 68 (1967): 293-303. Subsequent discussions of acquiescence, in particular the extensive debate between Block on the one side, and Jackson and Messick on the other, have only served to strengthen my conviction that the dangers of acquiescence have

no validity. Certainly, we lack the systematic evidence necessary to decide whether introspective data encourage greater or lesser error than do other types of data in the measurement of *particular psychological attributes*. There is no need for an unqualified commitment to the validity of introspective data. We should put the question in specific terms rather than in the abstract. That is, we ought to ask whether in measuring a particular trait, considering the costs of measurement alternatives, there is sufficient reason to trust a particular set of responses obtained from a particular sample of persons, not whether we may rely on introspective data under all (or any) circumstances.

In the measurement of self-esteem, the question of social desirability poses an obvious threat. To the extent that there is an overriding tendency for respondents to present themselves in a socially desirable light, my measures of self-esteem will be systematically in error: respondents unwilling to admit undesirable qualities in themselves will tend to be classified as high, not low, in self-esteem.[63]

---

been greatly overrated. See P. M. Bentler, Douglas N. Jackson and Samuel Messick, "Identification of Content and Style: A Two-Dimensional Interpretation of Acquiescence," *Psychological Bulletin* 76 (1971): 186-204; Jack Block, "On Further Conjectures Regarding Acquiescence," *Psychological Bulletin* 76 (1971): 205-210; P. M. Bentler, Douglas N. Jackson, and Samuel Messick, "A Rose by Any Other Name," *Psychological Bulletin* 77 (1972): 109-113; Jack Block, "The Shifting Definitions of Acquiescence," *Psychological Bulletin* 78 (1972): 10-12; and Franz Samelson, "Response Style: A Psychologist's Fallacy," *Psychological Bulletin* 78 (1972): 13-16.

[63] In principle, two types of error are possible: respondents may not acknowledge undesirable qualities they actually have, or they may attribute to themselves desirable characteristics they do not actually possess. In this instance, we must be concerned about the first type of error, but not the second, because of the "unbalanced" character of the items in our questionnaire inventory. They consist predominantly of statements so worded that agreement with an item entails admitting possession of a socially undesirable characteristic. Our respondents, in effect, have a great many opportunities to avoid showing themselves in an undesirable light, but very few to present themselves in an undeservedly desirable one.

There is no entirely reliable way to estimate the extent
to which this type of error jeopardizes my three measures
of self-esteem. But on the basis of the scholarly literature
on response styles and the evidence of my own data, I tend
to discount the likelihood that social desirability is a critical
source of contamination of the particular measures I have
constructed for this study. My skepticism rests in part on
recent critical appraisals of response styles in psychological
assessment and in particular on Block's incisive analysis of
the problems of acquiescence and social desirability.[64] The
tendency to "fake good" can account for self-esteem scores
only if the two are strongly correlated, but the correlations
observed between measures of self-esteem and social desirability vary remarkably in magnitude and in many instances
are insignificant in size. Nevertheless, it would be surprising
never to uncover a relationship between the two, for as Block
has pointed out, measures of social desirability tend to be
made up of items remarkably alike in content which appear,
on their face at least, to tap a personality characteristic
rather like anxiety, a characteristic which, if properly measured, should be associated with low self-esteem.[65]

This suggests, in turn, that it is the validity of measures
of social desirability, not that of self-esteem, that should be
questioned. How compelling is the evidence that these
response-style measures actually measure what they purport
to measure? Again, I am inclined to skepticism, for there
are different conceptions of what is socially desirable. A
number of studies have found not only disagreement among
people about what is socially desirable but signs that the
notion of social desirability is made up of several distinct,
sometimes unrelated dimensions.[66] Beyond this, the two most

[64] Jack Block, *The Challenge of Response Sets* (New York: Appleton-
Century-Crifts, 1965).

[65] *Ibid.,* pp. 72-73.

[66] See Ruth Wylie's review of empirical studies bearing on this point.
Wylie, *The Self Concept*, pp. 29-30.

frequently used measures of social desirability — the Marlowe-Crowne Scale and the Edwards Scale — sometimes fail to show any relationship at all to one another.[67] The absence of association between them suggests that these two scales measure different things; but it is not apparent which scale measures what. In addition, the concept of social desirability has been construed in different ways at different times even by the same people. Originally, it referred to a property of an item to elicit agreement from a certain proportion of persons rather than to a characteristic of an individual to react to a collection of items, regardless of their content, in a particular way. Gradually, it became interpreted as an aspect of an individual's personality; but precisely which psychological trait or state is being tapped is far from clear. The tendency to disagree with any statements which imply that one is in any important sense imperfect or a failure can arise from any number of psychological needs and processes. To this, the work of Marlowe and Crowne, among the most systematic investigators of social desirability, bears witness. Differences in scores on the Marlowe-Crowne Social Desirability Scale, they first asserted, reflect differences in the strength of the need for social approval. The stronger such a need, the more a person wants to present himself in a socially approved or desirable light; the weaker such a need, the more independent and open about his faults a person can be. But in their subsequent work, Crowne and Marlowe attached a different interpretation to their Social Desirability Scale. Rather than measuring the need for approval, the scale measured at one extreme "the need to be perceived as free from any inadequacies" and at the other "the need to be regarded as self-critical or self-deprecatory."[68]

[67] L. I. Jacobson and L. H. Ford, Jr., "Need for Approval, Defensive Denial, and Sensitivity to Cultural Stereotypes," *Journal of Personality* 34 (1966): 596-609.

[68] Jacobson and Ford, Jr., "Need for Approval, Defensive Denial, and Sensitivity to Cultural Stereotypes." See also D. P. Crowne and D. Marlowe, *The Approval Motive* (New York: Wiley, 1964).

But which of the two interpretations — the first, which centered on a need for approval, or the second, which stressed a process of defensive denial — is the more correct? Or is there a third interpretation superior to those two?

There is some plausibility to the assertion that people who are entirely unwilling to admit to any degree of imperfection or fault, not even the slightest, are in fact motivated by a deep desire to protect themselves from knowledge of how serious their shortcomings are; that is, they are defending themselves against a sense of low self-esteem. But what ought one to make of persons who are too ready to concede their shortcomings, persons who exhibit an unusual willingness to present themselves in a socially *un*desirable light? One might contend, as Crowne and Marlowe have, that such persons have either a weak need for approval or a strong need to be self-critical. Alternatively, one might argue that those who are excessively self-critical are attempting to elicit sympathy, attention, and aid from other persons. In short, both low and high social desirability scores may be signs of low self-esteem. The empirical studies faithfully reflect this conceptual confusion, sometimes reporting a positive association between measures of social desirability and self-esteem, sometimes a negative relationship between the two, and sometimes no relationship at all.[69]

[69] Some studies reporting a positive relationship are: D. P. Browne, M. W. Stephens, and R. Kelly, "The Validity and Equivalence of Tests of Self-Acceptance," *Journal of Psychology* 51 (1961): 101-112; D. T. Kenny, "The Influence of Social Desirability on Discrepancy Measures Between Real Self and Ideal Self," *Journal of Consulting Psychology* 20 (1956): 315-318; A. L. Edwards, *The Social Desirability Variable in Personality Assessment and Research* (New York: Holt, 1957); W. S. Kogan, R. Quinn, A. F. Ax, and H. S. Ripley, "Some Methodological Problems in the Quantification of Clinical Assessment by Q Array," *Journal of Consulting Psychology* 21 (1957): 57-62. For reports of no relationship or a negative one, see E. L. Cowen and P. N. Tongas, "The Social Desirability of Trait Descriptive Terms: Applications to a Self-Concept Inventory," *Journal of Consulting Psychology* 23 (1959): 361-365; and V. Crandall, "Personality Characteristics and Social and Achievement Behaviors Associated with Children's Social Desirability Response Tendencies," *JASP* 4 (1966): 477-486.

Yet, even when measures of self-esteem and social desirability are related, one may well ask which accounts for which. Social desirability is purportedly a measure of a tendency to respond to items on the basis not of what the item says but on how a particular response to it would be regarded. Hence, the common practice has been to assume that this is the factor that must first be taken into account. According to this view, only the variance in self-esteem scores unrelated to, and so uncontaminated by, this response style could conceivably reflect genuine differences in self-esteem. But as Block has pointed out in another context, either concept would logically account for the other.[70] Thus, the very fact that an individual lacks confidence in his own worth may well be the reason for his unwillingness to openly acknowledge personal failings. But if we are forced to choose between these two constructs, surely we should choose the one that has the greater heuristic value. And the choice to make on this ground is obvious. On the one hand, the concept of social desirability has little explanatory power. It is a postulate that some persons simulate the social virtues, a postulate, moreover, that is in essence methodological rather than theoretical. Its real purpose, the purpose for which it was originally introduced, was to account for error variance, that is, to identify an irrelevant determinant of responses to psychological tests. Outside the contest of measurement theory, it has little value. On the other hand, the concept of self-esteem is located at the center of several major personality theories and has rich and suggestive associations. It has stimulated empirical research in both experimental and non-experimental settings. Perhaps the most persuasive evidence of this concept's heuristic value is the number and variety of studies in which it is put to use. These studies include, among other things, research on attitude change, social interaction, conformity, creativity, opinion formation, psychological adjustment, and political participation and leadership. Thus, in the conduct of research, the concept

[70] Block, *Challenge of Response Sets,* pp. 81-84.

of self-esteem has been the source of an extraordinary range of hypotheses of substantive interest, while the concept of social desirability has been confined principally to the explanation of measurement error.

Social desirability, of course, remains a potential source of error. Therefore, in constructing this particular measure of self-esteem, the procedure was designed to give assurance, insofar as it is possible, that responses to these specific items are not a function of social desirability. As we noted, construction began with a factor analysis of the psychological and attitudinal scales of the PAB. If item responses reflected social desirability rather than self-esteem, that is, represented method rather than trait variance, the factor judged to assess self-esteem should be comprised of items decidedly more difficult for a person low in self-esteem to agree with. But agreement with items from scales in the other factors tend to be rated as more difficult, not less, for the person who either seeks approval or protection against acknowledgment of his personal inadequacies. That is, it is items from other factors, rather than those selected for these three measures of self-esteem, which manifestly deal with a person's unwillingness to describe himself in ways the society might judge undesirable. Similarly, items included in the three self-esteem measures have lower social desirability values than many of the items which were in the original item pool but were not selected for inclusion in the final versions of the three indices. Moreover, to construct the three separate indices of self-esteem, item-index correlations were computed. As noted above, in order for an item to be added to a particular index, it had to have a significant correlation with one index *and no other*. The aim was to locate items which assessed one and only one dimension of self-esteem. This insistence that the items added to each index measure different things minimized the chances that indices might measure the same thing, namely, social desirability.

Another aspect of the construction procedure was also designed to minimize contamination by social desirability. The instructions given to the panel of judges specifically requested them to classify indirect as well as direct indicators of low self-esteem. That is, a particular item on its face may not appear to concern a person's sense of worth; it may, for example, be an assertion about the qualities of persons in general rather than about the characteristics of the respondent in particular. The aim, of course, was to identify disguised indicators of low self-esteem, that is, items a respondent would not see as involving some form of self-evaluation, and would therefore feel free to respond to frankly and without any concern about presenting himself in a socially desirable light. A later part of the procedure fur thered this aim. The item-index correlations were explicitly intended to identify all items belonging to the same empirical domain, regardless of whether the content of an item, on its face, concerned self-esteem. The direct result of these two steps in the construction procedure is to incorporate in the self-esteem index a number of items which do not appear to involve self-rating, and therefore should not be affected by social desirability. Thus, in the personal unworthiness index, which is the aspect of self-esteem one might believe to be most strongly under the influence of a desire to deny faults and present a blameless appearance, three of the eight items ask for an opinion about people in general, not about the respondent himself. Of the remaining five items, at least two appear relatively free of influence by social desirability; agreement with these items (scored as a sign of low self-esteem) may in fact give the impression of a certain honesty about oneself and humility, an impression which, if anything, presents the respondent in a socially desirable rather than undesirable way.

For all these reasons, I doubt that social desirability seriously contaminates my measures of self-esteem.

In Retrospect

My three measures of self-esteem have their shortcomings. They certainly do not include all aspects of self-esteem, nor is there strong reason to believe that they are a representative sample of evaluative self-attitudes. Also, levels of self-esteem vary in expression with the development stage of the person. Thus, a marked concern for the status and social privileges which an occupation confers may emerge only at a later point in life. In short, my construction procedure is inevitably tied to the limitations — and opportunities — of secondary analysis.

On balance, I believe that these three measures do provide a somewhat crude, but relatively trustworthy, index to a person's self-esteem. The global concept of self-esteem has been reduced to simpler, more specific components, which ought at least to decrease conceptual vagueness. Each of these measures also appears homogeneous. A number of the construction procedures — the factor analysis of the scales, the regression analysis, the computation of item index correlations — were specifically selected so as to establish by a variety of methods the homogeneity of the measures. Moreover, I believe that the items included in these measures are a fair representation of those which I might have considered, had the questionnaire been explicitly designed for the purpose of measuring self-esteem. Certainly, there is nothing to suggest that respondents would be ranked in a different order, had many more items been available. Finally, the construction procedure was designed to provide a means of deciding which items to include and which to exclude, without relying on subjective judgments as to what an item assesses. With the exception only of the item ratings, performed by a panel with professional expertise and with no knowledge of the purposes of the larger study, the construction procedures used to determine which items belonged to the same conceptual domain were strictly objective.

Of course, no measure is error-proof. But then it is not my position that a relatively high score on the personal unworthiness index, for example, is proof-positive a person has low self-esteem, if for no other reason than the variety of meanings which have been attached to the notion of self-esteem. A search for the one "true" meaning is fruitless, for the notion is obviously complex and multi-faceted. For the same reason, there is no single, external criterion against which we might check a person's answers to the questionnaire items in the three indices to see whether "in fact" his self-esteem is high or low. In any event, as Paul Meehl has observed, what is important in the end is not whether what a respondent says is in fact so, but the fact that he or she says it is so.[71]

My construction procedure has included a number of major steps. Each step served as a hurdle, and items which could survive so many different obstacles merit some confidence. All these steps, however, constitute only the first phase in the justification of these measures. The second phase, which is equally demanding, will occur throughout the succeeding chapters. I shall demonstrate the construct validity of these measures by showing the close correspondence between the findings of previous studies and my results on the one hand, and between my results and my theoretical expectations on the other. A final assessment of the validity of my measures of self-esteem, therefore, must await the conclusion.

[71] Paul E. Meehl, "The Dynamics of 'Structured' Personality Tests," *Journal of Clinical Psychology* 1 (1945): 296-303. For a recent discussion of some of the issues Meehl's classic article raised and of subsequent empirical and theoretical work bearing on these issues, see Douglas N. Jackson, "The Dynamics of Structured Personality Tests," *Psychological Review* 78 (1971): 229-248.

Chapter 3 · THE SYNDROME OF SELF-ESTEEM

This chapter will explore the dynamics of self-esteem. It will sketch the larger syndrome of which self-esteem is but one part, suggesting what it means psychologically to be high or low in self-esteem and thereby establishing the basis for the specific hypothesis that succeeding chapters will test. The first step will be to outline a theoretical conception of self-esteem, the second, to survey the psychological correlates of my measures of self-esteem.

The Dynamics of Self-Esteem[1]

Self-esteem, as I have defined it, refers to evaluative self-attitudes. These attitudes are close to the surface of

[1] Below I have set down my "theoretical conception" of self-esteem, i.e., the understanding I have of the nature of the dynamics of self-esteem, an understanding which has guided to some extent the course of this study, suggesting, for example, hypotheses to test, strategies of analysis, and originally unanticipated possibilities of inquiry. A "theoretical conception," of course is not the same thing as a theory. I am attempting not to prove a theory, but to explain a theoretical position, so as to give the reader a guide to the reasoning underlying the specific arguments and hypotheses in this study. For that reason, I have omitted references to evidence supporting my point of view, and purely for convenience of exposition have set down arguments as though they were a matter of established fact. I have placed my greatest reliance on the following sources in developing my understanding of the dynamics of self-esteem: Morris Rosenberg, *Society and the Adolescent Self-Image* (Princeton: Princeton University Press, 1965); Stanley Coopersmith, *The Antecedents of Self-Esteem* (San Francisco: W. H. Freeman, 1967); George L. Engel, *Psychological Development in Health and Disease* (Philadelphia: N. B.

personality in two ways:[2] first, self-attitudes are relatively conscious, that is, they are available to awareness and self-report; second, they are partly determined by more deep-seated, unconscious processes such as long-standing habits, basic needs, or defense mechanisms. But this is not to say that these attitudes are epiphenomenal or lacking in dynamic power. On the contrary, I conceive them to be a central element in the structure of personality.

What, then, is the dynamic significance of self-esteem? Self-esteem, as I use the term, refers to the affect a person feels toward himself. Two types of affect can be distinguished — signal-scanning and drive-discharge.[3] The first type refers to affects such as pride or guilt which operates as a "warning or signal function and a 'How am I doing?' or scanning function, yielding judgments of good or bad, success or failure, pleasure or unpleasure."[4] The second type refers to affects such as anger involving some state of tension and feeling which the person must either discharge or block. Self-esteem, as I conceptualize it, is a signal-scanning rather than a drive-discharge affect.

What do different levels of self-esteem signal? In responding to this question, let us put to use some basic tenets of dynamic psychology. High self-esteem, I would suggest, is a sign of the success of the ego in dealing with the problems it characteristically confronts.[5] These problems may arise

---

Saunders, 1964); Hanna Fenichel and David Rapaport, eds., *The Collected Papers of Otto Fenichel* (New York: W. W. Norton and Company, 1954).

[2] For a discussion of various meanings of the notions of surface and depth in personality theory, see Nevitt Sanford, *Self and Society* (New York: Atherton Press, 1967). See especially pp. 90-91.

[3] For this distinction, see G. L. Engel, *Psychological Development in Health and Disease.*

[4] Engel, *Psychological Development in Health and Disease.*

[5] It is worth noting the increasingly close scrutiny being given to the emergence of ego psychology. For a recent extremely critical appraisal

from three sources — id, superego, and environment. For instance, favorable self-evaluation may indicate an overall record of success in the management of inner impulses. Everyone confronts the problem of coping with impulses such as sex and aggression. Such impulses can be dealt with in a variety of ways — for example, by deferring their gratification until a time of more appropriate circumstances or by altering their aim so as not to provoke disapproval — but these impulses must be brought under control, or the tension which they excite and the constant threat of their eruption will undermine a person's sense of worth and well-being.

Favorable self-evaluation also may indicate a record of success in satisfying the claims of the superego.[6] These claims encompass what a person believes he should or must do. Guilt is the price of failure to meet these claims. The person with high self-esteem has come closer to fulfilling the expectations of his superego than has the person with low self-esteem. That is not to say that a person who evaluates himself favorably is free of feelings of guilt. On the contrary, one of the cardinal features of high self-esteem is ability to tolerate *and* to put to profitable use the tension generated by both the inevitable sense of guilt a person feels and the equally inevitable frustration of instinctual energies he must suffer. I shall take up this point again shortly.

Last, favorable self-evaluation may be a sign of the ego's success in a third area — the external environment. Success in this area indicates an ability to deal effectively with others, to persevere in the face of external obstacles and characteristically overcome them, to meet the standards of achieve-

---

of the usage of the term ego in psychoanalytic theory, see Nathan Leites, *The New Ego* (New York: Science House, 1971).

[6] For a discussion of Freud's changing views on the relationships between ego-ideal and superego, see Roy Shafer, "Ideals, the Ego Ideal, and the Ideal Self," in Robert R. Holt, ed., "Motives and Though," *Psychological Issues*, 5, nos. 2-3, monograph 18-19, pp. 131-174. See especially footnote 3, p. 135.

ment and status — the conditions of worth, in Carl Rogers' phrase — established by the larger society and the social groups to which a person belongs.

No one, of course, attains success in any absolute sense. But there are important differences among people in the degree to which they have succeeded or failed. And a person's record of success and his sense of competence and self-confidence are likely to be intertwined. This sense of worth and competence encourages a person to perceive and react to his social world in a characteristic way. Enjoying the security his sense of worth and competence confers, the person with high self-esteem tends to be optimistic in outlook, to have confidence that other people are, on the whole, honest and well-intentioned, and to believe that his efforts will meet with success. This is not to say that he perceives himself as living in a world without obstacles or uncertainties, or for that matter, that he is not sometimes beset by inner impulses which he has difficulty dealing with. But because of his deep-rooted sense of worth and competence, he tends to view such problems as challenges which stimulate him to action rather than as forbidding dangers which threaten his security and well-being. High self-esteem, then, fosters a particular coping style — active, exploratory, and manipulative. For the person with high self-esteem, the world is malleable. It invites and rewards exploration, accomplishment, curiosity, involvement, and attempts at mastery.

Low self-esteem, by contrast, is a sign of a person's lack of confidence in his capacity to cope with the problems he confronts. Relative lack of success in dealing with such problems encourages a sense of unworthiness, helplessness, and vulnerability. The person who doubts his worth doubts also that others will think it worthwhile to come to his aid; he tends to feel, in Engel's words, "left out, let down, and deserted."[7] He sees a world which is at best indifferent to his needs, and at worst, actively hostile to them. It is in any event a world he cannot bring under control.

[7] Engel, *Psychological Development in Health and Disease.*

Thus, he sees himself as relatively powerless to overcome the problems he faces, whether those problems arise in the world outside or originate deep within himself. His sense of helplessness leads to an overreadiness to believe himself threatened and an overestimation of the seriousness of the threat. Here, then, are three elements in the dynamic of low self-esteem: helplessness, vulnerability, and anxiety.

Of equal importance is the fact that low self-esteem involves not only a judgment about the nature of the external environment but also a judgment about the quality of the person himself. It is not only the world which is out of joint but himself as well. Low self-esteem is a sign that a person blames himself, in part at least, for his relative failure. He may, and probably will, believe that external forces have worked against him; but he also believes that he ultimately lacked the capacity to overcome these forces, and that in consequence, the final responsibility for failure is his. The upshot is an amalgam of guilt and self-contempt which may attach itself to low self-esteem.

The fundamental reasons for these differences between persons with high and low self-esteem are unclear. Some take the position that self-esteem is related in some way to ego strength. As Fenichel has observed, one aspect of ego strength is the capacity for governance of instinctual energies.[8] The strong ego is able to defer gratification of an impulse when it would provoke disapproval, or if the ego is unable to hold the impulse in check, then it is able to substitute a culturally acceptable aim. The impulse whose immediate expression the ego blocks presses for discharge; the stronger the impulse, the more intense the pressure the ego must endure. A sign of ego strength, then, is the capacity to tolerate such tension.

Of course, this does not mean that the strong ego is able and likely to block any inner impulse. Ego strength is a matter of avoiding the two extremes of control:[9] under-con-

[8] See particularly Fenichel and Rapaport, *Collected Papers of Otto Fenichel.*

[9] *Ibid.*

trol leads to the immediate expression of inner drives, over-control to their repression, in the classical phrase, to the damming up of the instinctual energies.[10] Under-control and over-control are both signs of ego weakness; the sign of ego strength is the ability to tolerate inner impulses and the tensions they excite.

Ego strength has a second dimension. This dimension refers to the ego's weakness or strength in its relationships with the outer world. An ego weak in this respect lacks the ability to resist external pressures, to persevere in its intentions in the face of external obstacles, to arrive at accurate judgments about the source, aims, and likely consequences of human actions.[11] To be sure, the ego may be weak in one respect and strong in another. Indeed, it may owe its strength to its weakness; as Fenichel has observed, the source of the ego's power to repress permanently an instinctual drive may be its excessive fear of the outside world.[12] But on the whole, ego strength involves both the ability to govern inner impulses and the capacity to meet external demands.

High self-esteem, then, may be the sign of a strong ego, low self-esteem the sign of a weak ego. Certainly, ego strength carries with it the idea that a person is competent and is confident of his competence to deal with tensions generated by id and superego. And ego strength encourages activity, exploration, involvement, and accomplishment, while ego weakness, the result of anxiety,[13] "causes the organism to

[10] For quantitative empirical research in the concept of ego, see particularly the work of Jack Block. For example, Jack Block and Jeanne H. Block, "An Investigation of the Relationship Between Intolerance of Ambiguity and Ethnocentrism," *Journal of Personality* 19 (1951): 303-311; and Jeanne H. Block and B. Martin, "Predicting the Behavior of Children Under Frustration," *JASP* 51 (1955): 281-285.

[11] Fenichel and Rapaport, *Collected Papers of Otto Fenichel*, see Chapter 5, "Ego Strength and Ego Weakness," pp. 70-80.

[12] *Ibid.*, pp. 70-71

[13] *Ibid.*, p. 29.

turn away from the outer world, to withdraw into itself."[14]

Others take a position based more on learning theory than on a psycho-analytic perspective, contending that a person's self-esteem is a result of his reinforcement history.[15] This position has numerous variations, but typically holds that self-esteem is a sign of a record of success in achieving goals to which the society or the person attaches importance. The close connection between success and social rewards (such as approval or respect) or personal rewards (such as a sense of personal significance or competence) leads to self-reinforcing circles of success and failure. A consistent history of success leads to a more confident expectation of success, which, in turn, enhances the chances for further success. A history of failure sets the process in motion in the opposite direction: having failed, the person anticipates failure, accepting signs of failure while discounting evidence of success.

A third position suggests that the fundamental difference between persons of high and low self-esteem lies in the characteristic mechanisms of defense which they employ.[16] According to this view, the person with high self-esteem has a higher tolerance for experiences of failure without danger to his self-esteem because he relies on "avoidance" types of defense. Avoidance defenses (for example, repression or denial) allow the person to block out from awareness stimulus-objects which are personally threatening. Persons with low self-esteem, on the other hand, are said to characteristically rely on "expressive" types of defense. Expressive defenses (for example, projection) protect the individual by permitting him 'to act out' or in some manner express his inner conflicts

[14] *Ibid.*

[15] This point of view has been advanced by, among others, Arthur Cohen, "Some Implications of Self-Esteem for Social Influence," *Attitude Change and Social Influence* (New York: Basic Books, 1964).

[16] This position has been adopted by a number of investigators, including among others, Arthur Cohen.

and anxiety. In brief, this position asserts that persons with low self-esteem are more likely than those with high self-esteem to feel a sense of vulnerability and fear because avoidance defenses are more effective than expressive ones in blocking awareness of anxiety-arousing stimuli.

A final position suggests that it is not a person's specific methods of defense but his overall "defensive abilities" which are of importance.[17] In this view, high self-esteem itself confers on the individual a form of protection. It may do this, as Coopersmith points out, in two ways. First, a person's conviction that he is worthwhile and able carries with it a confidence in his capacity to take care of himself, if he were to face a threat. Second, whether a person appraises some stimulus or situation as a threat depends on his assessment of the likelihood of its inflicting harm; the person persuaded of his worth and abilities is less inclined to interpret a situation as threatening than the person who feels relatively helpless. For that matter, someone who is afflicted by a deep sense of unworthiness is more ready to believe that he is, or may shortly be, the object of attack — which may, for example, take the form of a disclosure of his shortcomings—than is the person with high self-esteem.

We cannot judge the relative value of these four positions. Further research may show that not one of them but several, perhaps in combination with other factors we have yet to take account of, provide the most adequate explanation of the differences between persons of high self-esteem and low self-esteem. Yet, I should like to emphasize that these various explanations are all consistent with the sketch of the dynamics of self-esteem that I have drawn. Low self-esteem is a sign that the ego confronts problems arising from an external or internal source which it feels it cannot deal with effectively. Reactions to the perception of such threats are varied and may include feelings of vulnerability, futility, isolation,

[17] The strongest argument for this position has been advanced by Stanley Coopersmith, *The Antecedents of Self-Esteem.*

and defensive avoidance. Low self-esteem encourages an overreadiness to perceive threats; high self-esteem protects against it.

This interpretation of the dynamics of self-esteem is, of course, incomplete. It also involves a large element of conjecture, assumptions and arguments which have little or no support in strictly empirical studies. What is worse, occasionally I have blithely made assertions such as, "high self-esteem is a sign of the ego's success over the id", which I have treated as if their truth were self-evident, when it should be obvious to all that I have not specified their exact meaning. In view of the state of current research, it could hardly be otherwise.

But the effort to articulate a basic conception of the nature and dynamics of self-esteem has some value. It provides a statement of the assumptions which underlie this study, some of which can be put to empirical test. It also makes more explicit the linkage between theory and hypotheses. Thus, it serves as a crude rudder, governing the direction we take in the analysis of the psychological correlates of self-esteem.

Feelings of Inadequacy

At the center of my interpretation of the dynamics of self-regard is the connection between self-esteem and self-confidence. The person with high self-esteem is more certain than the person with low self-esteem of his capacity to cope with problems he confronts. There ought to be, then, a close connection between a person's level of self-esteem and his sense of personal adequacy.

Table 3:1 shows the relationship between our three aspects of self-esteem and a number of questionnaire items which tap in different ways a general sense of inadequacy. A sense of personal adequacy, as I use the term here, refers to a person's confidence, or lack of it, in his abilities and achievements. The person who has low self-esteem is much more likely to concede that he frequently feels himself inferior to other persons than is the person with high self-esteem. Low self-esteem also encourages a measure of apprehensiveness. The person who doubts himself doubts also his chances of success. Indeed, he is more than uncertain about the prospects of success; he tends rather strongly to expect to fail. This expectation of failure inclines him to lower his aspirations sharply or to raise them unrealistically, both of which lessen chances for achievement.[18] It also makes him more apprehensive, more prone to worry about the misfortunes which may befall him. Thus, expectation of failure and fear of it become interlocked.

Table 3:1

THE RELATIONSHIP BETWEEN SELF-ESTEEM AND FEELINGS OF INADEQUACY[a]

Item	Personal Unworthiness			Interpersonal Competence			Status Inferiority		
	MB	PAB-F	PAB-L	MB	PAB-F	PAB-L	MB	PAB-F	PAB-L
I must admit that I often feel inferior to some of the people I meet.	.55	.46	.47	−.54	−.50	−.49	.44	.25	.37
I never try to do more than I can, for fear of failure.	.70	.73	.65	−.54	−.52	−.42	.26	.31	.34
I often feel that I am not good enough to succeed at something.[b]	.64			−.59			.37		
I worry over possible misfortune.[b]	.45			−.42			.39		
Median correlation	.59	.60	.56	−.54	−.51	−.46	.38	.28	.35

[a] The coefficients of correlation are gamma in this and subsequent tables in this chapter.
[b] Item available for Marginal Believer Study only.

[18] The reasoning for this contention has been best developed in work on the achievement motivation. See particularly, J. W. Atkinson and N. T. Feather, eds., *The Theory of Achievement Motivation* (New York: Wiley, 1966), and J. W. Atkinson, *An Introduction to Motivation* (New York: Van Nostrand Reinhold, 1964).

All three measures of self-esteem — personal unworthiness, interpersonal competence, and status inferiority — are strongly correlated with each of these items. There is, of course, some variation in the magnitude of the coefficients across the four items and over the three samples, but on the whole, the strength of these relationships is impressive (with the median being .430). This is not surprising since the notion of personal adequacy is so closely related to the meaning of self-esteem.

Implicit in my analysis is the assumption that low self-esteem is associated with a *general* sense of inadequacy, and high self-esteem with a characteristic sense of assurance and adequacy. This should not be taken to mean that a person's sense of adequacy never varies, but merely that it has a certain constancy which is apparent in many—though not of course in all—situations. Table 3:1 provides some support for this assumption, for the questionnaire items refer to a person's evaluation of himself relative to other persons in general, not to some specific person or groups, and the degree of his confidence in his ability to succeed in general, not in some specific situation or task. These data are suggestive, but not conclusive. That self-esteem engenders a general sense of adequacy, therefore, is more an assumption I make than a conclusion I demonstrate.[19]

Other studies have amassed considerable evidence in favor of this assumption. The question at issue is whether people develop a *relatively general* sense of their own adequacy, that is, whether they display a relatively generalized expectation of success or failure. This is obviously a matter of degree. Certainly, I do not mean to suggest that the person with high self-esteem always expects to succeed while the one with low self-esteem always expects to fail. A person may hold both a general belief about his ability to succeed and specific beliefs about his chances for success in a particular situation.

[19] Here we face a problem common to measurement of all but a very few personal attributes: to put the matter plainly, there is insufficient empirical data to establish the stability (over time) and constancy (across

One cluster of research studies bearing on this assumption is the work of Rotter and his colleagues.[20] These studies have focused in part on whether or not a person believes he can control in some important way the outcome of events. These beliefs, according to Rotter, constitute an enduring and important feature of an individual's makeup. People vary in the degree to which they believe that the outcome of a situation typically depends on external forces (such as fate, chance, the power of another person, or the working of a supernatural process) or on themselves. The Internal-External Scale was constructed to measure this attribute and has been put to use in a number of studies.[21] The work of Rotter and his colleagues has a different focus and background than mine, but there is some overlap. Persons with high self-esteem, I have argued, are more likely to feel able to deal effectively with the outside world, to enjoy a general confidence in their abilities and adequacy, which stimulates activity, curiosity, and achievement. Rotter's concept of internal-external control has obvious affinities with my interpretation of self-esteem. As he states:

> Perhaps the most important kind of data to assess the construct validity of the internal-external control dimension involves the attempts of people to better their life condition, that is, to control their environment in important life situations. It is in this sense that the

situations) of personal attributes. For a general overview of theoretical issues and empirical findings on human characteristics see Benjamin S. Bloom, *Stability and Change in Human Characteristics* (New York: John Wiley and Sons Inc., 1964).

[20] For a general introduction to the theoretical background behind this work, see J. B. Rotter, *Social Learning and Clinical Psychology* (Englewood Cliffs, N. J.: Prentice-Hall, 1954).

[21] S. Liverant and A. Scodel, "Internal and External Control As Determinants of Decision Making Under Conditions of Risk," *Psychological Reports* 7 (1960): 59-67; J. B. Rotter, "Generalized Expectancies for Internal vs. External Control of Reinforcement," *Psychological Monographs* 80 (1966): 1-28; J. B. Rotter and R. C. Mulry, "Internal vs. External Control of Reinforcement and Decision Time," *JPSP* 2 (1965): 598-604.

I-E scale appears to measure a psychological equivalency of the sociological concept of alienation in the sense of powerlessness.[22]

Rotter has summarized a number of studies which provide confirmation of this hypothesis,[23] and I shall examine some of these studies and the broader theoretical orientation which informs them in greater detail in Chapter 4. Here it will suffice to point out the convergence of numerous studies, directed by investigators working independently, focused on a variety of specific hypotheses, and conducted on various kinds of subjects (for example, university students, mental patients, and civil rights workers), showing that people do form relatively generalized expectations of success and failure.

The linkage between a sense of adequacy (or competence) and self-esteem is one reason for the close connection between self-esteem and anxiety. It is natural that a person who feels himself likely to fail should be more anxious than a person who is confident of his capacity to cope with problems he encounters.

Rosenberg's study of adolescents, among others,[24] finds clear-cut evidence of a connection between anxiety and low self-esteem. Persons with low self-esteem are more likely to suffer chronic and intense feelings of anxiety. Compared to those with high self-esteem, they more frequently report moods of apprehension, worry, uncertainty, fear, and indecision. They are also more likely to report other indicators of chronic anxiety — such as accelerated pulse rate, insomnia, fingernail biting, 'headaches,' and loss of appetite.

Of course, the causal influence may run in either direction. I have spoken as though it is low self-esteem that leads to

[22] Rotter, "Generalized Expectancies for Internal vs. External Control of Reinforcement," pp. 19-20.

[23] *Ibid.*

[24] Rosenberg, *Society and the Adolescent Self-Image,* Chapter 8, pp. 149-167.

high anxiety, but it may be the latter which leads to the former. As Mandler and Sarason point out, one reaction to anxiety, particularly common under stressful conditions, involves responses which impede completion of the assigned task — responses such as "feelings of inadequacy, helplessness, heightened somatic reaction, anticipations of punishment or loss of status, and implicit attempts to leave the test situation. It may be seen that these responses are self- rather than task-centered."[25]

The question of causal order is difficult. One alternative is that low self-esteem is merely a by-product of a kind of chronic anxiety, which gives rise to a pervasive sense of malaise that manifests itself in an indiscriminant willingness to report personal discomfort and mental agitation. Another alternative is that low self-esteem leads to anxiety. This point of view has been well stated by Ausbel, Schiff and Goldman: "Anxiety is conceptualized as an acquired reaction sensitivity in individuals suffering from impaired self-esteem to over-react with fear to any anticipated adjustive situation that contains a further threat to self-esteem."[26]

If pressed to choose between these alternatives, I would side with Lazarus. He challenges the conventional view that anxiety (a) serves as a signal of impending danger and (b) represents a drive that motivates instrumental efforts to reduce fear. He argues that it is more fruitful — in the analysis of psychological stress at least — to interpret anxiety not as a stimulus but as a response. It is essentially an affective reaction to an apprisal of threat.[27]

It is this conception of anxiety which best fits my interpretation of self-esteem. High self-esteem, I have argued, carries

[25] G. Mandler and S. B. Sarason, "A Study of Anxiety and Learning," *JASP* 47 (1952): 166-173.

[26] D. P. Ausbel, H. M. Schiff, and M. Goldman, "Qualitative Characteristics in the Learning Process Associated with Anxiety," *JASP* 48 (1953): 537-547.

[27] Richard S. Lazarus, *Psychological Stress and the Coping Process* (New York: McGraw-Hill, 1966) pp. 68-75 and pp. 71-72.

with it a sense of competence and confidence and fosters an active orientation to the external environment. Low self-esteem, by contrast, encourages a sense of powerlessness and vulnerability, which in turn leads to an overready appraisal of threat. Thus, persons who doubt their abilities and worth are overready to believe themselves faced with a threat, and because they lack a sense of competence and confidence, they are overready to exaggerate the seriousness of the threat they face — hence the close association between low self-esteem and feelings of fear, helplessness, and anxiety.

There is no way this study can determine empirically the causal order between anxiety and self-esteem. Rosenberg has presented some empirical evidence that low self-esteem precedes and produces anxiety, but I can neither confirm nor deny his findings.[28] For the purposes of this study, however, it is necessary only to establish the close association between self-esteem and anxiety, not their causal order.

Feelings of Futility

Feelings of low self-esteem, personal inadequacy, and anxiety should give rise to a deep-seated sense of futility. Table 3:2 shows the relationship between the three measures of self-esteem and questionnaire items which touch on aspects of a sense of helplessness and hopelessness.

The strong relationship between low self-esteem and a sense of futility manifests itself in several ways. Persons with low self-esteem, whatever the measure of self-regard, are much more likely than those with high self-esteem to believe their lives lack meaning or significance. One aspect of this lack of meaning is the belief that life has no purpose, or that whether one lives or dies is of little consequence, sentiments that persons with low self-esteem are much more likely to voice than persons with high self-esteem. Such a sense of purposelessness, as Dean has noted, is one of the

[28] Rosenberg, *Society and Adolescent Self-Image,* pp. 149-167.

Table 3:2

THE RELATIONSHIP BETWEEN SELF-ESTEEM AND FEELINGS OF FUTILITY

Item	Personal Unworthiness			Interpersonal Competence			Status Inferiority		
	MB	PAB-F	PAB-L	MB	PAB-F	PAB-L	MB	PAB-F	PAB-L
I have often felt that it doesn't matter much whether I live or die.	.50	.53	.35	−.44	−.38	−.34	.41	.32	.24
I am sometimes troubled by the thought that life really has no purpose.	.61	.34	.24	−.46	−.26	−.23	.47	.36	.19
With everything so uncertain these days, it almost seems as though anything could happen.	.55	.54	.45	−.41	−.38	−.26	.23	.33	.30
With everything in such a state of disorder, it's hard for a person to know where he stands from one day to the next.	.63	.65	.55	−.48	−.45	−.38	.36	.36	.40
I sometimes feel like a tiny cog in a huge machine.[a]	.42			−.26			.21		
The world is too complicated now to be understood by anyone but experts.[a]	.47			−.45			.37		
Median correlation	.52	.53	.40	−.45	−.38	−.30	.36	.34	.27

[a] Item available for Marginal Believer Study only.

quintessential elements in the classic notion of alienation, as formulated by Durkheim.[29]

But the notion of futility extends beyond a sense of purposelessness; it also involves a sense of powerlessness. Several of the items tap an individual's belief that he can understand and influence what is taking place in the world. Again, whatever the measure of self-esteem, persons with low self-regard are much more likely to confess that the world is too complex for them to understand. They are also more likely to belittle their own importance, perceiving themselves to be without power, seeing themselves, in effect, as "a tiny cog in a huge machine."

The connection between self-esteem and a sense of power-lessness helps us understand the nature of the anxiety which low self-esteem arouses. One facet of a sense of low self-esteem, as already noted, is a person's lack of confidence in his capacity to master the problems he confronts. But his doubts extend beyond the issue of mastery. They involve, more fundamentally, a sense of inefficacy. Table 3:3 shows the relations between the three measures of self-esteem and McClosky's scale of political futility.

The close association between low self-esteem and political futility is plain. Compared to persons with high self-esteem, those who doubt their worth or abilities are much more likely to exhibit feelings of political impotence. They are much more likely to doubt that they have any voice in politics and much more inclined to believe that a congressman or a political party will pay little attention to what they say or want. They see themselves as unable to exercise any influence in political affairs, believing that events in politics will continue to run the same course no matter what they want, say, or do.

The data, then, suggest that a person with low self-esteem may not merely lack a sense of efficacy; he may be afflicted

[29] Dwight G. Dean, "Alienation: Its Meaning and Measurement," *American Sociological Review* 26 (1961): 753-757. See also Elizabeth Douvan and Alan Walker "The Sense of Effectiveness in Public Affairs," *Psychological Monographs General and Applied*, Vol. 70, (1956): 1-19.

Table 3:3

THE RELATIONSHIP BETWEEN INDICES OF SELF-ESTEEM AND FEELINGS OF POLITICAL FUTILITY (PERCENTAGED DOWN)

	Personal Unworthiness			Interpersonal Competence			Status Inferiority		
	Low	Mid	High	Low	Mid	High	Low	Mid	High
PAB-Leaders	(n = 1434)	(n = 1072)	(n = 514)	(n = 580)	(n = 1286)	(n = 1154)	(n = 1050)	(n = 1395)	(n = 575)
Political Low	83	77	61	66	79	87	86	77	73
Futility Mid	10	19	29	24	18	11	12	18	20
High	2	4	10	10	4	2	2	4	7
PAB-Followers	(n = 407)	(n = 519)	(n = 558)	(n = 444)	(n = 503)	(n = 337)	(n = 351)	(n = 675)	(n = 458)
Political Low	53	35	16	18	36	55	41	35	23
Futility Mid	34	40	36	38	39	34	36	38	37
High	13	25	48	44	25	12	23	28	40
MB-Sample	(n = 287)	(n = 411)	(n = 384)	(n = 439)	(n = 352)	(n = 291)	(n = 315)	(n = 488)	(n = 279)
Political Low	61	41	18	20	37	65	50	38	23
Futility Mid	15	22	19	19	22	16	20	19	19
High	24	38	63	61	41	19	30	44	58

by a more deeply rooted sense of helplessness. Persons with low self-esteem are much more likely to see events in the world as entirely beyond their power to control or even to comprehend. Thus, 89% of persons in the Follower sample who lack a sense of interpersonal competence agree that "With everything so uncertain these days, it almost seems as though anyting could happen," compared to 69% of those who score in the upper third on this index. Similarly, among Leaders, 40% of those who score high on the index of Personal Unworthiness agree with the statement that "With everything in such a state of disorder, it's hard for a person to know where he stands from one day to the next," compared to only 9% of those who score low on this index.

Self-esteem, then, taps a person's beliefs about his capacity to cope with the environment. The person with high self-esteem has confidence in himself, in his ability to deal effectively with the problems he confronts, in his chances for success and achievement. Conversely, the person with low self-esteem lacks this self-confidence, characteristically feels inadequate, and in consequence, is afflicted by a sense of helplessness and the fear and anxiety that helplessness engenders.

Feelings of Guilt

This syndrome of low self-esteem, a sense of personal inadequacy, and feelings of futility may arise from two sources — the nature of the world or the character of the person. The first source gives rise to what Olsen labels "attitudes of incapability"[30] which represent a person's involuntary reaction to a world which is intractable and oppressive. The source of the difficulty may lie in one or more ways in which the social world frustrates and alienates the individual. For example, the social world may fail to provide cues indicating the actions which are appropriate to attain desired goals; it may fail to distribute the resources necessary for the achievement of these goals; or it may impose an illogical, meaningless structure of social relationships and

[30] Marvin E. Olsen, "Alienation and Political Opinions," *Public Opinion Quarterly* 29 (1965): 200-212.

expectations.[31] Whatever the reason, the fault lies with the world, not the person, and the end result is a deep-seated feeling of helplessness.

But self-esteem characteristically involves more than a sense of helplessness. Taken by itself, helplessness suggests that though the individual himself cannot deal effectively with the problems confronting him, others who confront similar problems can cope with them. Low self-esteem, however, encourages not only the belief that little can be done by anyone, but also the judgment that it is the individual's own fault (and not merely that of his external circumstances) that so little can be done. The individual with low self-esteem tends to doubt not only his competence but, what is equally important, his worth. He becomes, in Engel's terms, a victim of hopelessness as well as helplessness. And hopelessness involves a curious amalgam of futility and guilt, for as compared to the feeling of helplessness, "the feeling of giving up [of hopelessness] includes more despair, futility, 'nothing left;' the self-judgment that one is completely responsible for the situation that leads to the feeling that there is nothing he or anyone else can do to overcome the feelings or change the situation. Further, one is not worthy of help so that even if help is offered it cannot be accepted."[32] There should be, then, a strong association between low self-esteem and guilt.

As Table 3:4 shows, persons with low self-esteem, compared to those with high self-esteem, are much more likely to agree with statements where agreement is a direct or indirect indication of feelings of guilt. They are more likely to feel ashamed of themselves, to believe their outward appearance cloaks an inner reality they find shabby and repugnant, to feel apprehensive that their thoughts and desires will erupt and betray them publicly. Accordingly, in the MB sample, 74% of persons who score high on the measure of Status

[31] These sources of alienation correspond to three of Olsen's types of attitudes — guidelessness, powerlessness, and meaninglessness. *Ibid.*

[32] Engel, *Psychological Development in Health and Disease*, p. 175.

Table 3:4

THE RELATIONSHIP BETWEEN SELF-ESTEEM AND FEELINGS OF GUILT

Item	Personal Unworthiness			Interpersonal Competence			Status Inferiority		
	MB	PAB-F	PAB-L	MB	PAB-F	PAB-L	MB	PAB-F	PAB-L
Life is a constant struggle against temptation.	.58	.57	.53	−.33	−.31	−.23	.23	.29	.24
I sometimes feel I do not deserve the good life I have.	.33	.31	.44	−.17	−.21	−.26	.04	.01	.15
If people knew my inner thoughts I'm afraid they would think less of me.	.43	.59	.51	−.31	−.39	−.43	.21	.46	.37
I often feel ashamed of myself.	.59	.62	.61	−.44	−.38	−.38	.28	.34	.31
Median correlation	.50	.58	.52	−.32	−.34	−.32	.22	.32	.28

Inferiority agree that "Life is a constant struggle against temptation" compared to 57% who score low on this measure. Similarly, in the Follower sample, 29% who who score low on the measure of Interpersonal Competence confirm that "If people knew my inner thoughts, I'm afraid they would think less of me" compared to 9% who score high on this index.

These relationships were to be expected. After all, a sense of worthiness is one of the dimensions I believed to be most central to the concept of self-esteem. And not surprisingly, this index has considerably stronger relationships with items assessing guilt than do the other two measures of self-esteem.

Nevertheless, all three aspects of self-esteem are tied closely to feelings of guilt. Even excluding the personal unworthiness index from consideration, the median correlation between the indices of Interpersonal Competence and of Status Inferiority and these four items is .296. What is more, similar results have been reported by other studies using entirely different measures of self-esteem. For example, Moses and Duvall find that persons with large discrepancies between their Actual and Ideal Self tend to rate their task performance lower than do those whose Actual Self corresponds more closely to their Ideal Self; Moses and Duvall interpret this self-deprecation characteristic of persons with low self-esteem as a sign of self-hostility.[33] Also, Coopersmith and Rosenberg both report that persons with low self-esteem are significantly more likely than those with high self-esteem to confess that they frequently feel "ashamed" of themselves.[34]

Feelings of Disaffection

Self-esteem and disaffection are also related. By a sense of disaffection I mean a pervasive and deep sense of dissatisfaction. Disaffection is an amalgam of disappointment, frustration, resentment, and depression. It envelops the whole of a person's life, reflecting his overall feelings on the course his life has taken in the past and is likely to take in the future. In light of the data we have seen — the correlations between self-esteem and a sense of personal inadequacy, futility, and guilt — it is reasonable to expect a close connection between low self-esteem and disaffection.

Table 3:5 shows all three measures of self-esteem strongly associated with items tapping feelings of disaffection. Compared to persons with high self-esteem, those with low self-esteem are more likely to report that their lives and jobs

[33] M. Moses and R. Duvall, "Depreciation and the Self Concept," *Journal of Clinical Psychology* 16 (1960): 387-388.

[34] Rosenberg, *Society and Adolescent Self-Image;* Coopersmith, *Antecedents of Self-Esteem.*

Table 3:5

THE RELATIONSHIP BETWEEN SELF-ESTEEM AND FEELINGS OF DISAFFECTION

Item	Personal Unworthiness			Interpersonal Competence			Status Inferiority		
	MB	PAB-F	PAB-L	MB	PAB-F	PAB-L	MB	PAB-F	PAB-L
It often seems that we have to work too hard for what we get out of life.	.57	.56	.36	−.52	−.44	−.32	.46	.46	.38
I can't say I look forward to each day with much pleasure.	.47	.60	.49	−.43	−.41	−.40	.46	.45	.27
I hate to come back to work after a vacation.	.29	.21	.22	−.36	−.31	−.26	.38	.34	.33
I feel that I have often been punished without cause.	.61	.62	.58	−.36	−.31	−.41	.52	.47	.33
If I could live my life over again, I would do many things differently.	.53	.56	.51	−.35	−.33	−.30	.46	.52	.41
I am often in low spirits.[a]	.65			−.54			.49		
I think I suffer somewhat from wanting much more out of life than I am ever likely to get.[a]	.53			−.43			.54		
There are so many different things I want that I have difficulty knowing which ones I want most.[a]	.54			−.45			.41		
Median correlation	.54	.56	.49	−.43	−.33	−.32	.46	.46	.33

[a] Item available for Marginal Believer Study only.

are hard, drab, and unrewarding. Life has not worked out as they had hoped. Much that they had wanted to do they cannot, and much they have done they wish they had not. The overall tone is one of disappointment, some gloom, a certain resentment, and bitterness. For example, in the MB sample, 90% of persons who score high on the measure of Personal Unworthiness confess that "If I could live my life over again, I would do many things differently," compared to 55% of those who score low on this index. Similarly, those who score low on Interpersonal Competence are more than five times as likely as those who score high on this index to admit that they "are often in low spirits." Note also that all three aspects of self-esteem are strongly correlated with feelings of disaffection, though once again the relationships are strongest for personal unworthiness (the median correlations across samples are .535 for Personal Unworthiness, -.363 for Interpersonal Competence, and .451 for Status Inferiority).

Person Perception

What we are like and what we believe others are like are rather closely related, or so it is often assumed. This assumption may appear to be a truism, but in this instance at least appearances are quite deceiving. As Renato Tagiuri has noted, "There is a large number of studies on the relationship between person perception and the personality of the judge. . . . However, this line of empirical works has failed, so far, to identify the personality variables that seem to be consistently related to *how* we perceive others."[35] Yet, proceeding at a modest level, we can readily perceive a connection between the way a person feels about himself and the way he feels about others.

Table 3:6 shows the relationship between the three measures of self-esteem and five items assessing how other persons tend to be perceived.

[35] Renato Tagiuri, "Person Perception" in G. Lindzey and E. Aronson, eds., *Handbook of Social Psychology* vol. 3, pp. 395-449.

Table 3:6

THE RELATIONSHIP BETWEEN SELF-ESTEEM AND
PERSON PERCEPTION

Item	Personal Unworthiness			Interpersonal Competence			Status Inferiority		
	MB	PAB-F	PAB-L	MB	PAB-F	PAB-L	MB	PAB-F	PAB-L
It's all right to have friends, but you shouldn't let yourself get so attached that you're always having to do things for them.	.43	.38	.35	−.36	−.26	−.31	.29	.25	.23
You have to be pretty choosy about picking friends.	.42	.45	.41	−.22	−.16	−.22	.30	.33	.35
When you get right down to it, there are few people in this world you can really trust.	.55	.56	.42	−.34	−.36	−.31	.27	.38	.31
There are a lot of people in this world who are no good.	.37	.45	.44	−.30	−.25	−.21	.29	.38	.31
My way of doing things is apt to be misunderstood by others.	.54	.57	.45	−.46	−.36	−.35	.38	.29	.24
Median correlation	.43	.45	.42	−.34	−.26	−.31	.30	.33	.31

The person with low self-esteem places little faith in others. Caution, suspicion, reserve, and cynicism are his watchwords. He has little confidence in the good will of others. Given a chance, he is inclined to think others will attempt to take advantage of him, and deep down, he believes that most people in this world are simply "no good." Unable to believe in the good will of others, he is unable to trust them. Not only is he convinced that most people are indifferent to his well-being and some even mean him harm; he cannot trust others because they are not trustworthy, that is, dependable and predictable.[36] Specifically, he cannot trust them to see the world as he does; so on the one hand, he cannot depend on them to react to events as he would expect them to, and on the other, he cannot rely on them to understand what he does or why he does it. And it is partly their failure to understand which makes them a potential threat to his well-being. Ignorance can do as much damage as malevolence.

Accordingly, 31% of Leaders who score high on the index of Status Inferiority agree that "when you get right down to it there are few people in this world you can really trust," compared to 14% who score low on this index. Or, to note another example, 77% of Leaders who score high on the index of Personal Unworthiness, but only 42% of those who score low, agree that "There are a lot of people in this world who are no good." Thus, self-esteem and a particular orientation to others are closely linked. This orientation involves a mixture of elements — cynicism, anxiety, and hostility — and when coupled with a pervasive feeling of inadequacy, may assume the form of ressentiment. Stated less extremely, we may say that positive self-attitudes accompany positive attitudes toward others, and negative self-attitudes accompany negative attitudes toward others.

A number of studies have come to such a conclusion. Marlowe and Gergen, conceding at the outset the complexities of the relationship between person perception and the personality of the perceiver, still observe that ". . . one of the more consistent findings emerging from this area is a

[36] Julian B. Rotter, "Generalized Expectancies for Interpersonal Trust," *American Psychologist* 26 (May 1971): 443-452.

positive relationship between self-acceptance and acceptance of others."[37] They also refer to a number of studies[38] which made use of different measurement instruments, experimental subjects, and experimental designs, all of which confirmed a positive correlation between favorable self-rating and favorable rating of other persons.

Other studies furnish further evidence. In his study of adolescents, Rosenberg demonstrates there is a positive relationship between self-esteem and a "misanthropy" or "faith in people" measure, which in essence assesses whether or not a respondent believes others tend to be cooperative, concerned about one another, trustworthy, or relatively selfish, undependable, and exploitative.[39] Using the same measure of misanthropy but a different measure of self-esteem, Simmons found low self-esteem and misanthropic attitudes to be significantly correlated in a sample of college students.[40] Davids has studied a syndrome of five components — egocentricity, distrust, pessimism, anxiety, and resentment — which springs from a weakness of the ego.[41] He calls this syndrome self-alienation, but it bears some resemblance to the syndrome of low self-esteem in several respects.[42] The

[37] D. Marlowe and K. Gergen, "Personality and Social Interaction," in G. Lindzey and E. Aronson, eds., *The Handbook of Social Psychology,* vol. 3, pp. 590-665, especially p. 596.

[38] Marlowe and Gergen, "Personality and Social Interaction."

[39] Rosenberg, *Society and Adolescent Self-Image,* pp. 181-182.

[40] J. L. Simmons, "Some Intercorrelations Among 'Alienation' Measures," *Social Forces* 44 (1966): 370-372.

[41] A. Davids, "Generality and Consistency of Relationships Between the Alienation Syndrome and Cognitive Processes," *JASP* 51 (1955): 61-67; and A. Davids, "Alienation, Social Apperception, and Ego Structure," *Journal of Consulting Psychology* 19 (1955): 21-27.

[42] This is a general problem, which deserves fuller discussion than I give it here. What, for example, is the difference between "Alienation" as it is commonly described and low self-esteem as I have described it? I put this question aside because I have no adequate answer for it, not because I believe the answer has no importance.

self-alienated, he notes, have a tendency to see others as alienated, while those who are not alienated have a tendency to see others as not alienated, too. In this connection, it is worth noting Davids' observation that:

> In classic Freudian terminology the concept of projection was employed solely to describe the attribution of one's negative, undesirable traits onto other people. But the present results suggest that the concept of projection is applicable to positive attributes as well as negative attributes, with happy, contented, well-adjusted individuals tending to perceive others as similar to themselves, and, consequently, seeing them as less alienated than they really are.[43]

Lest this conclusion appear so clear-cut as to be self-evident, it is worth noting that the term projection may cover two very different processes: one in which the perceiver imputes an attribute to others which is similar to his own attributes, as the hostile person perceiving others to be hostile; the other in which the perceiver imputes to others an attribute which complements his own attributes, as the person with a persecution complex imputing to others the desire to harm him. Research presently provides no definitive clue as to when the principles of similarity or of complementarity will be operative.[44]

Ultimately, person perception appears to be the outcome of a complex process influenced by numerous factors in addition to the personality traits of the perceiver. Such factors include the complexity of the stimulus, the degree of psychological involvement in the stimulus situation, the number, explicitness, and consistency of the cues presented, and the task of judgment itself (for example, whether or

[43] Davids, "Alienation, Social Apperception and Ego Structure," p. 26.

[44] Donald Campbell, "Social Attitudes and Other Acquired Behavioral Dispositions," in Sigmund Koch, ed., *Psychology: A Study of a Science*, vol. 6, pp. 151-152.

not specific assessment dimensions are mentioned).[45] Then too, there may be an interaction between the characteristics of the stimulus person and those of the perceiver. As Shrauger and Altrocchi point out in a review of the experimental literature, authoritarians are more favorable than non-authoritarians in their judgments of high-status persons, but less favorable in their judgments of low-status persons.[46]

For the purposes of this study, it is not necessary to understand in detail the connection between self-attitudes and attitudes towards others; a broad outline will do. The essential point is the consistent finding that persons of high and low self-esteem differ in their characteristic evaluation of other persons: those with low self-esteem hold a more unfavorable view of others, a view which accents others' unreliability, their lack of concern and sympathy, their guile and deceitfulness, and their perversity, untrustworthiness, and hostility.

Defensive Withdrawal

People make judgments about what others are like, and they take it for granted that other persons make judgments about them. Both judgments may come from a common source — a person's judgment of himself. As we have just seen, persons with high self-esteem and low self-esteem differ in their assessment of others. Those with high self-esteem tend to perceive others as trustworthy, honest, and well-intentioned, a judgment that those with low self-esteem scarcely share. To the person who doubts his worth and abilities others are a potential source of harm. Note that it is most people who appear to him to be menacing, not merely those who pose a direct and obvious threat to his

[45] Tagiuri, "Person Perception." p. 430; see also S. Shrauger and J. Altrocchi, "The Personality of the Perceiver as a Factor in Person Perception," *Psychological Bulletin* 62 (Nov. 1964): 289-308.

[46] Shrauger and Altrocchi, "Personality of the Perceiver as a Factor in Person Perception," p. 297.

well-being. His fears and his feelings of ineffectiveness, working in combination, multiply the number of persons and situations he finds personally threatening. Thus, low self-esteem contributes to an enduring and pervasive sense of vulnerability. In turn, this vulnerability leads to a desire to avoid or withdraw from the company of others, for the greater the social or psychological distance between others and oneself, the less the danger.

Withdrawal, then, proceeds in part from one's judgment of others; it is a strategy of defense. But those with low self-esteem decide on such a strategy only in part because of their judgment of others. Their judgment of themselves may be equally involved. Low self-regard, we have observed, hinges on the person's sincere belief that he has failed to meet certain standards of worth which, to his mind, marks him as a person of little value. Persons with low self-esteem, persuaded that they are not worthy or honorable, naturally fear disclosure. They must conceal evidence of their personal failings in order to avoid exposure and social sanctions. Thus, a strategy of withdrawal further serves the person who lacks self-esteem, for by holding others at a distance from himself he can keep them in ignorance of his failings.

Withdrawal, of course, recommends itself as a method of defense particularly to the person who expects rough treatment at the hands of others. Those with low self-esteem come to anticipate such treatment in part because of the low opinion they hold of themselves and of others. But it is important to recognize that there is a basis in reality for their fears that others hold a poor opinion of them. Rosenberg's data have a direct bearing on this point. Trained nurses evaluated a number of "normal volunteers" admitted for research purposes to a NIMH Clinical Center.[47] The nurses had no knowledge of the subjects' scores on Rosenberg's self-esteem scale and the subjects had no knowledge of the nurses' evaluation of them. As Rosenberg reports, the nurses significantly more often described persons with low self-es-

[47] Rosenberg, *Society and the Adolescent Self-Image,* pp. 18-19.

teem, compared to those with high self-esteem, as less likely to be "well thought of," to make "a good impression," to be "often admired," and to be "respected by others."[48] In short, the person with low self-esteem is often correct in his assumption that others are likely to judge him unfavorably, or, in effect, to concur with his own evaluation of himself.

Defensive withdrawal becomes the more advisable the less protected a person is against social disapproval. It would be unnecessary for the person with low self-esteem to seek to make himself inconspicuous, were he able to dismiss or block out of his awareness the unfavorable reactions he encounters and comes to expect. But several studies have demonstrated that those with low self-esteem are more, not less, sensitive to criticism. Coopersmith asked his subjects to rate their degree of sensitivity to criticism.[49] Those with high self-esteem were more likely than those with low to judge themselves as relatively insensitive to criticism, while those with low self-esteem were more likely to judge themselves as extremely or quite sensitive to criticism. In addition, it is worth taking note of Rosenberg's summary of his feelings.

> People with low self-esteem, we find, 1) are much more likely to be sensitive to criticism, to be deeply disturbed when they are laughed at, scolded, blamed, criticized, etc.; 2) are much more likely to be bothered if others have a poor opinion of them; 3) are much more likely to be deeply disturbed if they do poorly at some task they have undertaken; 4) are much more likely to be disturbed when they become aware of some fault or inadequacy in themselves. In addition, among the normal volunteers described earlier, low self-esteem subjects are more likely to be described by nurses as "touchy and easily hurt."[50]

[48] *Ibid.*, p. 27.

[49] Coopersmith, *Antecedents of Self-Esteem*, p. 67.

[50] Rosenberg, *Society and the Adolescent Self-Image*, p. 158.

What is more, all psychological defenses do not afford the same kind of protection. It has become increasingly fruitful to think of defense mechanisms as lying along a continuum. According to Byrne,

> At one end of the continuum of defensive behaviors are those responses which involve avoidance of the anxiety-arousing stimulus and its consequence. Included here are repression, denial, and many types of rationalization. At the sensitizing extreme of the continuum are behaviors which involve an attempt to reduce anxiety by approaching or controlling the stimulus and its consequents. The latter mechanisms include intellectualization, obsessive behaviors, and ruminative worrying.[51]

Particular defensive strategies may matter as much as overall defensive abilities. Persons with high self-esteem characteristically rely on repression-type defenses, while those with low self-esteem depend on sensitization-type defenses, as already noted. In consequence, those with high self-esteem are better able to block or deny awareness of information that is anxiety-arousing. High self-esteem then, can serve as a protective shield in social interaction; and without this shield, a person is more vulnerable and so more inclined to withdraw from the company of other persons.

Table 3:7 shows the relationship between the three measures of self-esteem and items which tap a need for defensive withdrawal. Low self-esteem, it appears, encourages a person to be suspicious of others, particularly of efforts they might make to establish a close personal relationship. The person who lacks self-esteem has a need to fend others off. This need for inviolacy can find expression in many ways – in an insistence on the importance of privacy, for example, or in a resistance to making public one's own beliefs and failings, or in an opposition to dealing with other persons. But whatever the specific tactics, the fundamental objective is

[51] Donn Byrne, *An Introduction to Personality* (Englewood Cliffs, N. J.: Prentice-Hall, 1966), p. 178.

Table 3:7

THE RELATIONSHIP BETWEEN SELF-ESTEEM AND DEFENSIVE WITHDRAWAL

Item	Personal Unworthiness			Interpersonal Competence			Status Inferiority		
	MB	PAB-F	PAB-L	MB	PAB-F	PAB-L	MB	PAB-F	PAB-L
I must admit that I get very stubborn when people try to find out about my personal affairs.	.37	.34	.37	−.28	−.40	−.34	.26	.32	.31
Nowadays more and more people are prying into things that ought to remain personal and private.	.50	.57	.37	−.38	−.36	−.23	.29	.25	.26
The best policy is to keep things to one's self.	.43	.39	.31	−.39	−.24	−.33	.18	.28	.23
What a person thinks about politics is nobody else's business.	.29	.26	.21	−.35	−.32	−.19	.21	.14	.14
I don't really like the way some strangers will try to strike up a conversation with a person.[a]	.42			−.30			.32		
I like to have a small set of really close friends and then not be bothered with most people.[a]	.46			−.40			.40		
Median correlation	.42	.37	.34	−.36	−.34	−.28	.27	.26	.25

[a] Item available for Marginal Believer Study only.

the same — to find some protection from others — and the basic strategy is the same — to put the maximum distance between oneself and others. To cite only one example, 74% of Followers who are low on Interpersonal Competence agree that "I must admit I get very stubborn when people try to find out about my personal affairs," compared to only 43% of those who score high on this index. For every measure of self-esteem, for every item, and for every sample, persons with low self-esteem are much more likely than those with high self-esteem to strive for inviolacy by defensive withdrawal.

Social Estrangement

Clearly, self-esteem affects social relations. As we have seen, low self-esteem engenders anxiety, suspiciousness, inadequacy, hostility, and in extreme instances, ressentiment. This mixture of feelings inclines an individual to withdraw or avoid close ties with others. What is curious, though, is the extent to which individuals believe the opinions they hold toward themselves mirror the opinions others hold toward them. Thus, a person with a poor opinion of himself tends to think others have a poor opinion of him, too.[52] Moreover, it matters to him what others think of him, even — perhaps especially — when what they think is uncomplimentary. The person with low self-esteem tends to have a "thin skin."[53] The more a person doubts his worth, the more likely he is to be sensitive to the judgment of others, to be hurt by criticism or social disapproval, to anticipate that others will find fault with him, reproach him, or in some manner reject him. Thus, the absence of self-regard can lead persons to fear and to avoid close ties with others.

But persons with low self-esteem suffer from the absence of close ties with others, as well as from the fear of such ties. Withdrawal may serve as a method of defense, but it exacts a high price. It leaves the individual with few people

[52] Rosenberg, *Society and the Adolescent Self-Image,* p. 158.

[53] *Ibid.,* p. 209.

to trust, to confide in, or to turn to for aid or for company. Such withdrawal, of course, is relative, not absolute. Yet, it is sufficient to impair chances of obtaining social support and encouragement. Consequently, persons who lack self-esteem are often afflicted by feelings of isolation and loneliness.

As Table 3:8 shows, low self-esteem and feelings of isolation are strongly related. Those with low self-esteem are much more likely to confess that there are few people they can talk to and that they frequently feel they have been "left out."

Beyond a feeling of detachment, persons with low self-esteem may experience a sharp sense of dislocation. They tend to feel disconnected from others and "out of place"; not surprisingly, they are therefore more likely to feel forlorn. For every sample and for every measure of self-regard, those with low self-esteem are much more likely to confess that "deep down" they are lonely people.

This feeling of loneliness is one facet of a larger sense of estrangement; another is a feeling of disassociation. Interpersonal relations are impersonal: they lack genuine warmth, intimacy, concern; they tend to be superficial, short-lived, insincere. As we would expect, there is a strong association between low self-esteem and feelings of disassociation. In all samples, persons with low self-esteem are much more likely, compared to those with high self-esteem, to complain that most people have little concern or feeling for others, that friendship and friendliness are largely a sham, in short, that we live today in a cold and indifferent world where people no longer genuinely care for one another.

Another aspect of this sense of estrangement is social anxiety. Those whose negative feelings about themselves and others cause them to desire to avoid others are, not surprisingly, apprehensive when they find themselves in the company of others. As we see in Table 3:10, persons who lack self-esteem are much more likely to feel unsure of themselves, apprehensive, diffident, and awkward when they are with other people. Among Leaders, for example, those who score high on our measure of Personal Unworthiness are three times as likely as those who score low to agree with the statement, "When in a group of people I have trouble thinking of the right things to talk about."

Table 3:8

THE RELATIONSHIP BETWEEN SELF-ESTEEM AND FEELINGS OF ISOLATION AND LONELINESS

Item	Personal Unworthiness			Interpersonal Competence			Status Inferiority		
	MB	PAB-F	PAB-L	MB	PAB-F	PAB-L	MB	PAB-F	PAB-L
I wish there were more people I felt I could really talk to.	.51	.58	.49	−.48	−.42	−.44	.42	.41	.35
It seems to me that I am often left out of the things that other people are doing.	.63	.61	.60	−.53	−.50	−.51	.47	.44	.48
I may not always show it but deep down, I am often a quite lonely person.	.56	.58	.46	−.45	−.36	−.36	.45	.35	.39
The people around me usually don't like the things I do.	.45	.53	.44	−.28	−.31	−.25	.43	.44	.27
I often feel awkward and out of place.	.67	.67	.64	−.70	−.64	−.61	.42	.37	.41
I must admit I often feel lonely.[a]	.54			−.44			.38		
Median correlation	.55	.58	.49	−.46	−.42	−.44	.42	.41	.39

[a] Item available for Marginal Believer Study only.

Table 3:9

THE RELATIONSHIP BETWEEN SELF-ESTEEM AND DISASSOCIATION

Item	Personal Unworthiness			Interpersonal Competence			Status Inferiority		
	MB	PAB-F	PAB-L	MB	PAB-F	PAB-L	MB	PAB-F	PAB-L
People pretend to care more about one another than they really do.	.57	.56	.49	−.41	−.41	−.35	.37	.35	.37
What is lacking in the world today is the old kind of friendship that lasted for a lifetime.	.66	.62	.53	−.45	−.40	−.40	.28	.26	.27
People in big cities are too cold and heartless.[a]	.49			−.28			.27		
I feel I am liked and accepted by most of my neighbors.[a]	.21			−.36			.21		
Median correlation	.53	.59	.51	−.39	−.41	−.37	.27	.31	.32

[a] Item available for Marginal Believer Study only.

Several researchers have reported similar results. Rosenberg, for example, has observed that "interpersonal awkwardness" is characteristic of the person with low self-esteem: he is more likely to be "shy" and "easily embarrassed," hesitant to strike up conversations, tense in new situations, and uneasy about expressing his views.[54] Coopersmith has noted very similar tendencies in his studies of self-esteem.[55]

[54] *Ibid.*, pp. 171-176.

[55] S. Coopersmith, "Studies in Self-Esteem," *Scientific American* 218 (Feb. 1968): 96-106.

Table 3:10

THE RELATIONSHIP BETWEEN SELF-ESTEEM AND SOCIAL ANXIETY

Item	Personal Unworthiness			Interpersonal Competence			Status Inferiority		
	MB	PAB-F	PAB-L	MB	PAB-F	PAB-L	MB	PAB-F	PAB-L
I must admit I try to see what others think before I take a stand.	.38	.27	.16	−.40	−.29	−.13	.22	.28	.19
When in a group of people I have trouble thinking of the right things to talk about.	.46	.50	.41	−.60	−.59	−.62	.27	.22	.27
Median correlation	.42	.38	.29	−.50	−.44	−.38	.25	.25	.23

Children with high self-esteem are confident, active, at ease in their dealings with others; those with low self-esteem tend to be timid, passive, anxious. Clearly, high self-esteem encourages social confidence and competence; low self-esteem discourages them.

The Question of Spuriousness

These data point to an extensive web of connections between a person's level of self-esteem and his overall psychological makeup. To my mind, the various feelings we have surveyed together form a syndrome. Each influences, and is influenced by, every other. To take only one example, persons with low self-esteem characteristically feel insecure and ineffective. Consequently, they are more likely than persons with high self-esteem to be suspicious and apprehensive about the people they meet or know, to be chronically anxious, and to be easily threatened. Their sense of vulnerability strengthens their reluctance to form close attachments to others or even to participate in social interaction. Their reduced social contact further accentuates their feelings of estrangement and helplessness, but at the same time strengthens their need to maintain psychological distance from others in order to overcome a sense of vulnerability and guilt. In this manner each element strengthens the others, and the total pattern of needs and feelings which accompany low self-esteem thus tends to be self-reinforcing and self-perpetuating.

Conceivably the interrelationships we have observed are spurious, that is, are a product of some factor other than genuine differences among individuals in their personality characteristics. The charge of spuriousness has historically taken one of two forms — the first sociological, the second more psychological. The first is most forcefully put by Hyman and Sheatsley in their critique of *The Authoritarian Personality*.[56] They note that a relationship between any two variables may be the result of a third variable, and maintain that it is incumbent on the investigator to take account of such third variables, which an informed person may reasonably suppose might account for the original relationship. They then adduce numerous examples to suggest that many of the findings reported in *The Authoritarian Personality* may not be due to differences among individuals in psychological characteristics but may, instead, stem from differences in education.

The criticism of Hyman and Sheatsley is cogent, but their argument has proven so persuasive as to become an article of faith, which, many believe, largely undermines personality studies. Their objection is actually rather circumspect. They do not show or claim to have shown that the results reported in *The Authoritarian Personality* are a consequence of differences in education; they merely suggest that this may

---

[56] H. Hyman and P. Sheatsley, " 'The Authoritarian Personality' — A Methodological Critique," in R. Christie and M. Jahoda, eds., *Studies in the Scope and Method of the Authoritarian Personality* (Glencoe, Ill.: Free Press) 50-122.

be the case, chiefly by the use of vivid examples, deliberately selected, as they themselves concede, to buttress their argument. Nor do they suggest that even if education were found to have determined certain of these findings, or even the majority of them, the main contentions of *The Authoritarian Personality* would have to be regarded as "spurious" in the specific sense that test scores on the ostensible independent and dependent variable — authoritarianism and anti-semitism — are an artifact of differences in a third variable that is causally prior to the other two. Nevertheless, the years since the publication of their classic article have seen a swelling suspicion of personality studies, a suspicion based on the widespread belief that the findings of these studies can be accounted for largely, if not entirely, by social rather than psychological factors.

The suggestion that "personality" scales largely tap differences in social background rather than variations in psychological makeup deserves special consideration. The idea has frequently been put forward that a person's evaluation of himself, his self-esteem, depends in the main on his position within the society. To some theorists of society, status is the social badge of personal worth. People evaluate themselves and others, it is argued, by the standards of success and prestige their society lays down. The higher a person's status, the more he or she is a person to be reckoned with.

My data suggest that whatever is the case for personality scales in general, the scores on my self-esteem measures do not simply reflect variations in social status and background. Table 3:11 presents the relationship between my three measures of self-esteem and a number of social and demographic factors, Table 3:12 the relationship between the self-esteem measures and an array of psychological and attitudinal scales with social status and acquiescence, respectively, partialed out.

As Table 3:11 shows, the three measures of self-esteem have at best only a slight connection to such socio-demographic factors as income, occupational status, and education. Of these three factors, only with respect to education do

THE RELATIONSHIP BETWEEN INDICES OF SELF-ESTEEM AND EDUCATION (PERCENTAGED DOWN)

	Personal Unworthiness			Interpersonal Competence			Status Inferiority		
	Low	Mid	High	Low	Mid	High	Low	Mid	High
PAB-Leaders	(n = 1434)	(n = 1072)	(n = 514)	(n = 580)	(n = 1286)	(n = 1154)	(n = 1050)	(n = 1395)	(n = 575)
1. Grade school	2	5	6	5	4	2	3	4	3
2. Some high school	6	11	10	11	8	7	6	9	10
3. High school grad	11	12	15	14	13	9	10	12	15
4. Some college	23	27	26	27	25	24	23	25	31
5. College grad	58	46	43	43	50	57	58	51	41
PAB-Followers	(n = 407)	(n = 519)	(n = 558)	(n = 644)	(n = 503)	(n = 337)	(n = 351)	(n = 675)	(n = 458)
1. Grade school	10	18	33	29	19	11	17	21	26
2. Some high school	21	24	30	28	22	23	20	24	30
3. High school grad	29	29	21	26	29	21	32	26	21
4. Some college	19	18	11	11	19	20	17	16	14
5. College grad	21	11	5	5	11	24	13	12	9
MB Sample	(n = 287)	(n = 411)	(n = 384)	(n = 439)	(n = 352)	(n = 291)	(n = 315)	(n = 488)	(n = 279)
1. Grade school	13	24	29	38	24	10	17	30	36
2. Some high school	10	12	18	18	13	9	11	14	17
3. High school grad	37	32	28	28	36	33	36	34	24
4. Some college	16	15	7	7	14	19	17	11	9
5. College grad	23	16	6	7	13	28	19	13	13

Table 3:11B

THE RELATIONSHIP BETWEEN INDICES OF SELF-ESTEEM AND INCOME (PERCENTAGED DOWN)

	Personal Unworthiness			Interpersonal Competence			Status Inferiority		
	Low	Mid	High	Low	Mid	High	Low	Mid	High
PAB-Leaders	(n = 1434)	(n = 1072)	(n = 514)	(n = 580)	(n = 1286)	(n = 1154)	(n = 1050)	(n = 1395)	(n = 575)
1. Under 3,000	1	2	2	3	1	1	1	1	2
2. 3,000–5,000	5	7	9	8	7	5	6	7	7
3. 5,000–7,500	13	15	17	17	15	13	13	13	20
4. 7,500–10,000	19	19	19	22	18	19	19	19	20
5. Over 10,000	61	56	53	50	58	62	61	59	50
PAB-Followers	(n = 407)	(n = 519)	(n = 558)	(n = 644)	(n = 503)	(n = 337)	(n = 351)	(n = 675)	(n = 458)
1. Under 3,000	8	16	34	27	18	11	19	18	26
2. 3,000–5,000	29	37	35	39	33	28	33	35	33
3. 5,000–7,500	38	26	19	21	28	34	29	28	23
4. 7,500–10,000	14	11	5	5	10	16	10	9	9
5. Over 10,000	11	5	3	3	7	9	6	7	3
MB Sample	(n = 287)	(n = 411)	(n = 384)	(n = 439)	(n = 352)	(n = 291)	(n = 315)	(n = 488)	(n = 279)
1. Under 3,000	7	11	23	19	15	7	11	13	20
2. 3,000–5,000	48	48	50	55	44	45	45	51	48
3. 5,000–7,500	25	21	14	14	20	28	24	17	19
4. 7,500–10,000	7	7	3	4	6	9	6	6	6
5. Over 10,000	12	9	3	3	11	11	11	8	4

Table 3:11C

THE RELATIONSHIP BETWEEN INDICES OF SELF-ESTEEM AND OCCUPATIONAL STATUS (PERCENTAGED DOWN)

	Personal Unworthiness			Interpersonal Competence			Status Inferiority		
	Low	Mid	High	Low	Mid	High	Low	Mid	High
PAB-Leaders	(n = 1434)	(n = 1072)	(n = 514)	(n = 580)	(n = 1286)	(n = 1154)	(n = 1050)	(n = 1395)	(n = 575)
Low	4	5	6	4	6	4	4	5	6
Mid	42	40	44	46	42	39	40	40	48
High	54	53	48	48	51	56	54	54	44
PAB-Followers	(n = 407)	(n = 519)	(n = 558)	(n = 644)	(n = 503)	(n = 337)	(n = 351)	(n = 675)	(n = 458)
Low	38	52	65	66	53	38	50	51	57
Mid	47	37	23	26	36	49	37	36	30
High	12	5	2	3	6	11	6	7	4
MB-Sample	(n = 287)	(n = 411)	(n = 384)	(n = 439)	(n = 352)	(n = 291)	(n = 315)	(n = 488)	(n = 279)
Low	10	24	30	31	22	11	16	19	27
Mid	61	56	60	57	55	63	61	58	57
High	16	10	5	4	11	13	13	10	8

differences of any consequence occur, and these differences appear only at the extremes of the worst and the best educated. In truth, one would expect there to be some association between self-esteem and education, but such a relationship, I shall later argue, is evidence for my social learning hypothesis, not proof of spuriousness.

The major conclusion to draw from these data is plain enough: there is only a slight relation between major principles of social stratification such as income and levels of self-esteem. Where an individual falls in the society and how he feels toward himself are, to all intents and purposes, unrelated. The key to self-esteem, it appears, lies in how a person fares in meeting the demands of his immediate life space, not the standards of the larger society.

It has seemed so obvious as to be virtually self-evident that a person's social status and his self-regard were related, not perfectly related to be sure, but strongly related nonetheless. Those the larger society regards unfavorably — the poor, the black, the barely educated — regard themselves unfavorably for that very reason, or so it has seemed to a great many students of society. Following Rosenberg's suggestion, we may label this the stratification hypothesis.

For all its plausibility, the stratification hypothesis runs directly afoul of my findings. As a political scientist, my prime interest, of course, is in the consequences of self-esteem, not its sources. But it is important to note that my findings on this point are directly in line with those of other researchers. For example, Rosenberg finds only a weak (though significant) relationship between the self-esteem of children and the social class of their parents, which holds, however, chiefly for boys rather than girls.[57] Rosenberg then demonstrates that the relationship among boys is not due to social class *per se*; instead, it appears to be a function of the fact that father-son relationships are "closer" among the middle class than they are among the working class.[58] Following

[57] Rosenberg, *Society and the Adolescent Self-Image*, pp. 39-41.

[58] Rosenberg, *Society and the Adolescent Self-Image*, pp. 42-48.

up this line of argument, Coopersmith observed a nonsignificant association between the self-esteem of children and the social class of their parents.[59]

The lack of a close connection between self-esteem and socioeconomic status, I should emphasize, is no small boon. One reason research on authoritarianism, for example, floundered was precisely because the relationship between measures of this personality characteristic and, say, education were so strong as to make it virtually impossible to disentangle the two. Responses to the F scale could as readily be interpreted as a measure of the quality of the respondent's schooling as of the dynamics of his personality.[60] Consequently, it is no small advantage to know that our measures of self-esteem measure psychological traits, not social circumstances.

Nor is it socioeconomic status which accounts for the whole network of relationships we have uncovered. It could be argued, of course, that this syndrome reflects not apparent differences in psychological makeup but genuine differences in social circumstances and life chances. According to this view, those who are poorly-off or poorly educated might well have a consistent tendency to concede that they feel inferior to the people they meet, or confess that the world is too complicated for them to make sense of it, or admit that they hate to return to work after a vacation. All of this presumably flows directly from their actual conditions of life. It is superfluous, the argument runs, to conjure up so mysterious a notion as personality in order to understand patterns apparent in data such as mine.

But if socioeconomic status really does account for this syndrome of malaise, then the interrelationships should diminish appreciably in magnitude or disappear entirely, when we control for social status.

Table 3:12 shows the relationships between the measures

[59] Coopersmith, *Antecedents of Self-Esteem,* pp. 82-84.

[60] Gertrude Selznick and Stephen Steinberg, *The Tenacity of Prejudice* (New York: Harper and Row, 1969).

of self-esteem and an array of psychological orientations, after partialling out education, income, and occupational status. These data corroborate our earlier observations. Regardless of their social status, persons with low self-esteem, compared to those with high self-esteem, remain disproportionately likely to be hostile and suspicious, lacking in self-confidence, alienated, and psychologically disorganized.

The second form of the charge of spuriousness sees in the very multiplicity of psychological measures to which self-esteem is related and in the strength of these relationships a suspicious sign that our scales, indices, and items measure very much the same thing. It asserts that a person's scores on test A and on test B are related not because of any intrinsic connection between the variables these tests purport to measure, but rather because test scores are an index of a respondent's readiness to agree (or disagree) with a questionnaire item whatever its content.

Acquiescence is a conceivable contaminant, since my questionnaire items on the whole are worded in one direction. But before considering the risk of such contamination, let us take up briefly the nature of acquiescence.[61] A measure of acquiescence unfortunately measures more than acquiescence, if by that we mean merely a tendency to agree with a statement, regardless of what it says. The more acquiescent person also tends to be less careful in his judgment, less critical and reflective, and less likely to make fine discriminations in his thoughts and speech; the less acquiescent person tends to be more deliberate and thoughtful, to evaluate evidence for an assertion with greater care, and to be more alert to points which are ambiguous or need qualification. These differences in cognitive skills and style, quite apart from mere response set, contribute heavily to the readiness of the acquiescent person to agree with question-

---

[61] The following argument on the nature of acquiescence was suggested to me by Herbert McClosky. It appears (though not in fully developed form) in Herbert McClosky, "Consensus and Ideology," *APSR* 58 (1964): 379-380.

Table 3:12A

THE RELATIONSHIP BETWEEN THE THREE MEASURES OF SELF-ESTEEM AND A NUMBER OF PSYCHOLOGICAL SCALES

	Personal Unworthiness			Interpersonal Competence			Status Inferiority		
	PAB-F	PAB-L	MB	PAB-F	PAB-L	MB	PAB-F	PAB-L	MB
				With Education Partialed Out					
Guilt	.53	.52	.49	−.29	−.30	−.28	.26	.24	.19
Life satisfaction	−.37	−.23	−.09	.23	.16	.09	−.39	−.25	−.23
Need inviolacy	.32	.23	.34	−.17	−.16	−.27	.19	.13	.20
Alienation	.56	.45	.50	−.32	−.34	−.35	.41	.34	.40
Anomie	.63	.55	.56	−.36	−.38	−.39	.34	.29	.29
Paranoia	.55	.45	.45	−.24	−.27	−.25	.39	.27	.35
				With Income Partialed Out					
Guilt	.52	.52	.50	−.28	−.31	−.30	.26	.25	.20
Life satisfaction	−.36	−.22	−.07	.22	.15	.07	−.39	−.24	−.22
Need inviolacy	.32	.24	.38	−.18	−.16	−.14	.19	.14	.23
Alienation	.56	.45	.51	−.33	−.34	−.37	.41	.34	.41
Anomie	.63	.56	.59	−.38	−.39	−.45	.35	.30	.31
Paranoia	.54	.46	.49	−.25	−.28	−.30	.40	.28	.37

Table 3:12B

THE RELATIONSHIP BETWEEN THE THREE MEASURES OF SELF-ESTEEM AND A NUMBER OF PSYCHOLOGICAL SCALES

	Personal Unworthiness			Interpersonal Competence			Status Inferiority		
	PAB-F	PAB-L	MB	PAB-F	PAB-L	MB	PAB-F	PAB-L	MB
				With Occupational Status Partialed Out					
Guilt	.51	.52	.49	—.28	—.31	—.30	.25	.25	.20
Life satisfaction	—.36	—.22	—.09	.22	.16	.09	—.39	—.24	—.23
Need inviolacy	.33	.24	.37	—.19	—.17	—.31	.20	.14	.22
Alienation	.57	.45	.51	—.33	—.34	—.37	.41	.34	.42
Anomie	.64	.56	.59	—.37	—.39	—.45	.35	.30	.32
Paranoia	.55	.46	.48	—.25	—.29	—.30	.40	.28	.37
				With Acquiescence Partialed Out					
Guilt	.48	.46	.45	—.24	—.23	—.23	.20	.17	.13
Life satisfaction	—.36	—.24	—.19	.21	.16	.16	—.37	—.25	—.29
Need inviolacy	.16	.10	.21	—.08	—.06	—.18	.07	.03	.11
Alienation	.47	.36	.39	—.26	—.26	—.26	.32	.26	.33
Anomie	.54	.43	.44	—.32	—.28	—.31	.21	.16	.18
Paranoia	.42	.32	.32	—.16	—.16	—.15	.29	.15	.26

naire items, many of which are too broadly stated, overly simple and unqualified, or flatly dogmatic.

Thus, to partial out acquiescence is to remove the influence of individual differences in *both* response set and cognitive skill. The first is a source of measurement error, the second a genuine correlate of self-esteem, as the next chapter will confirm. In short, partialling out acquiescence removes a portion of the variance which is not an artifact of a response style but a genuine by-product of differences in self-esteem, though they should continue to be significant both statistically and substantively.

That is indeed what Table 3:12 shows. With acquiescence partialled out persons with low self-esteem, compared to those with high self-esteem, are likely to have stronger needs for inviolacy, more intense feelings of guilt and hostility, and a sharper sense of alienation. This holds for all three measures of self-esteem and all three samples. The MB study, which includes more clinical and socio-psychological indices, further confirms my judgment about the nature of the syndrome of self-esteem. Low self-esteem and psychological disorganization are strongly related, as is a lack of self-confidence and of self-esteem, even when acquiescence is controlled for. In short, the syndrome of psychological characteristics we have observed in this chapter appears to be a genuine by-product of self-esteem, not an artifact of acquiescence.

Psychological Traits and Psychological Syndrome—A Concluding Remark

By most standards, the measures I have built have done very well. They evidently measure a great many of the feelings and needs that other measures of self-esteem have in fact been shown to measure or that a measure of self-esteem ought in principle to measure — all of which is strong evidence indeed for the validity of the three measures. But the very plenitude of their success may be their undoing, for to some, at least, it may simply seem that "everything goes with everything else" — a suspicion not at all uncommon among skeptics of the survey approach.

For my part, I think that this suspicion has something to recommend it, though not for the reasons usually given. It is comparatively easy to separate personality traits conceptually; yet it can be extremely difficult to separate them empirically. The major problem is not inadequate theory or imperfect measures, though they complicate the problem. The root of the difficulty is nature. For better or worse, it is a stubborn, brute fact that a whole variety of sentiments of malaise run together in reality. Indeed, one reason self-esteem exercises the influence it does is precisely because it is not an independent trait at all, but merely one facet of a larger psychological syndrome.

While the thought that apparently "everything goes with everything else" is unsettling, basically what is at issue is an aspect of validity that rarely receives attention. All too often attention centers on whether a measure measures the attribute it purports to measure; only rarely does it center on whether the measure measures what it is supposed to *and only what it is supposed* to measure. In short, the problem of discriminant validity tends to be shunted aside.

We confront here what William McGuire has called the "principle of confounding."[62] My ostensible interest is in self-esteem, but my actual focus is rather different, for those who vary in self-esteem vary in so many other ways as well. For example, knowing that low self-esteem and high anxiety are strongly related, how can we say which is responsible for what? If we want to learn the impact of self-esteem, the solution is not "statistical controls." We ought not to set out to eliminate all traces of anxiety as though it were some form of contaminant. For good and proper reasons, the individual with low self-esteem on the average ought to have high anxiety. To ignore him entirely and concentrate instead on the exceptional case with low anxiety would be a very odd procedure indeed. Appearances to the contrary,

[62] William J. McGuire, "Personality and Susceptibility to Social Influence," in E. F. Borgatta and W. W. Lambert, eds., *Handbook of Personality Theory and Research* (Chicago: Rand McNally, 1968).

then, to focus on self-esteem is not to constrict attention to a narrow segment of an individual's psychological makeup; rather, such a focus takes in a surprisingly broad component of the personality system.

This problem, as confronted in this study, has a special twist. On the one hand, my three measures of self-esteem have very similar psychological correlates. Whatever the measure, those judged to be low in self-esteem tend to feel inadequate and insecure; they tend also to feel a sense of futility, of guilt, and of disaffection; they tend to be hostile and suspicious of others, they are tempted to avoid or withdraw from others, and they are afflicted therefore by a sense of loneliness and estrangement. In contrast, whatever the measure, those judged to be high in self-esteem tend to feel confident and sure of themselves; they tend to be more optimistic, more likely to believe they can and will succeed; on the whole they have confidence in others as well as themselves; they tend to feel at ease in the company of others, to have strong supportive personal relationships and to be active and self-assertive. These findings would appear to confirm that the three dimensions of self-esteem tap a common psychological orientation. Consequently, the three separate measures have been combined into an overall index of self-esteem.[63]

Yet, on the other hand, though my three measures of self-esteem measure much the same thing, they by no means measure exactly the same thing. Each index is designed to measure *one and only one* aspect of self-esteem. Several steps in the construction procedure were designed to assure exactly this, especially the item-index analysis and the panel ratings. My controlling assumption was that aspects of self-esteem are not always interchangeable, particularly when it comes to understanding the connection between personality and

[63] In each of the three samples split-half reliability coefficient for the overall indices have been computed. After the Spearman-Brown correction, the reliability coefficients for PAB Followers, PAB Leaders and MB are .77, .72, .76, respectively.

political involvement. Later chapters will test this assumption; however, I should point out that for convenience of exposition I have organized the analysis around the summary index of of self-esteem — unless the consequences of the separate indices in fact differ.

The task now is to explore the connections between the syndrome of self-esteem and the acquisition of political values.

Chapter 4 · THE ACQUISITION OF POLITICAL KNOWLEDGE

How does personality affect political belief? The question may seem to be too broad to tackle, for it is one thing to say that authoritarians tend to be anti-Semitic for this or that reason, or that compulsives tend to be isolationist for such and such reasons; it is quite another thing to attempt a general account that relates rigidity, authoritarianism and a large set of personality traits to political belief. Yet it seems a worthwhile strategy to frame the question in this way, if only to underscore the need to devise an explanatory schema that can fit a number of personality characteristics, not one tailored exclusively for self-esteem.

A Basic Schema

The study of personality and politics has yielded an extraordinarily varied crop of hypotheses, theories, and explanatory constructs. All manner of arguments have been made to account for the connection between personality and political belief. Nonetheless, analyses of the psychological foundations of political orientations conform to a remarkable degree to a common pattern, accounting for (1) adherence to a particular value (for example, conservatism) in terms of (2) the psychological rewards which acceptance brings (such as a reduction of fear) (3) to a person with a particular personality characteristic (for example, chronic anxiety).

The main approaches to the analysis of personality and political belief, though they disagree over the answers to give, agree on the basic question to ask. Consider the psychoanalytic approach. A classic example of this approach is, of course, *The Authoritarian Personality.* Its principal concern was to uncover the psychological foundations of anti-Semitism and fascist attitudes. It also provided a model of explanation which stimulated and strongly influenced subsequent studies of personality and political belief. These explanations share a number of characteristics: (1) an emphasis on unconscious determinants and processes; (2) a basic acceptance of the elements of personality largely as Freud conceptualized them (for example, superego, ego, id, egoideal), but more importantly, a heavy reliance on the defense mechanisms (such as projection, displacement, and identification with the aggressor) to account for causal processes, that is, "personality dynamics"; (3) a preference for genetic, developmental, historical explanations; and (4) an emphasis on the more "irrational," emotive personality forces.

Nevitt Sanford's case study of Mack is an excellent sample of the dynamic approach.[1] Sanford argued that in many instances attitudes such as anti-Semitism stem from an attempt on the part of an individual to overcome a basic fear of personal weakness. A complex configuration of psychological factors in the raising of the child — but most particularly, the failure to achieve an adequate solution to the Oedipal complex — lies behind this fear. In turn, the fear of being or of seeming weak leads the individual (by means of such psychological mechanisms as overcompensation, displacement, projection, and identification with the aggressor) to strive for power and status, to conceal or deny signs of weakness or dependency, and to attribute responsibility for any failing in himself to the operation of powers beyond his control. He thus is psychologically ready to

---

[1] Nevitt Sanford, "The Approach of the Authoritarian Personality," in J. L. McCary, ed., *Psychology of Personality* (New York: Logos Press, 1956).

believe that persons who are unfamiliar to him or who are in some respect dissimilar to him are untrustworthy, weak, inferior in character, resentful, envious, and, therefore, dangerous. Such persons and social groups come to embody features of his own character and inner feelings which he cannot consciously accept and acknowledge to be true of himself. His unacceptable impulses and desires become theirs: it is they who are weak and dependent, and he who is strong; it is they who flout the values of society, and he who defends them; and it is they who are resentful, discontented, belligerent, and intent on self-aggrandizement.

Here is one account of the psychological foundations of anti-Semitism and — in the opinion of the original investigators at least — of fascist attitudes. The core of this account, of course, is the construct of "the authoritarian personality." No reification of a single personality type was intended by the authors of The Authoritarian Personality. They acknowledged early and quite explicitly that there may exist a variety of "personality types" both among authoritarians and among non-authoritarians. In their view, there is no one personality type unique in its elements or their interrelationships and everywhere alike which gives rise to political authoritarianism; instead, there is a complex syndrome, variable in details from case to case, but still essentially similar in its psychological dynamics and appearance. The details in the investigation of authoritarianism obviously deserve attention in their own right.[2] But what is important here is not whether this account of the authoritarian personality is accurate and comprehensive in detail, nor even whether the original investigators were correct in their presumption that a prime source of anti-Semitism lay in the psychodynamics of personality. It is rather the claim of the original (and subsequent) investigators of the authoritarian

[2] For guides to the vast literature on authoritarianism, see Richard Christie and Peggy Cook, "A Guide to the Published Literature Relating to The Authoritarian Personality through 1956," Journal of Psychology 45 (1958): 171-199; and J. P. Kirscht and R. C. Dillehay, Dimensions of Authoritarianism (Lexington: University of Kentucky Press, 1967).

personality that the persuasive appeal of anti-Semitism is in its power to allay the individual's inner conflicts and needs.

The research on authoritarianism is of interest to us here because it provides a vivid illustration of the psychoanalytic approach to the analysis of the connection between personality and belief. This approach represents possibly the most widely known way of attempting to explain how psychological dispositions become translated into social attitudes and behavior, and it is an approach which has much to recommend it. The nature of the connection between attitude and personality, as conceived by psychoanalytic theory, was summed up by Sarnoff, who trenchantly observed that *"an individual's attitude toward a class of objects is determined by the particular role those objects have come to play in facilitating responses which reduce the tension of particular motives and which resolve particular conflicts among motives."*[3]

A second approach to the study of personality and political belief gradually emerged, partly in reaction to the sometimes overly simple notion of a "fit" between personality types and political orientations,[4] partly in reaction to the overly narrow range of political attitudes and action to which the ideas of depth psychology could be applied. The question to ask — in a now famous phrase[5] — was "of what use to a man are his opinions?" Holding an opinion, many investigators saw, might serve a number of functions, and these investigators evolved several variations of the functional approach. McGuire, for example, recognizes four functions

[3] Irving Sarnoff, "Psychoanalytic Theory and Social Attitudes," *Public Opinion Quarterly* 2 (Summer 1960): 261. Italics his.

[4] For an example of criticism of overly simple notions of a fit between personality and belief, see Gabriel Almond, "The Appeals of Communism and Fascism," unpublished paper presented at American Political Science Association 51st Annual Meeting, Boulder, Colorado.

[5] M. Brewster Smith, Jerome S. Bruner and Robert W. White, *Opinions and Personality* (New York: Wiley, 1964).

an attitude may serve.[6] Holding an opinion can be of service
to a person in the attainment of his goals — social adjustment,
for example — (the utilitarian or adaptive function); in the
conceptual organization of experience — permitting, for example, the perception of points of similarity and dissimilarity
among specific phenomena — (the knowledge function); in
providing a conduit for the outward manifestation of emotions or feelings (the expressive function); in the management
of inner conflicts — dealing with hostility towards parents
which cannot be consciously acknowledged, for example, by
adopting in defense excessively deferential attitudes towards
all forms of authority — (the ego-defensive function). Smith
and his associates, among the first to introduce the functional
approach, recognized three functions an opinion may serve
— object appraisal, social adjustment, and externalization
— "functions" which are more or less similar to those identified by Katz and his colleagues (namely, adjustment, ego-
defensive, value-expressive, and knowledge).[7]

Putting aside these differences in detail among particular
functional schemes, we may see the large common ground
of agreement shared by functional theorists. The way to map
out the linkages between personality and political belief, they
argue, is to identify the particular type of reward or favorable
consequence associated with holding a particular opinion for
a particular person. The idea of rewards is as broadly conceived as the notion of functions is vaguely defined, which
is to say, it includes all manner of ways an opinion may
be of service to a person.

In addition to psychoanalytic and functional interpretations, there is a third way to interpret the linkage between
personality and political belief, though it has begun to receive

[6] W. J. McGuire, "The Nature of Attitudes and Attitude Change," in
G. Lindzey and E. Aronson, eds., *The Handbook of Social Psychology*,
2d. ed. (Reading, Mass.: Addison-Wesley, 1969), vol. 3, pp. 136-314.

[7] See Smith, Bruner, and White, *Opinions and Personality;* and Daniel
Katz, "The Functional Approach to the Study of Attitudes," *Public
Opinion Quarterly* 24 (1960): 163-204.

attention only recently.[8] This third approach, variously called learning theory or behavior theory, has been applied to the study of personality and belief only occasionally and not very systematically.[9] The groundwork for using learning theory in the study of personality was laid by Dollard and Miller, and Mowrer.[10] They adapted and extended Stimulus-Response theory and fashioned a new approach to the familiar problems of clinical psychology, devising for example, explanations based on learning theory of neurotic conflict, repression, and transference. Political scientists have made little use of this early work or of writings produced by the more recent surge of interest in behavior therapy. But in principle learning theory promises to be a fruitful approach to the study of personality and political belief, for it provides a systematic introduction to the ways in which psychological states and traits mediate between the stimulus-object and situation on the one hand, and a person's acquired responses, both attitudinal and behavioral, on the other.

Learning theory is a rather broad canopy which covers a variety of distinctive theories. But whatever the differences among them wherever these theories have touched on the acquisition of social attitudes, their stress has fallen on the reward value of acceptance. It is the reinforcement contingency a person has experienced or comes to anticipate that determines attitude formation and change, whether the process of learning turns on simple classical or instrumental conditioning or involves more complex mechanisms of social learning such as imitation and vicarious conditioning. In this

[8] For a discussion of recent developments in this field, see Daniel E. Berlyne, "Behavior Theory as Personality Theory," in E. F. Borgatta and W. W. Lambert, *Handbook of Personality Theory and Research* (Chicago: Rand McNally, 1968), pp. 629-690.

[9] Berlyne, "Behavior Theory as Personality Theory."

[10] John Dollard and Neil E. Miller, *Personality and Psychotherapy* (New York: McGraw-Hill, 1950).

respect learning theories are similar to both the functional and the psychodynamic approaches, for they too focus on the way personality may heighten or diminish psychological rewards associated with acceptance of an idea, though of course the three approaches tend to define such rewards in very different ways.

These three approaches, despite their diversity and broad reach, can provide only a partial view of the role personality plays, for in the end the question which preoccupies each of them is how holding an opinion is of benefit to the individual. In consequence, each of the three approaches affords insight into only one of the several distinct processes involved in the translation of psychological predispositions into political beliefs.

Consider a common view of the connection between personality and ideology.[11] Societies, according to Levinson, develop sets of beliefs and values to further popular acceptance and support of the dominant institutions of the day. In a complex, pluralistic society there is often more than one system of values, and even idea systems which are more or less antagonistic to the prevailing social order may gain wide currency. Be that as it may, it is social groups (rather than individuals) which are the purveyors of idea systems. But not all individuals in the society embrace the same set of principles, and even among those who do share a common creed, not all interpret it in the same way or adhere to it with equal fidelity. It is personality, according to Levinson, which determines differential reactions to idea systems. The values a person comes to profess depend on the internal requirements of his personality as well as the external requirements of the society. Thus, a theory of personality and political belief must be "dualistic," incorporating the role both of the individual and of his society.

Levinson lays heavy emphasis on the necessity for a dualistic theory, presumably because of the importance he

[11] Daniel J. Levinson, "Ideas Systems in the Individual and in Society," in George K. Zollchan and Walter Hirsch, eds., *Explorations in Social Change* (Boston: Houghton-Mifflin, 1964).

attaches to personality; but let us examine more closely the role he accords to personality, for on inspection it turns out to be more circumscribed than it appears to be at first glance. He presumes that idea clusters are combined to form broader and more basic constellations of social values, such as autocratic and egalitarian ideologies, which are formulated and embodied in the institutions and "collective documents" of the larger society (for example, the folk culture or the formal constitution.) Members of the society choose from among the systems of values available in the larger society the one most congruent with their psychological makeup. Thus, authoritarian personalities are more receptive to autocratic ideologies, while non-authoritarian personalities are more receptive to egalitarian ideologies.

In the dualistic theory propounded by Levinson, then, personality serves mainly to account for the differential appeal of idea systems; it enhances the attractiveness of social values which are congenial to a person's inner needs and decreases the persuasiveness of ideas which are in conflict with them. Of course, once an individual has embraced a certain viewpoint, his personality characteristics can lead him to alter or embellish it, in order to bring his social values into closer conformity with his personal needs. Nonetheless, according to Levinson, personality exercises its chief influence on the acquisition of political values *by determining differential reactions to the ideas which society transmits to the individual.*

This account of the relationship of idea systems and individuals, though suggestive in many respects, fails to illuminate the *variety* of distinct ways in which personality may influence the process of political learning. It concentrates entirely on how personality may lead to differential reactions to idea systems, accounting for the variation in such reactions exclusively in terms of the rewards that acceptance (or rejection) of an idea system confers on the individual. Individual differences in personality characteristics such as self-esteem undoubtedly affect the rewards for acquisition; however, what has been overlooked — and what may prove equally important — is that personality may affect the conditions of acquisition, too.

To make clear the distinction between conditions of, and rewards for, acquisition, let us break down the process of political learning into some of its constituent phases. First, for a person to learn a particular orientation towards a public issue, exposure is necessary. No learning will take place unless and until he comes into contact with the information he is to acquire. Second, comprehension is necessary. A person is unlikely to learn a particular political orientation, even if he is aware of the issue, if he fails to understand the information about the issue which reaches him. Third, learning depends on the reward value of acceptance. Opinions differ in the extent to which holding or expressing them is positively (or negatively) reinforced. This elementary model, then, distinguishes three separate phases in the process of political learning — exposure, comprehension, and the reward value of acceptance.

Figure 4:1 presents in schematic form a basic paradigm of political learning and the role personality plays. The three components — exposure, comprehension, and the reward value of acceptance — are placed in separate boxes to mark off these steps in the learning process. The figure is drawn to point up the variety of ways in which personality may affect the process of political learning. The arrows connecting personality to the steps in the learning process illustrate the multiple forms of influence which personality can exert. The separation of the components underscores my conception of the process of political learning: the acquisition of political knowledge does not involve a direct response to a set of stimuli; instead it is the outcome of a complex mediational process consisting of several phases that may vary independently.

Such a conception of the learning process is by no means novel. It has been advanced on a number of occasions, though not exactly in the form given here. The "Yale group" have worked out the most elaborate of these mediational models. Hovland and Janis, for example, set out a formidably complex

Figure 4:1. An elementary model of personality and political learning

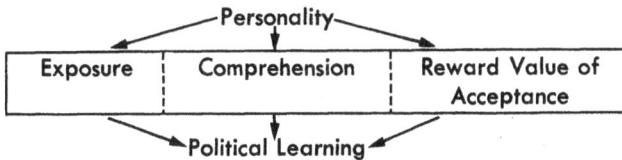

schema, which distinguishes, among other things, four steps in the learning process — attention, comprehension, anticipation, and evaluation.[12] McGuire more recently has elaborated an accordian-like schema which can be stretched to five behavioral steps — attention, comprehension, yielding, retention, and action — or squeezed to two steps — reception and yielding.[13] For the purposes of this study, I believe my three-step model of political learning is the most useful. Using that model, I propose to look at what has been overlooked previously: the relationships between self-esteem and the two conditions of acquisition of political knowledge — exposure and comprehension.

Determinants and Process

The degree and direction of the influence of personality on political learning depends on: (1) the personality characteristic; (2) the nature of the stimulus-object and the stimulus-situation; (3) the subject's other personality characteristics; and (4) the political belief.

A personality characteristic determines political belief to the extent that it affects exposure, comprehension, and the reward value of acceptance. It may affect one or more of these steps and it may be related differently to different steps. Figure 4:2 outlines how self-esteem affects political learning. The arrows in this figure, unlike those in the previous one,

[12] Carl I. Hovland and Irving L. Janis, *Personality and Persuasibility* (New Haven: Yale University Press, 1959), especially pp. 255-279.

[13] William J. McGuire, "Personality and Susceptibility to Social Influence," in E. F. Borgatta and W. W. Lambert, *Handbook of Personality Theory and Research*, pp. 1130-1188.

have signs (+ or -) to indicate whether the relationship is usually positive or negative. Thus, the figure suggests that high self-esteem tends to facilitate exposure and comprehension, while low self-esteem tends to inhibit them, a proposition which is under examination in the main part of this chapter. The double sign (both + and -) attached to the third arrow indicates that individual differences in self-esteem may either increase or decrease the reward value of acceptance; for obviously whether low self-esteem motivates a person to acquire or reject a belief depends, among other things, on the particular belief.

A personality characteristic such as self-esteem may, and frequently will, be related differently to the different mediating steps in the process of political learning. Thus low self-esteem may increase the reward value for acquiring a particular belief and yet decrease the exposure and comprehension needed to learn it. That is, the very same factor which motivates a person to acquire a particular point of view may prevent him from doing so.[14] This point has been overlooked too often in the study of personality and politics, largely because of the failure to think of the process of political learning as a series of steps which can vary independently with a personality characteristic such as self-esteem. Moreover, Figure 4:2 suggests, and this study will confirm, that individual differences in self-esteem have a strong impact on all three mediating steps in the process of political learning. And it is because of this pervasive impct on political learning that self-esteem is an especially significant personality characteristic for the study of socially relevant attitudes.

The degree and nature of the impact of self-esteem on political learning depend partly on the interaction of self-esteem with the stimulus-object and stimulus-situation. That is, not only is political learning situationally determined, but the extent to which — and the way in which — personality affects that learning is situationally determined too. Consid-

[14] See particularly Giuseppe DiPalma and Herbert McClosky, "Personality and Conformity: The Learning of Political Attitudes," *APSR* 64 (1970): 1054-1073.

Figure 4:2. An elementary model of self-esteem and political learning

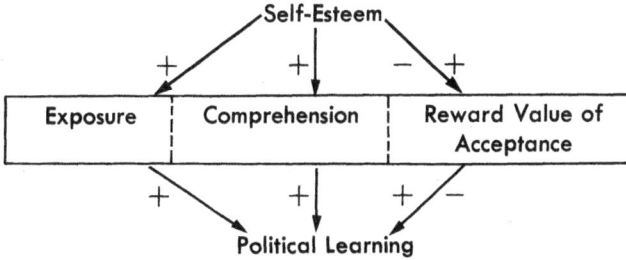

er, for example, how the characteristics of a persuasive communication and the self-esteem of the receiver interact to facilitate (or inhibit) attitude change. A number of researchers have found that persons with low self-esteem were more likely to change their opinions after receiving a persuasive communication than were those with high self-esteem, presumably because low self-esteem in some manner made the former more vulnerable to social influence.[15] But in these experiments the message always was simple and the source credible. When the communication was deliberately made complex, however, then subjects with high rather than low self-esteem were more likely to change their opinions, presumably because low self-esteem inhibited comprehension of the message, with the result that attitude change was checked.[16] Similarly, when the communication was threatening to the subject, more change took place among those with high than with low self-esteem, apparently because high self-esteem increases one's tolerance for threatening stimuli and therefore enhances the chances that one will devote the time and attention needed to understand and accept the position the persuasive communication presents.[17] In short,

[15] For an incisive review of these experiments, see W. J. McGuire, "Personality and Susceptibility to Social Influence."

[16] H. F. Gollob and James E. Dittes, "Effects of Manipulated Self-Esteem on Persuasibility Depending on Threat and Complexity of Communication," *JPSP* 2 (1965): 195-201.

[17] *Ibid.*

in the study of persuasive communications, the relationship between self-esteem and attitude change tends to be negative when motivation to change counts for a great deal and problems of learning count for very little; and the relationship tends to be positive when problems of learning become, for whatever reason, formidable.

Similarly, variations in the stimulus-situation can influence the impact of individual differences in self-esteem on the various steps in the learning process and thereby affect the outcome of the process itself.[18] For example, the classic studies of conformity showed that subjects with low self-esteem were more likely to succumb to pressure to conform to the group norm, while those with high self-esteem were more likely to resist them. These experiments took place, however, in a rather special set of circumstances. Consider the standard conformity experiment. In the classic studies of Asch and Crutchfield, it was made unmistakably clear to the experimental subject that he had deviated from the otherwise unanimous verdict of the group; his attention was focused directly on the group judgment, thereby supplying him with a salient yardstick with which to evaluate his own opinion; the alternatives open to him were limited and clearly defined: he could either reaffirm his original view or conform to the opinion of the group; finally, he knew he must make some response (that is, the option of 'leaving the field' was foreclosed), and the experimental situation limited the range of permitted responses to relatively simple reactions which the subject had already learned to perform. Not surprisingly, then, the influence of individual differences in exposure and comprehension was largely eliminated. A personality characteristic such as self-esteem would tend to affect the experimental outcome only insofar as it affected the reward value of acceptance.

In such circumstances, it is customary to find that low self-esteem leads to conformity. But in other circumstances,

[18] This argument has been developed by Giuseppe DiPalma and Herbert McClosky, "Personality and Conformity: The Learning of Political Attitudes."

when the stimulus-object and situation are more complex, less structured, or more ambiguous, self-esteem affects all three steps in the learning process, not merely the third, as the data from this and other studies will confirm. The number of steps affected may well determine the direction of relationship between self-esteem and conformity, for whatever interferes with the learning of norms diminishes the likelihood of conforming to them. As DiPalma and McClosky have shown,[19] a number of personality characteristics such as anxiety and low self-esteem, which tend to promote conformity in the laboratory, where individual differences in exposure and comprehension count for little, tend to promote deviation from social norms in the actual world, where such differences count for a great deal. In short, whether low self-esteem leads to conformity or to deviation may depend on whether its effect is chiefly on learning contingencies (exposure and comprehension) or on reinforcement contingencies (the reward value of acceptance), a matter which in turn may be situationally determined.

The connection between self-esteem and social learning also varies with individual differences in psychological make-up. Exactly how different configurations of personality characteristics affect the impact of self-esteem is far from clear, but two rather elementary points should be stressed. First, to speak of self-esteem as it is in the natural world, that is, as a relatively enduring aspect of personality, is to refer to a personality characteristic which is thoroughly "confounded" with a number of other personality characteristics.[20] Chapter 3 made plain the assortment of feelings, sentiments, fears, and desires which vary with variations in self-esteem. There is nothing spurious about such relationships, so far as we can tell. One element influences and is influenced by another and we cannot say which — the

[19] DiPalma and McClosky, "Personality and Conformity: The Learning of Political Attitudes."

[20] McGuire, "Personality and Susceptibility to Social Influence," pp. 1155-1161.

disaffection, the depressive affect, the sense of futility, or the lack of self-respect — is most basic. Part of what we mean when we say one person has high and another has low self-esteem is that they differ not only in their self-evaluations but in a host of other ways too. In short, self-esteem is embedded in a matrix of psychological attributes; to vary it is to vary them. So the impact of self-esteem on political learning should be attributed to this larger psychological matrix and not to self-esteem alone.

Second, of the personality characteristics likely to affect the relationship of self-esteem and political learning, perhaps the most important are cognitive abilities and skills. For any group of persons, the degree to which self-esteem inhibits exposure and comprehension depends on the average level and degree of variation of its cognitive ability. That is, the more extreme the group is in ability — whether it is very able or very poor — and the more narrow the range of differences in ability, the less effect variations in self-esteem will have on the capacity for political learning; conversely, the more widely the group is distributed along a gradient of intellectual ability, the more likely it is that individual differences in self-esteem will lead to systematic differences in social learning. This, of course, suggests a rough rule as to the validity of generalizing from survey studies to psycho-historical analyses. Many of the conclusions arrived at in this study about the connections between self-esteem and social learning, which are based on samples encompassing a considerable range of intellectual ability and skill, in all likelihood do not apply to the subjects of psycho-historical studies, who have tended to be men of exceptional abilities.

Last, the relationship between self-esteem and political learning varies with the political belief. Self-esteem shapes some opinions by its effect on learning contingencies, other opinions by its effect on reinforcement contingencies, and still other opinions, of course, by its effect on both kinds of contingencies. Thus, the relationship between self-esteem and certain political attitudes may be due largely to their inherent complexity and limited circulation within the society: to the extent low self-esteem impedes exposure and comprehension, low self-esteem will inhibit the learning of such attitudes, while high self-esteem will facilitate it. The relationship between other opinions and self-esteem depends largely on the power of beliefs or attitudes about certain subjects to evoke fairly deep-seated, intense feelings. For widespread beliefs with a strong emotional component, the connection to self-esteem is likely to be mediated largely by the reinforcement value of acceptance and very little, if at all, by differential comprehension and exposure.

In effect, I have drawn a crude distinction between two kinds of belief: in the first case, the connection to personality is due to a cognitive factor (for example, information which is difficult to learn because it is complex or because it is personally threatening); in the second case, the connection is due to an emotive factor (for example, an aspect of the belief may elicit support because it arouses and provides for the release of an emotion such as hostility). It is worth considering the connections these two kinds of belief may have with a personality characteristic such as self-esteem, for analysis of personality and belief has heretofore concentrated on the emotive and neglected the cognitive, a preoccupation which has proven seriously misleading, as the research on prejudice illustrates.

The Emotive and the Cognitive

Personality is commonly identified with the irrational, the aberrant, the emotional. Social science has reinforced the habit of drawing on the inner workings of personality as a mode of explaining individual reactions which are out of the ordinary or "out of place." Actions or reactions that a situation does not call for, that are so uncommon or intense as to be manifestly inappropriate — excessive hostility, disassociation between thought and action, and so forth — are seen as the proper field of study for psychiatrists and personality psychologists. By contrast, less esoteric explanations are sought where actions and reactions are less heavily laden with affect, more suitable to the external situation, more in line with the beliefs of others as to what is proper and improper, permitted and prohibited, true and false. There is, in other words, a more or less stereotyped identification of personality factors with emotive, non-cognitive forces.

Research on prejudice presents a striking example of a tendency to contrast the psychological and the emotive with the sociological and the cognitive. To attribute anti-Semitism to personality factors is, by common consent, to put forward an explanation which places major stress on the emotive quality of prejudice. One such explanation, advanced in *The Authoritarian Personality* and adopted by many subsequent investigators, suggests that the predisposition to prejudice arises out of a complex set of emotions and personality dynamics, which in the more or less ideal-typical case center on a person's hostility towards himself and (at least one of) his parents which is so intense as (1) to prevent the individual from consciously acknowledging and dealing with it and (2) to force him to find some means to express it in order to obtain relief from an otherwise unendurable tension. Prejudice is so congenial an attitude because it permits the expression or gratification of intense emotional states such as hostility. A set of beliefs such as anti-Semitism legitimates and encourages aggression in various forms — symbolic, verbal, and behavioral — and thus provides an outlet for hostility, as well as for the other emotional states such as anxiety and guilt which underlie prejudice. This condensation, while it oversimplifies the often subtle analysis of the psychodynamics of authoritarianism and prejudice, presents the main outlines of one approach to prejudice.

Psychodynamic explanations, it is worth noting, may take a rather different tack from traditional psychoanalytic theories. Thus, Bettelheim and Janowitz reject the view that a particular personality type or family experience in early childhood are critical determinants of prejudice.[21] They contend — and again, their argument is summed up more simply

[21] Bruno Bettelheim and Morris Janowitz, *Social Change and Prejudice* (New York: Free Press of Glencoe, 1964).

than it deserves to be — that it is punishing experiences in adult life (for example, downward social mobility) that arouse anxiety so acute as to undermine the individual's "personal controls," setting in motion a process that builds up a state of tension which can only be relieved by the expression of hostility.

Although Bettelheim and Janowitz view the dynamics of prejudice from the perspective of contemporary ego psychology rather than from the more classic Freudian standpoint of *The Authoritarian Personality*, they nonetheless essentially agree with the researchers on authoritarianism on the last links in the causal chain that tie prejudice and personality together: the connection between the two lies in the emotive character of anti-Semitism, that is, in the power of anti-Semitism to evoke and provide for the expression of intense emotions such as hostility.

The importance that personality-oriented theorists place on the emotive nature of prejudice has been subject to criticism, principally from sociologists.[22] This criticism takes many forms, but a basic theme running through it is that personality-oriented theories focus exclusively on the emotive component of prejudice and tend to overlook its cognitive component. As a consequence, such theories of prejudice give inordinate weight to the subtle interplay of forces taking place deep within the recesses of the individual's personality and pay only passing attention to the impact of the larger society and its institutions. Exploring this avenue of argument, Selznick and Steinberg characterize prejudiced attitudes thus:

> Viewed in their cognitive aspect, anti-Semitic beliefs are intellectually unenlightened. They are generalizations about an entire group, usually accepted uncritically and

[22] See, for example, E. H. Rhyne, "Racial Prejudice and Personality Scales: An Alternative Approach," *Social Forces* 41 (1962): 44-53; L. Weller, "The Relationship of Personality and Nonpersonality Factors to Prejudice," *Journal of Social Psychology* 63 (1964): 129-137; and especially, G. J. Selznick and S. Steinberg, *The Tenacity of Prejudice* (New York: Harper and Row, 1969).

on the basis of hearsay. When not patently false, they typically involve false inferences about Jewish motives and purposes. Viewed in this way, anti-Semitic beliefs are a small subset of a very large class of unsophisticated and cognitively primitive beliefs. Among their closest relatives are superstitions and magical beliefs, characteristic of almost any preliterate or semiliterate group.[23]

As they observe, the distinction between cognitive and emotive components is only analytic; in real life, the two may well be inseparable. Nevertheless, in their view, the cognitive may be the more decisive, for prejudice, as they understand it, ultimately belongs to a large set of primitive beliefs with wide circulation in the society which are accepted largely because one lacks the intellectual and normative criteria to reject them.

Selznick and Steinberg contend, to condense their argument, that there are two sets of values in American society — "the official culture, or ideal culture and the unofficial, or common culture."[24] The ideal culture is the repository of the values of tolerance, liberty, rationality, and pluralism which are the emblems of the society's institutions, while the values of the common culture, by contrast, are "not only prescientific and predemocratic but antiscientific and antidemocratic."[25] Prejudice thus goes hand in hand with the common culture.

Education, in their view, is the main institution for the transmission of the ideal culture. As the individual progresses through the educational system, he is brought into direct and increasingly close contact with the values of the official culture. Obviously education also cultivates the intellectual skills and style needed to understand these values and to appreciate their relevance to the affairs of everyday life. Not surprisingly, then, the further the individual progresses

[23] Selznick and Steinberg, *The Tenacity of Prejudice,* p. 136.

[24] *Ibid.,* p. 157.

[25] *Ibid.*

through the educational process, the deeper and firmer his grasp of the norms of the ideal culture. A lack of education, on the other hand, is likely to generate a "syndrome of unenlightenment." With little schooling one is ill-equipped to understand the complex values of the ideal culture. A poor education fosters "cognitive simplism" which gives rise not only to differential learning abilities but also to differential receptivity to certain values. Thus the unenlightened frame of mind is marked by "impatience with social problems, intolerance of dissent, attitudes of blame, and indifference to the suffering of others."[26] A lack of education poses so formidable an obstacle to entering the ideal culture in part because the educational system is the principal channel by which society passes on its ideal values, in part because a lack of schooling tends to block other channels of learning of these values. So the poorly educated are less likely than the well-educated to be exposed to the mass media (with the exception of television) and less likely to retain whatever information does reach them through the media.[27] For these and other reasons, Selznick and Steinberg conclude, first, that anti-Semitic beliefs are accepted for the same reason as other primitive beliefs, namely, a failure to acquire the cognitive skills and the values of the ideal culture which promote an antipathy to this syndrome of unenlightenment; and second, that education far more than any putative personality characteristic such as authoritarianism determines whether a person acquires the habits of thought that encourage him to reject the values of the common culture and accept those of the official culture.

The sociological criticisms of personality-oriented explanations of prejudice is persuasive on many points. Prejudice is very much like many primitive beliefs — overly simple, stereotypical, unsophisticated, and unsupported by reason or science. And education assuredly is a determinant of

[26] *Ibid.*, p. 141.

[27] *Ibid.*, pp. 148-152.

resistance to the primitive beliefs which are at the core of the common culture. Nonetheless, the sociological criticism falls wide of the mark in one vital respect. A basic aim of conceiving political learning in terms of a sequence of mediating steps is to call attention to the diverse nature of the intervening processes. The third step — the reward value of acceptance — is essentially emotive in character, the first two steps — exposure and comprehension — are basically cognitive; that is, the third step refers to reinforcement contingencies, the first two to learning contingencies. Low self-esteem and a lack of education have much the same effect on the first two steps in the process of political learning, as I shall show. Because they do, persons with high and low self-esteem differ in much the same ways as do the well- and the poorly-educated. In short, to contrast the psychological and the emotive with the sociological and the cognitive is to set up a false contrast, for self-esteem may be as closely tied to the cognitive component of belief as it is to the emotive. Indeed, the influence self-esteem has on the acquisition of political values is so pervasive precisely because it affects all three of the steps in political learning, not merely the final one.

Self-Esteem and Social Learning

Information is in constant circulation through the society. The process of social communication may be selective, self-selective, or some mix of the two. When it is selective, the distribution of information is limited to a particular audience, defined by some criterion such as profession or kinship which sets the target group off from the population at large. Social communication is self-selective (or nearly so) when information is 'indiscriminately' circulated (say, by the mass media), that is, when any individual by his own choice can become a member of the audience to which the communications are addressed. Whenever information diffusion is largely self-selective, whatever affects individual differences in exposure to the flow of information affects social learning. And a particularly important determinant of exposure is self-esteem, as we shall see.

Exposure

Exposure is a function of (1) location in the channels of social communication, (2) attentiveness, and (3) receptiveness. Let us consider each of these factors in turn.

Of the several channels of social communication, face-to-face contact is apparently of singular importance. Other channels such as the mass media may make information initially available but its diffusion through the population depends heavily on personal influence.[28] It is most often through his contact with others that a person acquires his opinions, or has them changed or strengthened, often without his being aware of it. The casual attention the average citizen pays to politics reinforces the power of social interaction to shape public opinion and voting behavior. In any event, because social influence is exerted with such force and frequency in the routine encounters of daily life, it is especially important to focus on the connection between self-esteem and social interaction.

Variations in self-esteem lead to marked differences in interpersonal orientation, as we saw in Chapter 3. Persons of high self-esteem hold a comparatively favorable image of others, judging them on the whole to be able, well-intentioned, honest, and trustworthy. Those with low self-esteem, on the other hand, have a decidedly unfavorable view of others, tending to emphasize their deceptiveness, unreliability, selfishness, and even aggressiveness; they harbor suspicious and apprehensive attitudes and fear that close relationships with others would leave them exposed and vulnerable, a frame of mind which is quite congenial to the idea of defensive withdrawal.

Not surprisingly, then, a number of studies have shown that low self-esteem inhibits the social exchange of informa-

[28] Elihu Katz and Paul F. Lazarsfeld, *Personal Influence* (Glencoe, Ill.: The Free Press, 1955).

tion. For instance, children with low self-esteem, as compared
to those with high self-esteem, participate less often in
extra-curricular activities;[29] belong to social clubs or take
part in such school activities as the glee club less frequently;[30]
and participate less often in classroom discussions and in
conversations outside the classroom "about matters of student government or general high school interest."[31] When
they do find themselves involved in a group discussion, as
in the normal course of events they must from time to time,
their preference is to assume a passive stand rather than
take an active part in the discussion.[32] Their aversion to
involvement, we may infer, grows out of their chronic anxiety
and self-doubts. Their low self-esteem encourages a fear of
what other persons may say or do if they were to speak out.[33]
It deprives them of a sense of ease and confidence, without
which they tend to doubt the validity of their own judgment[34]
and their ability to put their views across.[35]

Low self-esteem, then, raises a barrier to the social exchange of information: it blocks it, but of course, it does
not entirely shut it off. Depending on the circumstances,
low self-esteem may more or less tightly constrict exposure

[29] Morris Rosenberg, *Society and the Adolescent Self-Image* (Princeton,
N. J.: Princeton University Press, 1965).

[30] *Ibid.,* pp. 194-195.

[31] *Ibid.,* pp. 119-120.

[32] *Ibid.,* pp. 171-175 and pp. 185-186.

[33] Stanley Coopersmith, *The Antecedents of Self-Esteem* (San Francisco: W. H. Freeman, 1967), pp. 66-67; and Rosenberg, *Society and the
Adolescent Self-Image,* pp. 213-214.

[34] That doubt may be reality-oriented as some research indicates, see
Edward Levonian, "Self-Esteem and Opinion Change," *JPSP* 9 (1968):
257-259.

[35] Coopersmith, *Antecedents of Self-Esteem,* pp. 66-67; and Rosenberg,
Society and the Adolescent Self-Image, pp. 214-216.

to the flow of information. Research on children and adolescents adds credence to the view that the inhibitory effects of low self-esteem tend to be relatively generalized. Thus, behavior at play is much the same as in the classroom: children with low self-esteem participate less often, behave more passively when they do participate, demonstrate less verbal and physical aggressiveness, and avoid social interaction more often than children with high self-esteem.[36] Sociometric studies also confirm the social withdrawal hypothesis. Thus children and adolescents whose self-image is more unfavorable are poorly thought of and unpopular with their peers more often than are those whose self-image is relatively positive.[37]

These studies also clarify somewhat the nature of low self-esteem as a social motive. It is usually thought of as a motive which involves, among other things, a need for approval. Presumably, the person who is uncertain of his own worth, if he is to think well of himself, must rely on the opinions of others. Whether his attitudes towards himself are in some measure favorable depend on whether others' attitude toward him are favorable. To defend against his low self-esteem, then, he must secure their approval. Hence, low self-esteem is said to encourage social conformity — that is, a tendency to think and do what others consider desirable because they consider it desirable. Viewed in this way, low self-esteem may be thought of as an approach type motive.[38]

A very different way to conceive of self-esteem, which I shall only sketch out here, leaving the broad outline for later

[36] V. Crandall, "Personality Characteristics and Social and Achievement Behaviors Associated with Childrens Social Desirability Response Tendencies," *JPSP* 4 (1966): 477-486.

[37] Frances D. Horowitz, "The Relationship of Anxiety, Self-Concept, and Sociometric Status Among Fourth, Fifth and Sixth Grade Children," *JASP* 65 (1962): 212-214; and Rosenberg, *Society and the Adolescent Self-Image,* p. 203.

[38] See, for example, D. P. Crowne and D. Marlowe, *The Approval Motive* (New York: Wiley, 1964), pp. 189-205.

chapters to fill in, is that, instead of indicating a need to win approval, low self-esteem may reflect a need to avoid disapproval. The difference between the two parallels the difference between the motive to achieve success and the motive to avoid failure.[39] The need to avoid disapproval like the need to avoid failure is best conceived of as an inhibitory tendency. That is, both act as restraints, leading an individual to avoid the performance of certain actions. The need to avoid disapproval in this sense is a negative motive, for its chief effect is to motivate an individual *not* to do something. Viewed in this way, low self-esteem may be thought of primarily as a motive which inhibits the performance of actions expected to result in disapproval, and which, therefore, is often in opposition to the performance of actions expected to result in approval.

Low self-esteem as a social motive is best viewed as a primarily inhibitory tendency. One sign of its negative character is its association with social withdrawal: low self-esteem, evidently, motivates many persons *not* to do certain things. Such withdrawal tendencies are matters of degree; the outcome may be more or less complete inactivity or, as is more likely, it may be a diminution in the vigor of participation, leaving its mark in such personal characteristics as passivity and timidity. To refer again to evidence from studies of children, low self-esteem goes hand-in-hand with low expectations of success, a reluctance to seek recognition and approval, a tendency to avoid involvement in achievement activities — all of which suggest that those with low self-esteem are more strongly motivated by a need to avoid disapproval than by a desire to win approval.[40] It is worth noting that these findings held for both boys and girls, which is often not the case in research on self-esteem,[41] and

[39] See the chapter on "A Theory of Achievement Motivation" in J. W. Atkinson, *An Introduction to Motivation*, pp. 242-246.

[40] Crandall, "Personality Characteristics and Social Achievement Behaviors Associated with Childrens Social Desirability Response Tendencies."

[41] McGuire, "The Nature of Attitudes and Attitude Change."

more importantly, that they are drawn from observations of the behavior of children at play and not merely their responses to questionnaires administered in the artificial setting of the classroom.

Low self-esteem also inhibits face-to-face discussions. As Rosenberg has shown, high school students with low self-esteem are less likely than those with high self-esteem to engage in "discussions of matters of student government or general high school interest," are more likely to play a passive role when they do become involved in such discussions, and are less often asked what they think about such questions by their peers.[42] This is only one way, but a rather important way, that low self-esteem diminishes exposure to the flow of information about politics. Obviously, low self-esteem does not lead to a complete retreat from social life. Nor do individuals with low self-esteem find all social exchanges equally threatening or necessarily threatening at all. Nevertheless, low self-esteem does inhibit involvement in more informal and spontaneous social encounters as well as in larger, more formal, and organized gatherings.

There is a second way that low self-esteem affects exposure: it reduces attentiveness to information about politics. This hypothesis finds considerable support in other studies, though most of them do not deal directly with self-esteem. In particular, Seeman has carried out an extensive series of studies on the sense of powerlessness, a notion which is linked to low self-esteem as we saw in Chapter 3. Powerlessness is measured by a modified version of the I-E (Internal-External control) scale, developed originally by Liverant and Rotter. In a study of tuberculosis patients in a hospital, Seeman found that those who tended to see events as largely beyond their power to control had poorer knowledge about health matters than did those who believed they could exercise some influence over the outcome of events.[43] Note

[42] Rosenberg, *Society and the Adolescent Self-Image,* pp. 199-200.

[43] M. Seeman and John W. Evans, "Alienation and Social Learning in a Hospital Setting," *ASR* 27 (1962): 270-284.

that the two groups of patients which were compared, those high in powerlessness and those low in powerlessness, were matched with respect to hospital experience and standard socio-demographic factors such as age, education, and social class.

How does a sense of powerlessness affect the acquisition of knowledge? Seeman's answer to this question would likely run as follows: a sense of powerlessness implies a belief that events cannot be controlled, that the outcome is basically a matter of some external force, be it fate, luck, or whatever; if a man believes he has little or no influence over the outcome of events, he is less likely to take an interest in them and as a consequence, he is less likely to acquire information about them. So the causal sequence is more or less: a sense of efficacy ⟶ interest in external events ⟶ attentiveness ⟶ acquisition of information.

But does a sense of powerlessness inhibit the acquisition of knowledge about politics? The evidence is affirmative. A study of male workers in Sweden, for example, found a negative relationship between powerlessness and political knowledge; powerlessness is also negatively related to interest in politics, while political interest is positively related to political knowledge.[44] A later study of several student samples in Sweden turned up negative relationships between a sense of powerlessness on the one hand and general political awareness and information on nuclear testing on the other.[45] Is the inhibitory effect of powerlessness selective? That is, does it affect the acquisition of all kinds of knowledge or only information about certain subjects? On the basis of the available evidence, the impact appears selective rather than indiscriminate. Thus, a sense of powerlessness is associated with measures of political knowledge but not of cultural

[44] M. Seeman, "Alienation, Membership and Political Knowledge," *Public Opinion Quarterly* 30 (1966): 353-367.

[45] M. Seeman, "Powerlessness and Knowledge: A Comparative Study of Alienation and Learning," *Sociometry* 30 (1967): 105-123.

knowledge.[46] Similarly, a study of prisoners in a reformatory shows that powerlessness affects the acquisition of knowledge about some matters, but not about others. Prisoners who feel powerless, compared to those with more confidence in their ability to influence the outcome of events, are less likely to learn information about handling parole successfully, but are neither more nor less likely to learn information which concerns their situation at the reformatory or their long-range prospects for noncriminal careers.[47]

A proper explanation for the differential impact of powerlessness is rather hard to come by. Seeman has suggested that differential learning depends on whether interest is taken in the matter which, in turn, depends on whether information about it is useful to a person in "managing [his] destiny."[48] But it is difficult to credit the notion that citizens are interested in information about nuclear weapons because they believe that they can affect the outcome of nuclear war. And it does seem contrary to argue that knowledge about a reformatory is useless to prisoners living in it but knowledge about politics is useful to citizens at large. Seeman suggests that differential learning depends on differential interest across domains of knowledge; the more knowledge of a domain affects a person's control of his life chances, the more likely it is he will take an interest in the domain. Yet it is hardly persuasive to point to politics as an example of a domain where the average person is likely to take an interest. Although in some objective sense politics undoubtably affects the life situations of citizens, most of them pay only passing and casual attention to it.

Two points ought to be made. First, along with Seeman, I believe that a sense of powerlessness — and I might add, a feeling of low self-esteem - has a selective effect on

[46] Seeman, "Powerlessness and knowledge."

[47] Seeman and Evans, "Alienation and Social Learning in a Hospital Setting," pp. 270-284.

[48] *Ibid.*, p. 270.

learning. There is no reason to believe that low self-esteem invariably reduces exposure and comprehension to the same degree. Unlike Seeman, however, I suspect that differential learning may be due less to differences in content and more to a matter of variations in attention and intrinsic difficulty. Second, powerlessness (and self-esteem) may have a relatively generalized impact on social learning, which affects the acquisition of knowledge in a number of domains, among them, politics. One reason there is less of a selective effect than Seeman would have us believe is because personal characteristics such as low self-esteem tend to build a habit of inattentiveness. Beliefs about personal efficacy have a tendency to be self-reinforcing: the man who has doubts about his competence is less likely to try for the kind of success that would shore up his self-confidence. The more he doubts that he is able to influence the outcome of events, the less likely it is that he will be aware of or attach importance to cues which suggest he is able to affect the outcome. And the less attentive he is to a particular domain such as politics, the less information about it he is likely to acquire.[49]

The hypothesis cannot be given a direct test, since the data lack a measure of attentiveness. But in the MB study, there is a measure of the interest people take in politics. Table 4:1 presents the relationship between political interest and the combined index of self-esteem. The index of political interest is a five-item measure, which assesses the amount of attention a person ordinarily pays to politics. The focus, then, is everyday concern, not the special interest elections excite. Clearly, low self-esteem dampens political interest. Persons with low self-esteem are three times as likely to be disinterested in politics as those with high self-esteem; conversely, those with high self-esteem are four times as likely to be interested in politics as those with low self-esteem.

[49] Attentiveness enters into the learning process in other ways, chiefly in its effect on comprehension, which is considered below.

Table 4:1

THE RELATIONSHIP BETWEEN SELF-ESTEEM AND
POLITICAL INTEREST (PERCENTAGED DOWN)
MB SAMPLE ONLY

		Self-Esteem		
		High (n = 392)	Mid (n = 207)	Low (n = 483)
Political Interest	High	49	27	13
	Mid	40	55	50
	Low	12	19	37

Finally, variations in self-esteem are related to individual differences in receptivity. In fact, the link between the two greatly tightens the contention that low self-esteem is basically an avoidance rather than an approach type motive, for the relationship between reception of information and self-esteem permits us to evaluate these two rather different interpretations. If low self-esteem is conceived of as involving a need for approval, one might expect it to encourage greater sensitivity and responsiveness to social cues which convey what is expected and desired, since taking account of the approved standards would enhance the chances of gaining social approval. By this reasoning, the relationship between levels of self-esteem and reception of information ought to be negative, since those with low self-esteem have a stronger need for approval than do those with high self-esteem. If, however, low self-esteem is conceived of as involving a tendency for defensive denial, another result must be expected. Scholars offer different reasons for believing that low self-esteem and defensive denial are connected — some contend that low self-esteem makes greater reliance on defensive behavior necessary in order to maintain a sense of security,[50] others argue that it encourages a greater use of expressive

[50] Coopersmith, *Antecedents of Self-Esteem,* pp. 42-44.

as opposed to repressive types of defenses[51]—but there is general agreement as to the consequence of this connection: those with low self-esteem have a stronger tendency to "ward off" emotionally charged, evaluative stimuli. The defensive denial interpretation represents low self-esteem as an avoidance rather than an approach type motive, which is consistent with the earlier argument over whether a lack of self-esteem involves more of a need to avoid disapproval than a need to obtain approval. The defensive denial interpretation also leads to a different prediction about the relationship between reception of information and self-esteem than does the need for approval interpretation, as Jacobson and Ford have pointed out.[52] The relationship between receptivity and self-esteem ought to be positive, for the tendency to block out "self-threatening information becomes somewhat generalized and therefore results in a generally lessened sensitivity to information from the socio-cultural environment."[53]

There is considerable circumstantial evidence that supports the defensive denial interpretation. Coopersmith, for example, has reported the results of a word-recognition test, using three kinds of words — neutral, threatening, and pleasant.[54] His assumption was that self-esteem is one determinant of the threshold of recognition of self-threatening stimuli: the more confidence a person has in himself, the more readily he will acknowledge a potentially threatening stimulus. In line with this assumption, he found that boys

[51] See A. Cohen, "Some Implications of Self-Esteem for Social Influence"; for discussion of the Repression-Sensitization distinction, see Donn Byrne, *An Introduction to Personality* (Englewood Cliffs, N. J.: Prentice-Hall, 1966), pp. 178 and 453.

[52] L. I. Jacobson and L. H. Ford, Jr., "Need for Approval, Defensive Denial and Sensitivity to Cultural Stereotypes," *Journal of Personality* 34 (1966): 596-609.

[53] Jacobson and Ford, Jr., "Need for Approval," p. 606.

[54] S. Coopersmith, "Studies in Self-Esteem," *Scientific American* 218 (Feb. 1968): 96-106.

with high self-esteem recognized threatening words quicker than did those with low self-esteem.

Exploring a similar line of reasoning, Gollob and Dittes hypothesized that self-esteem and persuasibility are likely to be negatively related when the message is easy to comprehend and acceptance of it is non-threatening; however, self-esteem and persuasibility are likely to be positively related, if the message in some way is menacing to the receiver.[55] Presumably, self-esteem and susceptibility to stress are negatively related: those with little respect for themselves or their abilities more readily perceive themselves as threatened than do those with greater confidence in their ability to succeed. Stress is thus presumed to interfere with the process of attitude change—perhaps by distracting attention, or perhaps by blocking comprehension of the message. The work of Gollob and Dittes gives some credence to this line of argument. They find that low self-esteem increases the chances of attitude change when the message is easy to comprehend and nonthreatening and decreases the chances of change when the message is more complex or when acceptance of it is more or less threatening.

In addition to this circumstantial evidence, one experiment at least was especially designed to determine which interpretation — need for approval or defensive denial — is superior. Jacobson and Ford had male undergraduates describe by means of a semantic differential the connotative meanings of two sets of figures. One set of figures was black, the other was white, but the two sets were otherwise identical. Several personality measures (all of the social desirability type) also were administered. The evaluations of these figures provide a measure of cultural sensitivity, for black is usually rated as more threatening than white. If the "need approval" interpretation is sound, then high scorers on Social Desirability measures should have been more sensitive to this difference than low scorers; and if the defensive denial

---

[55] Gollob and Dittes, "Effects of Manipulated Self-Esteem on Persuasibility Depending on Threat and Complexity of Communication."

interpretation is superior, than the reverse should have been the case. As it turned out, for two measures (the Marlowe-Crowne and the Ford Social Desirability scales, though not for the Edwards) low scorers perceived the black stimuli more negatively than the white, but high scorers did not. Admittedly, these results may not hold for other measures of self-esteem, but Marlowe and Crowne do interpret their scale as a measure of self-esteem (with a high score indicating low self-esteem) and the correlates of their scale do match those of standard measures of self-regard.[56] All in all, the evidence appears to favor the defensive denial over the "need approval" interpretation.

Our own data support the defensiveness interpretation. Table 4:2 presents the relationship between three measures of psychological inflexibility and the overall index of self-esteem. Inflexibility, as it has been conceptualized by McClosky and his colleagues, is a sign of (excessive) dependence on the defense mechanisms (repression, denial, identification with the aggressor, and the like).[57] Inflexibility is both a by-product of a struggle for defense and a mode of defense. It manifests itself, characteristically, in an aversion to the complex, the uncertain, or the unfamiliar, in needs for order and predictability, and in more extreme form, in compulsiveness and rigidity in thought and action. The Intolerance of Ambiguity, Rigidity, and Obesessiveness measures tap different facets of psychological inflexibility.

As Table 4:2 shows, self-esteem and inflexibility are strongly and negatively related. A high scorer on the Intolerance of Ambiguity scale, for example, has a strong desire for everything to be fixed and definite. Discomfort, anxiety, and

[56] For instance, high scorers on the Marlowe-Crowne Social Desirability Scale, compared to low scorers, are more persuasible, more likely to conform under social pressure to do so, and more anxious and vulnerable to criticism. See D. P. Crowne and D. Marlowe, *The Approval Motive.*

[57] H. McClosky, "Personality and Attitude Correlates of Foreign Policy Orientation," in James Rosenau, *Domestic Sources of Foreign Policy* (New York: The Free Press, 1967), especially pp. 86-88.

Table 4:2

THE RELATIONSHIP BETWEEN SELF-ESTEEM AND MEASURES OF PSYCHOLOGICAL INFLEXIBILITY (PERCENTAGED DOWN)

		Self-Esteem								
		PAB-Leaders			PAB-Followers			MB Sample		
		High (n = 1020)	Mid (n = 1274)	Low (n = 726)	High (n = 224)	Mid (n = 499)	Low (n = 721)	High (n = 392)	Mid (n = 207)	Low (n = 483)
Rigidity	Low	55	40	27	52	38	23	45	34	26
	Mid	26	32	32	26	29	23	28	36	25
	High	20	28	40	21	34	55	27	35	49
Obsessiveness	Low	39	28	21	44	37	30	37	36	29
	Mid	23	24	23	25	27	24	31	23	28
	High	39	49	56	30	36	46	32	41	43
Intolerance of Ambiguity	Low	50	32	15	51	39	15	46	35	15
	Mid	27	29	24	34	34	31	31	33	31
	High	24	39	62	15	27	54	22	32	55

anger come quickly to him, if he is unsure as to what another person—or even he himself—believes on some important issue. In his desire to know where everyone stands, he tends to over-simplify, often dividing everyone into two camps — for or against, friend or foe. In all three samples, those who are low in self-esteem are much more likely to be intolerant of ambiguity. In the MB study, for example, those with low self-esteem are more than twice as likely to score high on Intolerance of Ambiguity than those with high self-esteem; conversely, those with high self-esteem are three times as likely to score low on the ambiguity measure as are those with low self-esteem. Similarly, low self-esteem is related strongly to rigidity and somewhat less strongly to obsess- siveness.[58]

There is, evidently, a rather close connection between low self-esteem and defensiveness, as indexed by these measures of psychological inflexibility. This is but one manifestation of people's tendency to adjust their cognitive style to their adaptive needs.[59] To state the point somewhat differently, persons with low self-esteem find that a "closed" mind rather than an open one better fits their need to defend themselves against an outer world which they find threatening, and often in addition, an inner world which they can not acknowledge or cope with. In self-protection, they close themselves off. And an immediate consequence of their defensiveness is a diminution in their reception of information.

There is an alternative line of explanation, which may prove a useful supplement to the defensive hypothesis and which, in any event, does not contradict it. The basic idea, simply put, is that high self-esteem may play a positive role in promoting the reception of information, quite apart from any negative role low self-esteem may play in blocking it. Such an idea, however, goes to the very roots of a theory

[58] We shall take up in more detail the relationship between self-esteem and obsessiveness in Chapter 7.

[59] Milton Rokeach, *The Open and Closed Mind* (New York: Basic Books, 1960), Chapter 1.

of motivation. Such basic questions, of course, are well outside of the scope of this study, but one or two brief observations may be in order. In the wake of renewed interest in ego psychology has come a new emphasis on the idea of intrinsic motivation. This type of motivation differs from the more familiar idea of extrinsic motivation in at least two respects:[60] (1) whereas extrinsic motivation turns on the idea of tension reduction (for example, the tension generated by viscerogenic needs such as hunger or sex or the arousal of anxiety), intrinsic motivation (for example, innate striving for stimulation or the production of effects) does not; (2) intrinsic motivation (such as motives for exploratory, manipulative, curiosity, and play behavior) is an "independent" source of energy, that is, it is not a "derivative" of fundamental drives directed at overcoming some state of deficiency. From the point of view of extrinsic motivation, low self-esteem is conceived to represent a deficiency state of some kind (such as insecurity or a need for status) which is an irritant, stimulating various sorts of activities (following either a drive-stimulus model of learning theory or the hydraulic model of Freud) aimed at eliminating the deficiency; high self-esteem signifies the relative absence of such a deficiency state. From the point of view of intrinsic motivation, however, high self-esteem is itself a source of energy. It is a positive stimulus and not merely the absence of a negative one. High self-esteem is an intrinsic motive because it is rooted in our inherent striving to be effective, to be active, to know, though the exact nature of the connection is far from clear.

An example may bring out more clearly the distinctive quality of this view of self-esteem. The defensive hypothesis contends, in effect, that low self-esteem establishes an avoidance tendency which impairs the reception of information; those with high self-esteem are more receptive because they are less disabled. A quite different hypothesis, based on the

[60] Robert W. White, *Ego and Reality in Psychoanalytic Theory*. See especially Chapter 3, "A Way of Conceiving of Independent Ego Energies: Efficacy and Competence," pp. 24-43.

connection between self-esteem and intrinsic motives to be effective, to be active, to know, may be called the exploratory hypothesis. The exploratory hypothesis asserts that high self-esteem positively motivates a person to acquire more information. And evidence can be cited that accords with this hypothesis too. Coopersmith, for example, reports that children with high self-esteem, compared to those with low self-esteem, are more imaginative and exploratory in their intellectual style. They are more likely to seek out, and to be pleased by, information which is novel, or complex, or presents a challenging problem to solve.[61]

But this example also illustrates the difficulty of determining the relative merits of the defensive and exploratory hypotheses, for both fit the facts on hand equally well. There is no evidence at this moment which supports one hypothesis, without also supporting the other. Nor has anyone suggested a 'crucial experiment' which might enable us to decide between them. Preferences for one or the other depend heavily on attitudes toward very basic issues of theory and method (such as humanist and ethnological revisions of the theory of motivation), which are not likely to achieve immediate resolution. So whether one wishes to subscribe to one or the other hypothesis or to both is at present largely a matter of individual choice; but both hypotheses point to a positive relationship between self-esteem and receptivity to information, which is repeatedly found in experimental and survey data and which is, for the purpose of this study, the important point.

Comprehension

The linkage between self-esteem and social learning is not merely a matter of exposure. No doubt there are circumstances where persons of high and of low self-esteem do not differ with respect to access or receptivity to the flow of information. Yet learning contingencies may still vary with self-esteem, for persons of high and low self-esteem are likely

---

[61] Coopersmith, "Studies in Self-Esteem."

to differ in their capacity to comprehend the information to which they are exposed.

How do variations in self-esteem affect comprehension? The data in Chapter 3 supply a clue. The connection between self-esteem and worry and emotional tension was noted: individuals with low self-esteem, more often than those with high self-esteem, complain of loneliness, insecurity, a sense of ineffectiveness, estrangement, and fear. And it is largely because low self-esteem is one element in a psychological syndrome reflecting a person's characteristic level of emotional arousal that variations in self-esteem directly affect comprehension.[62]

To begin with, level of emotional arousal is evidently a determinant of the direction of attention.[63] Consider the situation of an individual engaged in the performance of a somewhat difficult task. The more anxious individual tends to divide his attention between himself and the task facing him. The focus of his attention, to the extent it is directed at himself, tends to be his weakness and inadequacies; he worries about whether he will do well at the test, whether he can do well at it, whether others will do better than he, whether he is proceeding as well as he should be, and

[62] This position is shared by a number of others, for example, Richard H. Walters and Ross D. Parke, "Social Motivation, Dependency, and Susceptibility to Social Influence," in L. Berkowitz, ed., *Advances in Experimental Psychology* (1964), vol. 1, pp. 232-277; L. Berokowitz, "Social Motivation," in G. Lindzey and E. Aronson, *Handbook of Social Psychology,* vol. 3, 50-135, see especially p. 103; A. Bandura and R. H. Walters, *Social Learning and Personality Development* (New York: Holt, Rinehart, and Winston, 1965); and Irving L. Janis and Howard Leventhal, "Human Reactions to Stress," in E. F. Borgatta and W. W. Lambert, *Handbook of Personality Theory and Research,* pp. 1041-1085.

[63] Encouraged by a recent article reviewing the research literature on test anxiety and attention, I have amplified somewhat my original argument in this section. See Jeri Wine, "Test Anxiety and Direction of Attention," *Psychological Bulletin* 76 (1971): 92-104. My original argument and her review of relevant experimental results coincide on the points important for my purposes here, though I should note that there are a few points on which her views and mine differ.

so forth.[64] Such self-focusing tendencies are obviously distractive, preventing the individual from giving his full attention to performance of the task at hand and so significantly cutting down on his chances of success. More generally, emotional arousal interferes with comprehension of external events. To the extent that attention tends to be directed away from what is taking place outside the individual and toward what is taking place emotionally within him, his capacity to understand the world around him tends to be impaired.

Emotional arousal is likely in other ways to impair cognitive efficiency.[65] Strong levels of arousal, as Janis and Leventhal observe, are likely to lead to indiscriminate vigilance.[66] In such a condition the individual shows excessive alertness, as it were, coupled with an overreadiness to react, both of which enhance the probability of his interpreting inaccurately or responding inappropriately to situational cues. Then, too, arousal is likely to lead to "cognitive constriction," as evidenced by a tendency to rigidity and a narrowing of the range of cues made use of, the more so the more complex the cues.[67]

One consequence of emotional arousal, I have been arguing, is to alter the threshold of perception. Arousal is also likely to alter the threshold of response. Simply put, arousal strengthens the likelihood that cues or stimuli which are

[64] This is a paraphrase of a quote, cited by Wine, "Test Anxiety and Direction of Attention."

[65] For an example of perceptual and ideational distortions induced by factors such as obsessive compulsiveness or anxiety, see David Shapiro, *Neurotic Styles* (New York: Basic Books, 1965).

[66] A more elaborate version of some of the hypotheses to follow predicts a curvilinear relationship between arousal and cognitive efficiency, a track I would follow if my analysis involved a comparison between two learning tasks (or one task in two different sets of circumstances), one of which was notably more complex and difficult than the other. See I. L. Janis and H. Leventhal, "Human Reactions to Stress."

[67] Janis and Leventhal, "Human Reactions to Stress," p. 1052.

normally low in salience will elicit a response. Such heightened readiness to respond makes a person more readily distractible and so more likely to respond inappropriately in a learning situation — a tendency which grows in strength as the task increases in complexity.

Psychological states such as anxiety or low self-esteem, when sufficiently intense, are likely to impair perceptive and apperceptive processes, though it would be wrong to think their effect is always to increase error.[68] Nevertheless, research on stress suggests that emotional tension leads to an increase in stereotyped behavior and a decrease in variability.[69] Concentrating on cognitive performance, we may describe some of the changes which accompany stress as follows: a shift to concepts of greater category width, a decrease in the sensitivity and multiplexity of classification criteria, and stimulus fixation as evidenced by repetitiveness and stereotypy. The result is a greater use of more primitive constructs applied in a more indiscriminate fashion.

Defense mechanisms also enter in. To judge from the clinical literature, a number of aversive personality characteristics, among them low self-esteem, lead to a heavy dependence on the classic mechanisms of defense, particularly those which strengthen the chances of perceptual errors and distortion. Note that these defenses do not simply represent an effort to evade reality testing; indeed, they are frequently called on in an attempt to comprehend reality. Bettelheim and Janowtiz, for example, observe that the anti-Semite may be pressed to invent a delusional system, perhaps persuading himself of the existence of an all-powerful conspiracy, in order to rationalize attacks against Jews who would other-

[68] For a view of some of the complexities of this question, and in particular, the "executive-intending" function of personality, see George S. Klein, *Perception, Motives, and Personality* (New York: Alfred A. Knopf, 1970).

[69] R. H. Walters and R. D. Parke, "Social Motivation, Dependency, and Susceptibility to Social Influence."

wise appear harmless.[70] In any event, excessive reliance on such defense mechanisms enhances the likelihood of misperceiving or misunderstanding what other people believe, why they act as they do, what they are like, or how they are likely to behave in the future. More generally, aversive personality traits tend to introduce systematic biases in perceptual and cognitive processes, and so introduce error into social perception and learning. The anxious personality is quicker to believe harm threatens, the paranoid quicker to suspect a conspiracy at work. Of course, this is the sort of thing that most have in mind when they think of personality impeding perception, though the experimental evidence on such processes is sketchier than is commonly supposed.[71] Perhaps it will suffice merely to observe in a general way that an individual with low self-esteem is likely to be decidedly more vulnerable than one with high self-esteem to the varieties of perceptual distortion and error.

Low self-esteem not only impairs cognitive efficiency in general; it hampers social learning in particular. Consider the major mechanisms of social learning. Two of the most important means by which a person learns are through observation of others (including models which are symbolic as well as models which are real) and the administration of secondary reinforcements (both positive and negative) contingent on his performance.[72] But the efficacy of both mechanisms of social learning depends on the focus and level of attention.[73] As Walters and Parke have noted,

[70] Bettelheim and Janowitz, *Social Change and Prejudice,* p. 138.

[71] Tagiuri strikes a note of caution, which is worth remembering. See R. Tagiuri, "Person Perception," in Lindzey and Aronson, eds., *Handbook of Social Psychology,* vol. 3, pp. 395-449.

[72] Walters and Parke, "Social Motivation, Dependency, and Susceptibility to Social Influence."

[73] As the reader will have noticed, the concept of attention (or some cognate, such as vigilance) has appeared with some regularity in my discussion. For the record, I should point out that this apparently simple concept may actually prove to be somewhat complex, embracing several

In the first place, imitative learning is most likely when the attention of the observer is focused on the responses of the model; in fact, rather precise imitation will not occur unless the observer attends carefully. Secondly, attending to the actions of others . . . the observer is aware of the expressions of approval and disapproval and the manner in which their responses are associated with his own behavior.[74]

But development of "the habits of orienting and attending to others" depends on, among other things, self-esteem, for emergence of these habits characteristically turns on a willingness to trust significant others and, within limits, a desire to turn to them for aid and approval, particularly in childhood.[75] Here it is worth recalling that social withdrawal is an integral part of the syndrome of self-esteem. Persons with low self-esteem, compared to those with high self-esteem, report fewer and less satisfying attachments to others. They feel themselves alone and alienated, and at the same time, are apprehensive that others will approach and come into too close contact. Afflicted by such fears, they are unlikely to rely readily on others, to turn to them for aid or companionship. Habits of avoidance and social inattention tend to be self-reinforcing. As we saw earlier, the absence of self-regard limits exposure to others, and as we see here, it affects not only the likelihood of exposure but its efficacy as well. Lacking the habits of orienting and attending to others, persons of low self-esteem, even when involved in social interaction, are less likely to be attentive to or aware of what others say or do, of what they believe or value, and even of when they express approval or disapproval.

The data confirm in several ways that low self-esteem obstructs comprehension. In Table 4:3 we see that the

distinct elements. See Michael I. Posner and Stephen J. Boies, "Components of Attention," *Psychological Review* 78, no. 5 (1971): 391-408.

[74] Walters and Parke, "Social Motivation, Dependency, and Susceptibility to Social Influence," p. 244.

[75] *Ibid.,* pp. 232-277.

THE RELATIONSHIP BETWEEN SELF-ESTEEM AND MEASURES OF COGNITIVE CAPACITY (PERCENTAGED DOWN)

		Self-Esteem								
		PAB-Leaders			PAB-Followers			MB Sample		
		High (n = 1020)	Mid (n = 1274)	Low (n = 726)	High (n = 224)	Mid (n = 499)	Low (n = 721)	High (n = 392)	Mid (n = 207)	Low (n = 483)
Anomie	Low	83	61	26	68	36	8	69	38	14
	Mid	15	35	52	27	47	36	27	39	37
	High	1	5	22	5	17	57	5	24	48
Bewilderment	Low							56	36	14
	Mid							32	43	37
	High							12	21	50
Acquiescence	Low	69	40	21	62	41	15	60	35	17
	Mid	28	46	40	33	40	34	30	43	32
	High	3	14	38	5	19	51	11	22	51
Intellectuality	Low	7	13	22	11	20	36	16	30	42
	Mid	25	30	36	29	37	41	35	37	36
	High	68	57	42	61	43	23	49	33	22
Mysticism	Low							41	23	11
	Mid							39	41	35
	High							20	36	53
Awareness	Low							20	35	53
	Mid							37	39	32
	High							43	26	15

Anomie scale and the Self-Esteem index are strongly and negatively related. The McClosky Anomie scale may serve as a measure of cognitive disorientation.[76] The high scorer confesses his inability to understand the world about him. Everything changes so quickly, anything can happen, no one can really know what to expect or what rules to follow. It is not merely a matter of his seeing flux and disorder in the world; what is far more critical is his own uncertainty about what to do or believe. In every sample, those with low self-esteem are much more likely to be anomic than those with high self-esteem. Among the Followers, for example, 57% of those with low self-esteem, but only 5% with high self-esteem, score in the upper third of the Anomie scale, while 68% of those with high self-esteem, compared to 8% of those with low self-esteem, fall in the lower third.

The Bewilderment scale in the MB study taps, in addition to the element of cognitive disorganization, a feeling of helplessness. The high scorer feels, characteristically, that the government is too large and too complicated to be understood or to be influenced. Like the Anomie scale, the Bewilderment scale is strongly and negatively related to self-esteem: those with low self-esteem are four times as likely to score at the high end of the Bewilderment scale, while by about the same margin those with high self-esteem are more likely to score at the low end.

Moreover, there is a clear connection between acquiescence and low self-esteem, as Table 4:3 makes plain. It is rather less clear what to make of this connection. To conceive of acquiescence merely as response error will not do. Measures of acquiescence tend to be multi-faceted; at a minimum, they assess both response set and cognitive capacity. People likely to score high on acquiescence measures tend to be more disorganized intellectually, less reflective and attentive, more uncertain of their own opinions, and more likely, therefore, to wind up agreeing with statements which are

[76] For a discussion of the construction procedure for the Anomie scale, see H. McClosky and John H. Schaar, "Psychological Dimensions of Anomy," *American Sociological Review* 30 (1965): 14-40.

vague, ambiguous, exaggerated, or too broadly put. A score on an acquiescence test indicates the probability of one type of error, to be sure; but it also is a revealing even if crude measure of cognitive capacity, as its negative relationship with education, or with intellectuality, would suggest. This is particularly true for the McClosky acquiescence measures, for they are built from item pairs which express opposite opinions on the same issue. The items, though, are scattered through the lengthy questionnaire, and it requires a fair measure of concentration, skill, and discrimination to perceive the logical relationship between two items of a pair. In short, the relationship between acquiescence and self-esteem is one more sign that unfavorable self-attitudes impair cognitive functioning.

A further sign is the positive association between self-esteem and Intellectuality, a scale which measures the value placed on the emblems of high culture such as appreciation of symphony concerts, time given to reading books, credence given anti-intellectual credos or slogans (such as, "the heart is as good a guide as the head"). Among the Followers those with high self-esteem are more than twice as likely to score at the high end of the Intellectuality scale, while those with low self-esteem are better than three times as likely to score at the low end. Even among the Leaders, whose educational and economic advantages incline them, on the average, toward intellectual and cultural values, the Self-Esteem index and the Intellectuality scale remain strongly and positively correlated.

Such patterns of correlation are found not only with regard to symbols of rationality and high culture. The differences between persons with high and low self-esteem carry over to attitudes in everyday life. Particularly revealing is the belief, far more widespread among those with low self-esteem than among those with high self-esteem, that the occult is a key that will unlock the future. This belief signals a lack of confidence in reason and its allies, science and technology, and a reversion to more primitive, animistic ways of understanding, the closest ally of which in our culture is superstition. Table 4:3 shows the strong, negative relationship between self-attitudes and the Mysticism scale: 53% of those with low self-esteem score at the high end of this scale, compared to 20% of those with high self-esteem; conversely, 41% of those with high self-esteem, but only 11% of those with low self-esteem fall at the low end of Mysticism.

Finally, low self-esteem clearly inhibits the acquisition of political knowledge. On two tests of political awareness, constructed in very different ways, those with high self-esteem are more likely than those with low self-esteem to be politically knowledgeable. The Political Awareness scale in the MB study comprises nine items, each of which involves an assertion about American politics that is either true or false, with which the respondent is asked to agree or disagree. To answer correctly, it must be stressed, requires only a modicum of information. A typical statement asserts, "The United States never joined the League of Nations," another that "There are about 100 members in the U.S. House of Representatives." Obviously, this test of awareness is very crude; it can discriminate only those at the extreme pole of political benightedness rather than the variations in information over the entire gradient of political awareness. Yet there is a clear and strong relationship between political awareness and self-esteem: 43% of those with high self-esteem, but only 15% of those with low self-esteem, score in the upper third of the Political Awareness index; conversely, 53% of those with low self-esteem, compared to 20% of those with high self-esteem fall in the lower third.

The Political Awareness index built for the national PAB Followers is, if anything, cruder. The Index cumulates by respondent the number of "don't know" or "no answer" responses to 43 items in the questionnaire. Precautions were taken to assure that variations in item format exerted no undue influence over total scores. And for convenience the distribution of total scores was converted to stanine scores. This index is a less direct test of knowledge of politics than is the Awareness index of the MB. The PAB index requires no information about the structure of American political institutions; it only requires the respondent have an opinion, or a willingness to express one, on longstanding major issues (such as how much reliance the U. S. should place on the United Nations). But despite the crudeness of this measure, there is a quite substantial relationship between self-esteem and political awareness, offering a further indication of the extent to which low self-esteem impairs comprehension and thereby inhibits the acquisition of political knowledge.[77]

Recapitulation

This chapter has attempted to lay a foundation which succeeding chapters can build on. To that end it was necessary to consider how personality characteristics can affect the acquisition of political knowledge. The process of political learning may be conceived as a sequence of steps. As we observed, the study of personality and political belief, for all its apparent variety, has concentrated attention on the final step in the process — the reward value of acceptance. The main task of this chapter was to illuminate two earlier steps in the process — exposure and comprehension. In brief, low self-esteem tends to inhibit the acquisition of political knowledge by impeding exposure and comprehension, quite apart from whatever influence it may exert to incline an individual toward (or away from) acceptance of certain opinions or attitudes toward politics.

Conceiving of political learning as a multi-step process pays a number of dividends. It allows us, first, to recognize some of the quite different ways in which self-esteem affects political belief, a matter the following chapter will explore further. It also provides a framework in terms of which the influence of personality characteristics other than self-esteem can be interpreted, and thus reduces somewhat the need to devise an entirely unique explanation for every characteristic selected for study. In addition, it has some

---

[77] The following chapter will present the data in such a way as to back the causal language which I use somewhat loosely at this point.

value in accounting for certain nonmonotonic effects of self-esteem and interactions of stimulus, situation, respondent and response factors. Last, it permits us to see in a rather different light the connection between personality and democratic commitment, a task we turn to in the following chapter.

DEMOCRATIC COMMITMENT AND THE DEMOCRATIC PERSONALITY

Chapter **5** .

The idea of the "democratic personality" is both an ancient notion and a modern one. Plato and Aristotle, for example, insisted that there is a connection between a man's character and the type of government for which he is best suited and which he is most inclined to support. The belief in an affinity between the character of the citizens and their political system persists. Indeed, it is this belief which has inspired much of the work on personality and politics.[1]

But although the idea of a democratic personality enjoys a long history, it suffers from a scarcity of empirical research. Consequently, one of the aims of this chapter is to add to the existing stock of knowledge which is largely impressionistic and rather unsystematic. The addition, it should be understood, will be a modest one, for we shall examine only the ties between commitment to democratic values and individual differences in self-esteem, leaving for another time and other investigators a broader search for the psychological correlates of democratic commitment.

[1] See, for example, Alex Inkeles and Daniel J. Levinson, "National Character: The Study of Modal Personality and Socio-Cultural Systems," in G. Lindzey and E. Aronson, eds., *The Handbook of Social Psychology* (Reading, Mass.: Addison-Wesley, 1969) vol. 4, pp. 418-506.

This chapter has an additional aim. The notion of the democratic personality provides an opportunity to put to a test the basic arguments developed in the preceding chapter. There I considered the connection between personality and political belief. My object was to develop a general model of this relationship — general in the sense that it could be applied to psychological characteristics other than self-esteem and a model in the sense that it permitted a formalized representation of the various causal forces at work. The idea of the democratic personality offers an opportunity to explore this model of the relationship between personality and political beliefs.

First, however, the idea of the democratic personality needs to be spelled out and critically analyzed.

Democratic Character: A Paradigm by Lasswell

Harold Lasswell, in a pioneer essay, undertook a reformulation of the notion of the democratic personality.[2] Social scientists have since elaborated certain of his points, laid less stress on others, in some instances clarified his somewhat cryptic arguments,[3] and in others translated them into more precise propositions which could be put to an empirical test. But the main outlines of his formulation remain unchallenged. Since I intend to challenge Lasswell's view, I will begin by recapitulating it.

To anchor his analysis, Lasswell fastens his theory of the democratic personality to a particular conception of a 'democratic community.' This form of political organization he defines as ". . . one in which human dignity is realized in theory and fact. It is characterized by wide rather than narrow participation in the shaping and sharing of values."[4]

[2] Harold D. Lasswell, "Democratic Character," in H. D. Lasswell, *The Political Writings of Harold D. Lasswell* (Glencoe, Ill.: The Free Press, 1951), pp. 465-525.

[3] Fred I. Greenstein, "Harold D. Lasswell's Concept of Democratic Character," *Journal of Politics* 30 (1968): 696-709.

[4] Lasswell, *Political Writings*, pp. 475-476.

The fundamental values are eight in number — power, respect, affection, rectitude, well-being, wealth, skill, and enlightenment. By seeing what promotes popular participation in these values we can discover the hallmarks of a democratic polity. Thus, power — to take one example — is shared when the norms of the polity favor participation in decision-making, when participation in fact is widespread, when men in office and their decisions can be criticized legitimately and with impunity, and when there is "an effective presumption against the politicizing of human relations" and "against the use of power in great concentration, particularly in the form of regimentation, centralization, and militarization."[5]

Character affects men's orientations toward a democratic community. It refers to a part of the personality system. As Lasswell defines it, *"By character we mean the self-system of the person, together with the degree of support, opposition, or non-support received from the unconscious part of the personality.* When we say that a man has a steadfast character it is implied that he has sufficient command of the resources of the whole personality to maintain the self-system despite environing conditions which may be adverse."[6]

The self-system of the democratic personality has, according to Lasswell, four outstanding attributes. The democratic character is, first, marked by "the maintenance of an open as against a closed ego."[7] An "open ego" refers to a certain orientation toward other persons, particularly a capacity to invite and form genuine personal relationships. In Lasswell's words, "the democratic attitude toward other human beings is warm rather than frigid, inclusive and expanding rather than exclusive and constricting. We are speaking of an underlying personality structure which is capable of

[5] Lasswell, *Political Writings,* p. 476.

[6] *Ibid.,* p. 482.

[7] *Ibid.,* p. 495.

'friendship,' as Aristotle put it, which is unalienated from humanity."[8]

Second, the democratic character incorporates many values rather than a few and is "disposed to share rather than to hoard or to monopolize."[9] In Lasswell's view, for a man to center his energies on one value — be it power, respect, or whatever — jeopardizes his ties to others. He becomes self-centered and compulsive. Other people become means to his ends. His needs dwarf theirs. As a result, he fails to see their desires and fears, or he sees them as threats to his own gratification.

Third, the democratic character holds a certain attitude toward his fellow men.[10] He believes they are, by and large, able and well-intentioned. Others are worthy of his trust, or can be assumed so, unless they act to the contrary. Basically, people are honest and friendly. In short, his attitude toward his fellow man is essentially positive and optimistic, rather than distrustful and fearful.

Last, the democratic character is psychologically well-integrated. Psychological integration, as Lasswell uses the term here, refers to a state in which the unconscious energies of the individual are not at odds with other elements of his personality (for example, the superego) and where the individual is relatively free from anxiety.[11] Integration of the personality is a key aspect of the democratic character, because the individual is otherwise likely to deviate from the democratic creed, even if he consciously accepts it and believes he conscientiously adheres to it. As Lasswell points out, a process of reaction formation against anxiety and the destructive tendencies it arouses can lead a person at the conscious level to accept democratic values. Yet there may

[8] *Ibid.*

[9] *Ibid.*, p. 494.

[10] *Ibid.*, pp. 502-503.

[11] *Ibid.*, pp. 503-514.

be a flat contradiction between his beliefs and his behavior. Underlying anxiety and hostility may give rise to a rigid and intolerant personality. As a consequence, though he professes to be a democrat, he may occasionally or habitually act in an autocratic manner, entirely unaware of the domineering spirit of his actions; or while complying to the letter of these values he may apply them so rigidly as to violate their spirit; or he may have opinions on specific issues which sharply depart from the democratic values he swears by in the abstract.

These character traits of the democratic personality are interdependent, for they spring from a common source. According to Lasswell, the *"failure to develop Democratic Character is a function of interpersonal relationships in which low estimates of the self are permitted to develop."*[12] Thus the person with little self-esteem thinks little of others. Compared to the person with respect for himself, he is less likely to think well of others, more likely to suspect their motives and to distrust their ability and character, less likely to acquire interpersonal ties which might lend him a sense of safety and security, and more likely to be rigid, anxious, and hostile. In sum, he is more poorly adjusted socially and psychologically.[13] As Lasswell writes, "Democratic character develops only in those who esteem themselves enough to esteem others. . . ."[14]

Other scholars have sketched portraits of the democratic personality, in the main filling in details that Lasswell's description hints at, or leaves somewhat blurred. The pictures are essentially the same, whether drawn from the perspective of the democrat or the antidemocrat.[15] Thus,

[12] *Ibid.*, p. 521, Italics his.

[13] For Lasswell's view on this matter, see Harold D. Lasswell, *Power and Personality* (New York: Viking Press, 1962), pp. 161-164.

[14] *Ibid.*, p. 162.

[15] There are opposing views, of course. Maslow, for one, contends that there are so many different "types" of democrats that it hardly makes

the democratic personality, as Alex Inkeles sees him, is an individual confident of his own worth and the value of others, who accepts them as his equals and believes they are, by and large, rational and well-intentioned, who has no need to rule others or to submit to their rule, and who values tolerance, diversity in appearance and belief, and a willingness to conciliate, to compromise, and to change.[16] This configuration of values constitutes a distinct psychological type, according to Inkeles. The democratic personality, then, is flexible, tolerant of ambiguity and differences, relatively free from anxiety, and open rather than closed-minded; he is able to control and to accept his inner impulses, he accepts himself and others, he is well-integrated psychologically and socially, and he is not hostile, compulsive, suspicious, or alienated.

A similar sketch of the democratic personality is drawn by Rober Lane.[17] At first glance, it may appear less similar than it really is, because the descriptive terminology differs. Lane divides the "pathologies of Democratic man" into three categories — "those focusing primarily on the self, those primarily relating the self to others, and those primarily relating the self to society."[18] Under each, he enumerates congeries of personal attributes—beliefs, needs, patterns of behavior, and psychological states — which diminish a man's desire or capacity to be a democrat. Thus, under

---

sense to speak of *the* democratic character. See A. H. Maslow, "Power Relationships and Patterns of Personal Development," in Arthur Kornhauser, ed., *Problems of Power in American Democracy* (Detroit: Wayne State University Press, 1959), pp. 92-131.

[16] Alex Inkeles, "National Character and Modern Political Systems," in Francis L. K. Hsu, ed., *Psychological Anthropology: Approaches to Culture and Personality* (Homewood, Ill.: Dorsey Press, 1961), pp. 178-200, especially pp. 195-197.

[17] Robert Lane, *Political Ideology* (New York: The Free Press, 1962), "Notes on a Theory of Democratic Personality," pp. 400-412.

[18] *Ibid.*, p. 400.

the heading of social and cultural pathologies fall alienation from society, pervasive cynicism, traditionalism, single-valued belief systems, and a deep-seated belief that "the world is a jungle,"[19] and under pathologies of the self, a loss of identity (both personal and social), self-estrangement, a lack of self-control, irrationality, and an aversion to self-analysis and insight.[20]

In Lane's eye, these various pathologies cohere and form a distinctive psychological type, "the impoverished self"[21] which is the mirror image of Lasswell and Inkeles' conception of the democratic personality. The idea of an impoverished self is a composite notion, built from three basic components — low self-acceptance, low self-esteem, and low ego-strength. Low self-acceptance, as Lane uses the term, actually reflects certain aspects of low self-esteem, as I use that term. Very broadly, self-acceptance implies the person is "not in conflict with his unconscious and not rejecting his social member-ships."[22] Low self-acceptance, then, brings in its train guilt, anxiety, distortion of reality, self-alienation, and the like.[23] Low self-esteem is a similar source of the pathologies of the non democrat. For the person who sees little value in himself, the world lacks value. He is more prone to distrust and dislike other persons, to believe they are weak and inadequate. He is thus given to cynicism, a sense of malaise and alienation, doubt and confusion as to his inner values, and feelings of anomie.[24]

[19] *Ibid.*, pp. 402-409.

[20] *Ibid.*, p. 410.

[21] The nondemocrat *lacks* the qualities (e.g., rationality, trust, security and the like) a citizen must contribute to a democratic community, and it is for this reason Lane describes such a person as "the impoverished self." See Lane, *Political Ideology*, p. 409.

[22] *Ibid.*, p. 410.

[23] *Ibid.*, pp. 410-411.

[24] *Ibid.*, pp. 411-412.

A lack of ego strength, that is, an absence of "self-control, [and of] a sense of mastery over the environment" is the third basic feature of the impoverished self. The man with little power over himself is likely to feel powerless, to see himself at the mercy of others in a world which lacks order and security. He can neither understand nor deal effectively with other persons or problems. And his political outlook betrays his lack of efficacy and his inability to govern his impulses in an exaggerated emphasis on the possibility of chaos, a paranoid-like predilection to believe conspiracies are at work, and a deep-seated anxiety and irrationality.[25] Taken together, these three deficiencies — low self-esteem, low ego-strength, and a lack of self-acceptance — signify a basic impoverishment of the self, which is the characterological basis of the antidemocrat.

Personality Type and Political Ideology

These character portraits of the democrat and nondemocrat are vivid and, to a point, revealing. But they rest on several assumptions, which on examination appear unpersuasive, suggesting that we need to think of the relationship between personality and democratic commitment in other terms.

As a starting point, we may ask how the term "type" ought to be used. This question, though not the most important, is so often overlooked that it surely deserves attention. Lasswell and others speak of the democratic character (or the antidemocrat) as if it were a personality type. The democrat (or antidemocrat) is described by a list of psychological attributes—anxiety, guilt, low self-esteem, and the like, and the presumption is that these traits all fit together to form a personality type. Briefly, the question is what the term "type" ought to signify.[26] Should it refer only to a

[25] *Ibid.*, p. 412.

[26] For another approach to this question, using different categories and terminology, but seeing a vital distinction between the correlational and the noncorrelational uses of the type, see Harold D. Lasswell, "A Note on Types of Political Personality: Nuclear, Co-Relational and Develop-

certain set of attributes that co-vary? Or should it refer to a set of traits that are interrelated in such a way as to create a distinct entity or "type." In this second, and proper, sense of the term, a personality type is not a mere aggregation of traits but a unique configuration of them, which in its own right exerts an influence over thought and action.

The distinction between these two usages of "type" is not merely semantic; the two usages imply very different hypotheses as to what the "facts of the matter" actually are. The "democratic personality" may turn out to possess the numerous traits attributed to him (anxiety, low ego-strength, guilt, inflexibility, and the like), but this would hardly confirm that the democratic character was a personality type in the strict sense of the term. It may be, for example, that these traits contribute to the outcome separately rather than in combination. Thus, one hypothesis (a quite plausible one, I should add) is that paranoia and low self-esteem, though empirically related, constitute *independent* sources of opposition to democratic values.

Patently, the concept of a personality type in the strict sense makes certain very demanding assumptions as to the causal structure connecting personality and political ideology. With respect to the notion of a democratic character type, certain of the assumptions involved either have no support in empirical evidence or flatly contradict the data so far collected. For example, the idea of a democratic personality implies a distinct psychological type in some manner discontinuous with intermediate cases. But so far as one can judge from all the data reported and analyzed,[27] the relationship between attitudes toward principles of democracy and personality traits such as anxiety, guilt, and

---

mental," in Fred I. Greenstein and Michael Lerner, eds., *A Sourcebook for the Study of Personality and Politics* (Chicago: Markham, 1971), pp. 232-240.

[27] In this respect, the analyses being conducted by Herbert McClosky on the psychological correlates of democratic commitment — which I have had the opportunity to inspect — are vitally relevant.

the like is monotonic. Or to take another issue, two traits, for example, low self-esteem and inflexibility, may both undermine commitment to democratic values, but they may do so for very different reasons. Lumping them together as mere facets of a basic, underlying personality type, then, effectively blocks a view of the diverse mix of causal forces at work.

My quarrel is not with the notion of a personality type. Rather, it is with the indiscriminate use of that notion. Plainly, we have no reason to conceive of the "democratic personality" as if it were a distinct psychological type. The idea of a "democratic personality" does imply the existence of a unique and organized set of psychological traits characteristic of citizens committed to democratic values, but rather than assume there is a single character type, at this stage of research it would be far more reasonable to look for a variety of personality traits which strengthen democratic commitment. Evidence does not support the contention that these various personality characteristics form but one personality type, and in view of the complexity inherent in psychological processes of this sort, it is more plausible to assume that a number and variety of patterns may lie behind support for democratic values.

In any event, the same psychological characteristics said to typify the nondemocrat (anxiety, guilt, misanthropy, and so forth) are also reported to characterize the conservative.[28] Shall we then put forward the concept of the "conservative personality"? And if so, how shall we decide its merits as opposed to those of the "democratic personality," or for that matter, the rather large number of political and social attitudes and actions which are associated with similar sets of psychological characteristics — for example, ethnocentrism, isolationism,[29] and extreme left- and right-wing values.

[28] Herbert McClosky, "Conservatism and Personality," *APSR* 52 (1958): 27-45.

[29] See Herbert McClosky, "Personality and Attitude Correlates of Foreign Policy Orientation," in James Rosenau, ed., *Domestic Source of Foreign Policy* (New York: The Free Press, 1967), pp. 51-110.

In order to avoid the "type" fallacy, we must resist the temptation to reify trait correlations into psychological types; we must, instead, think in terms of continuous variations. The starting point for inquiry must be the linkage between democratic commitment and specific personality traits. This is not an argument for conceptual "reductionism"; it is more a plea for a measured increase in intellectual modesty and clarity. For that reason, this chapter concentrates entirely on the connection between adherence to democratic values and individual differences in self-esteem. I should add that attention is confined to self-esteem not out of a belief that it is the Rosetta Stone to deciphering the workings of personality; rather, this focus stems from a judgment that at this stage of research we would profit from an analysis of exactly how a particular personality trait affects the acquisition of democratic values.

Further pointing up the need for this type of analysis are two additional assumptions underlying scholarly work on the democratic personality. The first we may label, following the suggestion of Almond,[30] the principle of congruence.[31] This principle holds, in effect, that adherence to political beliefs and belief systems depends largely (though not entirely) on whether the ideology "fits" or "matches" a man's particular psychological makeup. It follows that different personality types over the course of time would tend to gravitate to their appropriate place on the ideological continuum. Citizens, depending on their personality characteristics, would either be drawn to the democratic creed, or be repelled away from it.

[30] Gabriel Almond, "The Appeals of Communism and Fascism," unpublished paper, presented at American Political Science Association 51st Annual Meeting, Boulder, Colorado.

[31] Virtually identical in meaning is the notion of 'immanence' proposed by Daniel J. Levinson, "The Relevance of Personality for Political Participation," *Public Opinion Quarterly* 22 (1958): 3-10. I shall refer to congruence only, though for the purpose at hand the two terms are interchangeable.

Some such principle of congruence is imbedded in the literature of the democratic personality, as it was in the early research on authoritarianism. In the latter a complex construction of psychological attributes was shown to encourage a susceptibility to (potential) fascism. But a clamor shortly arose drawing attention to the implausibility of postulating a one-to-one correspondence between personality and political ideology. There were, it turned out, authoritarians of the left as well as the right.[32] Presumably, the pole of the ideological spectrum one chooses to embrace depends more on the social (and cognitive) forces at work than on the dynamics of authoritarianism.

Also, as it developed, there was little sign of a number of distinct personality types propelling persons in a number of distinctive political directions. The evidence turned up on the authoritarian, the anti-Semite, or the communist pointed not to three distinct psychological entities but to a vaguely defined neurotic state, indicative of personal maladjustment and little else, which was more or less common to these varieties of belief. In short, one is hardly justified in presupposing a distinct democratic personality which in some manner is congruent with democratic values.

The principle of congruence is obviously in need of specification. This principle in its present form is inadequate for three reasons. First, the concept of congruence covers a variety of linkages between personality and political ideology, which ought to be sorted out, if only because the criticism of congruence[33] is usually directed at simple-mind-

[32] See, for example, Edward A. Shils, "Authoritarianism: Right and Left," in Richard Christie and Maria Jahoda, eds., *Studies in the Scope and Method of "The Authoritarian Personality"* (Glencoe, Ill.: The Free Press, 1954), pp. 24-49; Roger Brown, *Social Psychology* (New York: The Free Press, 1965), Chapter 10.

[33] There should be no need to say that congruence is not used here in its more technical and more easily specifiable sense, as in Osgood and Tannenbaum's congruity theory of attitude change. For a comprehensive exposition of various congruence and balance theories of cognitive consistency, see R. Abelson et al., *Theories of Cognitive Consistency: A Sourcebook* (Chicago: Rand McNally, 1968).

ed, almost literal usage of the concept (such as we find in the literature on the democratic personality). A political ideology may "match" or "fit" a personality type (or trait) in several senses. For example, the political belief may be a direct expression at a social level of an orientation at the personality level, as an intolerance of diversity may be a reflection of an intolerance of ambiguity. In this instance, the attitude mirrors the personality trait. A different kind of example is provided by the hostile personality who becomes a Quaker by reaction formation; in this instance the attitude is the mirror-image of the personality trait. Clearly, there are many instances when the process of inference from either thought or action to the underlying personality dynamic is extraordinarily complex; thus the metaphor which described Frued's classic analyses of neurosis is hardly "mirror" or "mirror-image"; "labyrinth of mirrors" would be more apt. The issue is not whether some version of a principle of congruence (or immanence) is valid, but under what conditions it is a useful principle in understanding the connection between personality and political belief. Any effort to reduce the complex interplay between political ideology and personality to merely a matter of congruence, as the literature on the democratic personality essentially does, grossly oversimplifies the problem and oversteps the proper limits of the principle of congruence.

The second reason why the principle of congruence is inadequate is that personality is but one factor in the field of forces. Social and historical circumstances may decisively affect the play of personality. Almond, for example, demonstrated that "the appeals of communism" depended heavily on a country's political system and customs. As he notes,

> where the [communist] party is a small but deviant movement as in the United States and England it is likely to be a haven for disturbed personalities and marginal social types. Where, however, the party takes on mass proportions as in France and Italy, such deviants are the exceptions, and the appeal of Communism

has to be understood in terms of deep-seated social and political problems, political tradition, and historical experience.[34]

Obviously, there are an enormous number of situational factors (such as family socialization, peer group pressure, and idiosyncratic life experiences) which can either elicit the ideology where the individual lacks the appropriate personality characteristics, or suppress it where he does. Less obviously, there are a variety of personal attributes which can affect the direction in which a trait such as low self-esteem moves a person. To take another example from Almond's study of communism, the same personality structure may lie behind right-wing nativism and communism; but the choice between them may depend on an individual's cognitive attributes, for the more intellectual he is, the more likely he is to be attracted to communism, if only because ideologies of the left, as compared to those of the right, have proven, since the nineteenth century certainly, to be more comprehensive in scope, more elaborate in detail, and more thoroughly worked out, and therefore, not surprisingly more congenial to the intellectual.[35] In sum, because beliefs are determined by a complex field of interacting forces, no one-to-one congruence personality type and political ideology is to be expected.

The third reason why the principle of congruence is inadequate is not as familiar as the first two, but it is lodged at the center of this study's approach to self-esteem and political belief and therefore deserves mention. The habit of analysis in personality and politics is to conceive of the impact of personality on belief in motivational terms, as we observed in Chapter 4. Personality arouses, impels, stimulates, and guides thought and action, or so most of us believe. This process may be described in various terms — in the

[34] Gabriel Almond, "The Appeals of Communism and Fascism," pp. 26-27.

[35] *Ibid.*, pp. 29-30.

language of early Freudianism, of latter-day ego psychology, of functionalism, or of learning theory. But the emphasis on psychological dynamics of goal-accented behavior remains the same. It follows that to unravel the skeins of the influence of personality on politicial thought the proper course to follow is to concentrate on the connection between a person's ideas and his motives.

In Chapter 4 we outlined a supplementary course to follow. Self-esteem affects political thought in part because it affects social learning. To be sure, persons with low self-esteem are motivated to embrace certain ideas about politics, while those with high self-esteem are motivated to accept rather different notions. But it is useful to separate out the two processes — the one motivational, the other social learning — which link personality and political belief, if only to consider the implications of the two influence processes for a theory of personality and democratic commitment. Thus, persons low in self-esteem may reject the norms of democratic politics not because they are motivated to do so but largely because their negative self-attitudes have impeded the learning of these values. I will shortly develop this argument but it should be evident even at this early point that emphasizing the learning process rather than the principle of congruence may carry analysis and interpretation in a different direction.

Finally, in addition to the type fallacy and the principle of congruence, there is a third assumption associated with the idea of the democratic personality which, on examination, strikes many in the social sciences as dubious, to say the least. I shall only mention this assumption, for the arguments on all sides are quite familiar, and in any event, the issue can best be examined in the context of the empirical evidence I shall present. Briefly, some would argue that the democrat, after all is said and done, turns out to be the "well-adjusted" person, while the nondemocrat is poorly adjusted socially and psychologically. Thus the nondemocrat is said to be suspicious, misanthropic, lacking in self-confidence, alienated, and anxious. The democrat, by contrast, is psychologically well-integrated, open and warm in his personal relationships, self-assured, optimistic, and high in self-esteem. This amounts, some would say, to identifying the democratic creed with mental health and regarding deviation from these values as a form of illness.

This synopsis oversimplifies the matter, of course. Nonetheless, discussions of the democratic personality by social scientists such as Lasswell, Lane, and others are couched in the language of mental pathology, and the failure to adhere to the values intrinsic to democratic politics, when it stems from some aspect of an individual's personality, is seen as a sign of some psychological aberration or deficiency. No doubt this view is sometimes justified. But is it justified for countries where the prevailing norm is non- or antidemocratic? The answer to this question lies outside the scope of the present study, but I would like to offer one comment. Should it turn out that self-esteem affects the acquisition of democratic values more by its impact on learning than reinforcement contingencies, this result would suggest that in political regimes with authoritarian norms it ought to be those who have high self-esteem (and not those who lack it) who are the most likely to reject democratic values, if only because they are more able — and therefore, more likely — to learn the political values their society prizes. In sum, if the emphasis I have given to self-esteem and social learning is deserved, the very same personality trait which in the United States reinforces democratic commitment may elsewhere promote political authoritarianism of the left and of the right.[36]

Let us now turn to the specific problem of how self-esteem affects the learning of the democratic creed.

Self-Esteem and Democratic Commitment: Basic Assumptions and Arguments

Since the Revolution the official culture in the United States has celebrated the principles of political democracy,

---

[36] Another likely alternative is that the same personality trait which promotes tolerance in the United States, taken as a whole, may promote intolerance in specific sub-cultures within the larger society.

however imperfectly it has honored them in practice. These principles have been defined in different ways; at different times the same principle has been given broad or narrow interpretations; and depending on historical and political circumstances different facets of the democratic creed have stood out more prominently at various times. But despite the difficulties in arriving at a full and fair definition of the democratic creed, one idea in particular has appeared to be of central importance under most, if not all, circumstances. Following the suggestion of Lipset and Raab,[37] we may call it the idea of democratic restraint.

The quality of restraint, as they point out, is essential to the well-being of democracy. Without it, the political marketplace must shut down, or be forced to operate under pressures which either diminish substantially public competition in ideas and policies or eliminate it entirely, leaving only the form and not the substance of a democratic politics.

Restraint is the guarantee of liberty. But who and what must be placed under restraint? Since John Stuart Mill, the classic answer has been state and society. It is easy to see at the very start of the liberal tradition the need to place checks upon the government, to put it under constant surveillance through the freedoms of press and of speech, and to call it to account for its actions, at least periodically, through the institution of elections. Beyond all this, the Bill of Rights testifies to the drive to curb the powers of government and also, as Lipset and Raab point out,[38] to the *negative* character of democratic restraint, for it lays out what the government can*not* do (for example, it "shall make no law abridging the basic freedoms") rather than spelling out what it ought to do. But while the fear of the state has been at the center of attention, at least as important (though less frequently mentioned) has been the fear of society. *On*

[37] Seymour M. Lipset and Earl Raab, *The Politics of Unreason* (New York: Harper and Row, 1970), see especially pp. 432-433.

[38] *Ibid.,* p. 432.

Liberty warns of the rising power of social conformity.[39] For Mill, society was more to be feared than the state, in part because social influence appeared more natural, and therefore, less visible or odious than political influence, in part because the emergence of the middle class had brought about new and more intense pressures to conformity than had been hitherto known. The remedy, Mill said, lay in restraints against social influence. Whereas restraint against the state took the form of prohibition, restraint against society assumed the form of tolerance. Men could find protection against society only where they were free to differ — in their opinions, appearance, practices, and styles of life. So the idea of democratic restraint came to incorporate two elements — juridicial prohibition and social tolerance.

The idea of democratic restraint may at times come into conflict with other elements in the democratic creed, for example, the idea of egalitarianism.[40] And certainly the democratic creed and its constituent elements assume different forms in different countries, but then it is worth noting that the ascendency of constitutionalism in the United States pushes the idea of democratic restraint into a position of prominence it does not always enjoy, and since this is a study of American values, the focus on restraint is well justified.

The notion of democratic restraint is an idea which is hard to understand and therefore difficult to learn. It turns on ideas such as due process, the freedom of conscience, association, and expression, and the panoply of civil liberties and rights citizenship confers. These ideas are complex, rooted in traditions of human history and political theory which are themselves difficult to grasp. In addition, these ideas have raised a host of vexing questions which even theorists of democracy are hard pressed to sort out, let alone arrive at some definitive and widely agreed upon answer. How ought

[39] John Stuart Mill, *Utilitarianism, On Liberty, Essay on Bentham,* ed., Mary Warnock (Cleveland: Meridian, 1962).

[40] Lipset and Raab, *Politics of Unreason.*

a democratic society to balance the claims of a majority against the rights of a minority? Are certain rights (for example, voting) more basic than others (for example, property)? Which should take precedence in the event of a conflict between them, and to what degree does the answer depend on the precise circumstances that prevail at the moment? What is a society obliged (or required) to do in order to assure the equality of citizens before the law, or for that matter, to guarantee (or to work toward a guarantee) that the governmental process is representative and fair?

These questions elude easy or exact answers. Indeed, they have no fixed answers, for over time their meaning tends to alter — sometimes subtly, sometimes sharply — as the circumstances of political and social life change. Thus, the removal of some restrictions on suffrage in the late eighteenth and early nineteenth century lent great impetus to the growth of political egalitarianism, ultimately finding popular expression in the rise of Jacksonian democracy. In our time the explosive struggle over the status of blacks is, perhaps, the most dramatic illustration of the continuing process of interpretation of central articles of the democratic creed such as equality and representation. But more than this, the democratic faith, by virtue of the very principles it affirms, is itself a constant stimulus to change. As Robert Dahl observed, ". . . because democracy has never been fully achieved, it has always been and is now potentially a revolutionary doctrine. For every system purporting to be democratic is vulnerable to the charge that it is not democratic enough, or not "really" or fully democratic. The charge is bound to be correct, since no polity has ever been completely democratized."[41] In sum, the task of learning the norms of democratic politics is difficult because the norms are both complex and variable. The democratic creed is a body of ideas which are alive, whose anatomy is as complicated as that of the human body. It has not been reduced

[41] Robert Dahl, *After the Revolution? Authority in a Good Society* (New Haven: Yale, 1970), p. 4.

to a lifeless catechism, easy to memorize and simple to apply.

In this respect the democratic creed may differ significantly from political ideologies such as communism, which can readily take two different forms: the esoteric doctrine, or the elaborated version of the ideology, confined principally to upper political echelons, and the exoteric doctrine, or popularized version, intended for mass circulation and consumption. The idea of democratic restraint has never developed a truly exoteric form, a popularized version which in any sense is a counterpart of vulgar Marxism. To be sure, citizens attach a value, which with few exceptions is strongly positive,[42] to the abstract statement of political rights such as freedom of speech or belief tied to the notion of democratic restraint. But those "rights" still remain, on the whole, abstract to them. So the idea of due process, which surely is central to the principle of restraint, has remained an essentially esoteric notion to all but a few, and as a consequence, occupies a place far removed from the center of attention in the minds of most.

The abstractness of these ideas poses a further problem in learning the democratic creed, for it is necessary to master not only the values but also the many specific beliefs needed to link the abstract ideas to a concrete situation. To apply correctly the idea of democratic restraint to some political or social question, or even to appreciate its relevance, is often a difficult task. It requires a large fund of information, a habit of attentiveness to politics, and skill in judgment and discrimination acquired through practice and experience. Lacking these three, even those who sincerely support the principle of democratic restraint may not see its relevance to an issue at hand, as a person who is committed to the right of free speech may be blind to its bearing on the question of permitting a "radical" to speak on a university campus. They may also be slow to appreciate threats to democratic values which may be implicit in political goals on which the

[42] See, for example, Herbert McClosky, "Consensus and Ideology," *APSR* 58 (1964): 361-382.

society places a high premium such as achieving "national security" and maintaining "law and order."

Then, too, the democratic creed is difficult to learn because it is pluralistic rather than monistic in character. It encompasses a large and diverse number of principles — popular sovereignty, due process, political egalitarianism, rights of conscience, advocacy and association, and the like. One principle may not always bear an obvious connection to all the others, or two or more of them, under certain circumstance, can be locked in irreconcilable conflict. In this respect, perhaps the most difficult idea to accept is that of democratic restraint, for not infrequently compliance with this principle requires a person to flatly oppose a policy (for example, rooting "communists" out of government) which he and a majority of his fellow citizens favor, or which he feels to be fully in accord with his deepest moral convictions. Not to do what one "knows" to be right, merely because to do it would violate the "right" way to do things in democratic politics is a very difficult idea to accept.

A monistic ideology, built on a single sovereign principle from which all else follows, is of course less troubled by this kind of "inconsistency" than a pluralistic ideology which combines several master ideas that may, depending on the circumstances, be mutually reinforcing or mutually exclusive. What is more, ideologies may invest the power of authoritative interpretation in a supreme institution, as Marxism does in the Communist party and Roman Catholicism does in the pope. This frequently proves a handy device for dealing with whatever inconsistencies or confusion may arise as political and social conditions change, and even in the normal run of affairs, having at hand an outstanding figure anointed to serve as the authoritative source of interpretation is of no small value in teaching a political ideology to a mass of citizens. By contrast, the democratic creed has no single voice. In the United States, the Supreme Court, of course, comes to mind, but its pronouncements are issued in the language of lawyers and addressed to the specifics of the case immediately at hand, and as a consequence, are often neither clear nor persuasive to many citizens, if, indeed, they catch popular attention at all. What is more, though the democratic creed does have certain sacred texts such as the Bill of Rights, it is at bottom an extraordinarily complex and intangible compound, which owes its inspiration and much of its content to political theorists as diverse and as distant as Locke and Hobbes, or Rousseau and the Utilitarians. It is, in short, an outgrowth of a tradition of thought which so far at least has resisted codification and popularization.

These are some of the reasons the democratic creed, and in particular, the idea of democratic restraint, are inherently difficult to learn. But not all people find the task equally formidable. The degree of difficulty depends on the person as well as the task. As we have seen, low self-esteem is very often a handicap to social learning. By comparison to persons with high self-esteem, those who lack confidence in their own worth are less frequently found in the main channels of social communication, and in any event, are less attentive and receptive to information which passes along these channels. In addition to being more poorly exposed to information circulating through the society, persons with low self-esteem are also less likely to understand correctly the information which they do receive.

Low self-esteem may not inhibit information processing in all areas of life, or inhibit it with equal severity under all circumstances, but there is good reason to believe it significantly blocks political learning. As we saw, the person with low self-esteem is less likely to be interested in, or informed about, politics. He has, therefore, less opportunity and reason to learn the values of the political culture. Because he pays less attention to politics and less often takes part in discussions about it, he is less likely to hear expressions of others' beliefs or, for that matter, to express his own. As a result, misperceptions, distortions, errors in reasoning, and misconceptions on his part are more likely to pass unnoticed and uncorrected.

It is but a short step to suggest that those low in self-esteem are less likely than those high in self-esteem to adhere to the democratic creed and that the difference between the two arises less out of a dislike for democratic values inspired by low self-esteem (though this, too, is involved) and more from the impediments to social learning raised by low self-esteem. In America, the ideal culture celebrates democratic values, and those with high self-esteem are more likely to be exposed to and comprehend such complex values than are those with low self-esteem. Because this particular society prizes the idea of democratic restraint, understanding promotes acceptance. In addition, because high self-esteem promotes an enlightened and informed outlook, the person with confidence in himself stands a better chance of being aware of why freedom is so widely valued — of the benefits other men have believed flow from liberty, of the deceptive disguises that threats to the idea of democratic restraint can assume, and of the sacrifices men have made to defend liberty. Then, too, the person with high self-esteem is more likely to offer the principle of democratic restraint consistent support because he is better able to perceive its relevance to the specific and often confusing controversies of political life.

Even though low self-esteem often induces a strong desire to conform, it is less likely than high self-esteem to motivate a person to conform to the official values of the political culture. Because of individual differences in exposure and comprehension, the person with low self-esteem is not only more likely to deviate from the norms of his society; he is also less likely to be aware that his views in fact are deviant. The effect, of course, is to diminish the strength of any drive to change his views in order to conform to the more socially desirable position. In this respect, it is worth recalling the by now familiar observation that many citizens have only a shallow understanding of the democratic creed.[43] It follows that the social pressure to conform to democratic values is often weak and inconsistent, which further decreases the chances a person with low self-esteem will learn that his views do deviate from the values of the political culture or

[43] *Ibid.*

will be so rewarded as to change his opinions to conform to the democratic creed.

Of course, the relationship between self-esteem and democratic commitment is not due solely to the impediments to social learning which low self-esteem raises. There is a complex misture of motivational forces at work. The democratic creed has a differential appeal to different persons, depending on how it and ideas with which it is closely associated resonate with their inner needs and basic psychological orientations. To illustrate this, let us take as an example the image of the democratic citizen in democratic theory.

Democratic theorists to a large degree have shared a common image of the citizen. On the whole, they have placed an emphasis on the citizen's capacity for deliberation, prudence, openness to persuasion, and civic trustworthiness. This image of the citizen involves a strong presumption that by and large people are capable of rational political choice, willing to play within the "rules of the game," and able and willing to give some thought to the public business, at least occasionally.

No doubt there is an element of idealization, of exaggeration, in democratic theory. People are not blessed with perfect intelligence, information, or character. They are imperfect in many respects and as empirical studies have repeatedly confirmed, the majority bear poor resemblance to the portrait of the informed and attentive citizen painted by some democratic theorists.[44] But democratic theory requires no assumption that people are faultless. Madison, for one, based his celebrated theory of political scale precisely on the power of larger political units to check the ambitious and contentious spirit inherent in the citizenry. Nevertheless, the image of the democratic citizen on the whole is a positive one, and hence is likely to have far greater appeal to persons

[44] Bernard Berelson, Paul F. Lazarsfeld, and William N. McPhee, *Voting* (Chicago: Chicago University Press, 1954); Herbert McClosky, "Political Participation and Apathy," David Sills, ed., *International Encyclopedia of the Social Sciences* (Macmillan, 1968), pp. 253-265.

who tend to have faith in people than it is to those who are deeply suspicious and misanthropic.

As we have already noted, individuals who think poorly of themselves tend to think poorly of others. They lack confidence in the honesty and amiability of others, and their suspicion, coupled with hostility, invites a deep cynicism about democratic government. As Rosenberg has shown,[45] persons with low self-esteem are less likely to have faith in their fellow men than those with high self-esteem. A lack of self-approval ought to incline an individual to the view that most people lack the understanding and temperament to participate responsibly in the political process: the important issues of the day are beyond the grasp of most citizens, and their choices of candidates for public office are unlikely to be either informed or sensible. The person with low self-esteem is also likely to have little confidence in public officials. The hostility and suspiciousness which low self-esteem engenders tend to be pervasive. Thus, the person who thinks little of himself ought to think little of those in public life. He should prove, for example, more ready than the person high in self-esteem to believe that politicians are people of small ability, untrustworthy, hypocritical, and more intent on serving their own interest than the public welfare.

This cynicism is likely to extend from the people in politics to the political institutions themselves. The man with little faith in his fellow citizens and the candidates they elect to office is not likely to have much faith in elections as a way to determine public policy. Unhappily, the man with low self-esteem has little faith in himself either. Thus, he tends to feel unable to influence the political process, and he may attribute the same inefficacy to others. A natural consequence of such a feeling of futility is the belief that the

[45] Morris Rosenberg, *Society and the Adolescent Self-Image* (Princeton, N. J.: Princeton University Press, 1965), pp. 181-182; idem, "Misanthropy and Political Ideology," *American Sociological Review* 21 (1956): 690-695; and idem, "Misanthropy and Attitude Toward International Affairs," *Journal of Conflict Resolution* 1 (1957): 340-345.

political process is unresponsive: politicians don't care what the citizens want and most citizens are in no position to make their voice heard, let alone secure the benefits they desire. In short, by encouraging futility as well as cynicism, low self-esteem ought to undercut a person's commitment to democratic politics.

Earlier I stressed one aspect of the democratic creed, the idea of democratic restraint. Democratic politics places a premium on the ability to tolerate disagreement and diversity.[46] The exercise of liberty requires the right of individuals to pursue their own ends, to criticize and experiment, to differ from one another in their tastes, convictions and character, and within limits, to be free to resist the pressure of state and society. But this freedom to disagree and to differ is always under pressure, for it persists only so long as citizens check the desire to compel those in the society who differ from them to conform. Restraint and freedom, then, are two sides of one coin.

It is not hard to see how low self-esteem undermines the commitment to restraint, whether the commitment takes the form of juridical prohibition or social tolerance, or both. In Chapter 3 we noted that low self-esteem is one aspect of a broader psychological state characterized by a sense of vulnerability, chronic anxiety, and stress. Those who think poorly of themselves think poorly of others. Their attitude toward others has a strong component of hostility and suspicion. And insofar as low self-esteem inclines an individual to feel insecure and in some danger, it strengthens his desire to strike out against others. Because his sense of vulnerability is diffuse, he is overready to mistrust others and to believe they pose a danger to the community, perhaps only because their views are unconventional or their appearance unfamiliar.

Persons with high self-esteem, compared to those who lack it, tend to have faith in people. And the stronger that faith,

---

[46] Much of this argument was suggested by Robert Lane, *Political Ideology*, pp. 26-40, 94-112, 400-412.

the more likely they are to grant others broad leeway in their actions and opinions. Trust promotes tolerance, and tolerance is vital to the principle of democratic restraint, for without it there is little willingness to abide persons whose ideas or actions are perceived to violate the conventions which define what is socially acceptable, expected, or desirable.

In addition, trust in people buttresses the commitment to democratic procedures. The need for democratic restraint arises, in part, out of the stresses of political life. Uncertainty and conflict are hallmarks of democratic politics. The political process is organized around the collision of interests and opinions. It is designed to give expression to divergent viewpoints. But while citizens will inevitably disagree about what is desirable, there is no one yardstick to measure who is right and who wrong, and there never can be, so long as the society remains democratic. Moreover, conflict and competition for public office are essential, as Schumpeter argued. And the battle between elites for office guarantees uncertainty and confusion as politicians are driven both to understate their differences on the issues in order to pick up the support of most citizens, and to overstate them in order to obtain the backing of party activists or a particular constituency.

One consequence of this uncertainty and competition, of course, is that democratic politics can easily appear a disorderly and unintelligible process, serving no apparent purpose, producing only conflict and confusion. Viewed in this light, it is not an appealing sight to a person already persuaded of the absence of personal security in the world. Thus, the person with little confidence in himself ought to prove more susceptible to appeals to take direct action against those he regards as dangerous to the community. He most likely will give less weight to protecting legal and political rights than will the person who has confidence in himself and others when honoring these rights might increase the chances of harm. In short, low self-esteem inclines an individual to be overready to perceive a threat, and the perception of this threat weakens his commitment to the restraints democracy lays down on the actions state, society, or citizens can take against a possible source of danger.

These, then, are some of the reasons we expect persons low in self-esteem to reject the democratic creed and those high in self-esteem to accept it. Let us examine now the empirical evidence on the connection between self-esteem and democratic commitment.

Self-Esteem and Democratic Commitment: Empirical Evidence

A commitment to democratic institutions does not demand an absolute faith in those who hold public office or in the citizens who elect them. Indeed, some men, particularly the more intellectually inclined, may be led to support the democratic process precisely on the ground that it is the form of government which best promises to check man's inherent fallibility, contentiousness, and inevitable drive for power and pre-eminence. But if the democratic creed does not demand absolute faith, it does benefit from a willingness to entrust the public business to the public and to the public officials they elect. And as Table 5:1 shows, whether a person's overall orientation toward politics emphasizes trust or cynicism strongly depends on his level of self-esteem.

Elitism is a sign of political cynicism. The Elitist scale assesses the general belief that men differ greatly *in ways that should disqualify many from participating in the political process.* The high scorer on this scale is likely to believe that " 'Issues' and 'arguments' are beyond the understanding of most voters," and that "Most people don't have enough sense to pick their own leaders wisely." The items in this scale also touch on aspects of elitism which are not political — for example, the contention that men are not born 'equal' — but overall, the scale tends to focus on whether citizens ought to be treated as equals in the political process. As we see in Table 5:1, the relationship between self-esteem and elitism is strong and negative. In all three samples, low self-esteem inclines a person toward elitist attitudes. Among the Followers, for example, 52% of those who are low on

Table 5:1

THE RELATIONSHIP BETWEEN SELF-ESTEEM AND MEASURES OF POLITICAL CYNICISM AND POLITICAL TRUST (PERCENTAGED DOWN)

| | | Self-Esteem | | | | | | | | |
| | | PAB-Leaders | | | PAB-Followers | | | MB Sample | | |
		High (n = 1020)	Mid (n = 1274)	Low (n = 726)	High (n = 224)	Mid (n = 499)	Low (n = 721)	High (n = 392)	Mid (n = 207)	Low (n = 483)
Elitism	Low	57	39	22	45	29	11	53	32	22
	Mid	33	37	40	35	42	37	34	43	40
	High	11	24	38	20	29	52	13	25	39
Political Cynicism	Low	74	53	31	55	33	14	49	29	13
	Mid	24	38	47	34	46	42	40	44	44
	High	3	10	22	10	21	44	12	27	43
Political Suspiciousness	Low	78	64	47	58	42	18	44	28	13
	Mid	18	28	36	32	38	46	39	34	43
	High	4	8	17	10	20	36	17	38	44
Political Moral Indulgence	Low	51	37	27	44	29	14	39	26	15
	Mid	43	51	52	43	54	42	38	39	29
	High	6	12	21	13	18	44	23	35	56

the self-esteem index, but only 20% of those who are high on it, score at the high end of the Elitism scale; conversely, those high in self-esteem are more than four times as likely to score low on Elitism as those who are low in self-esteem.

This connection between elitism and low self-esteem is entirely consistent with the data presented in Chapter 3, which showed that negative self-attitudes and negative attitudes toward other persons are related. Table 5:1 also illustrates another aspect of the connection between low self-esteem and political cynicism. Not only does the person with low self-esteem hold a low opinion of the common man; he also thinks little of men in public life. His elitist attitude is less an expression of the conviction that there are persons of superior abilities and merit than it is a reflection of a pervasive distrust and dislike of people in general. The Political Cynicism, Suspiciousness, and Moral Indulgence Scales all assess negative attitudes toward political leaders.[47] Thus, the high scorer on the Political Cynicism Scale is likely to feel that politicians are hypocritical. Their only concern is to win the election; they tell citizens whatever helps their chances to win and not what they really believe; once in office, they don't pay attention to ordinary citizens or care what they think. The Political Suspiciousness scale further elaborates this view, assessing whether the individual feels that politicians can be trusted or not, while the Political Indulgence scale assesses whether the individual believes that some corruption and dishonesty are inevitable in politics.

As Table 5:1 shows, a negative self-image and a negative orientation toward politics are closely linked. In the MB study, for example, 43% of those with low self-esteem score high on the Political Cynicism scale, compared to 12% of those with high self-esteem; conversely, those with high self-esteem are nearly four times as likely to score low on the Political Cynicism scale. The results are essentially the

[47] For a thorough exploration of these scales, and the attitudinal domain from which they are drawn, see Jack Citrin, *Political Disaffection in America* (Englewood Cliffs, N. J.: Prentice-Hall, forthcoming).

Table 5:2

THE RELATIONSHIP BETWEEN SELF-ESTEEM AND MEASURES OF DEMOCRATIC VALUES (PERCENTAGED DOWN)

| | | Self-Esteem | | | | | | | | |
| | | PAB-Leaders | | | PAB-Followers | | | MB Sample | | |
		High (n = 1020)	Mid (n = 1274)	Low (n = 726)	High (n = 224)	Mid (n = 499)	Low (n = 721)	High (n = 392)	Mid (n = 207)	Low (n = 483)
Procedural Rights	Low	7	11	22	16	27	38	14	22	36
	Mid	21	32	38	44	44	46	41	51	47
	High	72	58	40	40	29	16	45	28	17
Tolerance	Low	11	15	27	18	26	42	28	35	45
	Mid	20	22	25	17	24	26	26	24	24
	High	69	63	48	65	50	32	45	41	32
Faith in Democracy	Low	7	13	27	9	23	40	13	23	29
	Mid	39	47	52	54	52	51	49	50	55
	High	54	40	22	38	25	9	38	27	16
Democratic Commitment Index	Low	6	16	36	10	22	50			
	Mid	25	38	40	31	38	38			
	High	70	47	24	59	40	13			

same for Political Suspiciousness. Among the Followers, those low in self-esteem are nearly four times as likely to score high on the suspiciousness scale as those who are high in self-esteem, while 58% of those with high self-esteem, but only 18% of those with low self-esteem, fall at the low end of the Political Suspiciousness scale.

The Political Indulgence scale shows a virtually identical pattern: low self-esteem strongly predisposes an individual to a negative view of politics. Note also that although political leaders, as a group, have a much more positive image of politics than the average citizen, self-image and image of politics are strongly related among Leaders, too. Thus, Leaders with low self-esteem are four times as likely to score high on the Political Suspiciousness scale; conversely, 78% of those with high self-esteem, compared to 47% of those with low self-esteem, score low on the Suspiciousness scale.

Since the central concern of this study is with democratic commitment, not political estrangement, it should be pointed out that to say that low self-esteem leads to a disillusionment with politics is not the same thing as saying that low self-esteem undercuts commitment to the norms which specify how democratic politics ideally should operate. As Table 5:2 demonstrates, however, democratic commitment and self-esteem are strongly and positively related.

At the center of the democratic creed, as I have approached it here, is the idea of democratic restraint. The idea of restraint has several components, among them, the notion of juridical prohibition. The state and its citizens are under the restraint of the law even when dealing with a threat to the law. The guarantee of due process, for example, is a classic expression of juridical prohibition, for it forbids the state or society to suspend any of the legal and political rights the constitution confers. Citizens are guaranteed the right to a fair and speedy trial and are entitled to be presumed innocent until found guilty by a duly constituted court; they cannot be convicted on evidence obtained illegally; they have a right to avoid self-incrimination, and so forth. All citizens have all of these rights (in principle, but unhappily not in practice). No one ought to lose any of them because of his opinions, political convictions, or style of life.

The Procedural Rights scale is designed to assess commitment to juridical protection, broadly conceived. The items ask, among other things, whether the government has the right to arrest a person on mere suspicion, if people ought to be compelled to testify against themselves, whether congressional committees investigating "dangerous subversives" must stick to the rules, or if convictions obtained by illegal evidence should be struck down. As we see in Table 5:2, self-esteem and support for procedural rights are positively related. In the MB study, for example, those with high self-esteem are nearly three times as likely to score high on the Procedural Rights scale as those with low self-esteem; conversely, 36% of those with low self-esteem, compared to only 14% of those with high self-esteem, score low.

In addition to juridical prohibition, tolerance is a central component of democratic restraint. Men may come to the defense of diversity only out of the desire to curb the power of state and society. The right to differ, then, may be based only on the fear that authority will overreach itself. But there has also been a conviction that diversity in opinion is itself of benefit to a democratic society. This more positive view of diversity, which finds expression in an attitude of tolerance, is rarely buttressed by a highly organized set of arguments, though it derives directly from the tradition of liberal thought. The classic expression of this view, of course, is John Stuart Mill's. It was precisely on human fallibility that he based his defense of human liberty. For him, history was a storehouse of examples of state and society attaching a yoke to the necks of individuals, condemning their beliefs, silencing them all in the name of some faith other individuals and other ages "have deemed not only false but absurd."[48] The value of diversity springs from the near-inevitability of error. Mill thought that ". . . on any matter not self-evident, there are ninety-nine persons totally incapable of judging

[48] John Stuart Mill, *Utilitarianism, On Liberty, Essay on Betham*, p. 144.

it for one who is capable; and the capacity of the hundredth person is only comparative; for the majority of the eminent men of every past generation held many opinions now known to be erroneous and did or approved things which no one will now justify."[49] The only remedy is to encourage competition in the marketplace of opinion. The more vigorous the challenge to received opinion, the more likely it is knowledge will drive out error and ignorance. The principle of this marketplace is not self-interest but self-correction; restraints on the free competition of ideas diminishes the profits reaped by pitting two points of view, each somewhat in error, against the other.[50] It follows, of course, that it is to the benefit of all not only to protect but to encourage the right to differ in opinion. The well-being of a democratic society, then, depends on its tolerance of diversity.

The Tolerance scale is a gauge of the importance a person attaches to freedom of opinion and of advocacy. The low scorer on this scale is likely to agree with an assertion such as, "The idea that everyone has a right to his own opinion is being carried too far these days," while the high scorer is likely to agree with a sentiment such as, "People who hate our way of life should still have a chance to talk and be heard." The scale does not delve into the reasons tolerance is of importance to a democratic politics; but it does assess the degree of commitment to the value of tolerance.

As Table 5:2 shows, high self-esteem promotes a tolerant outlook; low self-esteem inhibits it. What is particularly noteworthy, perhaps, is the strength of the impact of self-esteem among political leaders. Political influentials, as a class of persons, have displayed a much higher level of commitment to democratic principles than has the ordinary citizen.[51] And as we can readily see, the Leader sample scores significantly higher on the Tolerance and Procedural Rights scales

[49] *Ibid.*, p. 145.

[50] *Ibid.*, pp. 180-181.

[51] See, for example, Herbert McClosky, "Consensus and Ideology."

than the Follower sample. But even though political leaders, as a group, have a deeper commitment to the norms of democratic politics than any comparable group of citizens, nevertheless, individual differences in self-esteem are of comparable significance in shaping the attitudes of the political leaders and of the ordinary citizens towards democratic values. Thus 69% of Leaders with high self-esteem score high on the Tolerance scale, compared to 48% of those with low self-esteem; conversely, Leaders with low self-esteem are approximately two and a half times as likely as those with high self-esteem to score low.

Note finally that the impact of self-esteem on democratic commitment is not confined to the idea of democratic restraint. Suppose, for example, that low self-esteem led a person to believe that communists are not entitled to the protection of the law, but that nonetheless he was as likely to uphold the principle of due process in the abstract as a person with high self-esteem. We would have to conclude, then, that low self-esteem might interfere with the application of the principle, but not with the acquisition of the value. Or we might assume that low self-esteem can impede the learning of democratic norms where these norms prohibit taking action against persons or groups considered to be a threat; that is, low self-esteem might reduce commitment to the idea of restraint but not to other more populistic democratic principles. But in Table 5:2 we find a strong and positive relationship between self-esteem and Faith in Democracy, a scale which assesses the degree of confidence an individual has in the ability of citizens to make worthwhile use of the ballot box. And observe the relationship between self-esteem and the Index of Democratic Commitment. This index combines a number of separate scales — Faith in Democracy, Elitism, Procedural Rights, and Faith in Freedom — so as to provide a broad representation of diverse aspects the democratic creed. Clearly, taking into account more of the elements of the creed leads to an even stronger relationship between self-esteem and democratic values: among the Followers, for example, those high in self-esteem are about five times as likely to score high on the Democratic Commitment Index, while those low in self-esteem are five times as likely to score low.

High self-esteem evidently promotes commitment to democratic values; conversely, low self-esteem increases the susceptibility to extreme political views. Table 5:3 presents the relationship between the self-esteem index and a number of scales which assess extreme political orientations. Direct Action, for example, is a scale which taps, among other things, the belief that "There are times when it almost seems better for the people to take the law into their own hands rather than wait for the machinery of government to act." In all three samples there is a strong, negative relationship between self-esteem and Direct Action. Among the Followers, for example, those low in self-esteem are nearly three times as likely to score high on the Direct Action Index, while those high in self-esteem are nearly three times as likely to score low. Moreover, a similar pattern appears on other measures of extreme belief: Populism, extreme Left Wing, extreme Right Wing, and Totalitarianism indices; in every instance, those with low self-esteem are much more likely to endorse extreme values than are those with high self-esteem.

This relationship between low self-esteem and extreme belief is scarcely surprising. As we saw in Chapters 3 and 4, persons with low self-esteem are likely to see the world about them as confused and threatening. Low self-esteem diminishes the incentives, opportunities, and capacity for social learning. As a consequence, it reduces the ability to understand what is taking place, particularly in a world where change is always taking place. The world outside appears, therefore, to lack order and meaning, and it is for this reason all the more bewildering and threatening. Low self-esteem, moreover, gives rise to fear and suspicion of others. There is no need to review in detail evidence presented earlier, except to recall how close the connection is between a lack of faith in oneself and a lack of faith in others. And as we have seen, anxiety and hostility are a natural outgrowth of low self-esteem, leading in turn to a tendency for

Table 5:3 THE RELATIONSHIP BETWEEN SELF-ESTEEM AND MEASURES OF EXTREME BELIEF (PERCENTAGED DOWN)

		Self-Esteem								
		PAB-Leaders			PAB-Followers			MB Sample		
		High (n = 1020)	Mid (n = 1274)	Low (n = 726)	High (n = 224)	Mid (n = 499)	Low (n = 721)	High (n = 392)	Mid (n = 207)	Low (n = 483)
Direct Action	Low	69	48	29	59	43	21	56	38	20
	Mid	19	26	26	21	23	24	20	28	28
	High	13	26	45	20	34	56	24	34	52
Totalitarianism	Low	79	58	37	64	36	13	51	32	15
	Mid	18	34	40	31	44	35	35	34	34
	High	3	8	23	5	21	51	15	34	51
Populism	Low	56	41	26	58	37	12	51	29	14
	Mid	38	48	50	32	41	36	34	49	38
	High	7	11	24	10	22	53	15	22	48
Right Wing	Low	64	43	23	62	40	12	62	44	21
	Mid	28	41	43	32	40	39	28	32	40
	High	8	16	34	7	21	49	10	24	39
Left Wing	Low	81	69	51	74	51	22	71	54	31
	Mid	15	25	37	21	34	36	21	28	35
	High	4	6	12	5	15	43	8	18	33
Fascist	Low							64	43	28
	Mid							30	42	44
	High							6	16	28

defensive withdrawal, a desire to protect the self by keeping others away. Unfortunately, the effect is to strip those who lack self-esteem of external as well as internal sources of support, thereby reinforcing their susceptibility to feelings of helplessness and unworthiness.

For people thus afflicted, extremist creeds offer several benefits. These beliefs at once provide a simple explanation for the unhappy state of the world and an attractive solution. They confirm, in effect, that a person is seeing the world as it really is. It would be foolish of us to underestimate the strength of the desire to comprehend reality, perhaps especially among those who appear to have the most difficulty in doing so. Extremist creeds, whether on the political left, right or center, not only provide a description of reality that is easy to grasp but also an explanation of why affairs of the world so often appear bewildering. In addition, of course, these explanations typically fix blame for the present unhappy state of affairs on some group or institution in the society. Extremist individuals are thus both free of responsibility and free to accuse. It is not they who are at fault but the world which is out of joint. Condemnations of conspiracies, then, provide an opportunity for persons with low self-esteem to counter feelings of personal unworthiness by — to mention only one mechanism of defense — projecting blame for their lack of well-being onto some handy external source — Jews, Negroes, intellectuals, politicians, foreigners, communists.[52]

Extreme political creeds, moreover, play on the psychology of crusades. Those on the extreme right, for example, see America in imminent danger of a takeover by the left, while those on the extreme left believe the country is about to fall into the hands of the extreme right. But both extremes are in agreement on the need for an aggressive campaign to wipe out a public evil. Their definition of that evil differs, but not their insistent call for action. Thus, these creeds

[52] See T. W. Adorno et al., *The Authoritarian Personality* (New York: Harper & Row, 1956). For a review of scapegoat theories and group conflict, see L. Berkowitz, *Aggression* (New York: McGraw-Hill, 1962).

202 . PERSONALITY AND DEMOCRATIC POLITICS

provide opportunities to vent hostility and to overcome a sense of helplessness.

One scale in particular captures the "totalistic" quality of this crusading spirit. The Totalitarianism scale assesses a state of mind of total commitment to a political ideology: all values — moral, aesthetic, intellectual, religious — are to be subordinated in the service of the cause; whatever advances the cause is justified. So the spirit of the crusade is reflected in the belief that "To bring about great changes for the benefit of mankind often requires cruelty and even ruthlessness." Then, too, the psychology of the crusade has other qualitites — for example, the sense of high drama and moral urgency — which are of particular appeal to the person who is afflicted by a sense that he is unworthy and that life is meaningless.

These are some of the reasons we see so strong a relation between the Self-Esteem index and the Totalitarianism scale. Among the Followers, for example, those low in self-esteem are nearly ten times as likely as those high in self-esteem to score high on the Totalitarianism scale; conversely, those high in self-esteem are more than five times as likely as those low in self-esteem to score low. To be sure, there is a very important difference between scoring high on such a paper-and-pencil test and taking action on behalf of an extreme cause. Indeed, some of the very factors that strengthen the chances of obtaining a high score on a test of extreme belief — for example, the sense of helplessness, inadequacy, or confusion — weaken the chances of actually becoming actively involved. Nonetheless, low self-esteem clearly renders the individual susceptible to extreme appeals of all varieties, a susceptibility which under the pressure of circumstance can swell the ranks of political extremists.

In addition, it is worth nothing that low self-esteem leads to extremism of both the left and the right. At first, this might appear an absolute inconsistency. The Right Wing scale contains items which assert, for example, "It is tragic to realize that both major parties in this country have been pretty much taken over by the left-wingers," and "When you see the things the newspapers print, it almost seems as though the press of this country has been taken over by left-wingers." The Left Wing scale, on the other hand, includes items which assert, among other things, that "Both major parties in this country are controlled by the wealthy and run for their benefit," and "When you consider that the newspapers of this country only print the views of the ruling classes, the so-called freedom of the press gets to be pretty much of a joke." Low self-esteem, then, inclines people to accept some assertions which on their face appear contradictory. But it would be misleading to interpret this simply as a manifestation of inconsistency. Extreme left and right wing views often mirror a common psychological state, in large measure because both points of view are extreme: they share, therefore, a "totalistic" quality, a strong component of aggression, a focus on "scapegoats" and secret conspiracies, a tendency to see things in "black and white" terms, an emphasis on the urgency of action, and a rejection of the restraints of democratic politics.[53] The beliefs of the extreme left and right, therefore, may be psychologically consonant, although logically inconsistent. Thus, low self-esteem can induce a generalized disposition to extremism.[54]

In any event, these data further testify to the power of high self-esteem to strengthen democratic commitment and of low self-esteem to weaken it. There remains, however, some question as to the nature of the relationship between self-esteem and democratic commitment. To understand more fully how a personality trait becomes translated into a political belief, we need a more exact picture of the causal processes at work, a matter I should now like to consider.

[53] The basis of this argument is laid out in Herbert McClosky, "Personality and Attitude Correlates of Foreign Polity Orientation," in James Rosenau, ed., *Domestic Sources of Foreign Policy* (New York: The Free Press, 1967).

[54] See Paul M. Sniderman and Jack Citrin, "Psychological Sources of Political Belief: Self-Esteem and Isolationist Attitudes," *APSR* 65 (1971): 401-417.

Motivation and Social Learning:
A Model of Psychological Influence

How do individual differences in self-esteem affect the level of democratic commitment? Up to this point, I have enumerated a large number of specific forces which play some part in connecting the two. Feelings of aggression, anxiety and unworthiness, the tendency to dichotomize and think in black-white terms, a distrust and dislike for others, an attitude of suspicion and cynicism — all of these and more enter in. But to further our understanding of how personality becomes translated into political belief, we need a model of the basic causal influences which link together self-esteem and democratic commitment, and it is my aim to develop such a model.[55]

More than one kind of causal model is possible of course; and different models make different assumptions. It is important at the outset to take particular note of one of these assumptions, for more than any other it will govern the form our model will assume.

My object is to design a mathematical representation of the causal process which links self-esteem and democratic commitment. The flow of causal influence can be variously represented, but here it is conceived as strictly unidirectional: no variable which is an effect of a variable can be a cause of that same variable. In making this assumption, I am of course imposing a strict prohibition on the forms the model can take: it specifically excludes from consideration "causal"

[55] For an incisive discussion of the multiple meanings of the term, 'Model,' see May Brodbeck, "Models, Meanings, and Theories," in May Brodbeck, ed., *Readings in the Philosophy of the Social Sciences* (London: Macmillan, 1969), pp. 579-600. The literature on empirical causal analysis is large and growing. See especially H. M. Blalock, Jr., and Ann Blalock, eds., *Methodology in Social Research* (New York: McGraw-Hill, 1968); H. M. Blalock, Jr., *Causal Inferences in Non-Experimental Research* (Chapel Hill: The University of North Carolina, 1964); H. M. Blalock, Jr., *Theory Construction* (Englewood Cliffs, N. J.: Prentice-Hall, 1969); Herbert A. Simon, *Models of Man* (London: Wiley, 1957); and Edgar F. Borgatta and George W. Bohrnstedt, eds., *Sociological Methodology, 1969* (San Francisco: Jossey-Bass, 1969).

Figure 5:1. An elementary model of self-esteem and political learning

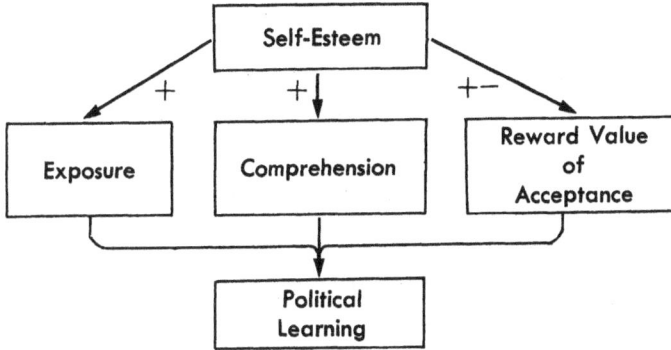

relationships which are reciprocal, that is, relationships where two or more variables *both* influence and are influenced by each other. In short, the causal model must be recursive.

In Chapter 4, I broke down the process of political learning into three components — exposure, comprehension, and the reward value of acceptance. Figure 5:1 presents a graphic representation of how self-esteem affects political learning. The main point the diagram is intended to convey is that individual differences in self-esteem can, and frequently do, have an independent effect on the separate components of the learning process. This point is graphically represented by the three arrows from self-esteem to the three components.

No arrows, however, connect the panels which encase the three components of the learning process. This is equivalent to saying that no causal relation among them can be represented, although in actuality there may well be a causal connection of some sort among them. On the face of it, the inability to represent the connection among the three components may seem unreasonable, for at first glance, there appears to be a definite and natural order in which these components take place. To learn an opinion, one must be exposed to it, comprehend it, and finally receive a reward or anticipate one for learning the opinion. The three components may, therefore, be thought of as "steps" in a learning process which follow one another in some set sequence. This is in fact the position that some theorists such as McGuire explicity take.[56]

The drawback to this position for our purposes is that there is no fixed sequence in which these so-called steps take place. The likelihood of exposure to ideas circulating through the society, for example, will vary with the history of reinforcement; and ability to comprehend may well determine likelihood of exposure, for the regular experience of a failure to understand information received may evoke sufficient discomfort to promote a habit of inattentiveness and avoidance of information, especially where it concerns areas of social life such as politics which tend to be of peripheral interest to the ordinary person. In short, although the components of exposure, comprehension, and the reward value of acceptance undoubtedly are causally related, the relationships are so complex and interdependent as to be better conceived as reciprocal rather than recursive processes of influence. For this reason, the schema of political learning outlined in Chapter 4 will not do for a recursive causal model.

Let us review the arguments of this chapter, for they may suggest an alternative way to conceive of the relationship between personality and political belief. I have contended that because low self-esteem encourages an amalgam of hostility and mistrust it discourages commitment to democratic values. As a consequence, persons with low self-esteem, compared to those with high self-esteem, are more elitist, cynical, suspicious, and alienated in their attitudes about politics. The hostility and suspicion engendered by low self-esteem undercuts a willingness to trust and to accept other persons and bolsters a belief that the practices of democratic politics — by encouraging diversity and freedom of expression — may prove dangerous. The person low in self-esteem is motivated then to reject the values of tolerance and of due process and is less likely than the person high in self-esteem

[56] William J. McGuire, "The Nature of Attitudes and Attitude Change," G. Lindzey and E. Aronson, eds., *The Handbook of Social Psychology* (Reading, Mass.: Addison Wesley, 1969), vol 3, pp. 136-314.

to develop a faith in democracy and a commitment to its values. In short, I have argued that motivation is a linkage between low self-esteem and rejection of democratic values, and more particularly that low self-esteem leads to hostility and rejection of other persons which, in turn, encourage an aversion to the idea of democratic restraint.

I have also argued that the connection between self-esteem and democratic commitment is partly due to social learning. Persons high in self-esteem, compared to those low in self-esteem, are more likely to be exposed to the flow of information through the society, and are more likely as well to comprehend the information they receive. It is the superior capacity for social learning of persons with high self-esteem, I have maintained, that strengthens their chances of learning the norms of the political culture, including, among others, the idea of democratic restraint. Democratic values are intrinsically complex and change over time; they turn on abstract ideas which require discrimination and training in order to be correctly applied in specific situations. Then, too, democratic values involve a pluralistic set of beliefs which sometimes appear to be inconsistent rather than mutually reinforcing. For that matter, the general public has a weak grasp of the principles of democratic politics, and so exerts little systematic pressure for complete compliance. In short, democratic values for a variety of reasons are not easy to learn, and whatever affects an individual's capacity for social learning also affects his chances of learning these values. Self-esteem is a determinant of the capacity for social learning, and thus, of the likelihood of learning democratic values.

According to my argument, then, motivation and social learning are the two linkages between self-esteem and democratic commitment. Rather than breaking political learning into three components — exposure, comprehension, and the reward value of acceptance — we may divide it into two intervening processes, as outlined in Figure 5:2. Under motivation, the first of these processes, I include all manner of affective states and traits which are a consequence of personality and are a cause of a consistent readiness to accept (or

Figure 5:2. Self-esteem and democratic commitment: a revised model

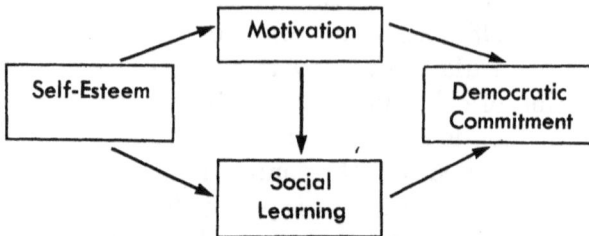

reject) a political belief, attitude, or point of view. Under social learning, the second of these processes, I include the set of psychological states and response habits which either facilitate or inhibit the learning of social and political values.

Several aspects of the model, as it appears in Figure 5:2, deserve comment. First, the model assumes that personality becomes translated into political belief in two ways — through motivation and through social learning; it explicitly predicts, therefore, that if the effects of the two were to be controlled for, or "partialled out," no relationship between personality and political belief ought to remain. Motivation and social learning, in other words, are the intervening causal mechanisms which account for the effect of personality on the acquisition of political belief.

Second, there is a definite relationship between the two intervening variables. The capacity for social learning is causally dependent on, among other things, motivation. This assumption is an entirely plausible one. It is possible to conceive of very uncommon circumstances where learning capacity might possibly affect the strength of a basic drive (for example, a persistent inability to learn — and consequently a chronic tendency to fail — might elevate anxiety level); but on the whole it is both common sense and common practice in the psychology of learning to treat learning capacity (and performance) as some function of the strength of such motives as anxiety, the need for approval, the desire for achievement, and the like.

The revised model of personality and political learning, despite its different appearance, is based on the same foundations as the original schema. It maintains the basic distinction between individual differences in exposure and comprehension (learning contingencies) on the one hand, and the reward value of acceptance (reinforcement contingencies) on the other. It asserts, in other words, that personality has an impact on political belief by affecting a person's capacity and willingness for social learning, quite apart from whatever degree of influence it may exercise in ways emphasized by students of psychology and politics in the past. To be sure, the revision omits the division between effects of personality on exposure as opposed to its influence on comprehension. But the loss is not a serious one because our main concern is to estimate whether the relationship between personality and democratic commitment is due to the impact of self-esteem on social learning as well as to its influence over motivation; whether the role learning does play is due largely to the impact of self-esteem on exposure or on comprehension is, at this stage of research, a matter of secondary interest.

This issue of the relative importance of motivation and learning capacity as mediators of the influence of personality is the principle question this model is designed to answer. The model is a formalized representation of (a) the causal mechanisms mediating the influence of personality on belief and of (b) the "paths" along which the influence of personality travels. For convenience, let us represent the personality variable by the number 1, motivation by 2, social learning by 3, and political belief by 4. The two causal mediators, of course, are variables 2 and 3. Less obviously, perhaps, the three paths may be represented as follows:[57]

$$\text{Path A} = P_{12}P_{24}$$
$$\text{Path B} = P_{13}P_{34}$$
$$\text{Path C} = P_{12}P_{23}P_{34}$$

[57] See especially Kenneth G. Land, "Principles of Path Analysis," in Borgatta and Bohrnstedt, eds., *Sociological Methodology*.

To illustrate the meaning of these three paths let us turn to the particular variables we shall analyze. Figure 5:3 represents the causal structure which (presumably) joins these variables. At the far left is self-esteem, the independent variable, and at the far right is support for democratic restraint, the dependent variable. As we have noted, the idea of democratic restraint has at least two facets, juridical prohibition and tolerance of differences in belief and expression. These two facets are interrelated but not interchangeable, and so we shall use two scales, Procedural Rights and Tolerance, in order to represent more fully affirmation (or rejection) of the principle of democratic restraint. In addition, using two scales doubles the number of tests that can be made of the causal model, and using both samples of the PAB study raises to four the number of independent tests of my hypotheses.

To serve as an index of the *motivational* linkage between self-esteem and democratic commitment I have chosen the Rejection-Hostility scale. This scale, better than any other available, gauges the psychological orientation most commonly thought to undermine the commitment to democratic values — a distrust and dislike for other persons. An inspection of the scale items, listed below, shows that the Rejection-Hostility scale directly taps an amalgam of suspicion and aggression.

Rejection-Hostility Scale

If someone doesn't like me he can stay out of my way.

It's a wonder there aren't more crimes with all the bad people in the world.

I like to see a good fight once in a while.

It's all right to have friends, but you shouldn't let yourself get so attached that you're always having to do things for them.

You have to be pretty choosy about picking friends.

There are a lot of people in this world who are no good.

The second intervening variable is anomie.[58] McClosky's

---

[58] Herbert McClosky and John W. Schaar, Psychological Dimensions of Anomie," *American Sociological Review* 30 (1965): 14-40.

Anomie scale is the optimal measure available to serve as an index of the *learning* process which links self-esteem and democratic commitment. Although by no means ideal for this purpose, the Anomie scale does provide a useful index of a person's capacity for social learning. The scale may be conceptualized in different ways, but it is evident on reading the scale items that it assesses, among other things, a state of cognitive disorganization which is the natural consequence of a persistent failure to understand what other people are doing, what their values are, what rules they generally abide by, and so on. To the person who cannot see the values which unite people, or for that matter, those which divide them, the world appears to be without purpose or design, unpredictable, with no apparent structure and order, and very often, therefore, thoroughly unintelligible. Insofar as the Anomie scale assesses the degree of a person's success in perceiving the norms which govern much of social conduct, it is a rough but ready sign of his capacity for social learning. Again, for the reader's convenience, I shall present the full list of items in McClosky's Anomie scale.

Anomie Scale

I often feel that many things our parents stood for are just going to ruin before our very eyes.

I often feel awkward and out of place.

It seems to me that other people find it easier to decide what is right than I do.

With everything so uncertain these days, it almost seems as though anything could happen.

Everything changes so quickly these days that I often have trouble deciding what are the right rules to follow.

With everything in such a state of disorder, it's hard for a person to know where he stands from one day to the next.

People were better off in the old days when everyone knew just how he was expected to act.

The trouble with the world today is that most people don't really believe in anything.

What is lacking in the world today is the old kind of
friendship that lasted for a lifetime.

There should be no need to say that neither the Anomie
nor the Hostility scale is perfect for our present purpose.
The Anomie scale, for example, provides only a crude index
of a person's learning proclivities; it discriminates at one
extreme those who have great difficulty in making sense of
their world. There are obviously many finer distinctions one
might wish to draw to encompass the varieties of abilities,
motives, and experiences the complex process of social learning includes. But there is no better measure available to us,
and it should be noted that the crudity of these procedures
works against — rather than for — the chance of confirming
my hypotheses and causal model.

The causal structure represented in Figure 5:3 may now
be set out in a straightforward way. The influence of self-esteem on support for democratic restraint travels along three
paths: first, the lower a person's self-esteem, the more hostile
he tends to be (for reasons detailed in Chapter 3); and the
stronger the hostility, the weaker his support for the values
of tolerance and of due process. Second, the lower a person's
self-esteem, the more likely it is his capacity for social
learning will be impaired (for reasons detailed in Chapter
4); and the greater the impairment to social learning, the
poorer the chances are for support for democratic restraint.
Third, low self-esteem leads to hostility, which in turn
inhibits the capacity for social learning, which further wor-
sens the chances for support for democratic values.

Figure 5:3. Self-esteem and democratic restraint: a causal model

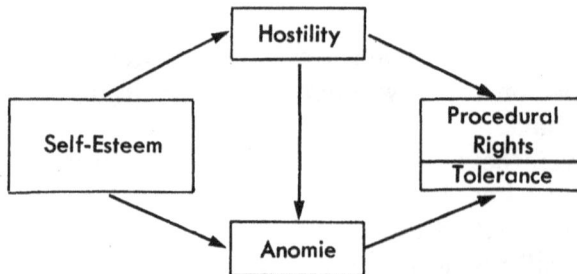

The structural equations for this model may be expressed as follows:

$$X_1 = U_1$$
$$X_2 = b_2X_1 + U_2$$
$$X_3 = b_{31}X_1 + b_{32}X_2 + U_3$$
$$X_4 = b_{43}X_3 + b_{42}X_2 + U_4$$

Where $X_1 \ldots X_4$ stands for the variables as identified above, $U_1 \ldots U_4$ for their respective disturbance terms, and $b_{21} \ldots b_{42}$ for the amount of change (expressed in terms of deviations about the mean) in, for example, variable 2 as a consequence of a one-unit change in variable 1. The model makes the standard assumptions for path analysis – normal distributions, linear additive relationships, and uncorrelated error terms.[59]

The causal model, as we noted, includes no arrow connecting Self-Esteem and Procedural Rights (or Tolerance). A missing arrow can be expressed in this instance as a prediction equation of the form:

$$b_{41.23} = 0$$

This amounts to an assertion that whatever effect the independent variable has on either of the dependent variables is due entirely to its effect on the two intervening variables. Naturally, then, if the influence of motivation and social learning (or operationally in this instance, of Rejection-Hostility and of Anomie) were partialled out, no relationship of consequence between self-esteem and Procedural Rights (or Tolerance) ought to remain; that, at any rate, is the prediction.

[59] One variable, acquiescence, can be interpreted as part of the error term, and if so, then it would be implausible to assume error terms are uncorrelated since scores on all the scales in the model are affected somewhat by acquiescence. Conceptually, it would be more proper to treat acquiescence as an endogenous rather than exogenous variable, in effect serving as a crude indicator of the same cognitive incapacity which the anomie scale taps; this was the gist of one of the arguments advanced in Chapter 2 on acquiescence and spuriousness. As noted earlier, this argument was originally suggested to me by Herbert McClosky. For many

Table 5:4 displays, first, the zero-order correlations between self-esteem and the Procedural Rights scale for both the PAB Leader and Follower samples, and then, in the row immediately below, the partial correlations between these variables, partialling out both the Hostility and Anomie scales. Clearly, when the influence of the two intervening variables is removed, the correlations drop to almost zero.

Table 5:4

ZERO ORDER AND PARTIAL CORRELATIONS BETWEEN SELF-ESTEEM AND PROCEDURAL RIGHTS

	PAB-Leaders	PAB-Followers
Zero Order Correlation Between Self-Esteem and Procedural Rights	.29	.29
Partial Correlation Between Self-Esteem and Procedural Rights, Partialing Out Hostility and Anomie	.03	.04

Table 5:5 displays the equivalent correlations for self-esteem and Tolerance. Again, when Hostility and Anomie are partialled out, the correlation between self-esteem and Tolerance virtually disappears. In short, for both samples and both measures of democratic restraint, self-esteem has no direct effect on democratic commitment, exactly as our model suggests; whatever influence self-esteem exercises is mediated by hostility and anomie.

In four independent tests, then, the data confirm the causal model. But my principal hypothesis holds that the tendency

people, this line of reasoning fails to be persuasive because of a tendency to view acquiescence as a measure of "error" and nothing but "error," which is highly resistant to extinction. Error or disturbance terms include more than "error," but operating on the assumption that some readers would be suspicious of any form of scale analysis which made — or appeared to make — no provision for the influence of response set (and particularly, of acquiescence) the path analysis was repeated for both Leaders and Followers, for both the Procedural Rights and the Tolerance scales, *for all persons with a middle score on the Acquiescence scale.* The results, which appear in Appendix C, confirm the conclusions of the analysis reported above.

Table 5:5

ZERO ORDER AND PARTIAL CORRELATIONS BETWEEN SELF-ESTEEM AND TOLERANCE

	PAB-Leaders	PAB-Followers
Zero Order Correlation Between Self-Esteem and Tolerance	.21	.29
Partial Correlation Between Self-Esteem and Tolerance, Partialing Out Hostility and Anomie	.02	.04

of students of personality and politics to account for the connection between self-esteem and democratic commitment largely — and very often exclusively — in terms of motivation is in error.

Figure 5:4. Path diagram of the relationship between self-esteem and procedural rights

PAB-Leaders

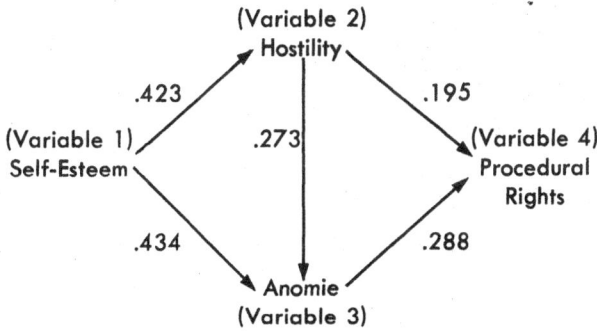

PAB-Followers

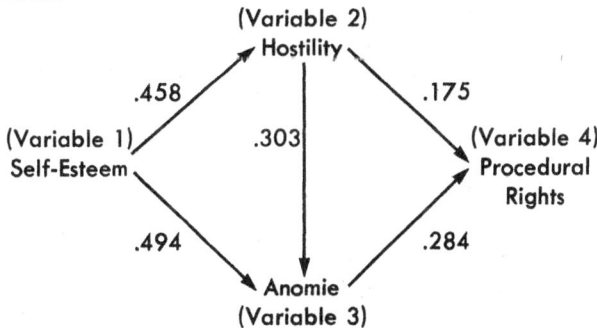

Figure 5:4 shows the relative contributions of Hostility and Anomie to scores on the Procedural Rights scale, and the contribution of self-esteem to scores on the Hostility and Anomie scales. Written beside every causal arrow connecting two variables is the value of the (standardized) regression coefficient, that is, the amount of change (expressed in standard deviation units) in the variable at the head of the arrow which is a function solely of a one-unit change in the variable at the tail of the arrow.[60] As is obvious from Figure 5:4, both Hostility and Anomie are important mediators of the relationship between low self-esteem and rejection of democratic restraint.

Figure 5:5 displays results of a similar analysis for the relationship between Self-Esteem and Tolerance. Again, the data clearly show both Hostility and Anomie — motivation and social learning — to be important mediators of the influence of self-esteem over democratic restraint.

What is more, if we compare how much of the relationship is due to the learning mediator and how much due to the motivation mediator, we find that learning is approximately one and a half times as important as motivation. Table 5:5 A and B present the compound path coefficients for the relationship between Self-Esteem and the Procedural Rights and Tolerance scales respectively. A compound path coefficient is the product of the simple path coefficients which together make up a causal path from independent to dependent variable. Thus, compound coefficients provide estimates of the relative contributions of causal paths in accounting for the correlation of independent and dependent variable. Path A is an estimate of the proportion of the total effect of self-esteem on Procedural rights (or Tolerance) which passes directly through motivation, while Paths B and C summed

---

[60] For convenience of presentation, plus and minus signs have been omitted. In the diagram, if one understands that an increase in low self-esteem means a decrease in support for procedural rights, all signs would be in the positive direction. With this rule in hand, the results of the path analysis can be readily interpreted.

Figure 5:5. Path diagram of the relationship between self-esteem and tolerance

PAB-Leaders

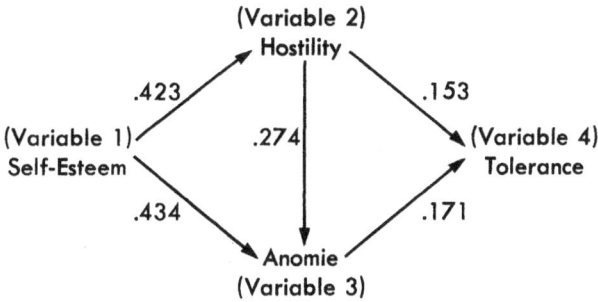

PAB-Followers

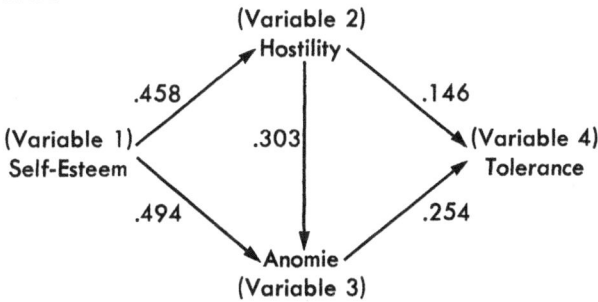

together[61] provide an estimate of the total effect mediated by learning capacity. For both Procedural Rights and Tolerance, and for both Leader and Follower Samples, the value of these two paths is approximately one and a half times as large as the value of Path A.

---

[61] The reason for summing Paths B and C rather than A and C is easy to see. Some might quibble that since C passes through the motivation mediator as well as the learning mediator, the decision to add it to B rather than A is an arbitrary one. But the key point is that the two mechanisms, motivation and learning, may often lead to different predictions. Thus, to put C together with A is to say that both paths invariably lead to rejection of democratic norms, for the motivational linkage (for example, hostility) is invariant across political systems; but to sum C with B is to recognize that for whatever reason (in this instance, the connection with hostility), low self-esteem hinders social learning, and hence the political correlates of low self-esteem may possibly vary (negatively) with the prevailing norms of political systems.

Table 5:5A

SIMPLE AND COMPOUND PATH COEFFICIENTS FOR THE RELATIONSHIP BETWEEN SELF-ESTEEM AND PROCEDURAL RIGHTS

PAB-Leaders

$$
\begin{aligned}
\text{Path A} &= p_{12} \cdot p_{24} & \text{Path B} &= p_{13} \cdot p_{34} \\
&= (.423) \cdot (.195) & &= (.434) \cdot (.288) \\
&= .082 & &= .125
\end{aligned}
$$

$$
\begin{aligned}
\text{Path C} &= p_{12} \cdot p_{23} \cdot p_{34} \\
&= (.423) \cdot (.273) \cdot (.288) \\
&= .033
\end{aligned}
$$

PAB-Followers

$$
\begin{aligned}
\text{Path A} &= p_{12} \cdot p_{24} & \text{Path B} &= p_{13} \cdot p_{34} \\
&= (.458) \cdot (.175) & &= (.494) \cdot (.284) \\
&= .080 & &= .140
\end{aligned}
$$

$$
\begin{aligned}
\text{Path C} &= p_{12} \cdot p_{23} \cdot p_{34} \\
&= (.458) \cdot (.303) \cdot (.284) \\
&= .039
\end{aligned}
$$

Table 5:5B

SIMPLE AND COMPOUND PATH COEFFICIENTS FOR THE RELATIONSHIP BETWEEN SELF-ESTEEM AND TOLERANCE

PAB-Leaders

$$
\begin{aligned}
\text{Path A} &= p_{12} \cdot p_{24} & \text{Path B} &= p_{13} \cdot p_{34} \\
&= (.423) \cdot (.153) & &= (.434) \cdot (.171) \\
&= .064 & &= .074
\end{aligned}
$$

$$
\begin{aligned}
\text{Path C} &= p_{12} \cdot p_{23} \cdot p_{34} \\
&= (.423) \cdot (.274) \cdot (.171) \\
&= .019
\end{aligned}
$$

PAB-Followers

$$
\begin{aligned}
\text{Path A} &= p_{12} \cdot p_{24} & \text{Path B} &= p_{13} \cdot p_{34} \\
&= (.458) \cdot (.146) & &= (.494) \cdot (.254) \\
&= .069 & &= .125
\end{aligned}
$$

$$
\begin{aligned}
\text{Path C} &= p_{12} \cdot p_{23} \cdot p_{34} \\
&= (.458) \cdot (.303) \cdot (.254) \\
&= .035
\end{aligned}
$$

Of course, the values of the various paths are only estimates and rather crude ones at that.[62] The exact importance of the two mediators — motivation and social learning — might have differed had I chosen scales other than Rejection-Hostility and Anomie to "stand for" the two mediators, or had I focused on a dependent variable other than the idea of democratic restraint; or had I selected a different personality trait to study. And one ought not to make a fetish of path analysis. It has its uses, but it also has its limits. To put it positively, path analysis encourages social scientists to turn to the analysis of the underlying causal structures which account for the relationships among variables. Or as Thomas Hobbes might say, path analysis is an example of the highest form of scientific reasoning, the resolutive-compositive method — that is, first breaking the object of analysis down into its constituent elements and afterwards putting the object together again — but then Hobbes insisted he could square the circle. Nonetheless, the consistency with which the data supported my model is encouraging. Very often investigators "test" a hypothesis (or "scale" an attitude or "build" a causal model) on the same data which suggested it to them, not infrequently, of course, because no alternative is open to them. By contrast, I was in a position to conduct genuinely independent tests on two different dependent variables in two independently drawn samples, and in every instance my basic hypotheses as to the connection between self-esteem and democratic restraint were confirmed.

In Sum

At the outset I took up an old theme in political theory and psychology — the idea of the democratic personality. The idea deserves examination for several reasons. It implies, among other things, that the connection between personality

---

[62] To facilitate comparison between two samples drawn from two distinct universes, I have standardized regression coefficients.

and ideology is permanently stamped in, regardless of culture and circumstance. It implies also that a country's citizens may be divided into two opposing camps — one more or less fixed in its commitment to democratic values, the other more or less fixed in its opposition to them.

As the data presented in this chapter suggest, there are indeed fundamental differences in psychological makeup between those who affirm the principles of democracy and those who fail to adhere as consistently to them. This chapter, of course, focused on self-esteem, but this should not be taken to mean that individual differences in self-regard are the sole, or even the principal, point of difference between the democrat and the nondemocrat. As McClosky and Bardach have shown in a much more thorough-going and ambitious analysis of the democratic personality,[63] democrat and nondemocrat differ in a large number of ways. As we saw, the democrat is more likely to have high self-esteem and less likely to be hostile. But they also show that he is less likely to be obsessive and intolerant of ambiguity, suspicious and anxious, paranoid and misanthropic, to cite only a few examples of the broad range of differences they find between democrat and nondemocrat.

But if self-esteem is not the whole of the story, it may yet provide a good clue as to how the story will turn out. The psychological profiles of democrat and nondemocrat may well be distinctive; also the distribution of personality characteristics in a social group on balance may favor democratic values. But if my results are credited, it need not follow that the democratic creed has a built-in constituency. On the contrary, the same psychological qualities that distinguish a democrat in the United States may well characterize a communist in Soviet Russia; for insofar as the linkage between personality and political ideology is a matter of social learning, then high self-esteem (and conceivably many other personality traits as well) ought to drive individuals

---

[63] See Herbert McClosky and Eugene Bardach, "Psychological Correlates of Democratic Commitments," unpublished.

towards accepting the norms of their political culture, whatever those may be.

This line of reasoning may also have some bearing on changing attitudes towards democratic politics. The standard presumption now, though it is often only implicit, is that opposition to democratic values that stems from the personality is for that reason "deeply" rooted and difficult to change. Further, this opposition is thought to be "dynamically" linked to personality. Efforts to build support for democratic norms must be organized around these personality dynamics. In this context the problem of attitude change takes on some aspects of therapeutic intervention, but more importantly, strategies of attitude change are narrowed down to persuasive efforts, well-suited to attitudes which mainly serve ego-defensive functions.[64] In contrast, the basic argument of this chapter suggests that failure to adhere to democratic values which arises from personality traits such as low self-esteem may be due largely to impediments to political learning, and therefore may be overcome more easily than is commonly thought. And, of course, strategies for change would vary considerably if opposition to democratic norms in the main represented a failure in social learning rather than the working out of complex dynamism of personality.

The problem of attitude change in this context deserves exploration, though the question must be framed in a better way if we are to answer it. I shall mention one problem only, for it goes to the heart of a basic limitation in the analysis and conceptualization of this study. Throughout the discussion of motivation and social learning, I have proceeded as if the two were essentially independent and the main question was to determine which of them is the more important link connecting self-esteem with support of democratic principles. Also, I have spoken as if low self-esteem (and hostility) affected social learning solely by impeding it — by

[64] Daniel Katz, "The Functional Approach to the Study of Attitudes," *Public Opinion Quarterly* 24 (1960): 163-204.

raising, in the language of information theory, the ratio of "noise" to "signal." But obviously a personality characteristic such as self-esteem can direct, as well as obstruct, social learning. Personality operates like a steering wheel in the learning of values, guiding people in rather different directions depending on their psychological makeup. In short, the sharp line I drew between social learning and motivation ought to be erased in subsequent research, for learning is obviously contingent on motivation, and it is the exact nature of the relationship between the two that students of personality and politics should now investigate.

In any event, individual differences in self-esteem evidently exercise a profound influence over attitudes to politics. Low self-esteem encourages distrust and disdain, and in their wake, an unwillingness to trust the political institutions of the society, the mass of the citizenry, and the public figures they elect to office. Political cynicism, suspiciousness, and alienation, then, feed on the inner frustration of the personality, and for that reason alone, remain a constant feature of the outer world of politics. Then, too, low self-esteem weakens commitment to the norms of democratic politics and strengthens susceptibility to the varieties of extremist politics. There is, then, much to recommend the basic insight of such scholars as Mannheim and Lasswell who perceived the connection between the character of men and the kind of society they favor. Whether the political values of citizens in fact affect the political order, however, is another matter. The answer obviously depends on a complex interplay of factors, not the least of which is whether the psychological makeup of citizens influences their chances of becoming involved in politics and, more importantly, of acquiring political influence. The remaining chapters of this study will therefore examine the connection between personality and political participation and leadership.

Chapter 6 · THE IDEA OF COMPENSATION

Political leadership and personality is an historic theme in political philosophy. The idea that political leaders are, or ought to be, different in their psychological makeup from ordinary citizens reaches at least as far back as the Greeks. It was the conviction that the well-being of the polity depends on the personality of the rulers that led Plato to devote *The Republic*, a dialogue ostensibly concerned with politics, in fact to education as a crucible for the moulding of character. That conviction has survived Plato, and along with it has gone the belief that political leaders and citizens differ in needs, temperament, aspiration, and (frequently) ability.

To be sure, confidence that governors and governed do indeed differ has ebbed — nowhere more sharply than in Hobbes' theory of representation — but with the twentieth-century surge in the empirical study of democratic politics, it has flowed back. For that matter, the presumption that the modal character traits of citizens and leaders differ has entered the popular folklore in the form of widely accepted stereotypes of the politician, who is commonly said to be extroverted, ambitious, gregarious, pragmatic, sociable, and power-oriented.

The contention that political leadership and personality are closely intertwined has won acceptance largely on the basis of discursive writing and argumentation. The experimental study of leadership delivered a sharp blow to trait theories of leadership.[1] On the one hand, leaders of experimental groups often are more self-confident, better adjusted psychologically, more sociable and outgoing, and more sensitive to the opinions of others than are other members of the group; but on the other hand, the importance of these traits varies, evidently, with the group's norms, structure, cohesiveness and goals, the specific character of the leadership role, and an assortment of other factors, all of which are somewhat untidily listed under the heading of situational characteristics. These findings have led to a greater emphasis on situational determinants of leadership at the expense of personality determinants.

Yet the exact lesson to draw from the experimental study of leadership is problematic. The idea of leadership has a rather special meaning in group research, as Gibb, for example, points out. "Group leaders," unlike political leaders, win no official posts which because of the powers invested in them or the force of custom and authority allow them to consolidate their leadership positions. Nor are group leaders in a position to control the behavior of group members by a judicious distribution of rewards and punishments, while political leaders frequently can allocate indulgences and in addition have recourse to the coercive sanctions of the state. Also, it is the group rather than the group leader that lays down the goals the group will concentrate on; and the social distance between group leader and group member is not great. Winning a leadership post and retaining it most often requires the group members' voluntary support.

The difference between the group leader and the political leader extends beyond the question of power to the matter of authority. "The [group] leader's authority is spontaneously accorded him by his fellow group members, and particularly by the followers. The authority of the head [for example, a political leader] derives from some extragroup

[1] For a review of the study of leadership, see Cecil Gibb, "Leadership," in G. Lindzey and E. Aronson, *Handbook of Social Psychology,* vol. 4, (Reading, Mass.: Addison Wesley, 1969), pp. 205-282; for trait theories of leadership, see especially pp. 218-228.

power which he has over the members of the group, who cannot meaningfully be called his followers. They accept his domination, on pain of punishment, rather than follow."[2]

The distinction can be overdrawn. Frequently a political leader will find himself in a situation not altogether unlike that of a group leader. Moreover, there are many different types of political leaders. Leadership of large-scale organizations is likely to differ in important respects from leadership of small groups, and both kinds of leadership may be found in the same political institution — the example of Congress and congressional committees comes readily to mind. Not surprisingly, then, the distinction between "leader" and "nonleader" may be exceedingly troublesome. In the present study, however, it is not.

In this study, the term political leader means simply any individual who attended the national convention of his or her party. Obviously, not all convention delegates or alternates have equal power, nor are all who have power convention delegates or alternates. Yet the opportunity to have a direct say in the nomination of one of two men who will be President of the United States would seem to bespeak a more than common measure of political influence. Beyond this, the national convention represented (at least at this time) a gathering of the politically powerful as well as the party faithful. Better than 60 percent of the convention (or Leader) sample held public office. So in speaking of political leadership I shall be referring to an assemblage of officials — governors, mayors, and city councilors; national, state and local committeemen; campaign organizers and fund raisers; those who held power openly and those who wielded it privately; those who had power but lost it and those who never had it but wanted to be close to those who did.

The connection between political leadership — as defined here — and personality remains an open question. Certainly, we must be very judicious in relying on the findings of experimental studies. The problems here are well known and

---

[2] Gibb, "Leadership," pp. 213.

need no lengthy elaboration.[3] For my purposes, perhaps it is most to the point to observe that experimental studies (with one exception)[4] have not dealt with on-going political groups conducting their routine activities. To the contrary, experimental groups consist in the main of college students and primary school children who usually are strangers to one another and who, at the outset at least, are on a more or less equal footing. Moreover, the task of the group is often an unfamiliar one and more often it is one to which few members of the group attach importance. Also, the participants know there is a predetermined length of time the experiment will run, even if they are unaware of exactly how long that will be; so they can carry out their experimental roles, knowing they need not do so on a continuing basis. Finally, it is implausible to assume that the distribution of personality characteristics under study in the experimental situation represents fairly the distribution of those same characteristics in real life. An experimental group consisting entirely of college students (and thus a group which is relatively homogeneous with respect to age, cognitive ability, and social status) on the average would show less variation on a dimension of personality such as self-esteem than would the population at large. That is, the relatively weak and frequently inconsistent relationships reported between personality factors and group leadership may be attributed, in some measure at least, to the narrow range of individual differences characteristically sampled in the experimental setting.

All this is not to argue that experimental studies of group leadership are invalid, or that they have no bearing on the study of politics. It is merely to insist on the very considerable differences between the group leader and the political leader and to suggest, for this reason, that the connection between political leadership and personality is by no means a closed question.

[3] See, for example, James Barber, *Power in Committees* (Chicago: Rand-McNally, 1966), especially pp. 8-10.

[4] James Barber, *Power in Committees.*

The Compensation Hypothesis:
Some Introductory Remarks

Of all the attempts to understand the connection between personality and political leadership, none has sparked more interest than the idea of compensation. This hypothesis, in its original version, was boldly put forward by Harold Lasswell: "Our key hypothesis about the power seeker is that he pursues power as a means of compensation against deprivation. *Power is expected to overcome low estimates of the self. . . .*"[5] According to this hypothesis, the drive to enter politics, insofar as it stems from personality, has its origin in damaged self-esteem. To overcome the doubts that low self-esteem arouses (and the deprivations that first led to the low self-esteem), men may strive to obtain approval, affection, respect, rectitude, but above all, power, for the possession of power provides assurance of indulgences and deference. For such men politics holds a special attraction because there power is concentrated and can be pursued openly and legitimately.

The classic version of the compensation hypothesis, then, may schematically be expressed as follows:
Low Self-Esteem→Power Motive→Political Activity. The relationships, of course, are not invariant. As Lasswell recognized, low self-esteem might lead to withdrawal and passivity as well as to compensatory striving. Nor is power the only value of consequence to a person with damaged self-esteem; achieving a sense of rectitude or obtaining social approval may be equally or more important to an individual struggling with a sense of unworthiness. Similarly, politics is not the only profession a man might enter in search of power; depending on circumstance and opportunity, such a man might even be drawn into the life of a university. But, of course, to acknowledge all of this is only to recognize that

[5] The entire passage is italicized in the original. Harold D. Lasswell, *Power and Personality* (New York: Viking Press, Compass Books edition, 1962), p. 39, italics in original. See also the whole of chapter 3, "The Political Personality," pp. 39-58.

Lasswell's compensation hypothesis is probabilistic, not de-terministic. Lasswell certainly means the hypothesis to be causal: low self-esteem leads to compensatory striving, which leads to accenting the value of power and acquiring certain skills, which in turn leads to a career in politics. The interre-lationships are not fortuitous and so should appear with regularity, though not, of course, with certainty.

At least a word on the idea of compensation is in order. The notion of compensatory striving is the key intervening variable in the developmental sequence beginning with low self-esteem and culminating in political leadership. Compen-sation, as used here, refers to a process of struggle set in motion originally by a sense of inferiority acquired in the formative years. Compensatory striving provides the psy-chological drive for the achievement of competence and skills necessary for success. Compensation, then, is a means by which a man, unsure of his worth, can prove it. But the proof is never conclusive, at least not in his own eyes. His worldly successes cannot extinguish his inner doubts, no more than living up to the approved standards of conduct can exorcise a deep-seated sense of guilt. Even the fullest measure of success cannot eliminate the self-doubt; it only takes the appropriate circumstances to awaken it. Further, the compensation hypothesis asserts that low self-esteem drives a man to seek high places in public life because of the importance he attaches to power. As Adler observed in an extreme but telling statement,

> . . . here is an individual who is striving incessantly from the sphere of insecurity and the feeling of inferiority towards a godlike dominance over his environment, is struggling for his significance, is attempting to force it.
>
> The actual form of expression and the deepening of this guiding thought could also be designated as *will to power.* . .[6]

---

[6] Heinz and Rowena Ansbacher, *The Individual Psychology of Alfred Adler: A Systematic Presentation in Selections from His Writings* (New York: Harper Torchbooks, 1967), p. 244.

In short, the compensation hypothesis, as originally formulated by Lasswell, predicts that political man will characteristically suffer damaged self-esteem, for it is low self-esteem which gives rise to the efforts at compensation which in the end orient him towards power and so politics.

A Review of the Empirical Evidence: The Case for Compensation

Studies appearing to support the compensation hypothesis may be divided into three types: (a) cross-population comparisons (between political actives and citizens at large); (b) cross-sectional comparisons within one population; and (c) psycho-historical and historical studies. Each type of study has characteristic drawbacks. For example, the historical study tends to lack properly validated indicators of psychological states — low self-esteem, status anxiety, emulative envy — which are thought to play some vital role; so this type of study leans heavily on indicators which are indirect and of dubious validity. Similarly, the life history has its characteristic weaknesses. Thus, it may be argued that intensive study of the life history of one individual is worthwhile because that one individual was an exceptional political or historical figure; but the more exceptional the object of these studies are, the more difficult it becomes to say to whom and under what conditions the findings of such studies should be generalized. But instead of dwelling on such generic problems, I shall concentrate on the specific failings of particular studies.

(a) Cross-Population Comparisons

The most frequently cited example of a cross-population comparison said to confirm the compensation hypothesis is a study by Hennessey.[7] One group consisted of persons active in politics (n = 72), the other of persons who did no more than vote (n = 66). The two groups were matched in a number of respects (for example, age, education, and socio-

[7] Bernard Hennessey, "Politicals and Apoliticals: Some Measurements of Personality Traits," *Midwest Journal of Political Science* 3 (1959): 355-366.

economic status) to minimize the chances that psychological differences between them might be due to external social factors. Hennessey found, among other things, that politicals score significantly higher on a "power scale" than do apoliticals. That is to say, politicals exhibit a stronger desire to control, influence, or exercise power over things and persons than do apoliticals, a finding that would appear to support the compensation hypothesis.

Unfortunately, this study is unpersuasive, because it is incomplete. Briefly, the study omits the information one needs not only to evaluate its conclusion but also to attach any interpretation to the results it reports. Beyond the summary observation that a power orientation is "defined as the desire to exercise control over persons and things" one is told next to nothing about the "power scale." No list of scale items is given, nor is even a sample of them presented for inspection. There is no discussion of the psychological attribute the scale is intended to measure, as if the notion of a "power orientation" had an obvious and unequivocal meaning, which it certainly does not. Nor does Hennessey exploit the opportunities he does have to fix the meaning of a power orientation, as it is operationally defined by this particular scale. Presenting the intercorrelations of the power scale and the other psychological scales the study includes (for example, authoritarianism, willingness to compromise, tough-mindedness — tender-mindedness, willingness to risk) might have given some indication of what it meant to score high or low on the "power scale," though it must also be added that no evidence is presented as to the reliability or validity of any of his scales. In short, even if one were to ignore the other flaws in this study, the very most one could conclude is that "politicals" and "apoliticals" differ with respect to some attribute. What the attribute is and what bearing the difference might have on the compensation hypothesis are not clear.

Moreover, politicians and citizens may be much alike in their motivational structure, under some circumstances at least, as Browning and Jacob have reported.[8] In an eastern city "respondents were a random sample of twenty-three businessmen (not retired) who had been or were chairmen, had run for or held elective office (both local and state) in the city, or had held appointive patronage positions, usually only part-time in conjunction with political activity at the ward level,"[9] and eighteen businessmen who were politically inactive but otherwise "matched eighteen of the businessmen politicians with respect to type and size of business, career level and specific occupation, religion, ethnic background, urban residence, average education, and age."[10] Also interviewed were fifty elected local officials, two-thirds of those holding office, in two Louisiana parishes. Power orientation was measured by a variation of the Thematic Apperception Test, modeled after McClelland's work on the Achievement Motive. Imaginative responses to six pictures were recorded, and among other things, the frequency of acts of feelings involving "attempts to control others" were scored.

Browning and Jacob discovered, contrary to their original expectations,[11] no significant difference between politicians and citizens of comparable social and economic position in their power motive scores. Moreover, the scores of politicians varied considerably; that is, there was no evidence of a relatively uniform or characteristic tendency for politicians to have a power motive of a particular strength whether

[8] Rufus P. Browning and Herbert Jacob, "Power Motivation and the Political Personality," *Public Opinion Quarterly* 28 (1964): 75-90; see also Rufus P. Browning, "The Interaction of Personality and Political System in Decisions to Run for Office," *The Journal of Social Issues* 24 (1968): 93-110.

[9] Browning and Jacob, "Power Motivation and the Political Personality," p. 80.

[10] Browning and Jacob, "Power Motivation and the Political Personality."

[11] See Herbert Jacob, "Initial Recruitment of Elected Officials in the U. S.—A Model," *Journal of Politics* 24 (1962): 703-716.

high or low. However, Browning and Jacob did report that in the Eastern city but not in Louisiana politicians who held an office with high potential for power had substantially higher power motive scores than either politicians who held office with low potential for power or businessmen of similar status who were not politically active. Also, they noted that the opportunities for influence and advancement were greater in the Eastern city and the politicians there were more power-oriented than in Louisiana. Their conclusion, then, was that politics is likely to attract the power-oriented person when the political system and the public office has a clear potential for power. In other words, for power to spur men into political life, they must not only be motivated to attain it, but also have a reasonable expectation of success. Only where this is the case is their evidence consistent with the classic version of the compensation hypothesis.

It is not obvious what to make of these findings. On the one hand, there is a fair measure of plausibility to a hypothesis which treats the decision to participate in politics as a joint function of personal motives and situational opportunities. But on the other, there are puzzling questions which this study raises and fails to answer. These questions are of particular importance because of our interest in the compensation hypothesis. Assume for the moment that Browning and Jacob's measure of power orientation measures what it purports to measure, that is, the strength of the motivation to control or influence others. It is at least conceivable, however, that politicians have a higher power motivation than nonpoliticians because they have a greater interest in, rather than a stronger need for, power.[12] For politicians, power may chiefly serve an instrumental function; it may be a value necessary for them to acquire if they are to realize the values that actually drew them into political life. If so, their higher power orientation would be due to the demands of a political career, not to compensate for

[12] I owe the observation to Alexander L. George, personal communication.

self-esteem damaged in childhood. So even if Browning and Jacob's measure of power orientation is valid and reliable, their findings are by no means strong evidence for the compensation hypothesis. But what reason is there to believe that their measure is valid? Browning and Jacob present no evidence for its validity, and a recent comprehensive power motivation measure suggests that this measure may be measuring virtually the opposite of what it was intended to measure.[13]

Originally intended as a measure of the desire to gain or maintain influence, the frequency with which an individual indicates a desire to attempt to control others may in fact be inversely related to the chances that he will actually attempt to attain or maintain political power. After a comprehensive review of the scholarly literature, Veroff and Veroff suggest that an apparent power orientation chiefly appears to reflect feelings of inferiority, weakness, or personal failure. More importantly perhaps, a power motivation apparently interferes with attempts to succeed and so obtain power under at least three conditions: when power motivation becomes intense, when standards of achievement are clear, or — and this last condition may be the most vital for our purposes — when the individual's performance is under public scrutiny. Of course, power motivation may sometimes further effective action, but it is likely to do so where the "performance is one that is not publicly and clearly defined as power oriented."[14] All in all, this scarcely suggests that power motivation, by itself, is likely to prove a positive motive for involvement in politics, as the classic version of the compensation hypothesis suggests. If it is a measure of anything at all,[15] the thematic assessment of 'power motiva-

[13] Joseph Veroff and Joanne Veroff, "Reconsideration of a Measure of Power Motive," *Psychological Bulletin* 78 (1972): 279-291.

[14] Veroff and Veroff, "Reconsideration of a Measure of Power Motive," p. 287.

[15] Doris R. Entwisle, "To Dispel Fantasies About Fantasy-Based Measures of Achievement," *Psychological Bulletin* 77 (1972): 377-391.

tion' is a measure of precisely the feelings of inferiority and inadequacy which encourage, among other things, a sense of political inefficacy and a tendency to political passivity. Politicians in Browning and Jacob's study, we should emphasize, score higher than nonpoliticians on power-orientation only when they also score higher on achievement motivation.[16] And contrary to the compensation hypothesis, a desire to have power, by itself, evidently obstructs attempts to gain it, in politics at least.

(b) Cross-Sectional Comparison

A frequently cited study with direct bearing on the question of compensation is Barber's analysis of freshmen state legislators.[17] It is a broad-gauged study, taking in the perceptions and adjustive reactions of men who were new to the legislative role, but here we shall consider only that portion of it that touches on the compensation hypothesis.

Self-esteem is both positively and negatively related to political involvement, according to Barber. If political involvement refers to more or less common forms of participation such as voting in Presidential elections or discussing the campaign with friends, then self-esteem and participation ought to be positively correlated. The reasoning for this hypothesis runs as follows: the political culture (in America at least) endorses such forms of citizen participation; since high self-esteem signifies a more successful "adaptation" to cultural norms than low self-esteem, high self-esteem and citizen participation ought to be associated.[18]

But political involvement is not all of a piece. It embraces very different kinds of activities, running from "talking

[16] This is a judgment on my part based on my reading of Table 3 of Browning and Jacob, "Power Motivation and the Political Personality." Unfortunately the data are not presented in such a way as to allow the reader to make this judgement with certainty.

[17] James D. Barber, *The Lawmakers* (New Haven: Yale, 1965).

[18] *Ibid.*, pp. 219-221.

politics" to "logrolling." The key distinction, as Barber sees it, is between "normal" and "abnormal" politics. Normal politics refers to activities associated with the citizen's role, for example, voting; abnormal politics refers to activities associated with the role of political activist, for example, running for public office. Though it is hard to determine the exact dividing line between the two kinds of politics, the distinction turns, according to Barber, on "the degree to which the person's daily routine is disrupted."[19] As he points out, a politician is not merely doing more of, and more often, what a citizen does less often. While the American culture gives strong encouragement to citizen participation in politics, it holds an ambivalent view at best towards the idea of going very far beyond the normal activities of the citizen. Witness the pejorative meaning of the term "politician" and the favorable connotations of the phrase "being above politics." For many, going into politics also represents a sharp break with their past activities and even, on occasion, their self-image. No doubt such a departure from their established life style tends to generate uncertainty and tension, which they have to cope with prior to entering politics.

This element of "discontinuity" in entering politics suggests to Barber that self-esteem may bear very different relationships to "abnormal" and "normal" politics. On the one hand, persons high in self-esteem should be better able (because of their poise and self-assurance) to handle the strain that entering a political career generates. On the other, those low in self-esteem may well have a strong drive to change their present circumstances (which proved, after all, not sufficiently satisfying to shore up their sense of worth) for a political career, for "political officeholding can offer strong and specific rewards to the damaged self, bolstering up an ego here, offering an extra chance there, conferring a moral blessing in another place."[20] In that event, the drive

[19] *Ibid.*, p. 221.

[20] *Ibid.*, p. 224.

to enter politics may be of sufficient strength to propel a person low in self-esteem over barriers (for example, the strain and uncertainty in selecting a new career) which otherwise would block him from entering politics. Following these two lines of argument, Barber then suggests that the competition for public office should attract men disproportionately from the two ends of the continuum of self-esteem. As a consequence, of course, variation in self-esteem should be greater among political activists than the population at large.

This set of arguments, which for convenience I shall call the "discontinuity" hypothesis, represents a considerably revised version of the classic compensation hypothesis. Three points of difference stand out. First, the discontinuity hypothesis predicts that both those high and those low in self-esteem may have an incentive to enter politics, whereas the compensation hypothesis in its classic version only offers a prediction as to the latter. Second, the discontinuity hypothesis alters the original emphasis on childhood experiences triggering a process of compensatory striving, calling attention instead to the effect of frustrating adult experiences (such as thwarted ambition) on those with low self-esteem. Last, the discontinuity hypothesis attaches no special place to a power motive. Whereas the standard version of the compensation hypothesis holds that an accentuation of power as a value tends to be a consequence of low self-esteem, the discontinuity hypothesis suggests that the object of compensatory striving may involve no stress on gaining or maintaining power. Indeed, depending on character type, the man with low self-esteem who wins public office may well be passive and submissive, removing himself from the center of political contention and, frequently, removing himself from the legislature at the first opportunity.[21]

Is there reason to accept the discontinuity hypothesis as valid? Unfortunately, although the hypothesis is at the

[21] See Barber's summary discussion of Legislator Types, pp. 214-215.

center of Barber's study, he turns up no evidence which bears on it, or more accurately perhaps, the "evidence" he does muster is neither relevant nor reliable.

Consider first the issue of relevance. What evidence would one need to support the discontinuity hypothesis? The discontinuity version — and all other versions of the compensation hypothesis, for that matter — makes a prediction not about political activists, nor about ordinary citizens, but about a difference between the two. Regardless of the particular prediction — whether one contended self-esteem to be higher among the elite or among the mass — confirmation would require a comparison between these two groups. All of this is elementary. But Barber's study, unfortunately, deals with levels of self-esteem among legislators only, paying no attention at all to citizens at large. This is no minor omission to be corrected in the course of further study. Given the present level of measurement practice, "scores" in psychological tests have no intrinsic significance whatever the method of assessment. To say a person has "low" self-esteem is to say only that it is low by comparison to some other person. Barber classifies a number of freshmen legislators as low in self-esteem *compared to their fellow freshmen legislators*, but the issue on which his hypothesis turns is whether they are low in self-esteem *compared to some comparable group of citizens who did not enter politics*.

Beyond the question of relevance is the problem of the reliability and validity of the data Barber collected. Consider first the relative frequency of high and low self-esteem among state legislators, according to Barber's estimate. He divides his sample into four types — Spectators, Advertisers, Reluctants, and Lawmakers — by cross-classifying two criteria — willingness to return to the legislature for a further term and amount of activity in the legislature.[22] What is of interest — indeed, what some might find astonishing — is that all the types but one, or fully 65.9% of freshman legislators, suffer

[22] *Ibid.,* p. 20f.

low self-esteem, in one form of another.[23] Thus, it would appear that self-doubt reaches epidemic proportions among the politically influential, unless the measuring instrument which produced those results was at fault.[24]

How, then, does Barber measure self-esteem? The answer is certainly not obvious, for his questionnaire contains no questions about self-esteem. I reproduce below the only portion of his questionnaire that is possibly relevant, entitled "General Role-Definition and Self-Rating."[25]

1) How would you describe the job of being a state legislator — that is, what are the most important things that you should be doing here?
(What is the main duty of function of a state legislator?)
(What approach should a member take to his legislative work?)

2) Thinking of these various points, how do you think you have done so far as a legislator?
(How would you rate yourself as a legislator?)
(Which of these things do you think you have been more successful in doing?)
(Which of them have given you trouble?)

3) What would you say has helped you, personally, in doing these things?
(What have been some of the things that have hindered you?)

[23] *Ibid.,* Appendix B., p. 264. The calculation is mine.

[24] Another curious feature of Barber's analysis is that a legislator scores either high or low in self-esteem, never medium. This may be the result, of course, of dichotomizing the full distribution of self-esteem scores, but this interpretation presumes there is such a distribution (although no evidence of it appears) and leaves it a mystery why the particular dividing point between high and low self-esteem (which could not have been the median) was chosen.

[25] Barber, *Lawmakers,* Appendix C, especially pp. 276-281. In addition to this questionnaire Barber also conducted interviews with 27 of 150 freshmen legislators, but he does not reveal precisely what questions were asked in these interviews or how responses to them were evaluated.

As an inspection of these questions shows, none ask directly or indirectly about self-esteem. The legislators were asked their opinion as to how well they were doing in their legislative role, but no one can seriously contend that how a person rates his performance on the job and how he evaluates himself are the same thing.

It should be perfectly plain that my objection is not to the measurement method. The respective merits of different assessment techniques — the focused interview as against the fixed item battery — is not the issue. The question, quite simply, is how information about self-esteem was obtained at all.

It is likely that a respondent provided information about himself in the course of answering the questions on role definition Barber asked, and quite possibly, other questions which were included in the interview. But there are no grounds for arguing that information collected so fortuitously is a reliable or valid guide to a person's self-esteem.

For our purposes, the conclusion to draw is rather straightforward: the discontinuity hypothesis is yet to be tested.

(c) Psycho-Historical and Historical Studies

The final type of study bearing on the idea of compensation and political involvement is basically historical in character, though it frequently has a heavy psychological or sociological accent. Criticism of this type of study would carry me an embarrassing distance from my field of competence. It would better serve my purposes if I reviewed, briefly, two rather distinguished studies — the one psycho-historical, the other historical — for each suggests an interesting variant of the compensation hypothesis that can be put to a test against my data.

The best known psycho-historical study exploring the compensation hypothesis is the Georges' study of Woodrow Wilson.[26] They present a carefully documented account of

---

[26] Alexander and Juliette L. George, *Woodrow Wilson and Colonel House* (New York: Dover Publications, Inc., 1964).

Wilson's development through childhood, his tenure as president of Princeton and governor of New Jersey, and finally, his two terms as president of the United States. At the outset they note the rigid and terribly exacting standards Wilson's father demanded of him. The scathing criticism and punishment his father treated him to when he fell short of what was expected of him left the young Wilson with a permanent sense of inadequacy and inferiority. Later in his life, as he gradually discovered and put to use his uncommon ability for writing and public speaking, the damage to his self-esteem served to spur him on to seek higher and higher offices. In each office, his personal needs — to innovate, to exercise influence, to direct and dominate others, to obtain respect, approval, and deference, and to assuage his sense of inferiority and unworthiness — continued unabated, leading him first to enjoy a period of creativity and accomplishment and then one of intractable and ultimately self-defeating conflict.

The Georges' study is a rich and compelling account of the role self-esteem can play in the dynamics of political leadership. Their analysis develops a substantially revised version of Lasswell's original compensation hypothesis, and it is directed particularly at more refined and dynamic conceptions of the complex interplay of situational pressures and personality forces.[27] But that is not what is of most interest for my purposes. As part of their interpretation of Wilson's personality, the Georges' have pointed to the compulsiveness that periodically characterized his compensatory striving. They note, for example, how assiduously young Wilson drove himself to develop his abilitities as an orator and a writer; how he displayed a lifelong penchant for the writing of constitutions; how he often handled himself in the face of opposition in a manner so inflexible, aggressive, and unyielding as to be needlessly self-defeating. In his career

---

[27] For further comment on this elaboration of the compensation hypothesis, see Alexander L. George, "Some Uses of Dynamic Psychology in Political Biography, Case Materials on Woodrow Wilson," in Fred Greenstein and Michael Lerner, *Sourcebook for Study of Personality and Politics* (Chicago: Markham, 1969).

one can see a single-mindedness of purpose, an obsessive and narrow preoccupation with his own goals, an inability or unwillingness, when threatened, to acknowledge the legitimate concerns of others, a desire to impose order and rules on the world, an insistence on his own purity, importance, and selflessness, a rigidity which becomes apparent under stress—often in the guise of a refusal "to compromise principle." These traits, when taken together, testify to a strong element of compulsiveness in Wilson's character.

Accenting this element of compulsiveness — for the sake of argument — leads to a rather different view of the compensation hypothesis. In the standard version of the hypothesis, it is compensation for damaged or inadequate self-esteem which orients the individual toward politics. But it may be the *syndrome* of compulsiveness, and not merely the single *trait* of self-esteem, which accounts for the distinctively strenuous quality of compensatory striving. After all, low self-esteem is but one element in the overall syndrome, and it is not obvious on the face of it that only one element should be highlighted and all others excluded from attention. What is even more important, low self-esteem, taken by itself, discourages rather than stimulates political involvement, as I shall later show. This consideration of the Georges' case study of Wilson, then, suggests a revised version of the compensation hypothesis, which runs as follows: low self-esteem, by itself, inhibits political involvement but, in combination with rigidity, obsessiveness, and other elements of the compulsive syndrome, low self-esteem can have a very different effect and help propel a person into political life. This hypothesis I shall label the *obsessive-compulsive hypothesis*.

A final kind of historical study offering some encouragement to the compensation hypothesis is less biographical and more sociological in orientation.[28] This is actually a rather broad umbrella under which many very different

[28] At first glance historical studies of social mobility and political movements may seem to have no connection to the compensation hypothesis as Lasswell and others conceived it. The reader who wishes reassurance on this point is referred to Lasswell's consideration of

investigators can find shelter;[29] so I shall consider only one example of the genre, in order to identify one last version of the compensation hypothesis.

For this purpose, a sketch of Richard Hofstadter's analysis of the Progressive Movement in America will serve us well.[30] In the vanguard of Progressive politics, he claims, were the professionals and self-employed small businessmen who were losing, or were faced with the imminent loss of, their standing in the social order. In the wake of industrialization trailed a new economic and social order. Large-scale manufacturing and commercial organizations were midwife to a new class whose wealth and power were without precedent. The old middle class who were once the embodiment of the society's virtues — individualism, thrift, hard work, self-discipline — were displaced, in effect, from their position in the social order. They had lost their secure hold on social approval and deference, and with the threat to their status, self-assurance began to give way to self-doubt. The desire for status, the need to raise their self-esteem, was in Hofstadter's view one of the motives which led them to Progressivism, a movement which aimed to restore its adherents to the position of prominence they held before the age of organization and industrialization.

The variation of the compensation hypothesis implicit in Hofstadter's analysis of the Progressive movement may be put as follows: downward social mobility leads to damaged self-esteem which, in turn, produces status strains and involvement in status-oriented political movements. Unlike the

---

precisely these phenomena — upward mobility, status marginality, and the like. See Harold D. Lasswell, *Power and Personality* (New York: Viking Press, 1962), especially pp. 48-51.

[29] For a recent example, see Seymour M. Lipset and Earl Raab, *The Politics of Unreason* (New York: Harper and Row, 1970). See also Hadley Cantril, *The Psychology of Social Movements* (New York: Wiley, Science Editions, 1963); Richard Hofstadter, *The Age of Reform* (New York: Alfred A. Knopf, 1955).

[30] Hofstadter, *Age of Reform*.

standard version of the compensation hypothesis, damage to self-esteem tends to take place in the adult years or in late adolescence rather than in the early years of childhood. Also, the interpretive accent falls heavily on status, so the dimensions of self-esteem which tap one's sense of standing in the society are, presumably, more critical in triggering status-oriented compensatory striving than are dimensions which reflect, for example, a sense of one's moral worth. Finally, there may be a difference in the consequences of status-oriented compensation, though it is hard to be exact about this. On the whole, however, historians and sociologists have applied this hypothesis to the emergence of mass political movements rather than the development of political leadership, and very often to movements which in some sense were radical in character. To set this version of the compensation hypothesis apart I shall label it *"the mobility hypothesis,"*[31] and I shall test it[32] in the following chapter.

Evidence Against the Compensation Hypothesis

A number of studies report findings which go against the compensation hypothesis. One of them is McConaughy's pioneer study of state legislators.[33] The Bernreuter Personality Inventory and the Guilford Martin Inventory of Factors

[31] Other variations of this hypothesis hold that the crucial factor is not downward mobility but mobility *per se* (see, for example, Bettelheim and Janowitz); however, in the case of upward mobility, the intervening variable appears to be an *uncertainty* as to self-identity, rather than a belief as to self-inadequacy; but this distinction is often a fuzzy one, so I shall consider both upward as well as downward shifts in mobility.

[32] Any test I can make is very limited, for the independent variable, as Hofstadter speaks of it, is the downward shift of large numbers, in a short period of time, presumably with some awareness that the fall is not an individual phenomenon but a group one, for which they hold the society responsible. As it happens, in the period the data were collected, downward mobility was limited in degree and was much more an individual than a group process.

[33] John McConaughy, "Certain Personality Factors of State Legislators in South Carolina," *APSR* 64 (1950): 897-903.

(as well as two tests of social and political attitudes) were administered to eighteen South Carolina legislators. The two personality inventories were then in common use and scoring norms (records of test scores derived from representative populations which allow, among other things, an estimate of scale scores for the "average" person to take the test) had been developed for both, which permitted a comparison between the scores of the legislators and those of persons outside of politics. In general, McConaughy finds these political leaders, compared to the average adult male, to be better balanced emotionally, less given to worry or emotional upsets, more independent and self-sufficient, more masculine in their interests and opinions, less nervous and irritable, slightly more dominant and decidedly more self-confident, and finally, comparatively free from feelings of inferiority or inadequacy.[34]

The weaknesses in McConaughy's research design are obvious and it is hard to know what to make of his results. Do they, for example, apply to all political activists, only to public office holders, or possibly only to some state legislators in South Carolina? What is more important, one is given no idea as to the method of selection of respondents (or the rate of refusal, for that matter); as a consequence, it is impossible to judge to what extent the results reported may have been an artifact of the sampling procedure (for example, the rate of refusal may have been higher for legislators who were anxious than for those who were more self-confident). Further, the psychological tests are open to some question,[35] although in fairness it must be said that they were two of the better psychological inventories available at the time. The test norms, however, raise a rather sticky question: it is simply not at all clear whether the appropriate

[34] John McConaughy, "Certain Personality Factors of State Legislators in South Carolina," pp. 900-907.

[35] For an example of this criticism, see Brent M. Rutherford, "Psychopathology, Decision-Making and Political Involvement," *Journal of Conflict Resolution* 10 (1966): 387-407.

comparison is between political leaders and the adult male population, or a sample of that population whose socio-economic characteristics are comparable to those of the legislators.[36]

McConaughy's study, however imperfect, does find consistent support from a series of studies conducted by Rosenberg. In an exploratory study,[37] he identifies and illustrates some of the psychological determinants of political apathy. One of these factors is the "threat of ego-deflation." To a person whose self-image is vulnerable, becoming involved in a discussion about politics can threaten his self-esteem: he runs the risk of appearing ignorant, of being caught committing some error in logic, of being bested by some other person – and his humiliation will take place in full view of others.[38]

Vulnerable self-esteem in another way can encourage apathy: low self-esteem tends to give rise to a deep-seated sense of futility, which naturally strengthens the expectation of failure. But the motivation to act is grounded at least in part in the expectation of success: he who is without faith in his ability to achieve the goals in politics he desires is unlikely to participate. Of course, as Rosenberg points out, a sense of futility can be based on factors other than low self-esteem – for example, in a belief in the operation of all-powerful external forces.[39] Nevertheless, unfavorable self-attitudes (and most critically perhaps, a lack of confidence in one's ability to be effective) are at the very center of attitudes that dampen enthusiasm for political involvement.

[36] For an illuminating discussion of the issues involved, see Paul E. Meehl, "Nuisance Variables and the Ex Post Facto Design," in Michael Radner and Stephen Winokur, eds., *Analyses of Theories and Methods of Physics and Psychology*, Minnesota Studies in the Philosophy of Science (Minneapolis: University of Minnesota, 1970), vol. 3, pp. 373-402.

[37] Morris Rosenberg, "Some Determinants of Political Apathy," *Public Opinion Quarterly* 18 (1954-55): 349-366.

[38] *Ibid.*, pp. 353-354.

[39] *Ibid.*, pp. 355-358.

Such observations are suggestive, but they are by no means conclusive, as Rosenberg takes care to point out. The interviews were unstructured and frankly exploratory, conducted with a sample drawn on a nonrandom basis (though exactly how he does not say). A later study of adolescents, on which I have frequently drawn in the course of this study,[40] buttresses the contention that low self-esteem tends to inhibit political involvement. The proof is indirect, for Rosenberg focuses on social participation in a high school, but the threads of evidence, when woven together, appear of a piece with the larger fabric of social life. Persons high in self-esteem participate more in extracurricular activities and voluntary formal organizations than do those low in self-esteem;[41] and as one might expect, those with high self-esteem are not only more likely to participate, they are also more likely to occupy leadership roles in formal groups.[42] This active and assertive style carries over to social exchanges. As we noted before, those high in self-esteem more frequently take part in discussions about "matters of high school government or general high school interest," are more likely to be asked their views on such matters, and are less likely to assume a passive role when they find themselves in this kind of social interaction.[43] Finally, variations in dominance are also evident in the classroom. On the basis of sociometric data collected from a limited number of students, Rosenberg concludes that those low in self-esteem "(1) were less likely to be selected as a leader by two or more of their classmates; (2) were judged as less likely to be actually chosen by others if an election were held; (3) were less likely to be described as active participants in classroom discussion; and (4) were

[40] Morris Rosenberg, *Society and the Adolescent Self-Image* (Princeton, N. J.: Princeton University Press, 1965).

[41] *Ibid.*, pp. 193-194.

[42] *Ibid.*, pp. 196-197.

[43] *Ibid.*, pp. 199-202.

more likely to be described as relatively subdued and inactive in classroom discussions."[44]

What accounts for this connection between low self-esteem and low participation? Rosenberg points to a congeries of personal attitudes and characteristics: compared to those high in self-esteem, those low in self-esteem tend to distrust others, to assume that others dislike them, to be less assertive, and to be less popular as well.[45] A variety of elements are mixed in together here — self-confidence, faith in people, dominance, and social interest — and it is rather hard to sort out how one influences and is influenced by another. Nevertheless, the basic reasoning has some appeal, and it can be recast in a more abstract form so as to apply more directly to the connection between self-esteem and political involvement: whatever dampens social interaction decreases the chances of participation in politics.

Rosenberg's study, of course, deals with adolescents, but a number of studies of adults report similar findings, demonstrating a *positive* relationship between political participation and various aspects of a person's sense of self-esteem, or to other personality characteristics closely connected to self-esteem. These studies are of interest not merely because they deal directly with a range of political activities from voting to holding public office and a variety of people from citizens to lobbyists. Equally important, these studies further articulate the reasons for expecting low self-esteem to act as an inhibitory tendency. Indeed, I shall distinguish two hypotheses which agree on the prediction of positive relationship between self-esteem and political involvement, but disagree somewhat in the reasons each gives as the basis for this prediction.

The first hypothesis, which follows rather closely Rosenberg's analysis, shifts attention away from the global idea of self-esteem to one of its most salient dimensions. This

[44] *Ibid.,* pp. 197-198.

[45] *Ibid.,* pp. 202-205.

dimension of self-esteem refers to a specific form of self-confidence — a belief in one's capacity to deal effectively with other persons — a dimension I have labelled interpersonal competence. In two studies Milbrath reports that a rather similar personality characteristic facilitates political involvement.[46] His two studies differ somewhat in the way they conceptualize and measure this personality characteristic, which, in the first study, he calls "sociability," and in the second, "sociality," but both refer to a person's degree of skill, knowledge, assertiveness, and assurance in interpersonal relations. Also, the studies were conducted at different points in time and on two different populations, the first being financial contributors to a political party in North Carolina and the second, lobbyists in Washington.

Both studies report significant correlations between the "sociality" attribute[47] and various, though not all, forms of participation — a particularly impressive result in view of the uncommonly high level of political involvement (as compared to the general public) characteristic of the two groups, political contributors and lobbyists, that were studied. From these data Milbrath comes to the conclusion that sociability (or sociality) affects the height of the barriers to political participation: lacking social competence raises their height, thus discouraging political involvement, while possessing a sense of social competence lowers their height, thus facilitating involvement. We shall label this the *"interpersonal competence hypothesis."*

Other studies bolster the notion that low self-esteem presents an obstacle to political involvement, but in the

[46] Lester W. Milbrath, "Predispositions Towards Political Contention," *Western Political Quarterly* 13 (1960): 5-18; Lester W. Milbrath and Walter W. Klein, "Personality Correlates of Political Participation," *Acta Sociologica* 6 (1962): 53-66.

[47] The correlation between the sociality scale and a five-item self-esteem scale was r .64, which suggests that the two scales were essentially measuring the same thing, particularly if one considers the reliability of the sociality scale—Kuder-Richardson (corrected for attenuation) .67.

process advance a somewhat different set of reasons to account for the inhibitory character of low self-esteem. Thus Campbell and his colleagues devote attention to a personal characteristic closely connected to self-esteem, which they dub "personal effectiveness."[48] This trait essentially refers to a person's characteristic feelings of success and failure, feelings they theorize are a summary indication of his ego-strength.[49] The stronger a person's sense of personal effectiveness, the more confident he is of his ability to exercise control over events in the external environment and the needs or feelings that arise within himself.[50] Personal effectiveness is one source of feelings of political efficacy. Those with a strong sense of personal effectiveness are more likely to vote and to become involved in politics than those who lack this sense of effectiveness.

Elaborating this line of analysis, Campbell and his colleagues suggest that when the personality confronts a threat to its well-being, energy is required to maintain its psychological economy and meet immediate emotional necessities. This line of reasoning is derived from the classical Freudian view on the economy of personality defenses.[51] The amount of energy the ego must appropriate in mounting defensive operations may, if the threat is of sufficient intensity and persistence, squander the resources available to the personality for healthy growth and creative action. Only when the ego is strong can it afford the energy to sustain involvement in areas of secondary interest to the personality such as politics. I shall label this the *hypothesis of surplus energies*.

[48] Angus Campbell, Philip E. Converse, Warren E. Miller, and Donald E. Stokes, *The American Voter* (New York: Wiley, 1960), pp. 499-519.

[49] *Ibid.*, p. 516.

[50] *Ibid.*, p. 517.

[51] See Otto Fenichel, *The Psychoanalytic Theory of Neurosis* (New York: W. W. Norton, 1945).

One final hypothesis worth disentangling from the convolution of arguments on the idea of compensation remains. Originally, Lasswell's formulation of the compensation hypothesis was reduced to the following schema: Low Self-Esteem⟶Power Motive⟶Political Activity. Obviously, low self-esteem does not always propel people into politics: under certain conditions it will, under others it will not. What factors are necessary if low self-esteem is to stimulate political involvement, at least as Lasswell conceives the process of compensation? In *Power and Personality* he argues that the arousal of compensatory striving is unlikely if the individual cannot modify his expectations and desires when deprivation occurs, or if there are no indulgences which accompany the deprivation.[52] Low self-esteem is also more likely to be associated with compensatory struggles to attain power, if the individual has a favorable orientation to power; that is, if he himself has consistently won power in the past and with it the other values such as recognition and respect that holding power brings, or he has regularly observed others with such a record of success.[53]

The crux of the argument here is that it is not low self-esteem alone that triggers the compensation process. After all, compensatory striving is only one reaction to deprivation; another is withdrawal. Why is the outcome political acticity for one man and passivity for another? Obviously, the outcome may hinge on certain extrinsic conditions — for example, the scarcity or surplus of opportunities and resources to exploit.[54] Such conditions establish the *mixture of motives* at work. So Lasswell argues that for compensation to take place the deprivation must not be so severe as to rob the individual of faith in his ability to succeed, for without this fundamental element of self-esteem and self-confidence, the individual inclines to passivity and

[52] Lasswell, *Power and Personality,* pp. 40-41.

[53] *Ibid.,* p. 41.

[54] *Ibid.,* p. 53.

THE IDEA OF COMPENSATION . 251

withdrawal. As Lasswell writes, "confidence in the self is sustained by the *expectation that a better value position is possible; and that this possibility depends in part upon the taking of active measures by the self.*"[55]

According to this view, compensatory striving depends on some mixture of favorable self-attitudes as well as unfavorable ones, of high self-esteem as well as low self-esteem. The mixture is, admittedly, a complex one, for it may involve many varieties and degrees of self-esteem, and Lasswell's description of it, terse to the point of being elliptical, hardly gives one a firm idea as to the components of compensatory striving or the way they are combined or the way they become related in the developmental process. Nevertheless, one ought to set this version of the compensation hypothesis off from the others; it suggests that compensatory striving depends not on low self-esteem alone, but on some mix of high and low self-esteem. Accordingly, I shall call this the *"mixture hypothesis."*

In Retrospect

One purpose of this chapter was to convey something of the state and quality of research on the idea of compensation and political involvement. The research literature gives the impression of a conversation simultaneously conducted in a dozen tongues, many of which are foreign or at least unfamiliar to one's ears, so that one can only make out a phrase here, an exclamation there, about the results of studies which sometimes appear hopelessly at odds with one another. There are, then, studies which conclude that low self-esteem propels men into political life and others which argue it drives them to avoid political contention altogether, or whenever possible. Which conclusion is the more valid one cannot tell with assurance, certainly not on the basis of previous research, for these studies differ in too many

[55] Harold D. Lasswell, "The Selective Effect of Personality on Political Participation," in Richard Christie and Marie Jahoda, eds., *Studies in the Scope and Method of "The Authoritarian Personality"* (Glencoe, Ill.: The Free Press, 1954), pp. 197-225 (p. 215, italics his).

respects to be strictly comparable. There is no consistency, for example, in what is meant by self-esteem or how it is measured. Self-esteem refers, variously, to a sense of one's worth, importance, or personal adequacy, to a need for recognition, approval, or power over others, to a sense of inferiority which lies either at the surface of personality where it is easily visible or deeply buried, covered by the years of compensatory struggle. Sometimes the self-esteem measure involves a set of statements, and the respondent must select from among a predetermined set of responses (for example, agree-disagree type items); sometimes it involves a standard set of pictures about which the respondent is instructed to make up stories (for example, T.A.T. type tests); sometimes the test is essentially a judgmental process, more or less like a diagnosis, based on psychiatric case histories or historical materials; and at other times — perhaps, the majority of times — the measurement procedure is not described at all or not in sufficient detail for anyone to see in what respects it differs from, or resembles, other measures of self-esteem.

Then, too, the meaning of political involvement differs radically from study to study. Several of them focus on a comparison between "politicals" and citizens, in effect asking how self-esteem enters in the selection process to fill leadership roles (broadly conceived) in the political system. Other studies focus on a much lower pitch of political activity, analyzing the psychological differences between those who vote and take some interest in politics and those who are apathetic and indifferent to it. Yet another type of study zeroes in on men at the very summit of the political system, such as President Wilson.

Studies also vary enormously in analytic design, amply illustrating the variety of research techniques from studies of a single person to large-scale surveys. In addition, they encompass a most heterogeneous set of subjects — adult citizens selected at random, historical figures of heroic proportions, college students, state legislators, political 'leaders' chosen on some nonrandom (usually unspecified) basis, financial contributors to a political party, mental patients, and lobbyists. Where there is such diversity of evidence and method, how is one to weigh the findings of one study against another?

I have also pointed to shortcomings in studies. I have deliberately refrained, however, from preparing a compendium of methodological flaws, preferring instead to call attention to the perfunctory effort many researchers make to conceptualize and measure personality characteristics before hurrying off to devote themselves to a discussion of their "findings." Certainly, this stricture does not apply to all of them, or to all of them with equal severity, but it is clear that the field of personality and politics will make little progress until we attach more importance to determining exactly what we have measured, and how well we have done it.

The second purpose of this chapter was to lay out the various versions of the compensation hypothesis. The idea of compensation is in common circulation, and as a consequence, its edges tend to be worn smooth, but actually it occurs in several distinct versions. On examination one can see a number of different hypotheses loosely bundled together under the notion of compensation, each of which can be conceptually disentangled and empirically tested. Which are valid and which false is the question the following chapter will answer.

Chapter 7 · PARTICIPATION AND POLITICAL LEADERSHIP

This chapter explores the effect of individual differences in self-esteem on political involvement. Political involvement is a broad term, covering many different actions — the discussion of outstanding public questions, taking an interest in an election campaign, working on behalf of some candidate or public cause, running for public office, and the like. Most persons undertake few of these activities, a few undertake many of them, and some pick and choose among them.[1] A rough but meaningful line can be drawn between the involvement of citizen and of "political leader," and so throughout this chapter I shall consider the impact of self-esteem on both degrees and kinds of political involvement.

First Principles: Social Learning
and Political Involvement

Our point of departure is the relationship between self-esteem and social learning. To review briefly, we have found that persons high in self-esteem, compared with those low in self-esteem, are more exposed to communications about politics, can better understand the messages they receive, and as a consequence are more knowledgeable about politics and more likely to have internalized the modal values of the political culture.

[1] See, for example, Herbert McClosky, "Political Participation and Apathy," *International Encyclopedia of the Social Sciences,* David Sills, ed., (Macmillan, 1968), pp. 253-265; Lester Milbraith, *Political Participation* (Chicago: Rand-McNally, 1965).

From this, it is but a short step to see that those with high self-esteem are more likely to hold the values and attitudes that foster political involvement. The political culture, in the United States at least, legitimizes the role of the participant citizen. The political order is committed, however imperfectly, to democratic values, and that commitment in turn encourages the idea that all citizens should show an active concern with the public business. To that extent, the values of the society inculcate the ideal of participation.

Then, too, the culture of the society is fundamentally egalitarian. A political tradition of elitism — the view that birth or character qualify some to rule and others to be ruled — has never taken hold in America. The egalitarianism of the political culture undercuts the idea that the public business ought to be reserved as a matter of principle to a select few and, instead, gives strong encouragement to the view that citizens at least periodically should participate. To be sure, there are limits on the kind of political involvement the society regards as proper. But it is fair to say that the society looks with favor on the idea of popular participation in politics, and this idea is therefore more likely to be adopted and acted on by persons who understand and conform to the values of the society — in short, by persons with high rather than low self-esteem.

One way social learning affects participation, then, is by the transmission of civic values, that is, standards of conduct the society regards as desirable and exhorts its members to meet. Another way social learning enters in is by the development of political motives. People acquire through a rather complex process such motives as an interest in politics and a sense of their own political efficacy which tend to orient them either toward or away from political involvement. Although the details of this process are not well established, it is clear even at this early point in research that a personality characteristic such as self-esteem is a key determinant in the acquisition of such motives.

The connections among self-esteem, political interest (or efficacy), and political involvement are relatively straightforward. Less obvious, perhaps, is the way self-esteem leads to differential reactions to inconsistent social cues relating to involvement in politics. Societies tend to differ not only in the value, positive or negative, that they place on political involvement,[2] but in the consistency with which they encourage or discourage participation. In a culture as complex and pluralistic as America the image of politics that a person develops inevitably involves a process of selective learning. He selects from among the ideas current in the society — accepting, rejecting, emphasizing, embellishing. Thus, there are in the American political culture elements of cynicism and of faith in government. Some persons give themselves entirely over to distrust and suspicion, others to an unquestioning faith, and still others hold both attitudes in varying combinations.

Self-esteem is one determinant of this process of selective learning. As Chapter 5 showed, low self-esteem fosters a cynicism about politics — a belief that political leaders are untrustworthy and overready to advance their own interests at the expense of the general welfare, while citizens by and large cannot be trusted to make responsible choices. Persons high in self-esteem, by comparison, are more optimistic in their outlook and more likely to have confidence in the honesty and intelligence of elected officials and the electorate. In short, those low in self-esteem accent the element of cynicism in their view of politics, those high in self-esteem the element of faith.

Holding an image of politics which is, on balance, favorable ought to stimulate involvement; conversely, developing an image which is unfavorable ought to encourage avoidance and apathy. Thus, insofar as self-esteem determines the selective learning of positive or negative orientations toward politics, it ought to affect the likelihood of participation in politics.

[2] Gabriel A. Almond and Sidney Verba, *The Civic Culture* (Princeton: Princeton University Press, 1963).

The "Circle" Hypothesis
The argument up to this point may be laid out as follows: variations in self-esteem lead to individual differences in the learning of (1) social norms which call for political involvement; (2) social motives such as political interest and political efficacy; and (3) positive and negative orientations toward politics based on inconsistent social cues toward politics. All three, of course, flow from the connection between self-esteem and social learning.

In addition, insofar as self-esteem is an indication of both a person's expectation of success and his experience of it, it affects his motivation to participate. Aspiration and performance tend to influence, and be influenced by, each other. Cofer and Appley in their encyclopedic study of motivation observe that "A quite widely accepted generalization from experiments on level of aspiration is that successful performance leads to an increased level of aspiration and that unsuccessful performance (failure) leads to reduced level of aspiration. . . ."[3] Aspiration level (broadly conceived) offers an index to one's confidence in one's capacity to succeed at some task. And confidence that one will succeed strengthens, evidently, the chances that one will in fact succeed. So the Coleman report, as M. Brewster Smith notes, presents evidence that students who have a general sense of confidence in their ability to succeed do markedly better in school than those who lack this sense of confidence.[4]

Experiencing success and expecting it are reciprocally related. Causal influence runs in both directions: a history of success affects expectations of success and expectations of success affect the chances of success. Viewed as a process that extends over a lengthy span of time, this reciprocal

[3] C. N. Cofer and M. H. Appley, *Motivation: Theory and Research* (New York: Wiley, 1967).

[4] M. Brewster Smith, "Competence and Socialization," in John A. Clausen, ed., *Socialization and Society* (Boston: Little, Brown and Company, 1968), pp. 270-320, 286.

relationship gives rise to two developmental circles, which Smith has well described:

> developmental progress or deficit is typically a matter of benign circles or of vicious ones, not of persistent effects of clear-cut single causes (see Myrdal, 1944). In social life, there is much bitter truth to the Biblical maxim, 'to him who hath shall be given; from him who hath not shall be taken away even that which he hath." Launched on the right trajectory, the person is likely to accumulate successes that strengthen the effectiveness of his orientation toward the world while at the same time he acquires the knowledge and skills that make his further success more probable. His environmental involvements generally lead to gratification and to increased competence and favorable development. Off to a bad start, on the other hand, he soon encounters failures that make him hesitant to try. What to others are challenges appear to him as threats; he becomes preoccupied with defense of his small claims on life at the expense of energies to invest in constructive coping. And he falls increasingly behind his fellows in acquiring knowledge and skills that are needed for success on those occasions when he does try.[5]

The picture of self-reinforcing circles that Smith sketches in his account of the development of competence also appears in the analysis of social participation.[6] Greater social participation brings with it greater opportunities for familiarity and practice, which in turn further the acquisition of relevant skills and knowledge. The more skillfully and successfully the individual carries out the obligations of his social role, the more his fellows are likely to reward him with approval and other forms of social reinforcement. Thus, his sense of

[5] Smith, "Competence and Socialization," p. 272. See especially Smith's discussion of competence as differentiating vicious and benign circles of development, pp. 276-278.

[6] This account is adopted from Robert H. Coombs, "Social Participation, Self-Concept and Interpersonal Evaluation," *Sociometry* 32 (1969): 273-286.

personal worth and his desire to participate are strengthened by a combination of factors — achievement of the goal which was the original stimulus to participate, the satisfactions which come with success obtained by personal striving, the social reinforcements received from his fellows. Note finally that his increased confidence in his own abilities leads to improved expectations of success, which in turn strengthen the likelihood of further participation.

Of course, this account of participation somewhat distorts the character of the proccesses involved, describing the phenomenon as if it was deterministic and rather straightforward, when in actuality it is probabilistic and quite complex. But the oversimplification does focus attention on one ideal-type, the benign circle of participation, and heighten the contrast between it and another ideal-type, the vicious circle of passivity. The second circle begins as a person, perhaps unsure of himself at the start, takes part in some social encounter and fails in his purpose or suffers some other form of disappointment or social disapproval. Should he frequently suffer a similar fate thereafter, his apprehension is likely to grow, and he more often finds himself motivated to withdraw from or to avoid such encounters altogether. The less his exposure, the smaller his chances to acquire the knowledge and skills necessary for success and the greater the likelihood his performance in the future will fall short of established social standards. Gradually, he learns to expect failure and loses confidence in his ability to succeed in social interactions. The lower his self-confidence, the stronger his desire to avoid similar experiences. So the vicious circle continues, becoming stronger and wider.

The benign and the vicious circles are illustrations of the psychology of competence, which Smith has briefly sketched in his notion of the competent self.[7] The idea of competence has two aspects: one cognitive, the other motivational. The cognitive aspect refers to the knowledge and skills which enhance a person's chances for success at some task; the

[7] Smith, "Competence and Socialization," pp. 273-275 and pp. 283-287.

motivational aspect refers to some inner need (whether intrinsic or acquired) to be active and effective.[8] These two aspects, though analytically distinguishable, are empirically related. The stronger an individual's drive to be active and effective, the more likely it is that he will acquire relevant knowledge and skills; and the more knowledgeable and able he is, the more confident and strongly motivated he will be. By contrast, anxiety and the desire to avoid failure characterize the person who lacks competence. Doubting his chances for success, he tends to forego opportunities to acquire more knowledge and skills, thereby reinforcing over time his conviction that he cannot succeed, which in turn confirms and heightens his initial fears.

But to speak simply in terms of "competence" or "the competent self" *without specifying competence at what* may be misleading. Competence, like virtue, is multi-dimensional: one may very likely be good at something without being good at everything, or one may be good in some circumstances, but not in others. No taxonomy of the types of competence has been prepared, nor does one appear to be in the offing. Not unless a systematic program of empirical research is undertaken will we be able to determine the number and kinds of competence, the degree to which they may be interrelated, and thus the extent to which it makes sense to speak of "the competent self."

It is advisable at the present stage of research to focus not on the global idea of competence but on one facet of it, interpersonal competence, which is closely connected to social (and presumably political) involvement. This type of competence is associated with a syndrome of attitudes: the person with a sense of interpersonal competence tends to feel at ease and self-assured when in the company of others, to be articulate and persuasive, to take the initiative fre-

---

[8] The notion of such an intrinsic need is derived from White's concepts of effectance and competence; see Robert W. White, "Ego and Reality in Psychoanalytic Theory," *Psychological Issues,* Monograph 11 (1960), Vol. 3.

quently, to be outgoing, active, forceful; by contrast, the person who lacks a sense of interpersonal competence tends to be shy, retiring, inhibited, awkward, and anxious when dealing with other persons.

It follows that those who enjoy a sense of interpersonal competence would be encouraged to initiate contact with others, to respond positively to overtures others may make to them, to sustain and strengthen a range of social relationships, to participate more vigorously and more often in a variety of social encounters, to show greater persistence in the face of social opposition or to withdraw selectively and realistically rather than yield to a desire to leave the field entirely. Thus, interpersonal competence should encourage the benign circle of participation. Conversely, those who lack such competence ought to fall victim more often to a vicious circle of passivity and withdrawal, with repeated failure heightening their initial lack of confidence, anxieties, and desires to withdraw from or curtail their role in social interaction.

This line of reasoning suggests that political involvement is positively related to interpersonal competence and more strongly related to it than to a person's overall level of self-esteem. Of the three dimensions of self-evaluation that the overall index combines, interpersonal competence bears the most directly on a tendency to participate in politics. To become involved in politics is to become involved with others. To participate is to attend meetings, to work in campaigns, to make public speeches occasionally — or perhaps rarely — but to discuss politics frequently. Political life is social life. What is more, it is a species of social life that demands a considerable measure of self-confidence and assertiveness. It throws a man into close contact with other men, including many who are unfamiliar to him, whose status and social background differ considerably from his, whose motives may be hostile or — more frequently — unfathomable. At the same time much of political life lacks a well-worked out and well-understood structure of roles, incentives, expectations, sanctions, and cues. Briefly, politics is an uncertain enterprise; it tends to demand, therefore, a certainty of self.

Compensation or Competence?

The compensation hypothesis contends that men tend to enter politics to obtain, among other things, power as a means of redressing damaged self-esteem: it predicts, therefore, a *negative* relationship between self-esteem and political involvement. The competence hypothesis holds that whether a person will become involved in politics depends, in large measure, on his history of success and failure in social interaction: the more favorable the record, the greater his skills, motives, and opportunities; it predicts, therefore, a *positive* relationship between an aspect of self-esteem and political involvement.

Table 7:1 presents the relationship between the self-esteem index and a political participation scale. The participation scale, which appears only in the MB Study, is an index of a person's record of political involvement; it is intended to assess whether a person in fact is active in politics and if so, in what ways and to what extent; it is not merely a measure of whether his attitude toward involvement is positive or negative. The Participation index is a measure of behavior, not of attitudes. This scale takes account of a variety of ways a person may take part in politics — supporting a candidate by displaying a sign on one's car or wearing a button, voting, attempting to persuade family and friends to turn out or to support a particular candidate, writing a political leader, joining a civic organization, attending a political meeting and the like. Note, however, that though this scale takes in a considerable variety of ways a man may participate in politics, it only taps a limited *range* of political activity: at the high pole is the participant citizen, not the political leader.

As Table 7:1 shows, the self-esteem index and the participation scale are positively related, but only barely so. The participation scale is trichotomized, and 39% of those high

Table 7:1

THE RELATIONSHIP BETWEEN SELF-ESTEEM AND THE
POLITICAL PARTICIPATION INDEX (MB) (PERCENTAGED DOWN)

Political Participation	Self-Esteem		
	Low (n = 483)	Middle (n = 207)	High (n = 392)
Low	36	37	29
Middle	34	30	32
High	30	34	39

in self-esteem, compared to 30% of those low in self-esteem score at the upper end of the scale, a difference which is scarcely of consequence.

The weakness of the relationship is a further sign that citizen participation in politics is relatively independent of a rather large number of personality characteristics, including, among others, self-esteem. For example, the research on authoritarianism and political activity suggests that personality traits such as authoritarianism have only a weak effect on the kinds of participation citizens engage in, or none at all.[9] The reasons for this are close at hand. Politics in America lacks the power to engage deep-seated personality needs, except under very uncommon circumstances, and even then, it attracts relatively few. Politics, for the most part, falls at the outer fringes of the citizen's life space, or outside it entirely. Few take an active interest in politics or know very much about it, and as a consequence, politics rarely takes on sufficient psychological importance for it to acquire the symbolic and affective associations necessary to engage some basic personality characteristic such as hostility. In other words, for politics to engage personality needs it must be salient, which it rarely is.

Even when politics is salient, the need to satisfy basic personality needs is unlikely to carry many into political activity, for reasons which will be readily apparent as this

[9] See Herbert McClosky, "Political Participation and Apathy."

Table 7:2

THE RELATIONSHIP OF THE DIMENSIONS OF SELF-ESTEEM AND POLITICAL PARTICIPATION (MB) (PERCENTAGED DOWN)

Political Participation	Interpersonal Competence			Status Inferiority			Personal Unworthiness		
	Low (n = 439)	Middle (n = 352)	High (n = 291)	Low (n = 315)	Middle (n = 488)	High (n = 279)	Low (n = 287)	Middle (n = 411)	High (n = 384)
Low	42	32	23	35	35	29	32	31	37
Middle	32	33	32	33	32	32	30	35	32
High	26	36	45	32	32	40	38	34	32

chapter proceeds. At this point, it should suffice to observe that participation in politics offers no unique advantages in dealing with specific psychological needs or conflicts. These internal forces, of course, can spill over into the area of politics, as they can into other areas of social life, but there is no compelling reason to believe a priori that political involvement holds out a special promise of relieving inner distress.

Table 7:2 casts some further light on the motives that facilitate political involvement. It shows the relationship between the Participation scale and each of the three components of the Self-Esteem index. As anticipated, individual differences in interpersonal competence affect participation. The more effective and at ease a person feels in dealing with others, the more active in politics he is likely to be. Forty-five percent of those with a sense of interpersonal competence score at the upper end of the Participation scale, compared to 26% of those who tend to feel ineffective in interpersonal relations; conversely, 42% of those who lack a sense of interpersonal competence score low on the Participation scale, compared to 23% of those who are more sure of themselves. Also as anticipated, two dimensions of self-esteem bear little relationship to political involvement. A sense of personal unworthiness or of status inferiority, to all intents and purposes, make it neither more nor less likely a person will become active in politics.

These results lend credence to the circle hypothesis, and thereby suggest some of the dynamics of psychological involvement. One way to conceive of political participation is to think of it as a habit, not in the sense that a man who becomes active always remains so, or is always active in the same way, but rather in the sense that political involvement is an acquired tendency which can be established by mere repetition. Thus, a person taking part in politics finds himself more regularly in the company of people who also participate and who are likely to encourage him to continue in politics because of the high value they place on political involvement. Then, too, participation is itself likely to strengthen certain of the motives which originally led him to become involved. For example, the politically active find they exercise more political influence than does the average citizen, a discovery which has the happy consequence of further confirming the sense of political efficacy which facilitated their involvement in politics in the first place. A similar process of self-reinforcement tends to occur for many of the reasons which lead men to enter political life. Thus, the citizen who becomes involved because of his strong convictions on some public issue, or perhaps out of a sense of civic duty, often finds his initial commitments heightened after he is an active participant, if only because his involvement in politics pushes to the center of his attention concerns which previously were not as salient. In addition, close association with others in a common enterprise generates new patterns of friendship and primary groups, which acquire a power in their own right to sustain his original desire to participate. And over a period of time, the political parties, personalities, and issues become invested with strong feelings and symbolic meaning; over time, then, politics tends to become more rather than less salient. Participation, then, for a variety of reasons tends to be self-reinforcing.

People obviously participate in politics for many reasons, not the least of which are the benefits participation brings. Personality characteristics, however, may well have their chief effect on involvement by affecting the ability and willingness to learn the habits and skills necessary to reap those benefits of participation, or to be aware of them. Interpersonal competence affects political participation, whereas a sense of status inferiority or of personal unworthiness apparently do not. Interpersonal competence is both a sign and a source of those social habits, motives, and skills, most likely learned early in life, which allow a person to become involved readily in a wide range of social activities, including, among many other things, political activity.

This interpretation of the role of personality is in contrast with another view, which stresses the role of personality-based motives such as the desire for power that drives some into politics. To be sure, personality-based motives may predominate on occasion, but in the main, personality affects participation by affecting the learning of skills and habits a person must acquire in order to obtain the rewards participation may confer.

Consider the selective effect of self-esteem on some of the different ways a person can participate in politics. Table 7:3 presents the relationships between the three components of self-esteem and the individual items of the Participation scale. Note that the analysis of the Participation index (Table 7:2) and of the individual items in the index (Table 7:3) lead to a similar conclusion: interpersonal competence has more of an effect on more aspects of participation than do status inferiority and personal unworthiness.

In addition, the data in Table 7:3 suggest that the clearest effect of interpersonal competence is to enable a person to make contact with those in politics. The point of contact may be a political leader or a political group, and to make contact may require writing a letter or attending a meeting; however that may be, possessing a sense of social competence sharply increases the chances of bridging the gap between the world of everyday activities and the world of politics, as the strength of the relationship between competence and the first two items of the participation index indicate. Conversely, a sense of personal unworthiness impinges most directly on participation by inhibiting the tendency to make contact with those in politics. The belief that one is not worthwhile, apparently, makes one averse to the idea of approaching others, though the strength of this aversion ought not to be exaggerated. It also is difficult to say how generalized this aversion is, though there is reason to believe it is confined to those who fall outside a person's immediate life space, for a sense of personal unworthiness has no noticeable impact on the readiness to talk about politics with family and friends, as Table 7:3 indicates.[10]

[10] It is also worth noting that those with a sense of personal unworthiness are more likely to report that they vote always, or nearly so. One

Table 7:3

THE RELATIONSHIP OF THE DIMENSIONS OF SELF-ESTEEM TO THE ITEMS IN THE POLITICAL PARTICIPATION INDEX (MB) (GAMMA)

Item	Inter-personal Competence	Personal Unworthi-ness	Status Inferi-ority
I have never written a letter to any political leader in connection with any political issue.	−.35	.16	.00
I have never been to a political meeting of any kind.	−.35	.16	.00
I often put signs or stickers on my house, lawn, or car in support of candidates for political office.	.02	−.08	−.16
I make a special effort to hear the main radio speeches of candidates in a campaign.	.18	.06	.03
I have sometimes worn a button supporting the candidate I intend to vote for.	.13	.00	−.11
I try to get my family and friends to vote.	.12	−.07	.05
I vote at practically every election.	.13	.14	.02
I have belonged to organizations whose main purpose is to work for a better government.	.14	−.01	−.17
During a political campaign I try hard to talk my friends into voting for the man I support.	.15	−.03	−.17

A sense of status inferiority also has a selective effect on some aspects of participation, though here too it is worth keeping in perspective the strength of its impact, which falls, whenever it is discernible, somewhere between slight and moderate. This sense of social inferiority apparently restrains those afflicted with it from participating in ways that would

might suggest that the response stems from a desire to be perceived as in compliance with the norm of the political culture which calls for citizens to vote, and further, that this dimension of self-esteem is one source of the frequently noted "over-reporting" of voting.

openly and clearly identify their own preferences. Thus, it diminishes (though not very strongly) the chances they will wear a button which names their favorite candidate, try to persuade their friends to vote for a particular candidate, place sign or stickers on their house or car, or in other ways publicly advertise their preferences. It is as if they wish to conceal their political preferences, for fear their views will prove embarrassing or socially undesirable.

But of course political involvement can stretch far beyond the range of activities covered by the participation index. We have already noted the rough but useful distinction which can be drawn between the role of participant citizen and that of political activist or leader, and I would like to turn to consider the effect of self-esteem on political leadership.

"Political leadership" may be defined in a number of different ways. "Political leader" may refer to the occupant of a formal role at or near the top of a political hierarchy, or to one who holds an informal but nevertheless quite real position of dominance. As used in the PAB study, political leadership refers to a narrow stratum of political activists, operationally defined as those attending the national conventions of their parties. Obviously, not all who attended were leaders, but convention delegates are among the politically influential in America and represent a genuine, and perhaps central, facet of leadership in American politics.

Figure 7:1A, B, C and D display the mean scores and frequency distributions of the three sub-indices of self-esteem and of the overall index of self-esteem for the Leader and Follower samples.

Clearly, Leaders tend to have higher self-esteem than do Followers. The mean score on the overall index of self-esteem (where a high score is a sign of *low* self-esteem) for Leaders is 3.35, compared to 4.38 for the Followers. Leaders have lower scores than Followers on all three dimensions of self-esteem, but as is readily apparent, the critical dimension of self-regard which most sharply separates Leaders and Followers is interpersonal competence.

Figure 7:1A. The means and frequencies for the overall index of self-esteem for national leader sample and general population

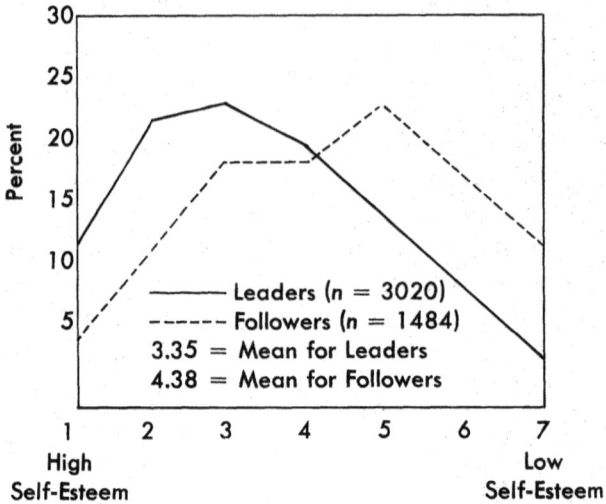

Figure 7:1B. The means and frequencies for the index of personal unworthiness for national leader sample and general population

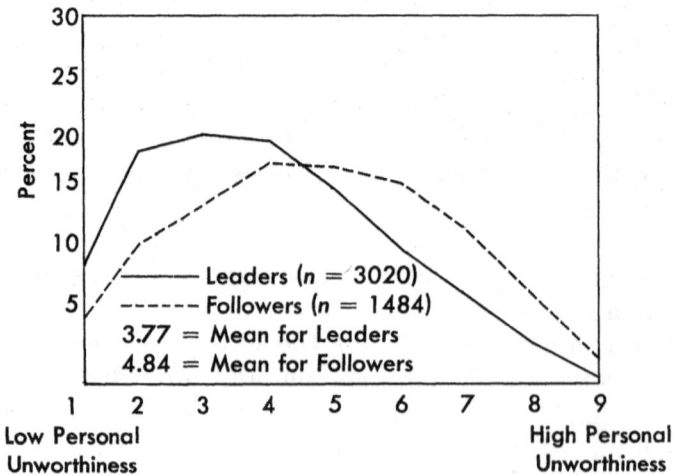

Figure 7:1C. The means and frequencies for the index of status inferiority for national leader sample and general population

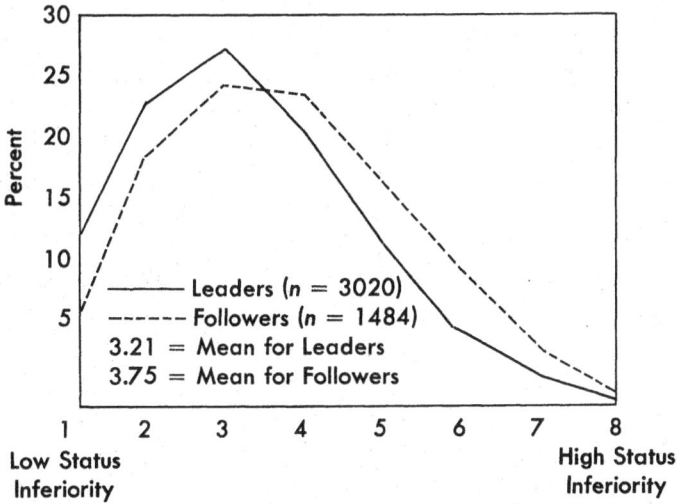

Figure 7:1D. The means and frequencies for the index of interpersonal competence for national leader sample and general population

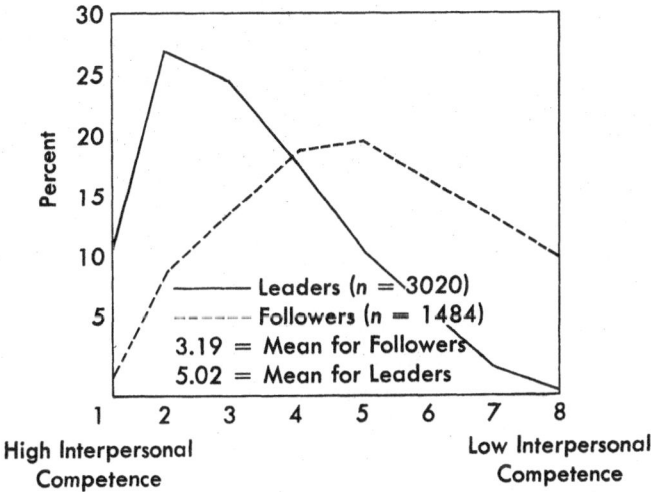

Figures 7:2A, B, C and D present the mean scores and frequency distributions of the overall index of self-esteem and of the three sub-indices of self-esteem for a sub-sample of Leaders and Followers who were precision matched with respect to four socio-demographic characteristics — education, income, occupational status and region (north-south). It is worth noting that the matching procedure was not merely designed to assure identical proportions in both sub-samples with respect to these social characteristics; rather, the sub-samples were so selected as to require that the *configuration* of these social characteristics was identical; for every Follower selected (at random), an exact counterpart (with respect to education and the like) was drawn from the Leader sample. In this way, variations in social background were controlled for, and whatever differences in psychological makeup remain are not "spuriously" related to differences in status between political Leaders and Followers.

As Figures 7:2A, B, C and D indicate, Leaders have only marginally higher self-esteem than Followers, after the influence of social factors is removed. These tables also show, however, that the critcal dimension of self-esteem still separating Leaders and Followers is interpersonal competence; it is this dimension of self-esteem, it will be recalled (Table 7:2), that most strongly affects the tendency of citizens to participate, in a limited way at least, in politics.

These findings run against the compensation hypothesis — in its standard version at least. And they buttress the earlier findings on more limited forms of political involvement and the basic contention I have been advancing as to the connection between personality and political involvement. This contention may be put as follows: political involvement is a learned form of social behavior, and whatever impedes the learning process it entails diminishes the chances of becoming politically involved.

The paradox of the compensation hypothesis — not to put too fine an edge on it — is that the personality factor thought to *motivate* a person to enter politics is very likely to be

Figure 7:2A. The means and frequencies for the index of self-esteem for the matched sample

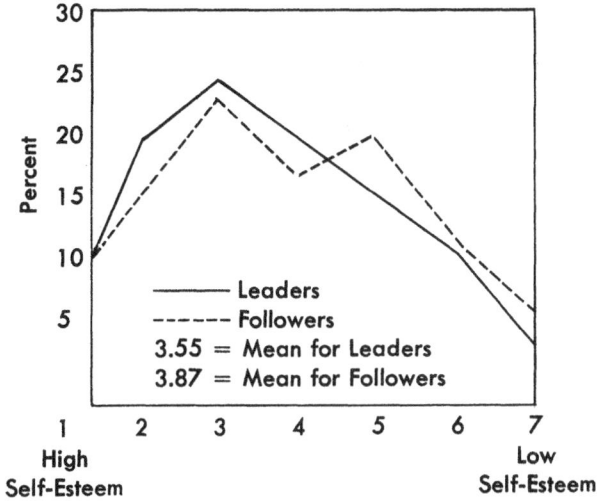

Figure 7:2B. The means and frequencies for personal unworthiness for the matched sample

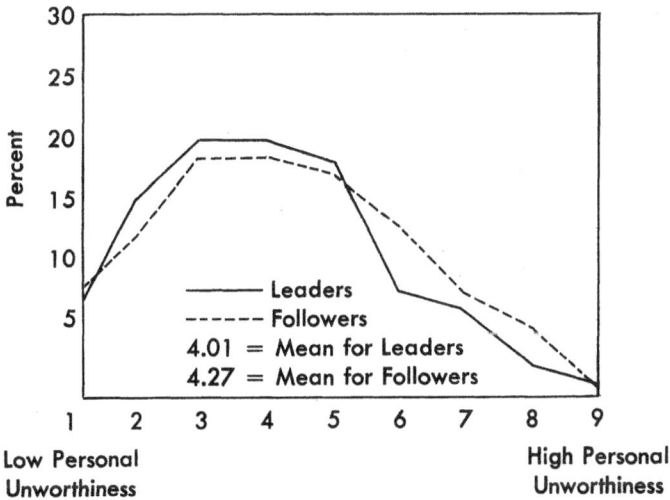

Figure 7:2C. The means and frequencies for status inferiority for the matched sample

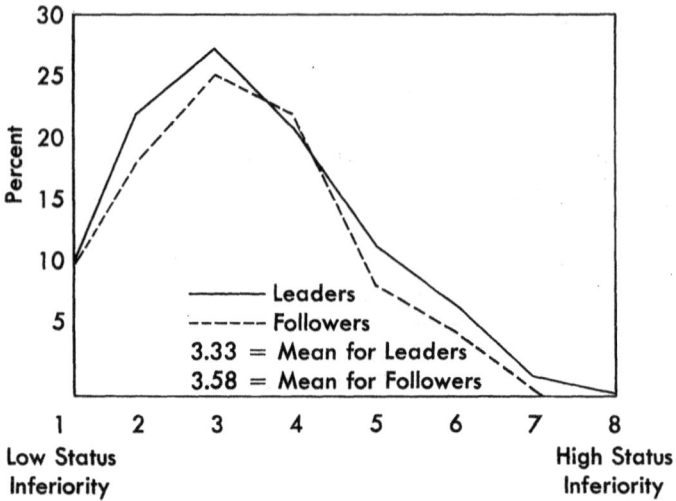

Figure 7:2D. The means and frequencies for interpersonal competence for the matched sample

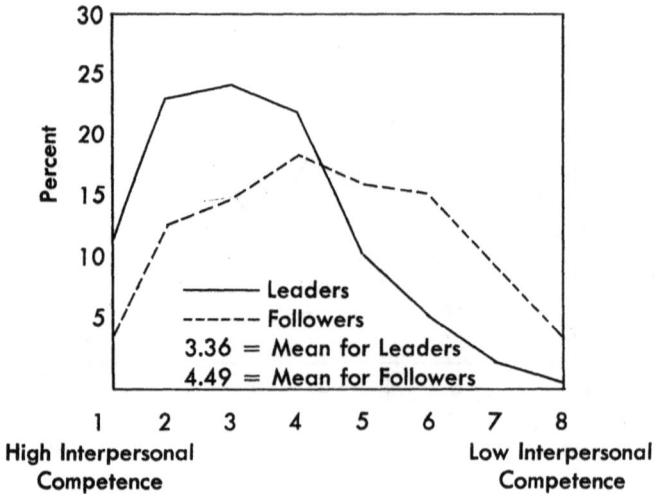

among the factors that frustrate his efforts *to learn* the skills and cues necessary. Even were we willing to assume that low self-esteem in a person has triggered a process of compensatory striving which has aroused a strong drive for power that can be met best, or met only, by entering politics, this person may easily fail to become politically active. Quite simply, there are relatively few cues to direct an individual to this course of action, and as I have argued many times over, low self-esteem is likely to diminish awareness of these cues.

To put the point more generally, psychological needs, even if they are strong and can be satisfied by only a few objects, regularly make themselves felt as relatively intense but vaguely defined states of stress or dissatisfaction.[11] This is most likely to be the case at and shortly after the point a need first emerges. Nevertheless, the object of such a psychological need remains to an appreciable degree permanently obscured, especially to the person harboring the need. Needs alone are insufficient to direct a man's actions: some learning is required. In particular, a man must learn of a specific end result (or consumatory act) which will satisfy his inner needs, and in addition, acquire knowledge and mastery of the particular steps he must take to attain his goals.

Now assume an individual has a strong desire to amass power. For him to enter politics, cues as to the goal and means are necessary: the drive itself is too indeterminate; it is cues which give a distinctive direction to men's strivings. We have no exact idea as to the number of cues which might direct men's attention to politics, their clarity, their frequency, or their saliency. But the mounting body of data on mass publics strongly suggests that such cues by and large occur infrequently, are perceived by only a few persons, and elicit a response from even fewer. What is more, insofar as

[11] For a theoretical discussion of this point, focused on the relationship between motivation and cognition, see George S. Klein, "Peremptory Ideation: Structure and Force in Motivated Ideas," in *Perception, Motives, and Personality* (New York: Alfred A. Knopf, 1970), pp. 357-412.

low self-esteem dampens political interest and inhibits the acquisition of political knowledge, those low in self-esteem ought to be less likely than those high in self-esteem to discriminate cues which would direct them into politics. In short, the very trait said to arouse a drive to enter politics interferes with the perception of the cues which direct a person towards 'politics.

Low self-esteem diminishes in other ways a person's chances of learning to do what it (presumably) motivates him to do. Even if low self-esteem were to arouse a drive to amass power, the person with low self-esteem is unlikely to make a successful entrance into politics or to stay at it very long, for low self-esteem itself tends to be an obstacle to the acquisition of skills a person needs in political life. Thus, the person with low self-esteem is likely to be timid, retiring, and lack the interpersonal skills to do well in political life. As Lasswell has earlier observed, success in a political career places a premium on the ability to form and maintain close personal relationships, a fair measure of flexibility and a high capacity to tolerate uncertainty, an ability to co-operate with others and to elicit their trust and respect, a capacity for reality perception, and the like.[12] In short, the personal characteristics which promote success in politics are precisely those a person low in self-esteem is likely to lack.

The assumption that low self-esteem tends to arouse a drive to enter politics is a dubious one. Even if we were willing to assume that low self-esteem implants a need for power, it is not at all clear that such a need on the average can be met best, or be met at all, by entering politics. Influence is unequally distributed in politics, and it is by no means obvious that the limited and often evanescent influence that

---

[12] Lasswell was speaking not of self-esteem but of power-orientation, presumably the intervening variable. See Harold D. Lasswell, "The Selective Effect of Personality on Political Participation," in Richard Christie and Marie Jahoda, eds., *Studies in the Scope and Method of "The Authoritarian Personality"* (Glencoe, Ill.: The Free Press, 1954), pp. 216-225.

the majority of men in public life possess, or can expect to obtain, is a sufficiently strong incentive to draw them into politics. As a consequence, there is no compelling reason to believe that holding a political office consistently offers better opportunities for self-aggrandizement than occupying a position of comparable status in, say, a business firm.[13]

In any event there is little reason to believe that participation in politics is of instrumental value in resolving a process of compensatory striving stimulated by low self-esteem, whether or not compensation lends to an emphasis on attaining or maintaining power. Clearly, the compensation hypothesis refers to a process which takes place over time: the individual is first seized by a sense of inferiority and personal inadequacy, invariably at an early period in life; then, with varying degrees of success, he overcomes these distressing feelings by compensatory striving for power or some other value. There is, in other words, a developmental process at work.

But this developmental process does not stretch over an indefinite period of time. The person who must find the means to deal with damaged self-esteem obviously would prefer to do so sooner rather than later. Now compensation, when it does occur, may involve a rather complex, continuing process of adjustment and re-adjustment as the individual works out a solution appropriate to the unique problems and opportunities posed by major stages in the developmental process. Yet it seems reasonable to assume that only a few of those with low self-esteem are likely to seize on a political career as a way to cope with their unfavorable self-attitudes, if only because the whole process begins so early in the developmental sequence. For most, politics acquires some psychological importance only as they approach adulthood. By this time, the individual who was faced with

[13] This is a concession Lasswell and others explicitly make in the distinction they draw between a functional and a conventional definition of politics, a distinction, however, that I am unable to make operational use of. See Lasswell, "The Selective Effect of Personality on Political Participation," p. 203.

a serious inner conflict, in all likelihood, has already developed and become attached to a set of preferred ways to cope with the intense and distressing pressures low self-esteem arouses. The opportunity or incentive to participate in politics usually comes too late to serve as a popular path to deal with the problems of self-esteem.[14]

It is also worth noting that the results of Figures 7:1A, B, C, and D not only run counter to the compensation hypothesis, they also undermine *the hypothesis of surplus energies*. That hypothesis, as set out above, contends that the inhibitory effect of low self-esteem on political involvement is a function of the depletion of energy available to the ego. According to this hypothesis, low self-esteem is a sign that the personality, for whatever reasons, must invest much of its resources into essentially defensive operations against a forbidden impulse or inner conflict which threatens to erupt. Investment of energy in massive defensive operations requires a large withdrawal, so to speak, from the fund available to the ego, leaving a balance too precarious to sustain activity in areas of secondary or even tertiary interest to the personality such as politics. High self-esteem, by contrast, is a sign of ego strength (or psychological integration). Free of the need to erect a costly set of defenses, the person with high self-esteem enjoys a surplus of energy, which he is free to expend as he pleases in political activity if he chooses.

The argument could be elaborated, but the metaphor at its center is straightforward and even persuasive to a point. But if the hypothesis of surplus energies is sound, then variations in a sense of personal unworthiness ought to best discriminate between the politically active and the passive citizen, for it is the dimension of self-esteem which most

[14] There are exceptions to this rule, of course, the most obvious of which is when politics is of uncommon salience to the parents of a developing child. In this respect, it is worth noting the importance the Georges attach to cues in Wilson's family milieu, which at a very early point oriented him towards politics. Alexander and Juliette L. George, *Woodrow Wilson and Colonel House* (New York: Dover Publications, Inc., 1964), Appendix.

directly taps the kind of inner conflict likely to drain energy from the ego. The high scorer on the personal unworthiness index is characteristically a person afflicted by a strong sense of guilt, unable to accept impulses within himself which, in his eyes, are unwholesome. In this sense, personal unworthiness is more deeply psychological than social inferiority and interpersonal competence, for it penetrates to a layer of impulse and conflict which is well below the surface of the personality, where an individual often cannot bring himself consciously to acknowledge the desires he feels.

The data are clearly counter to the hypothesis of surplus energies. Comparing first the participant citizen and the passive one (Table 7:2), we see there is little relationship between the personal unworthiness index and the political participation scale. Admittedly, there is some difference between Political Leaders and Followers (Figure 7:1 B). Nevertheless, personal unworthiness does not appear to be the critical dimension of self-esteem that separates leaders from followers, not certainly when compared to the far greater gap between them in terms of interpersonal competence (Table 7:1 D). To be sure, a sense of unworthiness does inhibit the chances of becoming a political leader, as do a number of basic psychological characteristics such as anxiety or inflexibility, for a number of reasons, among them possibly the damage it does to the psychological economy of the personality. But when Leaders and Followers are matched on social characteristics, the critical dimension of self-esteem on which they differ is plainly interpersonal competence (Figure 7:2 D) and not personal unworthiness (Figure 7:2 B) or social inferiority (Figure 7:2 C). In sum, self-esteem (or an aspect of it, such as a sense of personal effectiveness) does indeed affect the chances of political involvement, but in the main for reasons other than those the hypothesis of surplus energies would suggest.

More generally, political involvement hinges on competence rather than compensation. Individual differences in self-esteem influence the chances of political involvement, an influence which grows in strength as involvement increases in intensity. The more directly a dimension of self-esteem affects the acquisition of competence necessary for involvement, the stronger its influence. In short, the compensation hypothesis, as formulated by Lasswell, is in error. It is not empircally true that low self-esteem tends to drive men into politics to obtain power in order to compensate for their sense of inferiority, however plausible this reasoning may sound in the abstract. To be sure, low self-esteem in individual cases may propel some into political life, but as a rule it has exactly the opposite effect: to *inhibit* rather than stimulate political involvement.

A variation of the compensation hypothesis may be tenable even if the standard version of it is not, so we shall now examine the several variations of the compensation hypothesis Chapter 6 laid out.

Variations on a Theme

A person's self-evaluation, particularly of his ability to deal with others, affects the likelihood of his becoming politically involved. But the relationship is certainly not so strong as to preclude persons with low self-esteem from becoming active in politics; obviously, large numbers do. An important question, then, is why some men with low self-esteem become politically active, and others do not.

Let us distinguish two types of factors which can lead persons low in self-esteem to participate. The first comprises variables which induce all to participate, *regardless of their level of self-esteem*; the second comprises variables which stimulate political involvement *only among those low in self-esteem*.

Table 7:6 presents a selection drawn from the MB study of the first type of variables. All are familiar, and the reasons why they stimulate participation are well known. The table shows four groups:[15] those low in interpersonal competence and high on the Political Participation scale, those low on

---

[15] "High" and "Low" in every instance refer to scale scores which have been trichotomized.

Table 7:4

A COMPARISON BETWEEN THE POLITICALLY ACTIVE AND INACTIVE WITH DIFFERING LEVELS OF INTERPERSONAL COMPETENCE WITH RESPECT TO VARIABLES STIMULATING POLITICAL ACTIVITY (MB STUDY)

% High on Variables Stimulating Political Activity	Low Inter-personal Competence		High Inter-personal Competence	
	(n = 115) Politically Active %	(n = 182) Politically Inactive %	(n = 130) Politically Active %	(n = 68) Politically Inactive %
Political Disinterest Scale	24	48	6	27
Party Loyalty Scale	37	23	41	15
Political Futility Scale	49	70	9	35

both scales, those high on both scales, and those high on interpersonal competence and low on participation.

The question I am posing is why some persons who in some sense[16] have low self-esteem participate in politics, while others do not. Obviously, as Table 7:6 shows, in some measure they participate for much the same reasons that others do. For example, those who participate are more likely to have developed an interest in politics, regardless of their level of interpersonal competence. Among those with little confidence in their competence, those who are less politically active are twice as likely to score high on a measure of political disinterest as those who participate. And among those with a strong sense of their interpersonal competence, 6% of the politically active are high on political disinterest, compared to 27% of the less active. Similarly, those who participate tend to have stronger emotional attachments to the party and to be better educated than do those who are inactive in politics, again regardless of their level of interpersonal competence.

[16] Our concern is with the interpersonal competence index rather than the overall index of self-esteem, because only this one dimension of self-esteem had a significant relationship with the participation index in the MB study.

Nothing very surprising appears in Table 7:4, for the role these factors play in promoting political involvement is well established. But the data in Table 7:5 are another matter. There we see how a number of psychological factors — rigidity, obsessiveness, aspiration-ambition, and the like — affect political participation.

Obsessiveness, to take an example, *encourages* participation among those with a low sense of interpersonal competence: 47% of those who participate score high on a measure of neurasthenic obsessiveness, compared to 34% who are inactive. Yet obsessiveness has no effect on participation among those who have a firm sense of interpersonal competence. Rigidity also *encourages* participation among those with low interpersonal competence (as does intolerance of ambiguity to a lesser extent), but among those with a sense of competence the relationship *reverses* direction and rigidity inhibits political participation.

Of equal interest is the Material Aspirations scale. This five-item scale assesses the degree of importance a person attaches to accumulating money, expensive objects, and in

Table 7:5

A COMPARISON BETWEEN THE POLITICALLY ACTIVE AND INACTIVE WITH DIFFERENT LEVELS OF INTERPERSONAL COMPETENCE WITH RESPECT TO OBSESSIVE-COMPULSIVENESS

% High on Scales Measuring Aspects of Obsessive-Compulsiveness	Low Inter-personal Competence		High Inter-personal Competence	
	(n = 115) Politically Active %	(n = 182) Politically Inactive %	(n = 130) Politically Active %	(n = 68) Politically Inactive %
Obsessiveness	47	34	41	40
Rigidity	49	39	29	38
Intolerance of Ambiguity	51	45	25	21
Material Aspirations	54	36	38	47
Aspiration-Ambition	50	33	53	42

general a large stock of worldly goods. A sample item reads "I must admit I put a pretty high value on material things." Again we see material aspirations stimulates participation among those low in interpersonal competence: 54% of politically active citizens score high on this scale, compared to 36% of those who are relatively inactive. Among those with a strong sense of competence, however the relationship is the other way around: 38% of the politically active, as compared to 47% of the inactive, score high. The Aspiration-Ambition scale assesses a somewhat similar, though not identical, factor. This scale provides a rough measure of the strength of a person's desire for fame, distinction, elevation. Again we see that among those with little sense of social competence, aspiration-ambition is a spur to participate: 50% of the politically active, but only 33% of the inactive, score high on this scale; and although the relationship is in the same direction among those high in interpersonal competence, it is substantially weaker.

Observe the relationship of this second set of factors to political participation in the entire sample, which appears in Table 7:6. As is apparent, all but one of these psychological factors have a negligible relationship to political participation. Certainly these factors as a rule provide no strong stimulus to participate. Aspiration-Ambition does further participation but the strength of its impact is, at best, slight. The relationships between participation and these psychological factors are weak or non-existent.

These factors, then, do not normally increase political participation. But in combination with a lack of interpersonal competence there is an interaction effect and a characteristic such as rigidity encourages rather than inhibits involvement in politics.

These data, then, suggest that low self-esteem (or a certain aspect of it) may promote political activity when it is combined with certain other psychological characteristics, even though these, taken by themselves, may dampen a desire to become active in politics, just as low self-esteem usually does.

Table 7:6

THE RELATIONSHIP OF SELECTED PSYCHOLOGICAL
CHARACTERISTICS AND POLITICAL PARTICIPATION (MB STUDY)

Characteristic	Political Participation
Obsessiveness	.09
Rigidity	.04
Intolerance of Ambiguity	.08
Material Aspirations	.04
Aspiration-Ambition	.15

The exact psychological dynamism at work here is difficult
to pinpoint, but it appears to be closely connected to compulsiveness or obsessional determination.[17] Consider the various
personality characteristics which appear to play some role.
There is, evidently, a fusion between certain aspects of
inflexibility on the one side and a strong drive for recognition
and distinction on the other. It is this fusion which underlies
the incessant striving so characteristic of the compulsive
dynamism. Thus, the Rigidity and Obsessiveness scales
assess, among other things, the belief that one should set
a high standard for oneself and others should do the same
and that when one has started a job, one ought to see it
through to the end. There is a species of conscientiousness
here, a feeling one ought to let nothing interfere with or
interrupt one's work. There is also a strong desire for control
evident, for example, in the insistence that things be "carefully planned and organized," in the resistance to "doing
things impulsively, on the spur of the moment," and in the
aversion to the disorderly or unexpected — an effort, in effect,
to impose an order and discipline on the world. The Aspiration-Ambition and Material Aspiration scales bring out the
strong drive for recognition and distinction, which is an

---

[17] See the discussion of "obsessive-compulsive" in David S. Shapiro,
Neurotic Styles (New York: Basic Books, 1965), pp. 25-53. Also see Otto
Fenichel, *The Psychoanalytic Theory of Neurosis* (New York: W. W.
Norton and Company, Inc., 1945), pp. 268-311.

important element in the dynamism of compulsiveness.[18]

Compulsiveness involves a mixture of elements, one of which apparently is low self-esteem. These elements, including low self-esteem (or one aspect of it at least) by themselves encourage social withdrawal, or have no effect on political involvement, but in combination, they can propel a person into politics. It is not hard to see how the compulsive dynamism, with its stress on striving, persevering, attaining control, and meeting high standards of achievement and moral character, might stimulate political activity, though we have yet to see that it is a drive of sufficient strength to move men to become political leaders.

Table 7:7 presents data from the PAB studies bearing on *the compulsiveness hypothesis* comparable to the data presented in Table 7:5 from the MB study. In this case, however, the comparison is between political leaders and followers (who are 'matched' in their social characteristics) rather than between politically active and inactive citizens.[19] These data lend further support to the notion that it is compulsiveness which in part explains why low self-esteem on occasion stimulates involvement in politics rather than inhibiting it as it usually does.

The Inflexibility index is a composite measure of three scales — Intolerance of Ambiguity, Obsessiveness, and Rigidity. Consequently, it is a handy, if rough, gauge of an important facet of compulsiveness. Looking only at those with low self-esteem, we see that political leaders are much more likely to show signs of psychological inflexibility: 70%

[18] On this point see Alexander L. George, "Some Uses of Dynamic Psychology in Political Biography," in Fred I. Greenstein and Michael Lerner, eds., *A Sourcebook for the Study of Personality and Politics* (Chicago: Markham, 1971), pp. 79-98.

[19] Since Leaders and Followers differ with respect to all three dimensions of self-esteem, the overall index of self-esteem is used here and not merely one of its components as in the MB study. It should be noted that the data were also analyzed comparing persons high and low in interpersonal competence, exactly as done for the MB study, and the results are identical to those reported in Table 7:8.

Table 7:7

A COMPARISON BETWEEN "MATCHED" LEADERS AND FOLLOWERS WITH RESPECT TO SELECTED ASPECTS OF OBSESSIVE-COMPULSIVENESS—FOR PERSONS LOW IN SELF-ESTEEM AND PERSONS HIGH IN SELF-ESTEEM

% High on Measures of Obsessive- Compulsiveness	Low Self-Esteem		High Self-Esteem	
	Leader (n = 182) %	Follower (n = 243) %	Leader (n = 186) %	Follower (n = 150) %
Inflexibility	70	58	32	27
Aspiration-Ambition	48	28	37	27

of Leaders score *high* on the index of Inflexibility, compared to 58% of the Followers. Among those with high self-esteem, Leaders are also more likely to score high on inflexibility, but here the margin of difference between leaders and followers has been so reduced as to be nearly insignificant in size: 32% of the Leaders and 27% of the Followers score high on the Inflexibility index.

The pattern for the Aspiration-Ambition scale is virtually the same. Among those with low self-esteem, there is a very considerable difference running in the expected direction between leaders and followers. Thus, approximately 48% of Leaders score high on the Aspiration scale, compared to 28% of Followers. Among those with high self-esteem, however, the margin of difference is greatly reduced: 37% of Leaders, and 27% of Followers, score high on the Aspiration-Ambition scale.

These data, then, suggest something on the order of a catalytic reaction between low self-esteem and other psychological elements which together form the compound of compulsiveness. This reaction tends to propel men into political life, and any explanation of this tendency should not focus on one element of the compound, say, low self-esteem, to the exclusion of all other elements. It is the compound of these elements—or the dynamism of compulsiveness, if you will—which provides the critical stimulus, not merely one or another of its constituent elements.[20]

A variation of the compensation hypothesis, proposed by Lasswell himself, which hinges on the notion of an interaction among psychological attributes is *the mixture hypothesis*. Like the compulsiveness hypothesis, the combination hypothesis holds that there is an interaction. The interaction, however, is not between self-esteem and other psychological attributes as in the compulsiveness hypothesis; rather, it is between different dimensions of self-esteem. This hypothesis asserts, in effect, that it is a combination of favorable and unfavorable self-attitudes which generates the motive force to enter politics.

The data offer a trace of evidence supporting the mixture hypothesis. Among respondents with a weak sense of interpersonal competence no differences of consequence appear; however, among those with a strong sense of effectiveness when dealing with others, those who are politically active are more likely than those who are inactive to express feelings of social inferiority. As Table 7:8 shows, among the M. B. sample, 44 percent of the politically active score high on the Status Inferiority measure, compared to 26 percent of the politically inactive. I shall shortly comment on what I suspect is at work here, but for now two comments should suffice. First, no comparable result occurs if we compare

---

[20] My argument here seems congruent with the Georges' interpretation of Wilson, though there may be some difference of terminology and emphasis. What stands out about Wilson is the whole dynamism of his compulsiveness or obsessional determination (or as the Georges may prefer to put it, his compensation for his damaged self-esteem) and not merely, or even primarily, his low self-esteem. My data, then, may be interpreted as providing some support for the hypothesis of compensatory striving, though I should stress that the *main effect* of low self-esteem is exactly the opposite. Only under specific and limited circumstances is there evidence of an interaction, and then it offers some insight into why some with low self-esteem become involved in politics and others do not; it does not explain why those with low self-esteem are less likely to become politically active than those with high self-esteem.

leaders and followers (matched in socio-demographic characteristics). Second, it is worth noting that it is the two
dimensions of self-evaluation that bear most directly on one's
relationship with others which have an effect on participation, while a sense of personal unworthiness, which is less
socially oriented and more deeply psychological, makes very
little difference.

Up to this point we have considered interactions of two
kinds: between self-esteem and other psychological characteristics and among three dimensions of self-esteem itself.
Now let us turn to interactions of a third kind — between
psychological and social-situational characteristics. One
hypothesis centered on this type of interaction is *the discontinuity hypothesis*. It focuses on the interaction between
personal motives and social pressures that political recruitment generates. As outlined in Chapter 6, this hypothesis
holds that entering public life frequently involves so sharp

Table 7:8

**A COMPARISON BETWEEN THE POLITICALLY ACTIVE AND THE
POLITICALLY INACTIVE, WITH DIFFERING LEVELS OF
INTERPERSONAL COMPETENCE, ON MEASURES OF SELF-ESTEEM**

Measures of Self-Esteem (dichotomized)	Low Interpersonal Competence (MB) % High		High Interpersonal Competence (MB) % High	
	Politically Active (n = 115)	Politically Inactive (n = 182)	Politically Active (n = 130)	Politically Inactive (n = 68)
Personal Unworthiness	50	53	11	13
Status Inferiority	18	16	44	26
	PAB-Leaders[a] (n = 279)	PAB-Followers (n = 328)	PAB-Leaders (n = 367)	PAB-Followers (n = 318)
Personal Unworthiness	26	31	52	56
Status Inferiority	44	45	54	54

[a] PAB-Leaders and PAB-Followers for Matched Sample.

a break with one's past as to disproportionately attract those high in self-esteem and those low in self-esteem; further, it holds that though both of these types can manage the strain associated with entering politics, they are able to do so for very different reasons: those with high self-esteem have a greater tolerance for it because of their confidence in themselves and expectations of success, while those with low self-esteem have a stronger motive to endure the strain because of their need to obtain approval and to escape from lives they find dreary and frustrating, and which, more importantly perhaps, fail to give them a sense of being personally adequate or important or worthwhile.

Table 7:9 presents the magnitude of the variance for the three components of self-esteem and the overall index for the full Leader and Follower samples, and Table 7:10 for "matched" Leaders and Followers. The discontinuity hypothesis predicts, of course, that political leaders are drawn disproportionately from the extremes of the continuum of self-esteem; it follows that the variance of self-esteem among political leaders ought to exceed the variance among followers.

It is immediately evident that the data fail to confirm the discontinuity hypothesis. Rather than the variance in self-esteem being greater among leaders than followers, it is the other way around. The reason for this is readily apparent. The discontinuity hypothesis, as Barber argued it, suggests that politics disproportionately draws persons from the two extremes of self-esteem; there is, in other words, a bimodal distribution. But rather strong social and psychological pressures tend to work against the recruitment of those with low self-esteem, as we have already seen. The result, of course, is that the distribution of self-esteem among political leaders, as compared to that of the general population, tends to be skewed upwards.

The status (or mobility) hypothesis also focuses on the interaction of self-esteem and social pressures, but in this instance, it is not the passage into politics but a loss, or

Table 7:9

A COMPARISON BETWEEN THE VARIANCE IN SELF-ESTEEM AMONG ALL LEADERS AND FOLLOWERS

Leaders (n = 3020) Variance		Followers (n = 1484) Variance
2.49	Self-Esteem Index	2.80
3.15	Personal Unworthiness	4.08
2.17	Status Inferiority	2.54
2.34	Interpersonal Competence	3.29

Table 7:10

A COMPARISON BETWEEN THE VARIANCE IN SELF-ESTEEM AMONG THE MATCHED LEADERS AND FOLLOWERS

Matched Leaders (n = 646) Variance		Matched Followers (n = 646) Variance
2.53	Self-esteem index	2.71
3.34	Personal unworthiness	3.79
1.98	Status inferiority	2.46
2.52	Interpersonal competence	3.41

the threat of a loss, in status which generates these pressures. There is an element of ambiguity as to the exact nature of the interaction of social events and psychological characteristics which may take place. Usually, the status hypothesis runs more or less as follows: a precipitate decline in status, or the imminent threat of such a decline, arouses a strong need for status, a desire to retain or to win back one's social position, which in turn may lead to involvement in politics, particularly if a status-oriented movement exists to crystallize these sentiments. On occasion, however, the hypothesis is put in a slightly different way. Then it asserts that a drop in status (or the threat of it) may excite political involvement, depending on the person's psychological vulnerability to such changes in social status. The greater that vulnerability, the more likely the person is to become active in politics.

This hypothesis cannot be put to a fair test here. As it is usually formulated, the hypothesis is meant to apply to large-scale status shifts, where large numbers of persons belonging to a common social group (for example, middle-class professionals) are displaced from their position in the social order, or perceive themselves to be so displaced, and hold the society responsible. As it happens in the period when the present data were collected, by far the largest number in the sample had experienced a rise in status (as compared to their parents) and downward mobility on the whole was an infrequent occurrence.

Table 7:11 shows the relationship between social mobility and self-esteem. Downward mobility and low self-esteem which many observers would expect to be strongly related, are to all intents and purposes unrelated. As we noted earlier, self-evaluation in the normal course of affairs at least is more or less independent of one's particular position in the society, though of course there assuredly are times, societies, and social groups where this is not so. There is, however, a relationship between social mobility and political participation: a push down the social ladder apparently provides a push to get into politics, as Table 7:12 shows, though again it should be noted that these data are drawn from only one point in time, and it is not hard to imagine that in other circumstances social mobility might be a weaker (or stronger) stimulus to political involvement.

Of particular interest, however, is the interaction among mobility, self-esteem, and political participation presented in Table 7:13. Focusing on those whose social status was either worse than or the same as their parents, we see that whether they become politically active depends in part on their sense of interpersonal competence. Among those who feel themselves to be effective in dealing with others, 30%

Table 7:11

THE RELATIONSHIP BETWEEN INTERGENERATIONAL MOBILITY AND SELF-ESTEEM (MB STUDY ONLY) (PERCENTAGE DOWN)

Self-Esteem	Better off than Parents (n = 772) %	Same (n = 252) %	Worse off than Parents (n = 49) %
High	37	35	31
Middle	17	25	25
Low	46	40	45

Table 7:12

THE RELATIONSHIP BETWEEN INTERGENERATIONAL MOBILITY AND POLITICAL PARTICIPATION (MB STUDY) (PERCENTAGE DOWN)

Participation	Better off than Parents (n = 772) %	Same (n = 252) %	Worse off than Parents (n = 49) %
Low	33	38	22
Middle	34	31	27
High	33	31	51

of the politically active have failed to rise above their parents' status, compared to 18% of the politically inactive. However, among those who feel themselves to be *in*effective in dealing with others, there are virtualy no differences between the politically active and inactive.

These data suggest that the mobility hypothesis may have some validity, provided that it is substantially reformulated. Where the norm is a rise in status, a failure to rise or an actual decline in status can serve as a stimulus to political involvement. It is likely to elicit such a reaction, however, only among those who have confidence in themselves and who believe, therefore, they are able to better their position. The painful experience of failing to meet their status expectations is unlikely to move those who lack confidence in

Table 7:13

*A COMPARISON BETWEEN THE POLITICALLY ACTIVE AND THE
POLITICALLY INACTIVE WITH DIFFERING LEVELS OF INTERPERSONAL
COMPETENCE, ON INTERGENERATIONAL MOBILITY (MB)
(PERCENTAGE DOWN)*

	Low Interpersonal Competence		High Interpersonal Competence	
	Politically Active (n = 115)	Politically Inactive (n = 182)	Politically Active (n = 130)	Politically Inactive (n = 68)
Better off than Parents	67	71	69	82
Same	24	26	21	16
Worse off than Parents	8	2	9	2

themselves to take action, as we saw when we observed the interaction between interpersonal competence and status inferiority. A loss of status, then, will spark an interest in politics among those with self-esteem, not those who lack it.

One final hypothesis deserves consideration. Low self-esteem may inhibit political participation, but once a person (for whatever reason) becomes active in politics, do his unfavorable self-attitudes exert a decisive influence over his career in politics? Lasswell and others have suggested that aversive personality characteristics such as a fixation on power or compulsiveness tend to limit a person's political life chances, particularly (though not exclusively) in a democratic political system. Excessive anxiety, for example, leads to distortions in reality perception, compulsiveness to a lack of flexibility and adaptability, and hostility to the disruption of interpersonal relations. So Lasswell hypothesizes "Intensely power-centered persons tend to be relegated to comparatively minor roles." This we may call *the ceiling hypothesis.*

Table 7:14 presents the relationship between self-esteem and "political career." By the latter, I mean whether the person has won a public office, holds a party position, occupies a central role in party councils or a relatively peripheral one, and the like.

Table 7:14

THE RELATIONSHIP BETWEEN SELF-ESTEEM AND POLITICAL ROLE WITH PARTY CONTROL (PAB-L) (PERCENTAGE DOWN)

| | Self-Esteem | | | | | |
| | Low | | Middle | | High | |
Political Role	Republicans (n = 385)	Democrats (n = 635)	Republicans (n = 534)	Democrats (n = 740)	Republicans (n = 313)	Democrats (n = 413)
Hold Public Office Now						
Yes	59	54	61	57	68	57
No	30	42	35	41	31	40
Ever Held Public Office						
Yes	53	68	55	67	61	66
No	45	29	43	32	39	33
Party Position Held Now						
National	2	1	2	2	0	2
State Chairman	7	3	9	6	11	8
State Committee	11	4	9	8	13	7
County Chairman	21	15	19	14	17	16
County Committee	2	2	3	3	3	2
City	2	2	1	2	1	2
Ward	1	1	1	2	1	1
Village, Precinct, Town	4	7	4	4	7	5
Campaign Manager	0	0	0	0	0	1
Auxiliary Organization	4	3	4	2	4	2

| | Self-Esteem | | | | | |
| | Low | | Middle | | High | |
Political Role	Republicans (n = 385)	Democrats (n = 635)	Republicans (n = 534)	Democrats (n = 740)	Republicans (n = 313)	Democrats (n = 413)
Highest Party Position Held						
National	1	2	2	2	5	3
State Chairman	11	7	12	10	14	13
State Committee	11	8	8	9	12	7
County Chairman	27	20	21	17	20	22
County Committee	2	2	1	2	1	1
City	2	2	2	2	1	1
Ward	1	1	0	2	1	1
Village, Precinct, Town	2	4	3	3	3	2
Campaign Manager	0	1	2	1	1	2
Auxiliary Organization	7	5	8	4	10	5

As is apparent, variations in self-esteem make very little difference to political careers, at least insofar as the questions in Table 7:14 are a reliable guide. Those low in self-esteem are slightly less likely than those high in self-esteem to hold public office among Republicans, but the two differ only insignificantly among the Democrats. Again, among Republicans those low in self-esteem are slightly less likely to report they have ever held a public office, while among Democrats those low in self-esteem are more likely to say they have held public office at one time, but not significantly so.

Comparing the actual posts held in the party, we see persons low in self-esteem are somewhat less likely than those high in self-esteem in both parties to hold positions at the three highest levels[21] — national chairmen or committeemen, state chairmen, and state committeemen. But these differences are very slight in magnitude; what is more, these differences become even smaller if we turn from the question of the position a man now might hold and ask instead what was the highest position he has ever held.

Nor, apparently, does self-esteem affect political activity among political leaders, as Table 7:15 shows. In both parties, for example, virtually identical proportions of those high in self-esteem and of those low in self-esteem report working full-time in political activities. Nor are there any differences in terms of the numbers of hours they report giving each week to political activity, except among Republicans, and then the difference is not a great one.

In sum, individual differences in self-esteem evidently have little effect *among political leaders* on how high one rises in the party or public office or how hard one works for the party, though needless to say a more exhaustive battery of questions and analysis is necessary to explore all the possible connections between self-esteem and political careers.

The absence of a straightforward relationship between political careers and self-esteem has an interesting implica-

[21] No assumption should be made as to any one-to-one correspondence between formal level of position in the organizational hierarchy and organizational influence.

Table 7:15

THE RELATIONSHIP BETWEEN SELF-ESTEEM AND POLITICAL ACTIVITY WITH PARTY CONTROL (PAB-L) (PERCENTAGE DOWN)

| | Self-Esteem | | | | | |
| | Low | | Middle | | High | |
Political Activity	Republicans (n = 385)	Democrats (n = 635)	Republicans (n = 534)	Democrats (n = 740)	Republicans (n = 313)	Democrats (n = 413)
Full-Part Time Activity						
Full	9	14	6	12	11	13
Part	88	83	90	86	88	85
Hours per Week in Political Activity						
0–5	54	54	62	57	68	59
6–10	24	22	20	22	17	18
11+	23	24	19	21	15	23
Delegate-Alternate Previous Convention						
Delegate	49	60	49	60	54	64
Alternate	49	37	49	40	45	36

tion. Consider a possible objection to our finding that political leaders tend to have higher self-esteem than followers, even after removing the possibly contaminating influence of differences in their social characteristics. One might argue that leaders have higher self-esteem because, after all, they are leaders, persons in positions of influence and prominence, who by virtue of their stature enjoy social approval and rewards of all varieties. The objection asserts, then, that the higher self-esteem of political leaders may be a consequence of their assuming leadership roles, and not the other way around.

This objection is plausible to a point, but it is ultimately not persuasive. If it were sound, it would follow that the persons in politics with the highest self-esteem would be those in the highest places in politics, for surely they would receive more of the approval and rewards than would those who occupy the modest or lowly stations in the political order. If we consider our sample of "political leaders" it is obvious at once that it includes men of widely varying influence and prestige. At one extreme are the few who have a commanding say in the contest for the nomination and at the other the many who attend the convention in recognition of long years of faithful and, in the main, menial service to the party; and of course, there are the overwhelming numbers who fall at various points between the party chieftains and the party faithful. But as we have just seen, no indicator of these differences in prestige and power bears a relationship of any consequence to individual differences in self-esteem. These indicators (such as highest position held in the party) are admittedly crude but the results are consistent. There is good reason, then, to doubt that the higher self-esteem of the politically influential is a consequence rather than a cause of their involvement in politics.

The Clinical vs. the Actuarial Perspective:
A Last Look at the Compensation Hypothesis

Contrary to the compensation hypothesis, we have seen that political leaders tend to have higher self-esteem than ordinary citizens. But it may be objected that the compensation hypothesis has not been fairly tested because it has not been fairly stated. This objection deserves consideration.

I have spoken of low self-esteem leading to compensatory striving and so to an inclination toward politics. But the compensation hypothesis, as formulated by Lasswell and others, recognizes that the individual with low self-esteem may engage in compensatory striving, or alternatively, he may adopt the entirely different strategy of withdrawal. It may then be argued that the compensation hypothesis is meant to hold only for those who do compensate. And it should not be indiscriminately applied to all who have low self-esteem, regardless of whether they make attempts to compensate for damaged self-regard. Since this study lacks a measure indicating who has and who has not compensated, according to this argument, I have put the compensation hypothesis to the wrong test; I have lumped together all persons with low self-esteem rather than singling out those whose low self-esteem led them to compensate rather than withdraw.

Certainly, the compensation hypothesis does not contend that low self-esteem necessarily leads to compensatory striving; however, it does imply that low self-esteem frequently (and perhaps usually) leads to such striving. But what the compensation hypothesis suggests the facts of the matter are and what my analysis of the data shows them to be are quite different. As we saw in chapter 3, the person with low self-esteem characteristically feels that he lacks what it takes to succeed; that he ought to attempt only what he knows with certainty he can achieve for fear he is otherwise sure to fail; that he cannot properly comprehend or cope with the world in which he lives; that he feels unable to determine the outcome of events, unable certainly to influence the world of politics; that his work is hard and his spirits low; that he often feels uncomfortable in the company of others, unsure of what to say or do, afraid of making some mistake or gaffe. Surely, no one would claim this to be evidence of compensatory striving; on the contrary this syndrome is suggestive not of striving and activity, but of passivity, of acquiesence, of withdrawal. In short, I have not ignored the question of compensation. To judge by my data, damaged self-esteem is strongly related not to compensatory striving—as the compensation hypothesis implies—but to withdrawal and passivity. It may be argued that there are certain conditions under which low self-esteem leads to attempts at compensation. No doubt, there are.[22] But the fact remains that compensation for damaged self-esteem is the exception, not the rule.

Obviously some individuals with low self-esteem do compensate. Can we tell whether they are inclined toward politics — as the compensation hypothesis predicts — or by failing to distinguish them from those who do not compensate, have I made a fair test of the hypothesis impossible? Let us assume, for the sake of argument, the validity of the compensation hypothesis. Those compensating for damaged self-esteem, then, should turn up in disproportionate numbers in the Leader sample. Should this happen with any regularity, the distribution of self-esteem among political influentials ought to be bi-modal. For it would include disproportionate numbers of those high in self-esteem (to the extent that the competence hypothesis is valid) and of those low in self-es-

---

[22] The number of factors capable of determining whether power is used for compensatory purposes, to judge, at least, from Lasswell's discussion in *Power and Personality,* appears to be rather large indeed — for example, "ambitious and loving parents"; a sense of historical mission flowing from misfortunes of kin, clan, or country; elaborate requirements in childhood enforced with special intensity; "extremes of indulgence and deprivation" in the formative years; crisis conditions in modern society; the conflict inherent in middle-class values between demands on the self for both independence and dependence (the greater the conflict, the greater the extremities of indulgence and deprivation); status demands occasioned by mothers marrying "beneath" themselves, by groups or individuals holding "marginal positions" in their society, by "blighted careers"; by a wife's infidelity or by her death; actual or imaginary personal shortcomings, disfigurements, or illness or enforced inactivity especially in childhood. See Harold D. Lasswell, *Power and Personality* (New York: Viking Press, 1962), pp. 40-53. Of course, a hypothesis subject to so many exceptions is difficult to disconfirm — or to confirm.

teem (to the extent that the compensation hypothesis is valid). But as we have already seen, not only are self-esteem scores on the average higher among leaders than followers but the variance in these scores is significantly less among leaders than followers.

A second line of criticism contends that I have grossly over-simplified the compensation hypothesis and so not fairly tested it. Compensation for damaged self-esteem, as Lasswell and others are aware, does not automatically lead a person to a career in politics. Whether he strikes out for political office and influence depends also on his abilities, values, opportunities, and the like. Many variables intervene between compensatory striving and political involvement — for example, accenting power and other values especially appropriate to a life in politics — which I have, to all intents and purposes, ignored, Each of the variables in this complex process may be though of as a hurdle, and a person with low self-esteem is likely to enter politics only if he vaults them all. In short, by ignoring the complexities of the compensation hypothesis, I have made a "straw man" of a subtle argument.

This second line of criticism is wide of the mark, too. Consider the following two versions of the compensation hypothesis:

VERSION A

Low Self-Esteem→Power Motive→
 Political Involvement

VERSION B

Low Self-Esteem→Compensatory
Striving→Accentuation of
Power and other Values→
Skill Acquisition→Success
Experiences→Political
Involvement

For purposes of exposition, each version has the same, simple structure; each disregards possibilities of interaction; each takes account of one and only one causal chain. Now, assume that all links in the causal chain are of equal and exceptional strength. For convenience, suppose that the connection between each pair of variables immediately adjacent to one another is .5. Version B has 6 links in the causal chain, Version A but two. The critic has required, in effect, that the causal chain be lengthened so as to reflect with more fidelity the complexity of reality and to give the compensation hypothesis a fair trial. What, however, is a necessary consequence of this expansion of the causal chain? Quite simply, the correlation between the variables at either end of the chain — low self-esteem and political involvement — suffers a drastic decline in magnitude. In Version A of the hypothesis, granted our assumptions, the correlation between self-esteem and political involvement is $.5^2$, or .25, a correlation of considerable magnitude if actually observed between personality and actual behavior. In Model B, however, the correlation between low self-esteem and political involvement could not exceed $.5^6$, or rounded to two decimals, approximately .08. The price of inserting links in a causal chain is high, indeed. Nor can the problem be overcome by insertion of variables very highly intercorrelated, say, on the order of .8, for at that order of association, two variables become more or less the same thing, or at any rate, the actual value of each cannot be estimated independently because of among other things, the problem of multicollinearity. In short, the more complex a version of the hypothesis the critic insists is necessary, the weaker he acknowledges the relationship between low self-esteem and political involvement to be. Yet, however complex the version, the relationship should not be positive, which it in fact is, as we have seen.

A third line of criticism contends that the cross-sectional survey is a poor way to assess the compensation hypothesis, recommending instead the intensive study of individual lives. According to this argument, it is better to know a few people well than a great many superficially. To some students of personality and politics it seems plain that the more deeply an analyst delves into the details of a penetrating case study, the more likely he is to become aware of the exceedingly varied and frequently unique ways in which psychological dispositions find expression in individual lives. In their view, correlational analysis of large samples cannot do justice to the complexity and diversity of reality. To disentangle the true multiplicity of relationships — many of which may occur too infrequently to be detected in large samples — requires the case study approach, or so many contend. In short, the third line of criticism is prompted by a broader concern than the compensation hypothesis, for at bottom this criticism involves an argument for the superiority of the clinical over the actuarial approach.

My object is not to disparage the clinical approach. Plainly, it may be of inestimable value in the study of personality and politics. Nevertheless, I think the actuarial approach is better suited to the purpose of this study. My primary concern is to assess the validity of the compensation hypothesis (in all its versions). The actuarial approach tends to emphasize precise measurement, replicable procedures of observation (including selection of subjects), objective estimates of the direction and strength of relationships, and so forth. Not surprisingly, it is better suited to verifying hypotheses, while the clinical approach is better suited to suggesting hypotheses. All of this is familiar, though I should like to add one further point. It is precisely when researchers contend that the causal relations to be explored are exceedingly varied and complex — as they so frequently do when analyzing how psychological dispositions become translated into political behavior—that the actuarial approach becomes indispensable. On this point it is sufficient to note Jane Loevinger's trenchant comment:

> To say that in psychological research causes are manifold and complex is not to say that they do not exist or that they cannot be disentangled. To be realistic one must plan at the onset to contend with the basic fact that where there are many complex causes one must

expect the relations discovered to be numerically low.
There is no way of ascertaining low relations accurately
except through the use of a large number of cases.[23]

Perhaps the best prophylactic for criticism is a final statement of my findings. All I claim to have shown is that low
self-esteem tends to inhibit rather than encourage political
involvement. To the extent that the compensation hypothesis suggests the case is otherwise, it is wrong. Yet, low
self-esteem certainly does not preclude political involvement,
as my own results clearly indicate. Many with low self-esteem
become political activists and leaders, and many with high
self-esteem do not. Moreover, when low self-esteem is combined with various aspects of compulsiveness there is evidently a catalytic reaction. The outcome appears to be
something rather like obsessional determination. However
that may be, the insistence on achievement and high standards characteristic of this syndrome promotes political involvement. In short, under certain circumstances low self-esteem may incline a person toward rather than away from
politics. To the extent that this dynamism of compulsiveness
applies to many of the arguments advanced by Lasswell and
others, then the compensation hypothesis can be seen to have
an important element of truth to it. But the fundamental
point is evident. The actuarial method allows us to assess
whether low self-esteem typically leads to compensatory
striving and whether the latter, in turn, typically leads to
political involvement. Though this happens without question
in the lives of certain individuals, evidently low self-esteem
characteristically leads to passivity and withdrawal which,
in turn, characteristically inhibits involvement in politics.
In short, it is not that compensation does not occur—more
or less as the compensation hypothesis suggests. Rather, it
is that compensation does not characteristically take place
as many have supposed, and it makes all the difference to
learn that compensation is not the rule, but the exception
to it.

[23] Jane Loevinger, "Measuring Personality Patterns Women," *Genetic
Psychology Monographs* 65 (1962): 57.

Chapter 8 · CONCLUSIONS AND CONJECTURES

My concern has been to explore how individual differences in the ways in which people evaluate themselves affect the ways in which they embrace the democratic idea. Up to this point details of measurement and data analysis have been at the center of attention. Now I should like to consider some of the broader implications of the specific findings. For I believe these findings suggest certain marginal notes about larger questions in the study of personality and democratic politics. These notes are appropriately, and I hope usefully, modest. They are conjectures, not conclusions.

Political Extremism

The evidence seems plain, the conclusion obvious. Low self-esteem encourages a susceptibility to political extremism. Compared to those with high self-esteem, those with low self-esteem show markedly less tolerance, less support for procedural rights, less faith in democracy, and more cynicism about politics. They have a penchant for seeing conspiracies at work, a disenchantment with the established political order, an express desire for large-scale change by whatever means possible, at whatever cost necessary. They set little store by freedom of speech and assembly (unless it is theirs), the importance of diversity in an open society, the principle of equality. In sum, those with low self-esteem give evidence of a pronounced suspicion of — even a certain hostility toward — the democratic idea. Low self-esteem encourages extremist politics, or so it may appear.

Appearances can be deceptive. Low self-esteem works against democratic values; however, it need not work against democratic practice. To the extent that previous analysis of personality and political extremism has concentrated on the factor of motivation and overlooked that of social learning, it has presented a one-sided and possibly misleading picture. If we take account of questions of learning as well as pressures of motives, it becomes evident that the same psychological disposition may encourage extremist sentiments but discourage extremist politics. For example, a person low in self-esteem tends to be less attentive to politics and so less responsive to political cues — whether desirable or undesirable. Compared to the person with high self-esteem, he should be slower to learn of the emergence of a political demagogue, and less able to see the relevance of a demagogue's appeals to his own circumstances. To be sure, once aware of an extremist appeal, he may well be less likely to reject it than are persons with high self-esteem. Nonetheless, he is less likely to be exposed to such appeals, to pay attention to them, or to understand them.

Moreover, low self-esteem increases vulnerability to all the varieties of political extremism. As we saw in Chapter 5, a person with low self-esteem is more likely to embrace both extreme right-wing and extreme left-wing values. For example, he is at once likely to believe that the press is in the hands of left-wingers and that the laws of this country are "almost all 'rich man's laws.' " In short, he simultaneously takes his stand with extremist creeds at the very opposite poles of the ideological spectrum, a posture that is likely to prove not only awkward but self-defeating.

In addition, though low self-esteem encourages extremist views, it impedes political involvement. Thus, low self-esteem tends to weaken further the tenuous link between political attitudes and political behavior. More important perhaps, it inhibits the type of participation that is the key to being genuinely effective in a democratic society. When political scientists consider political participation, their attention is usually fixed on such *individual* actions as whether a person is likely to vote or to write a letter of complaint to an official or to contribute money to an election. But what counts most in democratic politics is what a citizen is able and willing to do with others, not what he is inclined to do on his own. As Tocqueville has remarked: "Among democratic countries . . . all the citizens are independent and feeble; they can hardly do anything by themselves, and none of them can oblige his fellow men to lend him their assistance. They all, therefore, become powerless if they do not learn voluntarily to help one another."[1] And the larger the political order becomes, the smaller the chances a citizen can influence the outcome of events by his independent actions. Now more than ever, "the art of association" becomes "the mother of action."[2]

The relationship between low self-esteem and political passivity therefore assumes additional significance. For low self-esteem not only impedes a citizen taking part in politics on his own — for example, by voting. More significantly, it inhibits him from taking part in politics with others. As we have seen, the individual with low self-esteem tends to avoid others, to be ill at ease in their company, to be reluctant to initiate or participate in conversation or social exchange, to be passive and withdrawn particularly in face-to-face contact with others who are unfamiliar to him or who in some way differ from him. Thus the very psychological needs that tend to motivate those with low self-esteem toward extremist politics tend to make it difficult for extremist movements to mobilize them.

Moreover, not only is a person with low self-esteem less likely to become active in politics, he is also less likely to become a leader in politics. His self-doubts stand in the way of attempting to lead a political organization or to organize one. He tends to lack the articulateness, assertiveness, and interpersonal skills necessary to advance himself or his cause

[1] Alexis De Tocqueville, *Democracy in America* (New York: Random House, 1945), vol. 2, p. 125.

[2] *Ibid.*, vol. 2, p. 115.

politically. And his lack of self-regard encourages an outlook likely to dampen or extinguish altogether his enthusiasm for political action. As he sees the world, few can be trusted and little can be done. Of course, I have painted a particularly dark picture of how the person with low self-esteem views the world, but he does tend to see the world of politics darkly or not at all. And his sense of political futility tends to undermine his chances of taking political action or gaining political power.

In short, the same personality trait which tends to make men strong advocates of extremist values tends to make them weak opponents of democratic institutions.

Elites and Masses

The irrationality of the mass emerged as a major theme in the group psychology of the late nineteenth century and the dynamic psychology of the early twentieth century. The mood then, as Rieff has pointed out, was conservative, pessimistic, and elitist, as psychological forces long hidden from awareness were increasingly uncovered and brought into sight.[3] Freud, Taine, and le Bon, among others, were struck by a new historical force: "the emotion of the masses."[4] Two themes became intertwined. The irrationality of the mass and the consequent fear of the mass, both of which are well illustrated in a letter written by Freud as a medical student in Paris: "The town and the people are uncanny; they seem to be of another species from us. I believe they are possessed of a thousand demons. . . . They are the people of psychical epidemics, of historical mass convulsions."[5] With the emergence of totalitarian politics, the fear of mass movements and mass politics deepened, the more so as classic studies of prejudice and civil liberties highlighted the role

[3] Philip Rieff, *Freud: The Mind of the Moralist* (Garden City, New York: Doubleday and Company, Inc., 1961), p. 249ff.

[4] *Ibid.,* p. 250ff.

[5] *Ibid.,* p. 250.

of the elite as a repository of democratic values.[6] By contrast, the mass appeared to be to political tinder, readily combustible.

Research on personality and politics has tended to deepen this fear of the mass. Indeed, as my own study has shown, the politically active and influential tend to have significantly higher self-esteem than does the average citizen. And to the extent that high self-esteem is a sign of psychological adjustment,[7] it might be argued that my findings add one further piece of evidence to the now classic theme of the relative irrationality of the mass. For my part, however, I think several findings of this study cast a somewhat different light on this classic problem.

I have considered one aspect of this problem in the discussion of personality and political extremism. But there is another aspect to consider — the relationship between personality and susceptibility to social influence. It is one thing to worry that low self-esteem may lead citizens to hold political values one regards as undesirable. It is quite another to worry that their emotional makeup makes them easy to manipulate politically. For if their psychological makeup renders them readily persuasible, then they may easily be caught up and tossed about by any sudden political storm. From this point of view what matters is not what ordinary citizens may believe but what they can be persuaded to believe.

This fear is far from specious. The experience of the thirties in Europe demonstrated the readiness of large numbers of

[6] See particularly, Herbert McClosky, "Consensus and Ideology in American Politics," *APSR* 58 (June 1964): 361-382; and Samuel Stouffer, *Communism, Conformity and Civil Liberties* (New York: Doubleday, Inc., 1955). For a recent dissent from this view based on a reanalysis of Stouffer's classic data see Robert W. Jackman, "Political Elites, Mass Publics, and Support for Democratic Principles," *Journal of Politics* 34 (Sept. 1972): 753-773.

[7] For a close examination of the extent of which this view is valid see Ruth Wylie, *The Self-Concept* (Lincoln: University of Nebraska Press, 1961).

citizens to embrace totalitarian ideologies. Of course, a variety of forces were at work but, no doubt, personality (and more specifically, authoritarianism) was among them. Authoritarianism as a dimension of personality, it is important to note, refers not to adherence to totalitarian values, but to "a *susceptibility* to anti-democratic propaganda."[8] Such a susceptibility is of special interest to us because of the long-established connection between low self-esteem and conformity. To the extent that low self-esteem leads men to submit to social pressure to conform to one set of political values and to insist that others conform to them too, it places the democratic idea in jeopardy.

The stronger the pressures for conformity, the greater the threat to diversity, to creativity, and ultimately to liberty itself. Increasingly, then, the danger to the democratic idea arises from the power of society and not that of the state to make men's convictions and conduct conform to a common mold, as John Stuart Mill argued in *On Liberty*:

> The circumstances which surround different classes and individuals, and shape their characters, are daily becoming more assimilated. . . Comparatively speaking, they now read the same things, go to the same places, have their hopes and fears directed to the same objects, have the same rights and liberties, and the same means of asserting them. . . And the assimilation is still proceeding. All the political changes of the age promote it, since they all tend to raise the low and to lower the high. Every extension of education promotes it, because education brings people under common influences, and gives them access to the general stock of facts and sentiments. Improvements in the means of communication promote it, by bringing the inhabitants of distant places into personal contact, and keeping up a rapid flow of changes of residence between one place and another. The increase of commerce and manufacture promotes it, by diffusing more widely the advantages of easy circumstances, and

---

[8] T. W. Adorno et. al., *The Authoritarian Personality* (New York: W. W. Norton and Company, Inc., 1950), p. 4. Italics are those of the authors.

> opening up all objects of ambition, even the highest, to general competition, whereby the desire of rising becomes no longer the character of a particular class, but of all classes. [And] a more powerful agency than even all these, in bringing about a general similarity among mankind, is the complete establishment, in this and other free countries, of the ascendancy of public opinion in the state.[9]

Men differ in their readiness to yield to established custom and public opinion. Low self-esteem in particular is thought to render a person susceptible to social influence. The person with low self-esteem lacks confidence in himself and in his opinions. As many experimental studies have shown, he is more likely to change his views if placed under social pressure, more ready to comply with social expectations, more likely to yield to social influence. He is more likely to be, in a word, a conformist.

Admittedly, to the extent that low self-esteem impedes social learning, it may lead a person to deviate from the official values of his society rather than conform to them. But the danger to the democratic idea remains; indeed, it may even be increased. For the individual is then unlikely to grasp the principle of democratic restraint and yet still insist on the urgency of conformity. He is all the readier, then, to join attacks on opinions that are unconventional or merely unfamiliar to him. He may be a conformist, without being a conformer.

Low self-esteem, it appears, encourages the desire for conformity and so threatens the principle of liberty. But on further thought the matter becomes more complex. It is plain that high self-esteem encourages the individuality and creativity that Mill so valued; however, it is by no means clear that low self-esteem promotes the societal mediocrity and conformity that Mill so feared.

Low self-esteem may not strongly foster the principles of diversity and creativity, but neither does it directly menace

[9] John Stuart Mill, *Utilitarianism* (New York: Meridian Books, 1962), pp. 203-204.

them. Mill and Tocqueville both feared that equality would promote uniformity. But democratic societies have generally proven to be pluralistic societies, comprising exceedingly diverse sentiments and social groups, rather than mass societies in which the largest number are more or less indistinguishable in conviction or vocation. In particular, one feature of American pluralism is the segmentation of society in such a way that only a relatively small fraction of citizens enters directly in the exchange of new ideas. The person with low self-esteem is little or no threat to commerce in this market-place of ideas, if only because low self-esteem so dulls his awareness of this market-place's existence or its daily activities.

The individual with low self-esteem may indeed favor conformity and may attempt to oppose ideas or practices which are novel or unfamiliar to him. But he is likely to prove a weak opponent, indeed, not because of the weakness of his desire to oppose diversity, but because of the poverty of his knowledge. Only when new ideas have won wide attention in the society is he likely to become aware of them. But by then those ideas will already have had the opportunity to win at least a foothold, and possibly even strong backing, among those in the society who pay attention to emerging ideas and who introduce and popularize fashions in opinion which the larger society tends — even if erratically — to follow. In short, low self-esteem makes it unlikely a person will frequent the market places for new and creative ideas, and thereby reduces the likelihood that he will impede the liveliness of the commerce in ideas on which both individual genius and social progress depend.

The root problem, of course, is broader than that of conformity, at least as Mill conceived it. What animated Mill was *fear for* genius; what has disturbed later observers more is *fear of* mass politics. The totalitarian movements of the twentieth century have dramatized the risks of mass politics — in particular, by revealing the apparent ease with which mass sentiments can be excited and manipulated. This problem cannot be considered in its entirety here, but the role that psychological characteristics such as low self-esteem are widely believed to play in it should be considered. The classic experimental studies of conformity and persuasibility show that low self-esteem increases the likelihood of yielding to social influence. Yet what many of our arguments to this point suggest is that it is precisely the person low in self-esteem who is the least likely to be susceptible to such influence, at least with respect to politics. The exercise of social influence depends on, among other things, the clarity of the transmission of socially approved standards. A person will tend to bring his behavior into line with such standards, other things being equal, as he becomes aware of (1) his departure from them; (2) the actions he must take to comply with them; and (3), the rewards and punishments contingent on compliance. But one consequence of low self-esteem is that it interferes with the reception of socially approved standards. Compared to the person with high self-esteem, the one with low self-esteem is more likely to deviate from these standards, despite his stronger desire to conform to them, because he is less likely to be aware of what the prevailing standards are; of whether he is actually deviating from them; of what he must do or avoid doing to bring himself into compliance; or of the rewards and punishments he may anticipate if he behaves in one way rather than in another. As we have seen, low self-esteem tends to diminish awareness and comprehension of socially approved standards, all the more effectively, in an area of life such as politics which is ordinarily not of great moment for the average citizen. In short, the person most willing to yield to social influence may often be the least susceptible to it. And both his desire to yield and his failure to do so may spring from the very same personality characteristic, low self-esteem.

However that may be, the contrast between political elites and ordinary citizens has been drawn increasingly sharply. Certainly, men drawn to political life are better informed about politics, more often articulate and aware, more interested in the important issues of the day, more deeply committed to the values of the American political culture and to the programs and philosophy of their party, and frequently better educated than ordinary citizens are.[10] As a consequence, political leaders, more often than the mass public, develop complex systems of ideas that permit them to organize large masses of information in terms of a manageable number of abstract categories and thereby to organize in a relatively consistent manner the variety of opinions they hold on specific subjects.[11] It is understandable, then, if some students of politics go on to draw the inference that political leaders, compared to the mass public, are more rational (in some sense of the term) and further, that personality, or more generally, non-logical "irrational" psychological forces, on the average have little effect on the political elite.

It is understandable, but it may well be wrong, or at least seriously misleading. In the data presented here, self-esteem appears to affect the opinions and values of political leaders as it does those of the general population. Certainly, self-esteem need not always have the same effect on leaders and followers. But we must not lose sight of the forest for the trees. On the whole, personality characteristics such as self-esteem appear to have much the same impact on the beliefs of elites as on those of citizens.

Self-esteem not only has much the same impact on political leaders and followers, it also affects their opinions in much the same way. Students of personality and politics traditionally have concentrated on the connection between personality and motivation. A person's beliefs or behavior have been explained in terms of the rewards experienced or anticipated for adopting a particular point of view or commiting a particular act. In this study, I have presented a different view of the connection between personality and belief, a view

[10] See for example, Philip E. Converse, "The Nature of Belief Systems in Mass Publics," in David Apter, ed., *Ideology and Discontent* (New York: Free Press, 1964).

[11] For this distinction see Carole Pateman, *Participation and Democratic theory* (Cambridge: Cambridge University Press, 1970).

intended to supplement, not replace, the viewpoint of previous research. Briefly, my aim has been to show that a personality characteristic can affect the acquisition of political opinions by affecting social learning as well as motivation. And as we have seen, this model of political learning applies as well to political leaders as to average citizens.

At a minimum, then, the findings of this study give us good reason to believe that the relevance of personality constructs is not limited to the analysis of mass politics. Personality characteristics such as self-esteem also play an important role in determining what political leaders believe, and very probably, how they behave.

Participatory Theories of Democracy

It has become increasingly fashionable to divde democratic theorists into two camps — one labeled elitist, the other participatory.[12] Up to this point, the contention between the two has turned on the values each supposedly promotes. But which of the two is the more satisfactory must depend in the end on the facts of the matter. All the facts are certainly not in hand, but some of my findings do sound a note of caution against certain claims advanced by participatory theories of democracy.

Before considering the evidence, I think it would be useful to state more clearly the difference between these two conceptions of democratic theory, particularly since the label "elitist" is both invidious and misleading. Both conceptions favor popular participation in politics. They differ not in the value they place in citizen involvement but in the role they assign to it. Citizen participation may be viewed as a political means to *public* ends. In this view, popular involvement promotes the good management of the public business. On this point, both camps of democratic theorists

[12] The distinction between the two functions of participation have been taken from Carole Pateman's *Participation and Democratic Theory*, p. 28.

are in agreement, though specific arguments vary from theorist to theorist. Participatory theorists, however, go on to contend that political participation is a political means to a specific *private* end—enhancement of the self. According to Mill, for example, participation in civic affairs improves the character of the citizen. It enlarges his intellectual and moral capacities, promoting a character type hailed by Mill as "active" and by G. D. H. Cole as "non-servile," a character type said by Pateman, a contemporary theorist of democracy, to involve "the belief that one can be self-governing, and confidence in one's ability to participate responsibly and effectively, and to control one's life and environment."[13] Thompson, another contemporary theorist, concurs, contending that participation may be a path to "self-realization."[14]

What distinguishes participatory theories is the view that becoming involved in the political process is likely to work important changes in the basic character of citizens. It is not merely that political participation may increase a person's sense of political efficacy. The claim is broader, if vaguer. Participation is a particularly promising means to affect fundamental changes in the citizen's self-image — to strengthen his sense of confidence and competence, to impress on him his own worth and dignity, in a word, to enhance his self-esteem. This notion that political participation may be a path to self-esteem and self-realization is worth noting, especially at a time when many argue that minorities historically excluded from political life ought to have assurance of office and influence in all major institutions of the society (political, economic, educational and the like), not only to secure representation of their interests, but to redress, at least partly, their damaged self-esteem.

The current emphasis on the self-enhancing function of participation is not without irony. Where contemporary

[13] See Pateman, *Participation and Democratic Theory*, p. 28ff.

[14] Dennis F. Thompson, *The Democratic Citizen* (Cambridge: Cambridge University Press, 1970), p. 64ff.

theorists contend that participation enhances, their prede-
cessors warned that power corrupts.[15] Whatever the reasons
for this shift in emphasis, it is now widely argued that
political participation can engender a sense of efficacy, of
self-assurance, and more broadly, of self-esteem.

Does participation in fact pay the psychological dividends
that participatory theorists claim it does? The findings of
this study bear on this question, though they certainly
provide no final answer to it. As we have seen, the politically
active have a stronger sense of efficacy, less anxiety, more
self-assurance and self-assertiveness, and higher self-esteem
than do those who are not active in politics. It is conceivable,
then, that participatory theorists may be right in advertising
the psychological benefits of participation.

It is conceivable, but in my opinion, unlikely for at least
two reasons. First, not all aspects of self-esteem are equally
related to participation. As we have seen, the lack of a sense
of interpersonal competence is strongly related to taking an
active part in politics, but feelings of personal unworthiness
or of social inferiority are related only marginally, if at all,
to political involvement. Thus participation, even if we were
to consider it a cause, rather than a consequence, of self-esteem, could be said to have only a limited power to change
self-attitudes. It may change how efficacious a person thinks
he is; it is much less likely to change how worthwhile he
believes he is. Second, high self-esteem most often appears
to be the cause and not the consequence of participation
in politics. The question of causal order, of course, is the
key to the problem. To sustain the claims of the participatory
theorists evidence must be amassed showing that the higher
self-esteem of political leaders appeared after and not before
they became involved in politics. The evidence available,
however, suggests that exactly the opposite is usually the
case. Thus there is some suggestive evidence that attitudes
toward the self, when they concern basic qualities of the

[15] For an interesting contemporary experimental test of Acton's Axiom,
see David Kipnis, "Does Power Corrupt?" *Journal of Personality and
Social Psychology* 24 (Oct. 1972): 26-32.

individual's character rather than particular capacities to perform specific tasks, develop early in childhood and are relatively enduring. Moreover, a recent experiment on the consequences of power found that having power did not lead to higher self-esteem.[16] Last, if participation did lead to more favorable self-attitudes, then the more active one is in politics, the higher one's self-esteem should be. But if by participation we mean more than prosaic acts of involvement such as voting — and I take it to be plain that by participation participatory theorists mean taking a genuine and vigorous part in political life — there is no relationship between degree of activity and level of self-esteem. As we have seen, among the sample of political activists, there is no relationship of consequence between self-esteem and how active a person is in politics, or how long he has been active in politics. Nor is there any relationship of consequence between level of self-esteem and position in political life (as indicated by public or party office held). These data do not support the hypothesis that participation in political life tends to promote self-approval. They suggest, instead, that the claims of participatory theorists for such psychological benefits are either exaggerated or erroneous. At a minimum, though the evidence at hand is merely suggestive, it would appear that such claims deserve far more critical scrutiny than they have yet received.

The Good Man and The Good Citizen

It is no small irony that a classical problem in political philosophy, the relationship between the good man and the good citizen, stimulated the scientific study of personality and politics. It was the pressure to understand the connection between the two in modern society, or more precisely the relationship between the bad man (defined psychologically) and the bad citizen (defined ideologically), that gave rise to the seminal studies of authoritarianism in the 1930s. The

[16] *Ibid.*

rise of fascism in Western Europe fixed the attention of some scholars — not a few of them refugees — on the sources of anti-Semitism. What made some men actually anti-Semitic, and thereby potentially fascistic? Conversely, what made others tolerant and egalitarian in outlook, and thereby well-disposed to the democratic spirit?

Part of the answer seemed to lie in man's psychological makeup. Achieving an understanding of some of the forces leading to totalitarianism of the right or the left entailed developing a psychology of ideology — an analysis of the personal needs, inner conflicts, fantasies, mechanisms of defense and strategies for adaptation that lie beneath anti-democratic creeds. So Aristotle's question, now substantially revised, proved the starting point for the psychological analysis of authoritarianism and thereby the scientific study of personality and politics.

My concern, too, has been with the relationship between personality and commitment to democratic values. My aim, however, has been to learn how such a relationship comes about, not merely to show that it in fact exists. For that reason, my findings both lend support to, and cast doubt upon, hypotheses of previous researchers. More important, the findings of this study help us to better understand the complexity of the connection between personality and political behavior.

Previous researchers have attempted to understand the connection between the two by focusing on the personal motives lying behind political values. Thus, Lasswell and others reasoned that the person low in self-esteem has less commitment to democratic values because he is more hostile, less tolerant, and so forth. And indeed the person with low self-esteem in fact is more hostile, less tolerant, and less committed to democratic values than the one with high self-esteem.

They made the right prediction, then, and for the right reasons, but unfortunately, for only some of the right reasons. As we have seen, the relationship between personality and belief is best thought of as a complex process, comprising a number of separate intervening steps. This process can be viewed in different ways. One alternative is to think of· it as involving three *steps* — exposure, comprehension, and the reward value of acceptance. Another alternative is to think of it as involving three *paths*, which account for the causal influence of personality on political belief as mediated by reinforcement contingencies (the reward value of acceptance) and learning contingencies (exposure and comprehension). Both of these conceptions make it plain that a personality characteristic can affect the acquisition of political opinions by affecting social learning as well as motivation. Thus, those with low self-esteem are less likely to acquire democratic values at least as much because of the barriers to social learning raised by low self-esteem as because of the personal motives that accompany it.

Recognizing that the relationship between personality and belief is mediated both by motivation and social learning helps us to understand both why and when the relationship between them will vary. Previous approaches, emphasizing only motivation, tend to suggest a one-to-one correspondence between a personality characteristic such as low self-esteem and a political orientation such as democratic commitment. Thus, Lasswell and others speak of a "democratic character" or the "democratic personality" as if the psychological profile of the democrat (and of the antidemocrat) tend to be always and everywhere alike. Such an approach pays no attention to the interaction of internal and external forces.

Self-esteem, as I have tried to suggest, may well lead to radically different outcomes, depending on the situation. When individual differences in exposure and comprehension are minimized, self-esteem is likely to affect the outcome only insofar as it affects the motivational orientations of individuals. For example, if we were to study a small policy-advisory group whose members were in close contact with each other and were equally able to understand the messages transmitted within the group, we might well expect low self-esteem to reinforce a tendency toward group conformity, or as Irving Janis has labeled it, "group-think."[17]

However, when individual differences in learning count for a great deal, low self-esteem is likely to lead to deviance, not conformity. Thus, in the circumstances of everyday life, low self-esteem tends to strongly inhibit exposure to and comprehension of the official values of the American political culture. As a result, low self-esteem weakens commitment to democratic values; that is, it leads to deviance, not conformity to institutionalized norms. Thus not only does the same personality characteristic lead to different outcomes, depending on the situation, but paradoxically, the same personality characteristic that motivates a person to conform frequently leads him to deviate.

This argument ought not to be taken as support for the contention of some scholars that personality constructs have little explanatory value because the same individual's behavior is so variable from one situation to another. Personality may well affect behavior, even if the former is constant across different situations. Indeed, a major aim of this study has been to develop an analytic scheme allowing us to suggest when self-esteem should lead to one outcome and when it should lead to another. Admittedly, this scheme is crude; nevertheless, it may be useful in understanding why personality may lead the same person to behave differently in different situations. However that may be, the choice between personality and the situation as determinants of behavior is a false choice. What may well matter most in explaining political belief and behavior is neither the influence of personality nor the impact of the situation *but the interaction between the two.*[18]

---

[17] For a provocative view of conformity forces in policy decision-making see, Irving L. Janis, *Victims of Group Think* (Boston: Houghton Mifflin Company, 1972).

[18] Henry Alker, "Is Personality Situation Specific or Intra-Psychically Consistent?" *Journal of Personality* 40 (March 1972): 1-16.

A one-to-one correspondence, then, between the good man and the good citizen is unlikely. Whether a citizen embraces democratic politics not only depends on the interaction between personality and the situation, it also hinges on the interaction among personality characteristics themselves. In this regard, the interaction between low self-esteem and psychological inflexibility is especially intriguing. As we have seen, a lack of self-esteem (and particularly, a lack of interpersonal competence) inhibits the tendency to participate in politics. Thus, rigidity raises a barrier to political involvement. Yet, if it is combined with low self-esteem, there is, so to speak, a catalytic reaction: these traits, in combination, potentiate rather than inhibit involvement in democratic politics.

This interaction between low self-esteem and inflexibility suggests something of the complex and as yet poorly understood processes by which personality dimensions become translated into action. Clearly much remains to be learned. But even at this early stage of inquiry, evidence of the interaction of self-esteem and other personality characteristics underlines the need for us to move from trait to profile analysis. Focusing on one personality characteristic is a useful strategy, especially in the early stages of inquiry. Yet it will become increasingly necessary to take account of the interaction among psychological and cognitive attributes, for the same personality trait may lead to very different outcomes, depending on the configuration of psychological characteristics in which it is imbedded.

Last, the interaction of personality and culture deserves mention. A paramount concern of this study has been the connection between personality and democratic citizenship. As we have seen, high self-esteem shows up democratic commitment and practice; low self-esteem undermines them. But the data for this study have been drawn only from the United States. We may expect that high self-esteem buttresses the values of democratic politics in other countries, but this may be so only where the democratic idea has legitimacy. The relationship between personality and political ideology may well differ where authoritarian values are at the center of political culture, for insofar as high self-esteem facilitates social learning, it may promote the learning of all socially approved values, whether democratic or not. And insofar as high self-esteem (and particularly, a sense of interpersonal competence) facilitates political involvement, it may encourage participation in political life, whether democratic or not. Ironically, then, the same personality trait which strengthens democratic commitment here may conceivably weaken it elsewhere.

The good man and the good citizen, Aristotle has argued, are the same — but only in the perfect society. The democratic personality may be the democratic citizen, I would suggest, but possibly only in a democratic society.

APPENDIXES

Appendix A

CHARACTERISTICS OF McCLOSKY NATIONAL POPULATION SAMPLE AND OTHER SELECTED SAMPLES

	AIPO Samples[a] (January, 1958) %	Michigan SRC Sample[b] (1956 Presidential Election) %	McClosky-PAB General Population Sample (January, 1958) %	Others %
	(N = 3024)	(N = 1762)	(N = 1484)	(1960 Census)
Sex				
Men	48	45	51	48
Women	52	55	49	52
Age (1)				
21–29	17		17	
30–49	46		45	
50+	37		38	
Undesignated	1		0	
Age (2)				
Under 35		30	28	
35–44		26	24	
45–54		19	21	
55+		25	28	
Race				
White		91	93	
Negro		8	7	

	AIPO Samples[a] (January, 1958) % (N = 3024)	Michigan SRC Sample[b] (1956 Presidential Election) % (N = 1762)	McClosky-PAB General Population Sample (January, 1958) % (N = 1484)	Others %
Rural-Urban				(1960 Census)
Urban (over 2500)		68	72	72
Rural (farm-nonfarm under 2500)		32	28	29
				PAB (Adjusted)
Region				
East	28	26	28	25[c]
Midwest	32	34	36	36
South	25	27	20	23
West	15	13	17	17
Education				
College	16	19	27	
High School	52	51	51	
Grade School	33	31	22	
Religion				
Catholic		21	22	
Jew		3	3	

			(Actual Congressional Vote, November, 1958)[e]
Prof., other, & NA	76	76	
Income			
Under 3000	24	20	
3000–5000	29	34	
5000–7000	26	27	
7500–10,000	11	9	
10,000+	8	6	
Refuse, NA, Dk	4	4	
Party Preference			
Democrat	56[d]	57	57[e]
Republican	44	43	43

Source: Herbert McClosky, "Consensus and Ideology in American Politics," APSR 18 (1964): 381–82, Table IX.

[a] The figures for the AIPO sample are averages computed from two national surveys conducted by the Gallup Poll in January, 1958. The information on the characteristics of these samples was supplied by the AIPO in a letter to the author.

[b] In most cases, the figures from the Michigan SRC sample are computed from the information supplied in the codebook for Deck 6 of Study 417, September 1956. Urban-rural figures are computed from a table in The American Voter, p. 454. Criteria for urban-rural are set out on p. 406.

[c] Michigan SRC included Md. and W. Va. in the South, while I had classified these states as Eastern. This column shows the PAB figures with Md. and W. Va. classified as Southern. SRC regional figures combine data from 1952 and 1956 (See The American Voter, p. 158).

[d] Data on party preference for the AIPO and the national congressional elections of 1958 are taken from a Gallup news release, May 24, 1959.

[e] Two-party vote only. PAB sample contained 821 Democrats, 623 Republicans, and 40 Independents, Other, and DK's.

Comparison of these figures confirms that the PAB Follower sample fairly represents, with one minor qualification, the general population of American adults in 1958. But, of course, it may be objected that these data are no longer representative, that the changes in American politics between then and now are so profound as to render the data of this study 'out of date.' The years between have been witness to the calamity of a war abroad and the failure of another at home; urban riots, universities become battlegrounds, political assassination; the rise and fall of the civil rights movement; the virtual overthrow of a president; a spreading sense of a steady deterioration in the quality of life; the faltering of the liberal spirit; even in some measure, a loss of confidence in the promise of America itself. How likely is it that the findings of a study of one era, critics may ask, will apply to another?

The question is argumentative, but I think it plain that the argument misses the mark, *given the objectives and design of this study*. My principal concern in this study has been commitment to democratic values and political involvement and leadership in a democratic society, both of which involve habits of mind and motives that are unlikely to change with every fluctuation in the political climate. I have deliberately chosen to avoid analysis of opinions toward specific issues of policy, largely out of the belief that some might summarily dismiss the larger study as time-bound, of historical interest only, and not in keeping with current preoccupations of political scientists. Wisely or not, I have concentrated on the enduring, not the ephemeral. To put the point plainly, there is no more reason to believe that the psychological sources of democratic values and political involvement observed in our data are highly variable than there is good reason to believe that the relationship between personality and, say, ethnocentrism changes every several years or so.

There is an inclination among political commentators to yield to the prophetic urge — at once sending out word of a new era beginning and taking to task those attached to the old one, in particular, those commited to the idea of regularity and predictability in human behavior. Of course, change occurs. Nothing is exactly as it was, and so political commentators interested in understanding the immediate present and future may dismiss as irrelevant a study based on data from the fifties.

For my part, I sympathize with the desire for up-to-the-minute information, but what is desirable is not always necessary, nor even especially useful. As decades of survey data testify, the impact of demographic factors (for example, education) on the type of basic political orientations examined in this study (such as political knowledge or commitment to democratic norms) is not highly variable. And until there is evidence to the contrary, it seems reasonable to assume a comparable constancy in the way in which basic personality traits such as self-esteem affect such basic political orientations.

Yet, my argument is not that we can assume a priori that the influence of personality tends to be constant. Rather, my contention is that we can begin to learn whether the impact of personality tends to be constant or variable, or more precisely, we can begin to learn the circumstances under which it is likely to be either, only by studying its role at different points in time. My study, in this sense, supplies a baseline for the study of constancy or change. Any query must begin at some point, sometimes even an arbitrary one, and from my point of view, McClosky's landmark studies offer the most attractive starting point. What some may regard as a weakness in this study — reliance on McClosky's data — I regard as one of its strengths. Construction of an omnibus inventory, permitting simultaneous assessment of a host of attitudes, group membership and identifications, socio-demographic factors and personality characteristics, and administration of this inventory to large-scale national samples of both political leaders and followers have created a set of data of unique value to the student of political psychology. It is not only that there are no data superior for my purposes; quite simply, there are no other data at all adequate to them.

Three further points are worth noting. First, the data, though all collected in the 1950s, were not all collected at the same time. The field work for the M.B. study was performed in 1955, the P.A.B. studies in 1958. An earlier study, the P.A.R., was conducted in 1951. McClosky's studies, then, cover a decade. All three are built around an omnibus questionnaire, the largest part of which is identical from study to study. As my formal analysis of the M.B. and P.A.B. studies have shown, and as informal observation of the P.A.R. study suggests, the relationships we have observed between personality and belief and political involvement reproduce themselves with remarkable fidelity on distinct samples drawn from quite different universes at widely different points in time. This may not persuade a critic who has already persuaded himself that the sixties or the seventies are so vastly different from the fifties that the conclusions from studies then could not be relevant now. Yet, to the critic who is skeptical but not cynical, the remarkable stability observed in this series of studies in the connections between personality and political behavior constitutes impressive evidence that there ought to be a presumption in favor of, and not against, the continuing relevance of my findings. Second, McClosky's surveys have been the major, but not the sole, source of empirical evidence for this study. Wherever possible, I have attempted to base my arguments on experimental and survey studies conducted by many different investigations, many of which were conducted in the mid-sixties and early seventies. The results of their studies and mine corresponded closely — even on "non-obvious" points. I showed, for example, that the relationship between self-esteem and such social conditions of worth as education, income, and occupation is surprisingly weak and, following Rosenberg, argued that a person's level of self-esteem depends on his success in meeting the standards of worth enforced by those with whom he regularly interacts, and not the standards of worth established by the larger society. If so, it follows that the level of self-esteem among blacks ought to be approximately the same as that among whites (if the two groups live separately). This prediction is surely not the obvious one to make, for race involves one of the most invidious comparisons in the United States. Compared to whites, blacks have less of all the advantages—jobs, housing, income, education, medical care, and opportunities for public esteem. If one accepts the common view that an individual's level of self-esteem depends heavily on the degree to which he matches the conditions of worth set by the larger society, then one would expect that a minority — habitually deprived, often oppressed, and frequently humiliated — should in some measure reflect the larger society's judgment that they are indeed inferior. As it happens, what appears to many to be self-evident is apparently false, or at any rate, far from being firmly established. Thus McCarthy and Yancey, among others, have produced careful evidence showing that blacks are not systematically and significantly lower in self-esteem than whites.[1]

[1] John McCarthy and William L. Yancey, "Uncle Tom and Mr. Charlie: Metaphysical Pathos in the Study of Racism and Personal Disorganization," *American Journal of Sociology* 76 (1971): 648-672.

My data, of course, do not allow systematic comparisons by race. But I have shown, again contrary to the conventional wisdom, that a person's level of self-esteem is only very weakly related to his standing in the social hierarchy of the society (as measured by his income, occupation or education). Again, a study undertaken in the summer of 1969 strongly confirms my study's findings on this "non-obvious" point. Yancey, Rigsby, and McCarthy examined both white and black samples, using among other measures Rosenberg's self-esteem scale. The investigators devoted a major part of their effort to identifying the impact on self-esteem of a host of demographic variables, including education, race, work-force participation, sex, maritial status, age, and place of residence. They concluded in part:

> . . . the inadequacy of the set of dimensions of social position in explaining variance in measures of affective state is revealing. A little more than 16 per cent of the variance in self-esteem and a little more than 13 per cent of the variance in symptoms of stress is explained by the seven dimensions of social position.[2]

I would add only that the virtually exact correspondence between their findings and mine on a point which is scarcely a truism, despite all the years separating their data and mine, argues strongly for the validity of my self-esteem measures and the pertinence of my specific findings.

More generally, political analysts appear to have a penchant for announcing new epochs in politics, sometimes rightly, often wrongly. But if "basic research" in the social sciences must always keep pace with the very latest pronouncements and alarums, the effect will be the same as harnessing it to a skittish horse: we will continually be dragged from place to place, by a power outside our control and largely beyond our comprehension, neither choosing nor knowing where we are going or where we have been, accomplishing nothing much other than kicking up the dust. My study is an attempt at scientific inquiry. So far as it has been successful, I believe its "relevance" is assured.

[2] William L. Yancey, Leo Rigsby, and John D. Butler, "Social Position, Self-Evaluation, and Race," *American Journal of Sociology* 78 (Sept. 1972): 338-359.

SCALES AND INDICES

With the exception only of the measures of self-esteem, all scales and indices were built by Herbert McClosky, in collaboration with Paul E. Meehl, Kenneth B. Clark, and others. As noted, construction methods varied, depending on the attribute being measured. Listed below are the scales used in this study and the number of items in every scale scored in the same direction.

Scale	Number of Items Scored in Same Direction
Alienation	9 of 9
Anomie	9 of 9
Aspiration-Ambition	4 of 7
Awareness	8 of 9
Bewilderment	7 of 7
Democratic Commitment	23 of 32
Direct Action	6 of 6
Elitism	6 of 9
Faith in Democracy	3 of 5
Fascist	8 of 8
Feelings of Political Futility	5 of 6
Intellectuality	5 of 9
Intolerance of Ambiguity	9 of 9
Left Wing	9 of 9
Life Satisfaction	6 of 9
Material Aspirations	4 of 5
Mysticism	10 of 10
Need Inviolacy	6 of 6
Rejection-Hostility	6 of 6
Obsessiveness	6 of 6
Paranoia	9 of 9
Political Cynicism	9 of 9
Political Interest	5 of 5
Political and Moral Indulgence	9 of 9
Political Suspiciousness	6 of 8
Populism	9 of 9
Procedural Rights	6 of 9
Tolerance	5 of 9
Totalitarianism	13 of 13
Rigidity	5 of 5

Appendix C

SIMPLE AND COMPOUND PATH COEFFICIENTS FOR THE RELATIONSHIP BETWEEN SELF-ESTEEM AND PROCEDURAL RIGHTS (FOR MIDDLE ACQUIESCENCE)

PAB-Leaders

$$\text{Path A} = p_{12} \cdot p_{24} \qquad\qquad \text{Path B} = p_{13} \cdot p_{34}$$
$$= (.273) \cdot (.205) \qquad\qquad\quad = (.369) \cdot (.181)$$
$$= .056 \qquad\qquad\qquad\qquad\quad = .067$$

$$\text{Path C} = p_{12} \cdot p_{23} \cdot p_{34}$$
$$= (.273) \cdot (.189) \cdot (.181)$$
$$= .009$$

AB-Followers

$$\text{Path A} = p_{12} \cdot p_{24} \qquad\qquad \text{Path B} = p_{13} \cdot p_{34}$$
$$= (.329) \cdot (.102) \qquad\qquad\quad = (.347) \cdot (.228)$$
$$= .034 \qquad\qquad\qquad\qquad\quad = .079$$

$$\text{Path C} = p_{12} \cdot p_{23} \cdot p_{34}$$
$$= (.329) \cdot (.302) \cdot (.228)$$
$$= .051$$

PAB-Leaders

$$\text{Path A} = p_{12} \cdot p_{24} \qquad\qquad \text{Path B} = p_{13} \cdot p_{34}$$
$$= (.273) \cdot (.157) \qquad\qquad\quad = (.369) \cdot (.129)$$
$$= .043 \qquad\qquad\qquad\qquad\quad = .048$$

$$\text{Path C} = p_{12} \cdot p_{23} \cdot p_{34}$$
$$= (.273) \cdot (.189) \cdot (.129)$$
$$= .007$$

PAB-Followers

$$\text{Path A} = p_{12} \cdot p_{24} \qquad\qquad \text{Path B} = p_{13} \cdot p_{34}$$
$$= (.329) \cdot (.123) \qquad\qquad\quad = (.347) \cdot (.158)$$
$$= .040 \qquad\qquad\qquad\qquad\quad = .055$$

$$\text{Path C} = p_{12} \cdot p_{23} \cdot p_{34}$$
$$= (.329) \cdot (.302) \cdot (.158)$$
$$= .016$$

PATH DIAGRAM OF THE RELATIONSHIP BETWEEN SELF-ESTEEM AND PROCEDURAL RIGHTS FOR MIDDLE ACQUIESCENCE

PAB-Leaders

(Variable 2) Hostility

.273   .205

(Variable 1) Self-Esteem   .189   (Variable 4) Procedural Rights

.369   .181

Anomie (Variable 3)

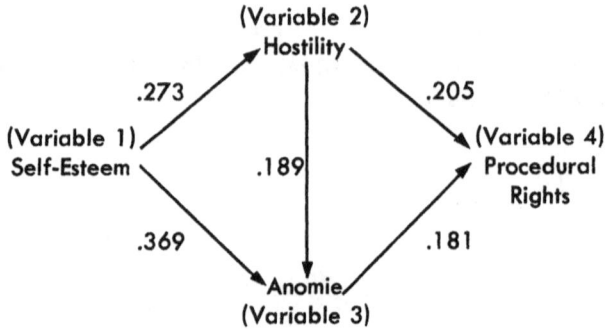

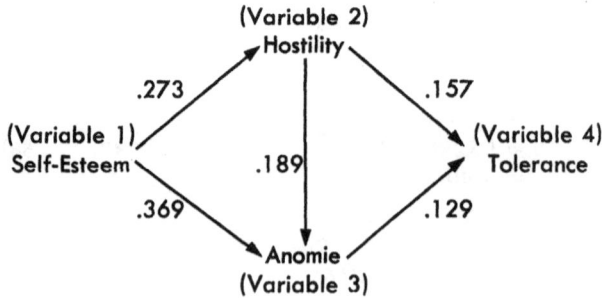

PAB-Followers

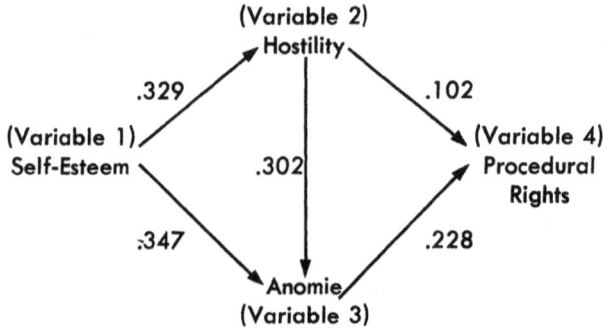

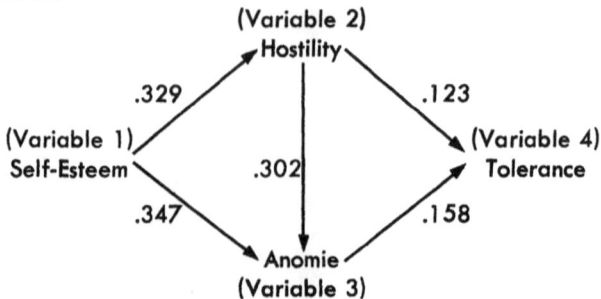

(Variable 2) Hostility

.329   .102

(Variable 1) Self-Esteem   .302   (Variable 4) Procedural Rights

.347   .228

Anomie (Variable 3)

PAB-Leaders

(Variable 2) Hostility

.273   .157

(Variable 1) Self-Esteem   .189   (Variable 4) Tolerance

.369   .129

Anomie (Variable 3)

PAB-Followers

(Variable 2) Hostility

.329   .123

(Variable 1) Self-Esteem   .302   (Variable 4) Tolerance

.347   .158

Anomie (Variable 3)

BIBLIOGRAPHY

APSR American Political Science Review
JASP Journal of Abnormal and Social Psychology
JPSP Journal of Personality and Social Psychology
POQ   Public Opinion Quarterly

Abelson, R., et al. *Theories of Cognitive Consistency: A Source Book*. Chicago: Rand McNally, 1968.

Ackerman, N.W., and Marie Jahoda, *Anti-Semitism and Emotional Disorder*. New York: Harper, 1950.

Adelson, Joseph, "Personality," in P. H. Mussen and Mark R. Rosenzweig, *Annual Review of Psychology*, Palo Alto: Annual Review, 1969, 217-252.

Adorno, T. W., Else Frankel-Brunswick, Daniel J. Levinson and R. Nevitt Sanford, *The Authoritarian Personality*. New York: Harper, 1950.

Albert, Robert S., "The Influence of Patterns of Conformity and General Reasoning Ability on Subjects Responses to an Inconclusive Message: A Preliminary Study," *Journal of Social Psychology*, 73 (1967), 241-251.

Alker, Henry A., "Is Personality Situationally Specific or Intrapsychically Constant," *Journal of Personality*, Vol. 40, No. 1, (March 1972), 1-16.

Allport, Gordon, "The Ego in Contemporary Psychology," *Personality and Social Encounter*. Boston: Beacon Press, 1964.

Almond, Gabriel A., *The Appeals of Communism*. Princeton: Princeton University Press, 1965.

———, "The Appeals of Communism and Fascism," unpublished paper, presented at APSA, 51st Annual Meeting, Boulder, Colorado.

———, and S. Verba, *The Civic Culture*. Princeton: Princeton University Press, 1963.

Ansbacher, H. L. and R. R. Ansbacher, eds., *The Individual Psychology of Alfred Adler.* New York: Harper and Row, 1964.

Argyle, Michael, *The Psychology of Interpersonal Behavior.* Baltimore: Penguin, 1962.

Armstrong, J. Scott, "Deviation of Theory by Means of Factor Analysis or Tom Swift and His Electric Factor Analysis Machine," *The American Statistician,* 21 (1967), 17-21.

Atkinson, J. W., *An Introduction to Motivation.* New York: Van Nostrand Reinhold, American Book, 1964.

———, and N. T. Feather, eds., *The Theory of Achievement Motivation.* New York: John Wiley and Sons, Inc., 1966.

Ausbel, D. P., H. M. Schiff, and M. Goldman, "Qualitative Characteristics in the Learning Process Associated with Anxiety," *JASP,* 48 (1953), 537-547.

Bandura, A., *Principles of Behavior Modification.* New York: Holt, Rhinehart and Winston, Inc., 1969.

———, and R. H. Walters, *Social Learning and Personality Development.* New York: Holt, Rhinehart and Winston Inc., 1965.

Barber, James D., *The Lawmakers.* New Haven: Yale University Press, 1965.

———, *Power in Committees.* Chicago: Rand McNally and Company, 1966.

Barocas, Ralph, and Leon Gorlow, "Self-Report Personality Measurement and Conformity Behavior," *Journal of Social Psychology,* 71 (1967), 227-254.

Barron, Frank, "Some Personality Correlates of Independence of Judgement," *Journal of Personality,* 21 (1953), 287-297.

Bell, W., R. J. Hill, and C. R. Wright, *Public Leadership,* San Francisco: Chandler Publishing Co., 1961.

Bennis, W. G., and D. Peabody, "The Conceptualization of Two Personality Orientations and Sociometric Choice," *Journal of Social Psychology,* 57 (1962) 203-215.

Bentler, P. M., D. N. Jackson and S. Massick, "Identification of Content and Style: A Two Dimensional Interpretation of Acquiescence," *Psychological Bulletin,* 76 (1971), 186-204.

———, "A Rose by Any Other Name," *Psychological Bulletin,* 77 (1972), 109-113.

Berelson, Bernard, Paul F. Lazarfeld, and William N. McPhee, *Voting,* Chicago: Chicago University Press, 1954.

Berkowitz, L., *Aggression.* New York: McGraw-Hill, 1967.

————, "Social Motivation," in *The Handbook of Social Psychology* IIEdition, eds., G. Lindzey and E. Aronson, pp. 50-153. Reading, Mass.: Addison-Wesley Publishing Co., 1969.

Berlyne, D. W., "Arousal and Reinforcement," in David Levine, ed., *Nebraska Symposium on Motivation,* pp. 1-110. 1967.

————, "Behavior Theory as Personality Theory," in E. F. Borgatta and W. W. Lambert, eds., *Handbook of Personality Theory and Research.* Chicago: Rand McNally, 1968.

————, *Conflict, Arousal and Curiosity.* New York: McGraw-Hill, 1960.

————, "Motivation Problems Raised by Exploratory and Epistemic Behavior," in S. Koch, ed., *Psychology: A Study of a Science,* Vol. 5, 284-364. New York: McGraw-Hill, 1959.

Bettelhein, Bruno, and Morris Janowitz, *Social Change and Prejudice.* New York: Free Press of Glencoe, 1964.

Bills, R. E., E. L. Vance, and O. S. McLean, "An Index of Adjustment and Values," *Journal of Consulting Psychology,* 51 (1951), 254-259.

Bing, James F., Francis McLaughlin, and Rudolf Marburg, "The Metapsychology of Narcissism," *The Psychoanalytic Study of the Child,* 14 (1959), 9-28. New York: International Universities Press.

Blalock, Hubert M. Jr., *Causal Inferences in Nonexperimental Research.* Chapel Hill: The University of North Carolina, 1964.

————, "Causal Inferences in Natural Experiments: Some Complications in Matching Designs," *Sociometry,* Vol. 30, No. 3 (Sept. 1967), 300-315.

————, "Correlated Independent Variables: The Problem of Multicollinearity," *Social Forces,* 42 (Dec. 1963), 233-237.

————, *Theory Construction.* Englewood Cliffs, N.J.: Prentice-Hall, 1969.

————, and Ann Blalock, eds., *Methodology in Social Research.* New York: McGraw Hill, 1968.

Block, Jack, *The Challenge of Response Sets.* New York: Appleton-Century-Crofts, 1965.

————, "On Further Conjectures Regarding Acquiescence," *Psychological Bulletin,* 76 (1971), 205-210.

————, "The Shifting Definitions of Acquiescence," *Psychological Bulletin,* 78 (1972), 10-12.

————, and Jeanne C. Block, "An Investigation of the Relationship

Between Intolerance of Ambiguity and Ethnocentrism," *Journal of Personality,* 19 (1951) 303-311.

———, and Thomas Hobart, "Is Satisfaction with Self a Measure of Adjustment?" *JASP,* 51 (1955), 254-259.

Block, Jeanne, and B. Martin, "Predicting the Behavior of Children Under Frustration," *JASP,* 51 (Sept. 1955), 281-285.

Bloom, B. S., *Stability and Change in Human Characteristics.* New York: Wiley, 1964.

Borgatta, E. F., "Traits and Persons," in E. F. Borgatta and W. W. Lambert, *Handbook of Personality Theory and Research,* pp. 510-528. Chicago: Rand McNally, 1968.

———, ed., and George W. Bohrnstadt, assoc. ed., *Sociological Methology 1969.* San Francisco: Jossey-Bass, 1969.

———, and W. W. Lambert, eds., *Handoook of Personality Theory and Research.* Chicago: Rand McNally, 1968.

Boulding, Kenneth E., *A Primer on Social Dynamics.* New York: The Free Press, 1970.

Breger, Louis, and Charlotte Ruiz, "The Role of Ego-Defense in Conformity," *The Journal of Social Psychology,* 69 (1966), 73-85.

Brehm, J. W., and A. Cohen, *Explorations in Cognitive Dissonance.* New York: Wiley, 1962.

Brodbeck, May, "Models, Meaning, and Theories," in May Brodbeck, ed., *Readings in the Philosophy of the Social Sciences* pp. 579-600. London: The MacMillan Co., 1969.

Brown, Roger, *Social Psychology.* New York: Free Press, 1965.

Browning, Rufus P., "The Interaction of Personality and Political System in Decisions to Run for Office: Some Data and a Simulation Technique," *The Journal of Social Issues,* Vol. 24, No. 3 (July 1968), 93-110.

———, and H. Jacob, "Power Motivation and the Political Personality," *POQ,* 28 (1964), 75-90.

Butler, J. M., and G. V. Haigh, "Changes in the Relationship Between Self-Concepts and Ideal Concepts Consequent Upon Client-Centered Counseling," in C. R. Rogers and Rosiland F. Dymond, eds., *Psychotherapy and Personality Change,* pp. 55-75. Chicago: University of Chicago Press, 1954.

Byrne, Donn, *An Introduction to Personality.* Englewood Cliffs, N. J.: Prentice-Hall, 1966.

Campbell, Angus, Philip Converse, Warren Miller, and Donald

Stokes, *The American Voter*. New York: John Wiley and Sons Inc., 1960.

Campbell, Donald T., "Social Attitudes and Other Acquired Behavioral Dispositions," in Sigmund Koch, ed., *Psychology: A Study of a Science*, Vol. 6. New York: McGraw-Hill, 1963, 91-177.

———, Carole R. Siegman, and Matilda B. Rees, "Direction-of-Wording Effects in the Relationships Between Scales," *Psychological Bulletin*, Vol. 68, No. 5 (Nov. 1967), 293-303.

Cantril, Hadley, *The Psychology of Social Movements*. New York: Wiley, Science Editions, 1963.

Christie, Richard, and Marie Jahoda, eds., *Studies in the Scope and Method of "The Authoritarian Personality."* Glencoe, Ill.: Free Press, 1954.

———, and Peggy Cook, "A Guide to the Published Literature Relating to *The Authoritarian Personality* through 1956," *Journal of Psychology*, 45 (1958), 171-199.

Citrin, Jack, *Political Disaffection in America*. Englewood Cliffs, N. J.: Prentice-Hall, forthcoming.

Cofer, C. N., and M. H. Appley, *Motivation: Theory and Research*. New York: John Wiley and Sons, Inc., 1967.

Cohen, Arthur R., *Attitude Change and Social Influence*. New York: Basic Books, 1964.

———, "Some Implications of Self-Esteem for Social Influence," in C. I. Hovland and I. Janis, eds., *Personality and Persuasibility* pp. 102-120. New Haven: Yale University Press, 1959.

Coleman, James S., "Implications of the Findings on Alienation," *American Journal of Sociology*, Vol. 70, No. 1 (July 1964), 76-78.

Combs, Arthur W., Daniel W. Soper, and Clifford C. Courson, "The Measurement of Self Concept and Self Report," *Educational and Psychological Measurement*, Vol. 23, No. 3 (1963), 493-500.

Converse, Philip, "The Nature of Belief Systems in Mass Publics," in David Apter, ed., *Ideology and Discontent*. New York: Free Press, 1964.

Coombs, Robert H., "Social Participation, Self-Concept and Interpersonal Evaluation," *Sociometry*, Vol. 32, No. 3 (Sept. 1969), 273-286.

———, and V. Davies, "Self-Conception and the Relationship Between High School and College Scholastic Achievement,"

Sociology and Social Research, Vol. 50, No. 4 (July 1966), 460-471.

Coopersmith, Stanley, *The Antecedents of Self-Esteem.* San Francisco: W. H. Freeman and Co., 1967.

———, "A Method for Determining Types of Self-Esteem," *JASP,* 58 (1959), 87-94.

———, "Relationship Between Self-Esteem and Sensory (Perceptual) Constancy," *JASP,* 68 (1964), 217-221.

———, "Studies in Self-Esteem," *Scientific American,* Vol. 218, No. 2 (Feb. 1968), 96-106.

Cowen, E. L., and P. N. Tongas, "The Social Desirability of Trait Descriptive Terms: Applications to a Self-Concept Inventory," *Journal of Consulting Psychology,* 21 (1957), 57-62.

Crandall, Virginia, "Personality Characteristics and Social and Achievement Behaviors Associated with Children's Social Desirability Response Tendencies," *Journal of Personality and Social Psychology,* Vol. 4 No. 5 (1966), 477-486.

Cronbach, L. J., "Proposals Leading to Analytic Treatment of Social Perception Scores," in R. Tagiuri and L. Petrillo, *Person Perception and Interpersonal Behavior,* pp. 353-379. Stanford: Stanford University Press, 1969.

———, and P. E. Meehl, "Construct Validity in Psychological Tests," in H. Feigl and M. Scriven, eds., *The Foundations of Science and the Concepts of Psychology and Psychoanalysis,* Vol. 1, pp. 174-204, in Minnesota Studies in the Philosophy of Science. Minneapolis: University of Minneapolis Press, 1956.

Crowne, Douglas P., and D. Marlowe, *The Approval Motive.* New York: John Wiley and Sons, Inc., 1964.

———, and Mark W. Stephens, "Self-Acceptance and Self-Evaluative Behavior: A Critique of Methodology," *Psychological Bulletin,* Vol. 58, No. 2 (1961), 104-121.

———, Mark W. Stephens and Richard Kelly, "The Validity and Equivalence of Tests of Self-Acceptance," *The Journal of Psychology,* 51 (1961), 101-112.

Crutchfield, Richard S., "Conformity and Character," *American Psychologist,* Vol. 10 (1955), 191-198.

Dabbs, James M. Jr., "Self-Esteem, Communicator Characteristics and Attitude Change," *JASP,* 69 (1964), 173-181.

Dahl, Robert, *After the Revolution: Authority in a Good Society.* New Haven: Yale University Press, 1970.

Dahlstrom, W. Grant, "Personality," in P. H. Mussen and Mark R. Rosenzweig, *Annual Review of Psychology,* Palo Alto: Annual Reviews, Vol. 21 (1970), 1-48.

Davids, Anthony, "Alienation, Social Apperception and Ego Structure," *Journal of Consulting Psychology,* Vol. 19, No. 1 (1955), 21-27.

———, "Generality and Consistency of Relationships Between the Alienation Syndrome and Cognitive Processes," *JASP,* 51 (1955), 61-67.

Dean, Dwight G., "Alienation: Its Meaning and Measurement," *American Sociological Review,* Oct. 1961, Vol. 26, No. 5 (Oct. 1961), 753-757.

Dicks, Henry V., "Personality Traits and National Socialist Ideology," *Human Relations,* Vol. 3, No. 2 (1950), 109-220.

Diggory, James C., *Self-Evaluation: Concepts and Studies.* New York: John Wiley and Sons, Inc., 1966.

DiPalma, Giuseppe, and Herbert McClosky, "Personality and Conformity: The Learning of Political Attitudes," *APSR,* 64 (1970), 1054-1073.

Dollard, J., and N. E. Miller, *Personality and Psychotherapy.* New York: McGraw-Hill Book Co., Inc., 1950.

Douvan, Elizabeth, and Alan Walker, "The Sense of Effectiveness in Public Affairs," *Psychological Monographs: General and Applied,* Vol. 70, No. 22 (1956), 1-19.

Eckhardt, William, and Alan Newcombe, "Militarism, Personality, and Other Social Attitudes," *Journal of Conflict Resolution,* Vol. 13, No. 2 (1969), 210-219.

Edinger, Lewis J., and Kurt Schumacher: *A Study of Personality and Political Behavior.* Stanford: Stanford University Press, 1965.

Edwards, A. L., *The Social Desirability Variable in Personality Assessment and Research.* New York: Holt, 1957.

Engel, G. L., *Psychological Development in Health and Disease.* Philadelphia: W. B. Saunders Co., 1964.

Engel, G., "The Stability of the Self-Concept in Adolescence," *JASP,* 58 (1962), 211-215.

Entwisle, Doris R., "To Dispel Fantasies About Fantasy-Based Measures of Achievement," *Psychological Bulletin,* Vol. 77, No. 6 (June 1972), 373-391.

Erikson, Erik H., *Gandhi's Truth.* New York: W. W. Norton, 1969.

———, *Young Man Luther.* New York: Norton, 1958.

Eulau, Heinz, *The Behavioral Persuasion.* New York: Random House, 1967,

———, *Micro-Macro Political Analysis.* Chicago: Aldine Publishing Co., 1969.

Farnham-Diggory, S., "Self-Evaluation and Subjective Life Expectancy Among Suicidal and Non-Suicidal Psychotic Males," *JASP,* 69 (1966), 628-634.

Farrar, Donald E., and Robert R. Glauber, "Multicollinearity in Regression Analysis: The Problem Revisited," *Review of Economics and Statistics,* 49 (Feb. 1967), 92-107.

Fenichel, H., and D. Rapaport, eds., *The Collected Papers of Otto Fenichel,* Second Series. New York: W. W. Norton and Co., 1954.

Fenichel, Otto, *The Personality Theory of Neurosis.* New York: W. W. Norton and Co., Inc., 1945.

Festinger, L., "A Theory of Social Comparison Processes," *Human Relations,* 7 (1954), 117-140.

Frenkel-Brunswik, Else, "Interactions of Psychological and Sociological Factors in Political Behavior," *APSR,* 46, No. 1 (March 1952), 44-65.

Freud, Anna, *The Ego and the Mechanisms of Defense.* New York: International Universities Press, 1966.

Freud, Sigmund, "On Narcissism: An Introduction" in *Collected Papers* Vol. 4, pp. 60-83. London: Hogarth, 1925.

Fromm, Erich, *Escape from Freedom.* New York: Holt, 1941.

Gardner, R. W., P. S. Holzman, G. S. Klein, H. B. Linton, and D. P. Spence, "Cognitive Behavior," *Psycholgical Issues,* Vol. 1, No. 4 (1959), 1-169.

Gelfand, D. M., "The Influence of Self-Esteem on Rate of Verbal Conditioning and Social Matching Behavior," *JASP,* 65 (1965), 259-265.

George, Alexander L., "Power As a Compensatory Value for Political Leaders," *Journal of Social Issues,* 24 (1968), 29-49.

———, "Some Uses of Dynamic Psychology in Political Biography, Case Materials on Woodrow Wilson," in Fred Greenstein and Michael Lerner, *Sourcebook for the Study of Personality and Politics.* Chicago: Markham, 1969.

———, and Juliette L. George, *Woodrow Wilson and Colonel House.* New York: Dover Publications, Inc., 1964.

Gergen, Kenneth J., *The Concept of Self.* New York: Holt, Rhinehart and Winston, Inc., 1971.

Gergen, K. J., and R. A. Bauer, "Interactive Effects of Self-Esteem and Task Difficulty on Social Conformity," *Journal of Personality and Social Psychology,* 6 (1967), 16-22.

Gibb, Cecil, "Leadership," in G. Lindzey and E. Aronson, eds., *Handbook of Social Psychology,* IV, pp. 205-282. Reading, Mass.: Addison-Wesley, 1969.

Goldhamer, Herbert, "Public Opinion and Personality," *American Journal of Sociology,* 55 (1950), 346-354.

Gollob, H. F., and J. E. Dittes, "Effects of Manipulated Self-Esteem on Persuasibility Depending on Threat and Complexity of Communication," *Journal of Social Psychology,* 2 (1965), 195-201.

Gordon, Robert A., "Issues in Multiple Regression," *AJS,* 73 (March 1968), 592-616.

Gough, Harrison G., *California Psychological Inventory,* Palo Alto: Consulting Press, 1957.

———, Herbert McClosky and Paul E. Meehl, "A Personality Scale for Dominance," *JASP,* Vol. 46, No. 3 (July 1951), 360-366.

———, Herbert McClosky and Paul E. Meehl, "A Personality Scale for Social Responsibility," *JASP,* 47 (Jan. 1952), 73-80.

Greenstein, Fred I., "Harold Lasswell's Concept of Democratic Character," Journal of Politics, Vol. 30, No. 3 (Aug. 1968), 696-709.

———, "The Impact of Personality on Politics: An Attempt to Clear Away the Underbrush," *The American Political Science Review,* Vol. 61, No. 3 (Sept. 1967), 629-641.

———, *Personality and Politics.* Chicago: Markham, 1969.

Griffitt, W. B., "Interpersonal Attraction as a Function of Self-Concept and Personality Similarity-Dissimilarity," *Journal of Personality and Social Psychology,* 4 (1966), 581-584.

Gustafson, Donald F., ed., *Essays in Philosophical Psychology,* Garden City, N. Y.: Doubleday Anchor Books, 1964.

Hall, C. S., and G. Lindzey, *Theories of Personality.* New York: John Wiley and Sons, Inc., 1957.

Hanley, C., "Eysenck's Tender Mindedness Dimension: A Critique," *Psychological Bulletin,* 53 (1956), 159-176.

Hanson, David J., "Personality and Politics," *International Review of History and Political Science,* Vol. 5, No. 2 (May 1968).

Hartz, Louis, *The Liberal Tradition in America.* New York: Harcourt, Brace and World, 1955.

Heiss, Jerold, and Susan Owen, "Self Evaluation of Blacks and Whites," *AJS,* 78 (1972), 360-370.

Helson H., and W. Bevan, *Contemporary Approaches to Psychology.* Princeton: D. Van Nostrand Co., Inc., 1967.

Hennessey, Bernard, "Politicals and Apoliticals: Some Measurements of Personality Traits," *Midwest Journal of Political Science,* 3 (Nov. 1959), 336-355.

Hilgard, Ernest, "Human Motives and the Concept of the Self," *American Psychologist,* 4 (1949), 374-382.

Hofstadter, Richard, *The Age of Reform.* New York: Alfred A. Knopf, 1955.

Hollander, E. P., and James W. Julian, "Leadership," in E. F. Borgatta and W. W. Lambert, *Handbook of Personality Theory and Research,* pp. 890-899. Chicago: Rand McNally, 1968.

Horowitz, Frances D., "The Relationship of Anxiety, Self-Concept and Sociometric Status Among Fourth, Fifth and Sixth Grade Children," *JASP,* Vol. 65, No. 3 (1962), 212-214.

Hovland, Carl I., and Irving L. Janis, *Personality and Persuasibility.* New Haven: Yale University Press, 1959.

Hyman, Herbert H., and Paul B. Sheatsley, " 'The Authoritarian Personality' — A Methodological Critique," in R. Christie and M. Jahoda, eds., *Studies in the Scope and Method of "The Authoritarian Personality,"* pp. 50-122. Glencoe, Ill.: Free Press, 1954.

Inkeles, Alex, "National Character and Modern Political Systems," in Francis L. K. Hsu, ed., *Psychological Anthropology: Approaches to Culture and Personality,* pp. 178-208. Homewood, Ill.: The Dorsey Press, Inc., 1961.

———, and Daniel J. Levinson, "National Character: The Study of Modal Personality and Socio-Cultural Systems," in G. Lindzey and E. Aronson, eds., *Handbook of Social Psychology,* 2d ed., Vol. IV, 418-506. Reading, Mass.: Addison-Wesley, 1969.

Jackman, Robert W. "Political Elites, Mass Publics, and Support for Democratic Norms," *Journal of Politics,* 34 (1972), 753-773.

Jackson, Douglas, "The Dynamics of Structured Personality Tests," *Psychological Review,* 78 (1971), 229-248.

———, and S. Messick, "Response Styles on the MMPI: Comparison of Clinical and Normal Samples," *JASP,* 65 (1962), 285-289.

Jacob, Herbert, "Initial Recruitment of Elected Officials in the U. S. — A Model," *Journal of Politics,* 24 (1962), 703-716.

Jacobson, L. I., and L. H. Ford, Jr., "Need for Approval, Defensive Denial and Sensitivity to Cultural Stereotypes," *Journal of Personality,* 34 (1966), 596-609.

James, William, *The Principles of Psychology.* New York: Dover Publications, 1950.

Janis, Irving L., *Victims of Group Think.* Boston: Houghton Mifflin Co., 1972.

———, and Howard Leventhal, "Human Reactions to Stress," in E. F. Borgatta and W. W. Lambert, *Handbook of Personality Theory and Research,* pp. 1041-1085. Chicago: Rand McNally, 1968.

Johnson, Homer H., and Ivan D. Steiner, "Some Effects of Discrepancy Level on Relationships Between Authoritarianism and Conformity," *Journal of Social Psychology,* 73 (1967), 199-204.

Kalleberg, Arthur L., "Concept Formation in Normative and Empirical Studies: Towards Reconciliation in Political Theory," *APSR,* 63 (1969), 26-39.

Kardiner A., and L. Ovesey, *The Mark of Oppression.* Cleveland: The World Publishing Co., 1962.

Katz, Daniel, "The Functional Approach to the Study of Attitudes," *POQ,* 24 (1960), 163-204.

———, Irving Sarnoff, and Charles McClintock, "Ego Defense and Attitude Change," *Human Relations,* 9 (1956), 27-46.

Katz, Elihu, and Paul F. Lazarsfeld, *Personal Influence.* Glencoe, Ill.: Free Press, 1955.

Kelman, Herbert, "Compliance, Identification, and Internalization: Three Processes of Attitude Change," *Journal of Conflict Resolution,* 2 (1958), 51-60.

Kenny, D. T., "The Influence of Social Desirability on Discrepancy Measures Between Real Self and Ideal Self," *Journal of Consulting Psychology,* 20 (1956), 315-318.

Key, V. O., *Public Opinion in American Democracy.* New York: Knopf, 1961, pp. 182-206.

Kipnis, David, "Does Power Corrupt," *JPSP,* 24 (Oct. 1972), 33-41.

Kirscht, John P., and Ronald C. Dillehay, *Dimensions of Authoritarianism.* Lexington: University of Kentucky Press, 1967.

Klein, George S., *Perception, Motives and Personality.* New York: Alfred A. Knopf, 1970.

————, "Preemptory Ideation: Structure and Force in Motivated Ideas," in *Perception, Motives and Personality.* New York: Alfred A. Knopf, 1970.

Kluckhohn, Clyde, Henry A. Murray, and David M. Schneider, eds., *Personality in Nature, Society and Culture,* 2d ed. New York: Alfred A. Knopf, 1964.

Kogan, W. S., R. Quinn, A. F. Ax, and H. S. Ripley, "Some Methodological Problems in the Quantification of Clinical Assessment by Q Array," *Journal of Consulting Psychology,* 21 (1957), 57-62.

Land, Kenneth C., "Principles of Path Analysis," in Edgar F. Borgatta and George W. Bohrnstedt, eds., *Sociological Methodology, 1969.* San Francisco: Jossey-Bass, 1969.

Lane, Robert E., *Political Ideology.* New York: Free Press, 1962.

————. "Political Personality and Electoral Choice," *APSR,* 49 (1955), 173-190.

————, *Political Thinking and Consciousness.* Chicago: Markham Publishing Co., 1969.

Lasswell, Harold D., "Democratic Character," in *The Political Writings of Harold D. Lasswell,* pp. 464-525. Glencoe, Ill.: The Free Press, 1951.

————, "A Note on Types of Political Personality: Nuclear, Co-Relational and Developmental," in Fred I. Greenstein and Michael Lerner, eds., *A Sourcebook for the Study of Personality and Politics,* pp. 232-240. Chicago: Markham, 1971.

————, *Power and Personality.* New York: Viking Press, Compass Books, 1962.

————, *Psychopathology and Politics.* New York: The Viking Press, 1960.

————, "The Selective Effect of Personality on Political Participation," in Richard Christie and Marie Jahoda, eds., *Studies in the Scope and Method of "The Authoritarian Personality,"* pp. 197-225. Glencoe, Ill.: The Free Press, 1954.

Lazarus, Richard S., *Psychological Stress and the Coping Process.* New York: McGraw-Hill Book Co., 1966.

League, B. J., and D. N. Jackson, "Conformity, Veridicality, and Self-Esteem," *JASP,* 68 (1964), 113-115.

Leites, Nathan, *The New Ego.* Science House, 1971.

Lerner, D., *The Passing of Traditional Society.* London: Collier-MacMillan Otd., 1964.

Lerner, Michael, "A Biographical Note," in F. Greenstein, *Person-*

ality and Politics. Chicago: Markham, 1969.

Levinson, Daniel J., "Idea Systems in the Individual and in Society," in George Zollchan and Walter Hirsch, *Explorations in Social Change.* Boston: Houghton-Mifflin, 1964.

———, "The Relevance of Personality for Political Participation," *POQ,* 22 (1958), 3-10.

———, "Role, Personality, and Social Structure in the Organizational Setting," *JASP,* Vol. 58, No. 2 (March 1959), 170-180.

Levonian, Edward, "Self-Esteem and Opinion Change," *Journal of Personality and Social Psychology,* Vol. 9, No. 3 (1968), 257-259.

Liberty, P. G., Jr., E. Burnstein, and R. W. Moulton, "Concern with Mastery and Occupational Attraction," *Journal of Personality,* 34 (1966), 105-117.

Lindzey, G., and E. Aronson, *The Handbook of Social Psychology,* 2d ed. Reading, Mass.: Addison-Wesley Publishing Co., 1969.

Lipset, Seymour Martin, *Political Man.* Garden City: Doubleday, Anchor, 1963.

Lipset, Semour M. and Earl Raab, *The Politics of Unreason.* New York: Harper & Row, 1970.

Liverant, S., and A. Scodel, "Internal and External Control as Determinants of Decision Making Under Conditions of Risk," *Psychological Reports,* 7 (1960), 59-62.

Loevinger, Jane, "Measuring Personality Patterns of Women," *Genetic Psychology Monographs,* 65 (1962), 53-136.

Lovejoy, A. O., " 'Pride' in Eighteenth Century Thought," *Essays in the History of Ideas.* New York: Braziller, 1955.

Lowe, C. Marshall, "The Self Concept: Fact or Artifact?" *Psychological Bulletin,* 58, No. 4 (1961), 325-336.

Lynd, H. M., *On Shame and the Search for Identity.* New York: Wiley Science Editions, 1966.

McCarthy, John, and W. Yancey, "Uncle Tom and Mr. Charley: Metaphysical Pathos in the Study of Racism and Personality Disorganization," *AJS.,* 76 (1971), 648-672.

McClelland, David C., *The Achieving Society,* Glencoe, Ill.: Free Press, 1961.

McClosky, Herbert, "Consensus and Ideology in American Politics," *APSR,* 58 (June 1964), 361-382.

———, "Conservatism and Personality," *APSR,* 52 (1958), 27-45.

———, "Personality and Attitude Correlates of Foreign Policy Orientation," in James Rosenau, ed., *Domestic Sources of*

Foreign Policy, pp. 51-110. New York: The Free Press, 1967.
———, "Political Participation and Apathy," *International Encyclopedia of the Social Sciences,* pp. 252-265.
———, "Survey Research in Political Science," in C. Y. Glock, ed., *Survey Research in the Social Sciences,* pp. 63-143. New York: Russell Sage Foundation, 1967.
———, and Eugene Bardach, "Psychological Correlates of Democratic Commitment." Unpublished manuscript.
———, Paul J. Hoffman, and Rosemary O'Hara, "Issue Conflict and Consensus Among Party Leaders and Followers," *APSR,* 54 (June 1960), 406-427.
———, and Paul E. Meehl, "Inflexibility." Unpublished manuscript.
———, and Paul E. Meehl, "Personality, Attitudes, and Liberal-Conservative Belief Systems." Preliminary draft, August 1967.
———, and John H. Schaar, "Psychological Dimensions of Anomy," *American Sociological Review,* 30 (1965), 14-40.
McConaughy, John, "Certain Personality Factors of State Legislators in South Carolina," *APSR,* Vol. 44 (Dec. 1950), 897-903.
McDougall, William C., *Introduction to Social Psychology.* New York: Barnes and Noble, University Paperbacks, 1960. especially Chapters 7 and 8.
McGuire, William J., "Attitudes and Opinions," *Annual Review of Psychology,* Vol. 17 (1966), 475-513.
———, "The Nature of Attitudes and Attitude Change," in G. Lindzey and E. Aronson, eds., *The Handbook of Social Psychology,* 2d ed., Vol. III, 136-314. Reading, Mass.: Addison-Wesley Publishing Company, 1969.
———, "Personality and Susceptibility to Social Influence," in E. F. Borgatta and W. W. Lambert, eds., *Handbook of Personality Theory and Research,* pp. 1130-1188. Chicago: Rand McNally, 1968.
McKeon, Richard, *Introduction to Aristotle.* New York: The Modern Library, Random House, Inc., 1947.
McNeil, E. B., "Personal Hostility and International Aggression," *Journal of Conflict Resolution,* Vol. 5, No. 3 (1961), 279-290.
Mandler, G., and S. B. Sarason, "A Study of Anxiety and Learning," *JASP,* 47 (1952), 166-173.
Mann, Richard D., "View of the Relationships Between Personality and Performance in Small Groups," *Psychological Bulletin,*

4 (July 1959), 241-270.
Marcus, G. E., "Psychopathology and Political Recruitment," *Journal Of Politics,* Vol. 31, No. 4 (Nov. 1969), 913-931.
Marlowe, D., and K. Gergen, "Personality and Social Interaction," in G. Lindzey and E. Aronson, eds., *The Handbook of Social Psychology,* Vol. 3, 2d ed., 590-665. Reading, Mass.: Addison-Wesley Publishing Company, 1969.
Maslow, Abraham H., "Authoritarian Character Structure," *Journal of Social Psychology,* Vol. 18 (1943), 401-411.
———, *Motivation and Personality.* New York: Harper and Row Publishers, 1954.
———, "Power Relationships and Patterns of Personal Development," in Arthur Kornhauser, ed., *Problems of Power in American Democracy,* pp. 92-131. Detroit: Wayne State University Press, 1959.
———, *The S-I Test: A Measure of Psychological Security-Insecurity.* Stanford: Stanford University Press, 1952.
Meehl, Paul E., *Clinical vs. Statistical Prediction.* Minneapolis: University of Minnesota, 1954.
———, "The Dynamics of 'Structured' Personality Tests," *Journal of Clinical Psychology,* 1 (1945), 296-303.
———, "Nuisance Variables and the Ex Post Facto Design," in *Analyses of Theories and Methods of Physics and Psychology,* Michael Radner and Stephen Wonokur, eds., Vol. III, Minnesota Studies in the Philosophy of Science, pp. 373-402.
———, "Problems in the Actuarial Characterization of a Person," in H. Feigl and M. Scriver, *The Foundations of Science and the Concepts of Psychology and Psychoanalysis,* Vol. I, in Minnesota Studies in the Philosophy of Science, pp. 205-222.
Milbrath, Lester W., "The Nature of Political Beliefs and the Relationship of the Individual to the Government," *The American Behavioral Scientist,* Vol. 12 (Nov-Dec. 1968), 28-36.
———, *Political Participation.* Chicago: Rand-McNally and Co., 1965.
———, "Predispositions Toward Political Contention," *Western Political Quarterly,* Vol. 13, No. 1 (March 1960), 5-18.
———, and Walter W. Klein, "Personality Correlates of Political Participation," *Acta Sociologica,* Vol. 6 (1962), 53-66.
Mill, John Stuart, *Utilitarianism and Selected Writings,* New York: Meridian Books, 1962.

Millman, Susan, "Anxiety, Comprehension, and Susceptibility to Social Influence," *Journal of Personality and Social Psychology,* Vol. 9, No. 3 (1968), 251-256.

Mischel, Walter, *Personality and Assessment.* New York: John Wiley and Sons, Inc., 1968.

Moses, M., and R. Duvall, "Depreciation and the Self-Concept," *Journal of Clinical Psychology,* 16 (1960), 387-388.

Murphy, G., *Personality.* New York: Basic Books Inc., 1966.

Murray, Henry A., "An American Icarus," in G. Lindzey and C. S. Hall, eds., *Theories of Personality: Primary Sources and Research,* pp. 162-175. New York: Wiley, 1965.

———, "Egoistic Self-Infusion and Unleashed Wrath in Captain Ahab," in G. Lindzey and C. S. Hall, eds., *Theories of Personality Primary Sources and Research,* New York: Wiley, 1965.

———, and Clyde Kluckhohn, "Personality Formation: The Determinants," in Clyde Kluckhohn, Henry A. Murray and David M. Schneider, *Personality in Nature, Society and Culture,* 2d ed. New York: Alfred A. Knopf, 1964.

Mussen, P. H., and L. W. Porter, "Personal Motivations and Self-Conceptions Associated with Effectiveness and Ineffectiveness in Emergent Groups," *JASP,* 59 (1959), 23-27.

Mussen, P. H., and A. B. Wyszynski, "Personality and Political Participation," *Human Relations,* Vol. 5, No. 1 (1952), 65-82.

Nelson, P. D., "Similarities and Differences Among Leaders and Followers," *Journal of Social Psychology,* Vol. 63 (1964), 161-167.

Nisbett, R. E., and A. Gordon, "Self-Esteem and Susceptibility to Social Influence," *Journal of Personality and Social Psychology,* 1967.

Noyes, A. P., and L. C. Kolb, *Modern Clinical Psychiatry.* Philadelphia: W. B. Saunders Co., 1964.

Nunally, Jung, *Psychometric Theory.* New York: McGraw-Hill, 1967, pp. 255-258.

Olsen, Marvin E., "Alienation and Political Opinions," *POQ.* Vol. 29, No. 2 (1965), 200-212.

Oskamp, Stuart, "Relationship of Self-Concepts to International Attitudes," *The Journal of Social Psychology,* 76 (1968), 31-36.

Pateman, Carole, *Participation and Democratic Theory,* Cambridge, England: Cambridge University Press, 1970.

Peabody, Dean, "Attitude Content and Agreement Set in Scales of Authoritarianism, Dogmatism, Anti-Semitism and Economic Conservatism," *JASP*, Vol. 63, (1961) 1-11.

Pepitone, A., *Attraction and Hostility*. New York: Atherton Press, 1964.

Perkins, Charles W., and Donald T. Shannon, "Three Techniques for Obtaining Self-Perceptions in Preadolescent Boys," *Journal of Personality and Social Psychology*, Vol. 2, No. 3 (1965), 443-447.

Phares, E. J., "Internal-External Control as a Determinant of Amount of Social Influence Exerted," *JPSP*, Vol. 2, No. 5 (1965), 642-647.

Posner, Michael I., and Stephen J. Boles, "Components of Attention," *Psychological Review*, Vol. 78, No. 5 (1971), 391-408.

Pye, L. W., *Politics, Personality and Nation Building*. New Haven: Yale University Press, 1964.

Rapaport, David, "A Historical Survey of Psychoanalytic Ego Psychology," *Psychological Issues*, Vol. 1, No. 1 (1959), 5-17.

Rhyne, Edwin Hoffman, "Racial Prejudice and Personality Scales: An Alternative Approach," *Social Forces*, Vol. 41, No. 1 (Oct. 1962), 44-53.

Rieff, Philip, *Freud: The Mind of the Moralist*. Garden City, New York: Doubleday and Company, Inc., Anchor Books, 1959.

Rieselbach, Leroy N., "Personality and Political Attitudes: A Bibliography of Available Questionnaire Measures." *Unpublished manuscript*, July 1966.

———, "Personality and Political Behavior: The Question of Relevance." *Unpublished manuscript.*

Rogow, Arnold, *James Forrestal: A Study of Personality, Politics and Policy*. New York: Macmillan, 1963.

Rokeach, M., *Beliefs, Attitudes and Values*. San Francisco: Jossey-Bass, 1969.

———, *The Open and Closed Mind*. New York: Basic Books, 1960.

Rorer, Leonard G., "The Great Response Style Myth," *Psychological Bulletin*, Vol. 65, (1965) 129-156.

Rose, A. M., "Alienation and Participation: A Comparison of Group Leaders and the 'Mass,' " *American Sociological Review*, Vol. 27 (1962), 834-838.

Rosenberg, Morris, "Misanthropy and Attitudes Toward International Affairs," *Journal of Conflict Resolution*, 1 (1957), 340-345.

————, "Misanthropy and Political Ideology," *American Sociological Review,* 21 (1956), 690-695.

————, *Society and the Adolescent Self-Image.* Princeton: Princeton University Press, 1965.

————, "Some Determinants of Political Apathy," *POQ,* Vol. 18 (Winter, 1954-55), pp. 349-366.

Rotter, Julian B., "Generalized Expectancies for Internal vs. External Control of Reinforcement," *Psychological Monographs: General and Applied,* Vol. 80, No. 1, Whole No. 609 (1966), 1-28.

————, "Generalized Expectancies for Interpersonal Trust," *American Psychologist,* 26 (May 1971), 443-452.

————, *Social Learning and Clinical Psychology.* Englewood Cliffs, N. J.: Prentice-Hall, 1954.

————, and R. C. Mulry, "Internal vs. External Control of Reinforcement and Decision Time," *JPSP,* Vol. 2, No. 4, (1965), 598-604.

Rutherford, Brent M., "Psychopathology, Decisionmaking, and Political Involvement," *Journal of Conflict Resolution,* Vol. 10, No. 4 (Dec. 1966), 387-407.

Ryle, G., *The Concept of Mind.* London: Hutchinson's University Library, 1949.

Samelson, Franz, "Response Style: A Psychologist's Fallacy," *Psychological Bulletin,* Vol. 78 (1972), 13-16.

Sanford, Nevitt, "The Approach of the Authoritarian Personality," in J. L. McCary, ed., *Psychology of Personality,* pp. 253-320. New York: Logos Press, 1956.

————, "Personality: Its Place in Psychology," in S. Koch, ed., *Psychology: A Study of a Science,* Vol. 5, pp. 488-592. New York: McGraw-Hill 1963.

————, *Self and Society.* New York: Atherton Press, 1967.

Sarnoff, Irving, "Psychoanalytic Theory and Social Attitudes," *POQ,* No. 2 (Summer 1960), 251-279.

Schacter, Stanley, "The Interaction of Cognitive and Physiological Determinants of Emotional State," in L. Berkowitz, *Advances in Experimental Social Psychology,* Vol. I, pp. 49-80. New York: Academic Press, 1964.

————, and J. E. Singer, "Cognitive, Social and Physiological Determinants of Emotional State," *Psychological Review,* 69 (1962), 379-399.

Scott, William A., "Attitude Assessment," in G. Lindzey and E.

Aronson, eds., *Handbook of Social Psychology,* Vol. II, pp. 204-273. Reading, Mass.: Addison-Wesley, 1969.

Sears, P. S., and V. S. Sherman, *In Pursuit of Self-Esteem.* Belmont, Calif.: Wadsworth Publishing Co., 1966.

Seeman, M., "Alienation, Membership, and Political Knowledge: A Comparative Study," *POQ,* Vol. 30 (Fall 1966), 353-367.

———, "Powerlessness and Knowledge: A Comparative Study of Alienation and Learning," *Sociometry,* Vol. 30 (June 1967), 102-123.

———, and J. W. Evans, "Alienation and Learning in a Hospital Setting," *American Sociological Review,* Vol. 27 (Dec. 1962), 772-782.

Selznick, G., and S. Steinberg, *The Tenacity of Prejudice.* New York: Harper and Row, Publishers, 1969.

Shafer, Roy, "Ideals, The Ego Ideal and The Ideal Self," in Robert R. Holt, ed., "Motives and Thought," *Psychological Issues,* 5, No. 2-3, Monograph 18-19, 131-174.

Shapiro, David, *Neurotic Styles.* New York: Basic Books, 1965.

Sherif, Musaerr, and H. Cantril, *The Psychology of Ego-Involvements.* New York: Wiley, Science Editions, 1966.

Shils, Edward A., "Authoritarianism: Right and Left," in R. Christie and M. Jahoda, *Studies in the Scope and Method of the Authoritarian Personality,* pp. 24-49. Glencoe, Ill.: Free Press, 1954.

Shrauger, Sid, and John Altrocchi, "The Personality of the Perceiver as a Factor in Person Perception," *Psychological Bulletin,* Vol. 62, No. 5 (Nov. 1964), 289-308.

Silverman, Irwin, "Differential Effects of Ego Threat Upon Persuasibility for High and Low Self-Esteem Subjects," *JASP,* Vol. 69, No. 5 (1964), 567-572.

———, Leroy H. Ford, Jr., and John B. Morganti, "Inter/related Effects of Social Desirability, Sex, Self-Esteem and Complexity of Argument on Persuasibility," *Journal of Personality,* 34 (1966), 555-568.

Simmons, J. L., "Liberalism, Alienation, and Personality Disturbance," *Sociology and Social Research,* Vol. 49 (July 1965), 456-465.

Simmons, J. L., "Some Intercorrelations Among 'Alienation' Measures," *Social Forces,* Vol. 44, No. 3 (March 1966), 370-372.

Simon, Herbert A., *Models of Man.* New York: John Wiley and Sons, Inc., 1967.

Smelser, Neil J., "Personality and the Explanation of Political Phenomena at the Social-System Level: A Methodological Statement," *The Journal of Social Issues,* 24 (July 1968), 111-126.

———, and W. T. Smelser, eds., *Personality and Social Systems,* II edition. New York: John Wiley and Sons, Inc., 1970.

Smith, G. M., "Six Measures of Self-Concept Discrepancy and Instability: Their Interrelations, Reliability, and Relations to Other Personality Variables," *Journal of Consulting Psychology,* 22 (1958), 101-112.

Smith, M. Brewster, "Competence and Socialization," in John A. Clausen, ed., *Socialization and Society,* pp. 270-320. Boston: Little, Brown and Company, 1968.

———, "Opinions, Personality and Political Behavior," *APSR,* Vol. 52, March 1958, pp. 1-26.

———, Jerome S. Bruner and Robert W. White, *Opinions and Personality,* New York: John Wiley and Sons, 1964.

Sniderman, Paul M., and Jack Citrin, "Psychological Sources of Political Belief: Self-Esteem and Isolationist Attitudes," *APSR,* 65 (1971), 401-417.

Spielberger, Charles, ed., *Anxiety and Behavior.* New York: Academic Press, 1966.

Steiner, Ivan D., and Homer H. Johnson, "Authoritarianism and Conformity," *Sociometry,* Vol. 26, No. 3 (March 1963), 21-34.

Stephenson, W., *The Study of Behavior.* Chicago: University of Chicago Press, 1953.

Stouffer, Samuel, *Communism, Conformity and Civic Liberties.* New York: Doubleday, 1955.

Strickland, Donald A., "The Non-vivus Psychoanalysis of Political Figures: A Review," *Journal of Conflict Resolution,* Vol. 11, No. 3 (Sept. 1967), 375-381.

Tagiuri, R., "Person Perception," in G. Lindzey and E. Aronson, eds., *The Handbook of Social Psychology,* 2d ed., Vol. III, pp. 395-449. Reading, Mass.: Addison-Welsley Publishing Company, 1969.

———, and L. Petrillo, *Person Perception and Interpersonal Behavior.* Stanford: Stanford University Press, 1969.

Thompson, Dennis F., *The Democratic Citizen,* Cambridge, England: Cambridge University Press, 1970.

Tocqueville, Alexis de, *Democracy in America,* Vol. II. New York: Random House, Vintage Books, 1945.

Turner, R. H., and R. H. Vanderlippe, "Self-Ideal Congruence as an Index of Adjustment," *JASP*, 57 (1958), 202-206.

Verba, Sidney, "Assumptions of Rationality and Non-Rationality in Models of the International System," *World Politics*, 14 (1961), 93-117.

Veroff, Joseph, and Joanne B. Veroff, "Reconsideration of a Measure of Power Motivation," *Psychological Bulletin*, Vol. 78, No. 4 (Oct. 1972), 279-291.

Walters, Richard H., and Ross D. Parke, "Social Motivation, Dependency, and Susceptibility to Social Influence," in L. Berkowitz, ed., *Advances in Experimental Psychology*, Vol. 1 (1964), 232-277.

Watson, R. I., *The Clinical Method of Psychology*. New York: Wiley, Science Editions, 1963.

Weller, Leonard, "The Relationship of Personality and Nonpersonality Factors to Prejudice," *Journal of Social Psychology*, Vol. 63 (1964) 129-137.

Werts, Charles E., and Robert L. Linn, "Path Analysis: Psychological Examples," *Psychological Bulletin*, Vol. 74, No. 3 (1970), 193-212.

White, Elliott, "Intelligence, Individual Differences, and Learning: An Approach to Political Socialization," *British Journal of Sociology*, Vol. 20 (March 1969), 50-68.

White, Robert W., "Ego and Reality in Psychoanalytic Theory," *Psychological Issues*, Monograph 11, Vol. III, 1960.

———, ed., *The Study of Lives*, New York: Atherton Press, 1966.

Williams, J. E., "Acceptance by Others and Its Relationship to Acceptance of Self and Others: A Repeat of Fry's Study," *JASP*, 65 (1965), 438-442.

Wine, Jeri, "Test Anxiety and Direction of Attention," *Psychological Bulletin*, Vol. 76, No. 2 (1971), 92-104.

Wisdom, J., *Other Minds*. Oxford: Blackwell, 1952.

Wittenborn, J. Richard, "Depression," in Benjamin B. Wolman, ed., *Handbook of Clinical Psychology*, pp. 1030-1057. New York: McGraw-Hill, 1965.

Wolfenstein, E. Victor, *The Revolutionary Personality*. Princeton: Princeton University Press, 1967.

Wylie, Ruth C., "The Present Status of Self Theory," in E. F. Borgatta and W. W. Lambert, eds., *Handbook of Personality Theory and Research*, pp. 728-787. Chicago: Rand McNally, 1968.

————, *The Self-Concept.* Lincoln: University of Nebraska Press, 1961.

Yancey, William L., Leo Rigsby, and John D. McCarthy, "Social Position and Self Evaluation. The Relative Importance of Race," *AJS,* Vol. 78 (Sept. 1972), 338-359.

Zellner, Miriam, "Self-Esteem, Reception and Influenceability," *Journal of Personality and Social Psychology,* Vol. 15, No. 1 (1970), 87-93.

Zillner, Robert C., "The Alienation Syndrome: A Triadic Pattern of Self-Other Orientation," *Sociometry,* Vol. 32, No. 3 (Sept. 1969), 287-300.

Zollchan, George K., and Walter Hirsch, eds., *Explorations in Social Change.* Boston: Houghton-Mifflin, 1969.

Zuckerman, M., and I. Monashkin, "Self-Acceptance and Psychopathology," *Journal of Consulting Psychology,* 22 (1957), 165-171.

INDEX

PAB study: attitudinal and psycholog-
ical scales of, 45, 60; defined, 17-20
Parke, Ross D., 156-157
Participatory theories of democracy,
315-318
Party conventions. *See* National party
conventions
Passivity, 259, 261
Pateman, Carole, 314 n. 11, 315 n.
12; on value of citizen political participation, 316
Path analysis, 213; limits of, 219
Pathologies, and the democratic personality, 169-170
Pepitone, A., 37
Perception, changes in by emotional
arousal, 154-156
Person perception, and low self-esteem,
88-92
"Personal effectiveness," and political
involvement, 249
Personal unworthiness: compared in political leaders and general population,
270; compared in political leaders and
"matched" followers, 272, 273; connected to feelings of inadequacy, 73;
defensive withdrawal and, 96-97; disaffection and, 86-87; guilt feelings and,
84; and hypothesis of surplus energies,
278-279; and influence of social
desirability, 61; items in analysis of,
53 loneliness and, 98, 99; person perception and, 88, 89; and political futility, 81; related to political
involvement and interpersonal competence, 287-288; related to political
participation, 264-265, 266, 267; related to self-esteem, 48, 49; and sense of
futility, 79
Personality: approaches to the study of
political belief and, 3-4 116-125; causal
mechanisms mediating political belief
and, 209-215, 319; and commitment to
democratic values, 1-3; connection of
to political involvement, 272-280; definitions of, 10-11; ideology and, 122-
123; role of in political learning, 124-
131, 207-209; social background vs.
psychology in tests of, 103-109; and
susceptibility to social influence, 309-
313. *See also* Democratic personality
Personality characteristics: effect of on
the relationship of self-esteem to political learning, 6, 129-130; emotive vs.

cognitive factors of in political beliefs,
131-136
Personality type, and political ideology,
171-179
Persuasability, 147
Persuasive communication, related to
self-esteem and attitude changes, 127-
128
Plato, 164, 223
Political Affiliation, Activity and Belief
study, (PAB), 17-20, 45, 60
Political apathy, 245
Political Awareness Scale, 158, 161-162
Political beliefs: effect of on the relationship of self-esteem to political
learning, 130-131; emotive vs. cognitive personality characteristics and,
131-136; and principle of congruence,
174-176; two variables effecting
personality and, 208. *See also* Extreme beliefs; Personality; Political
extremism
Political careers, influence of self-esteem
on, 293-298
Political cynicism, and low self-esteem,
188-189, 191-195
Political elite, 313-314. *See also* Elitism
Political extremism, and low self-esteem,
305-306
Political futility, 80-81
Political ideology, and personality type,
171-179. *See also* Ideology
Political interest, related to self-esteem,
144-145
Political involvement: as an acquired
tendency, 265-266; compensation
theory vs. competence hypothesis of,
262-280; defined, 254; interpersonal
competence as key factor of, 260-262;
as a learned form of social behavior,
272; self-esteem positively related to,
247-251; as self-reinforcing, 266; social
learning and, 254-262. *See also* Political participation
Political knowledge: conditions for acquisition of, 125; inhibited by a sense
of powerlessness, 142-144; low self-esteem and, 161-162
Political leaders: commitment of to
democratic principles, 197-198; compared to followers on obsessive-compulsiveness, 286; compared to group
leaders, 224-225, 226; data from studies of undermines surplus energies